INSIDE AutoSketch
Second Edition

A Guide to Productive Drawing Using AutoSketch

Frank Lenk

New Riders Publishing, Gresham, Oregon

INSIDE AutoSketch®
Second Edition

A Guide to Productive Drawing Using AutoSketch

By Frank Lenk

Published by:

New Riders Publishing
1025 E Powell, #202
Gresham, Oregon 97030 USA

All rights reserved. No part of this book may be reproduced or transmitted in any form or by any means, electronic or mechanical, including photocopying, recording, or by any information storage and retrieval system, without written permission from the publisher, except for the inclusion of brief quotations in a review.

Copyright © 1990 by Frank Lenk

Second edition 1990
Printed in the United States of America

2 3 4 5 6 7 8 9 0

Library of Congress Cataloging-in-Publication Data

```
Lenk, Frank, 1954-
Inside AutoSketch : a guide to productive drawing using
AutoSketch / Frank Lenk. -- 2nd ed.
     p.      cm.
  Includes index.
  ISBN 0-934035-96-2 : $22.95
  1. AutoSketch (Computer program)    I. Title.
TS385.L44  1990
620'.0042'0285369--dc20                       90-13394
                                                   CIP
```

Warning and Disclaimer

This book is designed to provide tutorial information about the AutoSketch computer program. Every effort has been made to make this book complete and as accurate as possible, but no warranty or fitness is implied.

The information is provided on an "as-is" basis. The author and New Riders Publishing shall have neither liability nor responsibility to any person or entity with respect to any loss or damages in connection with or arising from the information contained in this book.

If you do not agree to the above, you may return this book for a full refund.

Trademarks

AutoSketch and AutoCAD are registered trademarks of Autodesk, Inc.

IBM PC/XT/AT and IBM PS/2 are registered trademarks of the International Business Machines Corporation.

MS/DOS and OS/2 are trademarks of the Microsoft Corporation.

The publisher has attempted to identify other known trademarks or service marks by printing them with the capitalization and punctuation used by the trademark holders. New Riders Publishing attests that it has used these designations without intent to infringe on the trademarks and to the benefit of the trademark holders. However, the publisher disclaims any responsibility for specifying which marks are owned by which companies or organizations.

About the Author

Frank Lenk

Frank Lenk is senior editor of *Computing Now!* magazine, the leading Canadian microcomputing monthly. He has been a contributor to *Computers in Education* and *Electronics Today* magazines, and has served as editorial director of Moorshead Publications. He has also contributed to a number of industry and corporate in-house publications on subjects ranging from local area networks to telephone switching systems. In addition to *INSIDE AutoSketch*, Mr. Lenk has authored *INSIDE Designer* (with illustrations by his wife, Sû Allison-Lenk), also published by New Riders.

Mr. Lenk graduated from Queen's University, in Kingston, Ontario, with a B.Sc. in mechanical engineering. His interest in computing dates back to the mid-1970s, with undergraduate work on mini and mainframe computers. He assembled his first eight-bit microcomputer in the early 1980s. He has written extensively on the subject of software applications, with a particular emphasis on hands-on techniques and the human side of computing.

Acknowledgments

The author wishes to thank Autodesk, Inc. for its support throughout the preparation of both the first and second editions of *Inside AutoSketch*. Special thanks go to Patricia Pepper and Gloria Bastidas for extending that support. Very special thanks to Nik Grant for continuing advice and support and contributing many inside hints and tips.

The author would also like to thank the entire team at New Riders Publishing, who deserve a major part of the credit for both the form and content of this book. Particular thanks are due to Ken Billing for his expert guidance and unfailing attention to detail, and specifically for the many additional tips for AutoSketch owners who also use AutoCAD. Thanks also to Rusty Gesner for overseeing the production of the book, and specifically for contributing some of the exercises and drawings used in both the first and second editions. Credit is also due to Kevin Coleman for additional exercise development and illustration help.

Autodesk, Inc. supplied both pre-release and production copies of AutoSketch for use in creating this book. Xerox Corp. supplied Ventura Publisher. Microsoft Corp. supplied Word, used for final editing, and Windows, which was used to multitask AutoSketch during most of the creation of this book. Borland International, Inc. supplied Sprint, in which most of the writing was done. Inner Media supplied Collage Plus, which was used to capture AutoSketch screen images. Thanks also to Dell Computer Corp., for their assistance in providing the computer system on which most of the drawing and writing was done.

Special thanks to Harbert Rice and Jon DeKeles, who started it all. And to my parents, who admired the earlier edition without understanding a word of it.

Production

Editorial Director:	B. Rustin Gesner
Managing Editor:	Ken Billing
Technical Editor:	Kevin Coleman
Illustrations:	Frank Lenk, Kevin Coleman
IS Disk Development:	Ken Billing
Copyediting:	Christine Steel
Page Layout:	Margaret Berson

Contents

Introduction

    How *Inside AutoSketch* Is Organized   I–2
    How to Do the Exercises   I–3
    System Setup and the IS DISK   I–5
    Stepping Up to AutoCAD   I–7

PART ONE — Basic Drawing Tools

Chapter 1   Getting Started

Objects vs Pixels	1–2
The AutoSketch Screen	1–3
Coordinates and Units	1–9
Files	1–14
Quitting	1–22
File Practice	1–23
Summary	1–23

Chapter 2   Drawing Fundamentals

Points	2–1
Lines	2–3
Undo and Redo	2–4
Erase	2–5
Boxes	2–6
Polylines	2–8
Circles	2–9
Ellipses	2–11
Arcs	2–15
Polyline Arcs	2–16
Curves	2–18
Text	2–21
Command Practice	2–25
Map Drawing	2–31
Summary	2–37

Chapter 3 Basic Editing

Move	3–3
Copy	3–7
Rotate	3–8
Mirror	3–11
Scale	3–13
Stretch	3–15
Text Editor	3–17
Command Practice	3–19
Map Drawing	3–23
Summary	3–27

Chapter 4 Viewing Options

Zoom Box	4–3
Zoom X	4–6
Zoom Full	4–8
Zoom Limits	4–9
Pan	4–11
Last View	4–14
Redraw	4–16
Summary	4–17

Chapter 5 Drawing Effects and Setup

Color	5–2
Line Type	5–5
Text Effects	5–7
Layers	5–13
Show Properties	5–16
Change Property	5–17
Drawing Limits	5–19
Command Practice	5–22
Space Plan	5–25
Summary	5–29

PART TWO — Drawing Aids

Chapter 6 Advanced Drawing Tools

Curves	6–2
Frames	6–4

	Ortho Mode	6–6
	Grid Display	6–7
	Snap Mode	6–10
	Attach	6–14
	Command Practice	6–21
	Space Plan	6–23
	Summary	6–27

Chapter 7 Advanced Editing Tools

Break	7–2
Group	7–5
Ungroup	7–7
Parts	7–7
Macros	7–14
Command Practice	7–22
Space Plan	7–25
Summary	7–31

Chapter 8 Getting Output

Plot	8–2
Plot Area	8–5
Pen Info	8–10
Plot Name	8–12
Command Practice	8–14
Space Plan	8–17
Summary	8–19

PART THREE — Advanced Features

Chapter 9 Technical Drawing Tools

Getting Started	9–2
Arrays	9–3
Pattern Fill	9–11
Chamfers, Fillets, and Rounds	9–14
Polyline Width and Fills	9–20
Command Practice	9–25
Summary	9–29

Chapter 10 Technical Drawing Aids

Point	10–2
Coordinate Display	10–3
Bearing	10–5
Distance, Angle, and Area	10–6
System Variables	10–10
Dimensioning	10–12
Custom Dimensioning	10–20
Command Practice	10–29
Map Drawing	10–30
Space Plan	10–32
Summary	10–34

Chapter 11 File Transfers

Slides	11–2
DXF Files	11–5
Plot Files	11–8
Command Practice	11–14
Space Plan Viewing	11–14
Summary	11–16

Chapter 12 Advanced Applications

Business Applications	12–1
Isometric Drawings	12–10
Maps Made Easy	12–14
Site Plans	12–18
Tips for Schematic Diagrams	12–19
Summary	12–21

Appendix

Work-Arounds for AutoSketch 2.0	A–1
Saving Multiple Configurations	A–9
Hardware Help	A–11
File Management	A–13
Command Line Options	A–18
Prototype Drawings	A–19
Support and CompuServe	A–20

Introduction

AutoSketch is still an unusual piece of software, just as it was when we launched the first edition of this book — but perhaps not for all the same reasons. In the past two years, both AutoSketch and the software market have evolved. Today there is a wider selection of drawing products than ever. Yet AutoSketch remains unique and has even advanced relative to the competition.

Most important, AutoSketch retains its appealing simplicity and ease of use. No other product has quite the same blend of professional power and clarity of approach. There are many far more powerful products on the market, to be sure, including AutoSketch's "big brother," AutoCAD, but these products can sell for as much as twenty times the price!

Although it remains an easy program to learn, AutoSketch has acquired many exciting new features with the release of version 3. We believe that the program has now reached a technical plateau; AutoSketch 3 is capable of handling a remarkable range of drawing jobs. It's still a perfect program for beginners, but it's one that they won't soon outgrow.

To begin with, you can expect AutoSketch to be relatively simple to learn and easy to use. You can expect it to handle quick-and-dirty sketching jobs with unruffled grace. You can even expect it to accomplish fairly complex drafting tasks, once you take the time to learn how to get the most from its more advanced capabilities.

You should not expect AutoSketch to be a complete replacement for a professional computer-aided drafting (CAD) system. However, you can look forward to easily transferring your work from AutoSketch into more sophisticated programs such as AutoCAD.

Most important, you should not expect AutoSketch — or any other computer program — to instantaneously make a massive job trivial. Like any tool, AutoSketch still needs to be used creatively. However, while it can't whip up a complex blueprint at the snap of your fingers, AutoSketch can, with planning and care, handle a vast range of design and drawing problems.

AutoSketch is a vehicle that can help you automate the solutions to those problems, and this book is the road map. We'll show you some interesting places that the vehicle can take you, and throw in some tips on how you can become a better driver along the way.

If you find at first that AutoSketch is a bit slower or more difficult than traditional pencil-and-paper techniques, don't be alarmed. A certain amount of reorientation is normal — even for experienced computer users. Stick with it, and this book will teach you the skills and techniques you need to make AutoSketch a productive drafting tool.

How *Inside AutoSketch* Is Organized

Because AutoSketch is designed to meet a broad range of drawing needs, we've divided this book into three distinct parts. Each part covers an increasingly sophisticated group of AutoSketch commands and features. Based on your previous experience and the complexity of the drawing task you face, you should be able to start at a point that will give you instant gratification.

Part One deals with nontechnical applications — the sort of sketching that anyone might need to do. It assumes little previous knowledge of either manual or computer-aided drawing systems and presents the fundamental drawing, editing, and viewing functions available in AutoSketch. This part will give you a grasp of how the basic AutoSketch functions can be used to carry out simple drawing tasks. Topics include: getting to know your way around AutoSketch and its files; making drawings with lines, circles, curves, other basic geometry, and text; moving, copying, rotating, and distorting objects; viewing drawings in different ways; and changing drawing properties such as color and line type.

Part Two goes on to explore some of the higher-level features of AutoSketch. These CAD drawing tools allow dedicated users to complete moderately complex technical drawing jobs. Topics include: reference grids, snap, attach, drawing layers, macros, group object manipulation, creating individual parts, and printing or plotting.

Part Three deals with full-blown technical drawing applications. Topics include: pattern fill; wide polylines; object arrays; dimensioning; measurements; and transfer of drawing files to other software including AutoCAD, other graphics packages, and desktop publishing programs. Chapter 12 provides several examples of how AutoSketch can be applied to real-world drawing tasks, and gives some general advice on efficient and productive AutoSketch work habits.

Finally, a lot of useful information is compressed into the appendix. It deals with correct setup, use, and management of your computer's hardware and operating system. The appendix is no substitute for a good MS-DOS manual, but we'll try to provide some tips on how to set things up with the specific goal of getting the most from AutoSketch. We also provide information on support services and on PostScript output files.

How to Do the Exercises

The chapters in *Inside AutoSketch* are divided into sections that explain one command at a time. Each command is put into context, its behavior is detailed, and a reference exercise which demonstrates proper command usage is shown. You will also find time-saving tips used by AutoSketch experts.

Two types of optional exercises follow the command sections in most chapters. Practice exercises provide suggestions for further drawing experiments you can try. The drawing exercises use real-world examples that will give you a feel for how various AutoSketch commands can be used on actual projects. Most drawing exercises span several chapters, following the drawing process through all its stages.

You can do each chapter's exercises in sequence, or you can do them in two passes. That is, you can go through *Inside AutoSketch* once just reading the material and concentrating on the simple exercises, then go back and work your way through the more elaborate exercises. This method may give you a better feel for the continuity of the drawing process.

What you see below is a formatted exercise. You needn't bother to work through this one; it's only a sample, to illustrate the exercise format that you will encounter. The exercises are designed so that you can quickly see what to do. Instructions typically begin with key words (such as Pull down, Select, Click, or Pick) that indicate the action you take. Next is the item on which to act, such as the name of a menu (**Draw**), a command (**Line**), or an option (**OK**). To the right there may be additional instructions or information you need to know to perform the command. Whenever you need to type input, it is shown in bold type like the word **SCRATCH** below.

Example Exercise Format

```
Pull down File Select New                    Start a fresh drawing.
Pull down File Select Save As
Filename: SCRATCH                            Type SCRATCH.
```

Set the number of curve segments to 2, then draw a curve.

```
Pull down Settings Select Color
Click Blue                                   Set color to blue.
Click OK                                     Click the OK box.
```

Occasionally, a few complete lines of text will appear within an exercise sequence. These are usually instructions telling you to perform a series of commands that you should already be familiar with. "Set the number of curve segments to 2," above is an example of an exercise instruction. Sometimes we'll insert a text line or two just to clarify what should be happening as you proceed through the exercise.

With some command options, you make your selection by clicking your pointer on the appropriate box, which may have the option label inside it or along side. In either case, you want to click the box to select the indicated item.

Individual key presses are shown with angle brackets <>. For example, AutoSketch keyboard shortcuts are shown like this: <ALT-F2>. This is the same as A2 shown on the AutoSketch Draw menu, and means that you are to press the <F2> function key while holding down the <ALT> key. Whenever you're supposed to press a function key within an exercise, the shortcut sequence will be shown in bold: for instance, **<ALT-F2>**.

We always assume that you press the <ENTER> key (the same as <RETURN>) to complete text that you have typed in at a prompt.

If you somehow "lock up" AutoSketch, you may be able to recover control of your computer with <ALT-CRASH> — that is, type CRASH while holding down the <ALT> key. If it can, AutoSketch will give you a chance to save your current drawing to disk, terminate, and return you to the DOS prompt. This trick doesn't always work. However, you should need it only rarely, unless you've messed up your AutoSketch installation or have an unrelated hardware or software problem.

System Setup and the IS DISK

The exercises in this book make very few assumptions about your system setup. However, file operations assume that you have AutoSketch installed and configured on a hard disk C; in a subdirectory named \SKETCH3. These are the defaults assumed by the AutoSketch installation program. If you installed AutoSketch on a different drive or in a different directory, substitute their names wherever you see C:\SKETCH3. If you only have floppy disk drives, you'll want to substitute drive A: (and insert your AutoSketch program diskette) where we refer to AutoSketch's program files. Similarly, substitute drive B: (or drive A: if you only have one drive) and use a new, formatted diskette for loading and saving drawing files.

There is an optional Inside AutoSketch Disk (IS DISK) available that can save you time in doing the exercises. The IS DISK includes all the drawings that you will create in the exercises at various points of completion, as well as a few accessory files for your use and convenience. If you don't want to do all the exercises, or if you wish to jump into the middle of the book and do an exercise that uses a drawing created in an earlier chapter, the IS DISK drawings will keep you updated. You can also use the IS DISK drawings as a reference, to compare and verify your own results. You'll find an order form for the Inside AutoSketch Disk (IS DISK) inside the back of this book, or you can call New Riders Publishing at 1-800-541-6789.

To help you along in the exercises that benefit most from the IS DISK, we've included instructions with special symbols called icons. These icons show you what to do if you do (or don't) have the IS DISK.

 Do "this" if you have the IS DISK.

 Do "this" if you don't have the IS DISK yet.

The instructions which follow the IS DISK icons will tell you which file to load depending on whether you have the IS DISK. We've designed the exercises so you can choose to use the IS DISK files or not on an exercise-by-exercise basis. Each exercise creates the same drawing regardless of the disk, but you will load a different file if you choose to use the IS DISK file than if you decide to do the exercise from scratch. The filenames shown in the exercise instructions will be different only in the addition of an ending number. The IS DISK files for each complete drawing have a different number specifying their order in sequence. For example, to complete the space plan drawing in the book, you will continually work in a file named FLOOR if you don't have the IS DISK. If you have the IS DISK, the instructions following the IS DISK icons will refer to FLOOR1, FLOOR2, and so on. If you don't want to use the IS DISK files, simply follow the instructions as if you don't have the disk.

Installing the IS DISK

If you have the IS DISK, there are a few steps you should take before using the drawing files. First of all, as with any software or data, you should make a working copy of the disk with the DOS DISKCOPY command. Depending on your computer, you may have to enter the command differently from the example below. Refer to your DOS manual. For computers with one 5.25" floppy drive A: (with or without hard disk), issue the command:

```
C:\>DISKCOPY A: A:
```

Then follow the prompts. You'll be asked to insert the "source" disk in drive A: first. This is the IS DISK. Insert a blank disk when prompted for the "target" disk. If you don't have a hard disk, once the copying is complete, you are ready to go! Just use your working copy whenever you need to load an IS DISK file.

If you have a hard disk, make a new subdirectory for the IS DISK files under the \SKETCH3 directory. Save all your own drawings there while you are working on the book's exercises. This will help you keep them separate from your other files and make finding them easier. Use the following commands:

```
C:\>CD SKETCH3
C:\SKETCH3>MD IS-DISK
```

Then copy the IS DISK files into this new subdirectory with the DOS COPY command like this:

```
C:\SKETCH3>CD IS-DISK
C:\SKETCH3\IS-DISK>COPY A:*.* /V
```

If your 5.25" drive is not A:, substitute its letter for A: in the example above.

Stepping Up to AutoCAD

We've tried to make *Inside AutoSketch* valuable for AutoSketch owners who also have AutoCAD or may step up to it someday. You might find yourself wondering how AutoSketch stacks up against its much bigger and more capable sibling. Throughout *Inside AutoSketch*, we've included tips on the differences between the two programs. Wherever AutoSketch and AutoCAD share a command that has the same name, but acts differently, we tell you the difference. If they act in a nearly identical way, you'll appreciate the similarity if you ever use AutoCAD, but we don't bog you down by mentioning it. We also give you tips on the corresponding AutoCAD command to use for each AutoSketch command that has different name. They can be quite helpful if you someday move up to AutoCAD and need a little help on making the transition.

There are a few commands that AutoSketch has that AutoCAD does not, and many, many commands that AutoCAD users enjoy that set it apart from AutoSketch. Since pointing out all those differences would easily fill a book alone, we haven't included them here. Instead, we recommend that you get *Inside AutoCAD*, the pre-eminent reference and tutorial on AutoCAD.

That's enough formalities — let's get busy!

PART ONE

Basic Drawing Tools

In this first part of *Inside AutoSketch*, we'll introduce you to some AutoSketch fundamentals. After we lay the groundwork, we can proceed to examine the basic AutoSketch drawing commands and let you start using AutoSketch to do what it does best — make simple drawings quickly.

You will learn about these AutoSketch basics:

- **Getting Started** will take you on a tour of the overall structure of AutoSketch.
- **Drawing Fundamentals** teaches you how to create all the fundamental geometric objects.
- **Basic Editing** shows you some simple ways in which AutoSketch allows you to manipulate objects.
- **Viewing Options** allows you to look at your drawing from different perspectives.
- **Drawing Effects and Setup** looks at some ways to organize and embellish your drawings for better communication.

The drawing exercises in this part deal with a fairly common real-life project: creating a simple map like one you might use with invitations to a party. We'll ignore technical details such as scale for now, and concentrate on getting a feel for the various drawing, editing and viewing commands.

U.S. Capitol, Courtesy of Autodesk, Inc., and Jamie Clay

Chapter 1

Getting Started

Before you begin to learn how to operate AutoSketch, it's best to have an overall understanding of how the program works — and *why* it does things the way it does. Of course, you could learn to operate AutoSketch parrot-fashion, by simply memorizing the necessary commands. However, that approach won't necessarily yield productive drawing, and will work only as long as nothing unexpected crops up.

In the chapters to come, we'll be leading you through a carefully arranged sequence of exercises — some as simple as trying a single command, others as complex as creating a complete technical drawing. If you follow through each step, you'll finish up with a complete grasp of all the capabilities of AutoSketch.

In this first chapter, you'll get to know your way around inside AutoSketch and discover something of the philosophy underlying the program.

Here are the specific topics and commands that we'll be looking at in this chapter.

- Drawing Objects — the fundamental components that AutoSketch creates in building your drawing.
- The AutoSketch Screen — prompts, time display, memory meter, and menu bar.
- Pull-Down Menus — the control center you use to access all AutoSketch operations.
- Dialogue Boxes — used by AutoSketch to ask for detailed information relating to some of the more complex or powerful commands.
- Pointer and Rubberbands — the visual tools you use to draw on the AutoSketch screen.
- Coordinates — the standard numeric system used to specify locations within AutoSketch drawings.
- Files — used by your computer to store the drawings you create in AutoSketch.

Objects vs Pixels

Before you immerse yourself in a program like AutoSketch, we need to give you some background. A basic understanding of the principles of computer graphics can help you avoid a lot of confusion later.

Paper drawings consist of a series of pen strokes, brush strokes, or pencil marks, depending on the tool you happen to be using. Computer graphics programs create drawings in the form of electronic images on your monitor screen, or on paper in the form of plotter lines or printer ink.

Internally, all graphics programs deal with images in one of two different ways.

The simplest graphics programs are *pixel-oriented*. That is, they store and edit an image as an exact map of the actual dots that appear on your computer screen. These dots are known as *pixels* (PIcture ELementS). Pixel-oriented programs tend to be easy to use, and very versatile when dealing with subtle shades of color or photorealistic images. However, the images are forever limited by their actual resolution — the number of pixels they contain. Furthermore, detailed images can be edited only by modifiying potentially large numbers of pixels individually or in small groups.

AutoSketch belongs to the other category of graphics programs: those that are *object-oriented*. In AutoSketch, an image is a visible representation of data which describes each geometric object. Each AutoSketch object is created by a specific drawing command to much greater precision than pixels allow. In a sense, an AutoSketch drawing is simply a diary of all the commands used to create it. What you see on the screen, or on your printed or plotted output, is a summary of that diary information.

Object-orientation makes it very easy to create drawings of great precision. When you are drawing a circle, you can simply tell AutoSketch that you want it to have a radius of 3.125 inches, and that's exactly what AutoSketch will produce.

Object-orientation also provides great drawing flexibility. In an AutoSketch drawing, you are always free to "reach in" and take hold of any object. You can change the size, shape, or color of things you drew days or weeks ago, even if they've since become embedded in complex drawings. You can even build up complex drawings by combining portions of what you've already done.

With an object-oriented program like AutoSketch, your monitor or printer acts only as a window, allowing you to view the mathematically precise objects stored in your computer. The program always takes the best advantage of your output device. For example, most monitors have a relatively low resolution and will show a circle as somewhat rough, or jaggy. But a dot matrix printer has finer resolution; AutoSketch will automatically take advantage of that resolution to print the circle much more cleanly and precisely. Plotters and laser printers have even finer resolution. If you output the same circle on one of these devices, AutoSketch will be able to produce an almost perfectly smooth image. The drawing itself is the same in each case. If you buy a better monitor or printer, or merely transfer your AutoSketch drawings to a better-equipped system, you can instantly get better-looking results.

If this is the first time you have used AutoSketch, see your *Installing AutoSketch* manual for instructions on installing and configuring the program. Begin by loading the AutoSketch program.

Loading AutoSketch

```
C:\>CD \SKETCH3          Go to the SKETCH directory.
C:\SKETCH3>SKETCH        Type SKETCH. The screen appears.
```

The AutoSketch Screen

In order to use AutoSketch, you need to know what the program's display screen is all about — what mechanisms you use to talk to the program, and how it speaks back to you. The AutoSketch display has been kept deliberately simple, so you should have very little trouble picking up the basics.

When you start up AutoSketch, notice that there are two text areas marked off at the top and bottom of the screen. The top area is primarily for your *input*; it consists of the menu bar, a memory meter, and the current time display. The bottom area is for *prompt messages* from AutoSketch and coordinate display. Everything between the two horizontal lines is your drawing space.

You can move the arrow-shaped pointer freely around the screen. While in the drawing area, the pointer is your *pencil*. When you move it into the menu bar at the top of the screen, the pointer is used to select drawing commands. The pointer can be controlled from the keyboard, mouse, or digitizer tablet. The mouse is probably the most common and convenient device. A digitizer is the most accurate. We don't recommend using AutoSketch with the keyboard alone.

The AutoSketch interface is based on a very popular, standardized type of control — the *pull-down* menu. Commands are divided into logical categories. Headings representing each category are located in a row on the top line of the screen (often referred to as a *menu bar*). To get to a specific command, first select the category: move your pointer over the appropriate heading until it is highlighted and click the mouse or digitizer button. The full menu for that category will drop down from the menu bar. Commands on the menu are selected in the same way: point to the one you want and click the button.

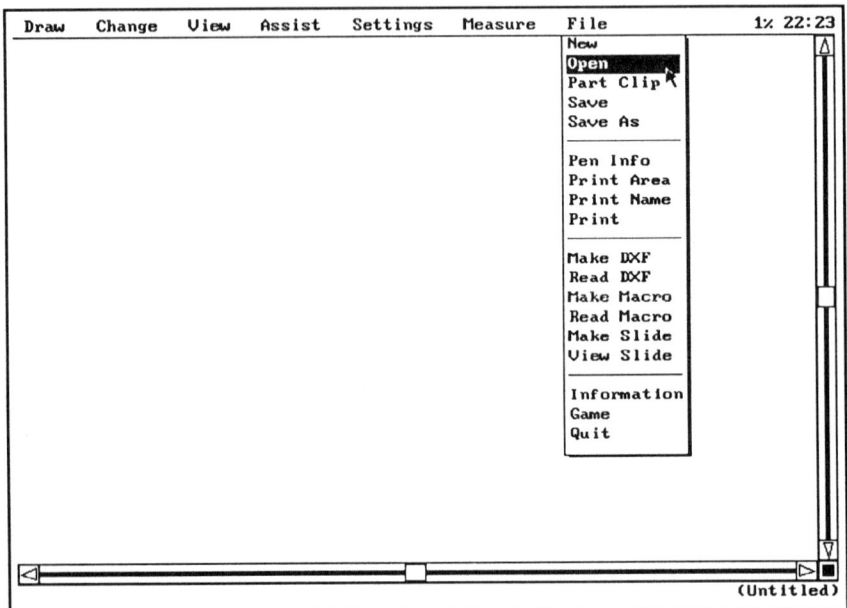

The File Menu

Pulling Down a Menu

Pull down **File** Select FILE from the menu bar.
The full menu rolls down.

This point-and-click organization ensures that you can eventually find any command you need without ever looking at the manual. Of course, you'll find things much faster if you understand how commands are organized.

Many commands are also accessible by means of keyboard combinations based on the function keys, <F1> through <F10>. (If you have an enhanced keyboard, function keys <F11> and <F12> are not used.) To provide more than ten command combinations, the function keys are also used in combination with the <ALT> and <CTRL> keys.

Next to some commands on the menu there is either an A, a C, or an F followed by a number. The A means an Alternate key, the C stands for the Control key, and the F means a Function key that can be used either alone, or in combination with an <ALT> or <CTRL> key, to execute the command. Thus, next to the Copy command on the Change menu, you'll see "F6"; that means you can invoke this command by pressing <F6>, without going through the menu. Next to the Circle command on the Draw menu, you'll see "A4"; this means that to start drawing circles without going through the menus, you should press <ALT-F4>. (That is, hold down the ALT key and then press the F4 key.)

As an extra convenience, most AutoSketch commands continue to repeat, once they have been selected. Thus, once you've selected the Circle command, you can continue to draw circles without constantly going back to the menu or the keyboard shortcut. To terminate circle drawing, or any other repeating command, just select another command, using either the menu or a keyboard shortcut.

Additionally, each AutoSketch pull-down menu remembers the last command you selected from it. The command is automatically highlighted the next time you click on the menu heading. Clicking on the heading once more will execute the highlighted ocommand without your having to move the pointer to it. For example, if you use the Circle command on the Draw menu, and then use the Move command from the Change menu, clicking twice on the Draw heading would execute the Circle command once again.

The bottom line of the screen gives extra information about your menu choices. In most cases, a brief prompt message will appear, asking you to complete a selection on the screen. Since AutoSketch commands repeat and many of them have similar prompts, such as to pick a point, the first word on this line is always the name of the active command, followed by its prompt message. In the exercise instructions which appear throughout this book, the repeating command name is omitted for clarity.

Two other constant read-outs appear on the screen. At the top right, a percentage number indicates how full your computer's memory is. On a 512K or 640K computer, it will take a very complex drawing to push this indicator anywhere near 100 percent. AutoSketch version 3.0 supports *expanded* memory (also referred to as LIM EMS or EEMS memory). If you run into memory limitations, consider adding extra expanded memory to your system. If you are using an 80386-based computer, you can add less-expensive *extended* memory, then use a memory management utility to make it act like expanded memory. Many 80386 computers include memory management software. Two excellent memory managers are also available commercially: QEMM, from Quarterdeck Office Systems, and 386^{Max}, from Qualitas. Your AutoSketch dealer should be able to supply one or the other of these. (See the appendix for some hints on memory management.)

Next to the memory meter, AutoSketch displays the current time. At the bottom right, you'll see the current drawing name. If your drawing hasn't yet been saved to disk, the indicator reads (Untitled).

AutoSketch can also provide some graphic viewing controls on the screen. When installing AutoSketch, you have the option of displaying *scroll bars*. These appear as bars down the right side and across the bottom of the screen. In the middle of each bar is a small square — the *elevator box*. You can click on this box and drag it the length of the scroll bar and click again to reposition your current display in relation to the current drawing (limits or extents, whichever is larger). You'll learn more about the limits and extents of a drawing later. If you click to either side of the elevator box, your display will pan one-half of the screen width or height in that direction, depending on whether you clicked on the vertical or horizontal scroll bar. You can click on the arrows at each end of the scroll bars to move the display one-quarter screen in relation to the entire drawing. Together, the elevator box, scroll bars, and arrows duplicate the Pan command, in an easy-to-use fashion that you can execute while in another command, and without having to use the pull-down menu. This allows you to view drawings that are much larger than the screen itself.

With the scroll bars displayed, you also have access to the *redraw button*, located at the lower right corner of the screen, where the two scroll bars meet. Clicking on this small square area causes AutoSketch to redraw the screen. This is occasionally necessary to tidy up after you've edited a drawing.

Other types of information appear in *dialogue boxes*. Dialogue boxes flash up in the middle of the screen on top of your drawing. They usually provide extra information or choices about the current command, such as a listing of the drawing files on your disk. Dialogue boxes are sometimes used to draw your attention to a potential problem — such as exiting AutoSketch without saving your current work.

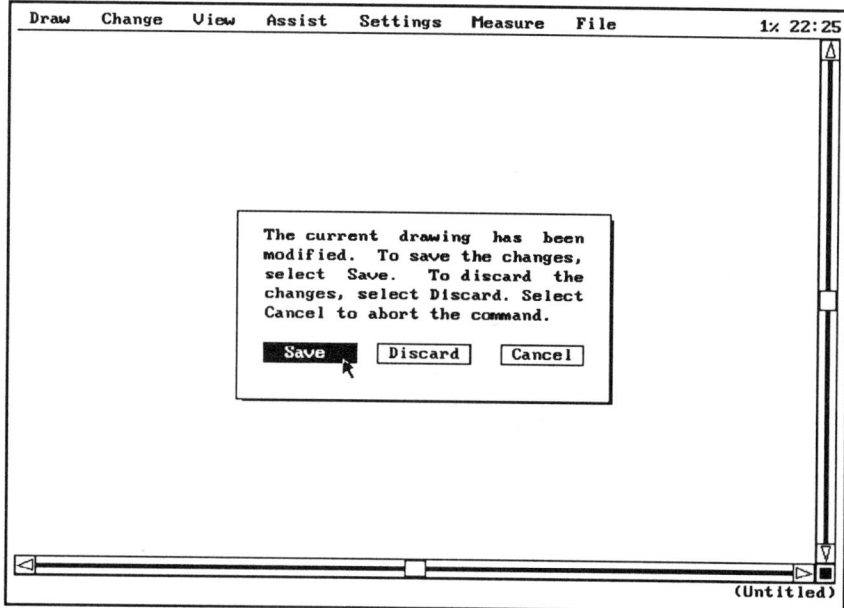

AutoSketch Screen With Dialogue Box Showing

Within a dialogue box, several smaller boxes may appear for you to enter information or confirm options. If such a box is expecting a filename or number, you can simply move your pointer to the box until it is highlighted, and type in a valid filename without the extension or an appropriate number. If the box has a check mark or the words Off or On in it next to a command option, you can toggle its current state depending on your preferences. If a scroll bar is present, use it to scroll through available options similar to the screen display scroll bars described above. You can drag the elevator box to quickly jump to different ranges in the list, click on the upper or lower scroll bars to scroll the list up or down one page at a time, or click on the arrows at either end to scroll the list up or down one selection at a time. Once you have read the information in a dialogue box, or set up all the options offered, close the dialogue box by clicking on the large OK button at the bottom of the dialogue box. The dialogue box will disappear, and if it displayed command options, your preferences will be in effect.

As you work with AutoSketch commands, your drawing pointer will change shape. When it appears as a hand with a pointing finger, AutoSketch is ready for you to select one or more objects on the screen.

To select a single object, simply click your pointing device when the fingertip is on the object you wish to select.

Besides selecting objects directly with the pointer, you can use a more powerful technique, the *Crosses/window* box. If you click your mouse or digitizer button when the hand pointer is not pointing directly at an object, AutoSketch automatically goes into Crosses/window mode. Then when you move the pointer, it stretches open a box on the screen. This box is not a real part of the drawing. It is more like a "net" in which you sweep up objects that you wish to select.

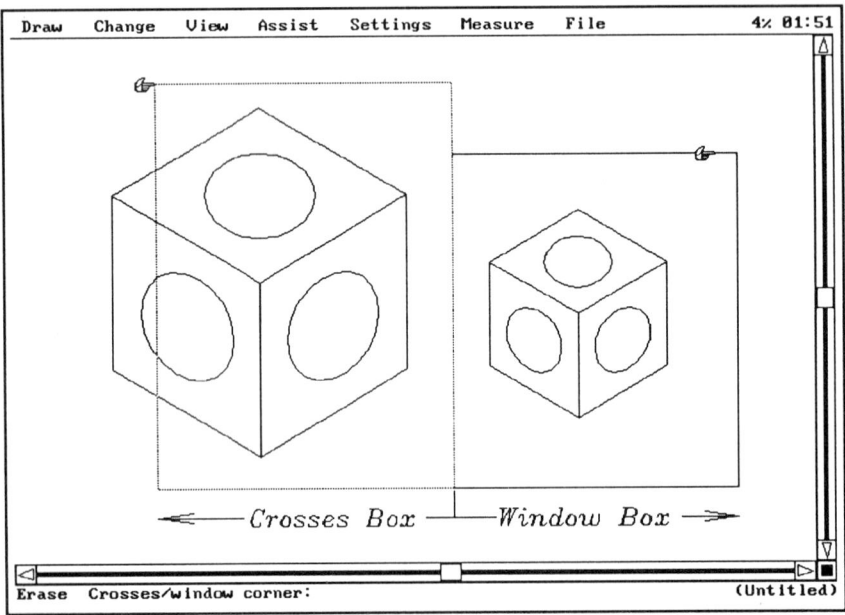

Hand Icon at Crosses/Window Corner

Pulling the pointer to the *right* creates a highlighted selector box. Only objects entirely surrounded by this "window" will be selected.

Pulling the pointer to the *left* creates a dotted selector box. Objects will be selected even if they lie only partially within this dotted "Crosses" box.

The Window selector provides fine control over what will be caught in the net. The Crosses selector is more of a catch-all, picking up anything that it touches or surrounds.

You can change from one selection method to the other any time you are in Crosses/window mode by dragging the rubberband selector box in the opposite direction beyond your original corner point. Unfortunately, this will usually take you in the opposite direction of whatever you were trying to grab. Simply select the command again, or enter the keyboard combination (for example, <F3> for Erase) and pick a new corner point that will work better for the selection method you want to use.

Obviously, you need to be careful which way you move the hand pointer with this and the other select commands or you'll end up catching the wrong objects in your selector net. Remember, you have the appearance of the box to guide you: dotted for *Crosses* mode, solid for *Window* mode. Also, notice that the word Crosses is the *left* word in the prompt, and window is on the *right*.

Picking up exactly the right object simply by pointing at it is not as easy as it might seem. This is partly because of the method AutoSketch uses to store these objects internally. For instance, to select *text*, you point at the invisible *baseline* that AutoSketch uses to locate the text. If this baseline were visible, it would appear as an underline directly below the entire text object. Also, objects on the screen can become crowded very closely together and you might end up erasing the wrong ones. This is where the Undo command can be very handy. You'll use the finger pointer and the Crosses/window box constantly in AutoSketch.

➡ *TIP: If you are an experienced AutoCAD user, you may notice that AutoSketch tends to select objects in the order that they were created in a drawing, instead of reverse order as AutoCAD does. This may require some adjustment on your part when selecting objects if you are accustomed to relying on AutoCAD to select the most recent object when you pick a point at which several objects intersect.*

For more information on picking objects and some aids to object selection, see *Frames, Snap Mode,* and *Attach* in Chapter 6, *Advanced Drawing Tools.*

Coordinates and Units

No matter what sort of pointing device you use, you always have the option of entering points directly from the keyboard using their coordinates. If you are unfamiliar with the concept of Cartesian coordinates, you may want to brush up on your geometry. However, we'll summarize what you really need to know.

Because AutoSketch stores all points as locations specified by their coordinates, you always have the choice of two techniques for entering points. The fast and easy method is simply to point at the desired location and click your pointer button. The slower, but more accurate, method is to enter coordinates directly from the keyboard. You are free to intermix pointer and coordinate input within a single command sequence.

Coordinates, by default, are normally measured from an origin point, initially located at the lower left-hand corner of your screen. This point's coordinates are (0,0). The coordinates of any given point consist of X and Y distances. The X distance is measured along a horizontal axis. Positive distances are to the right of the origin and negative to the left. The Y distance is measured along a vertical axis with positive distances above the origin, and negative values below it. On a VGA display, you'll initially find that coordinates with X values from 0 to about 14, and Y values from 0 to about 9 will be visible when you start AutoSketch. (Later on we'll discuss how you can view a larger or smaller portion of the virtually infinite coordinate *space*.)

Although it is conventional to specify coordinates surrounded by parentheses, AutoSketch does not require them for simple point entry. You can enter either 2,3 or (2,3) as a point. Coordinates based upon a 0,0 origin are known as absolute coordinates.

In addition, AutoSketch allows two variations in coordinate entry:

- **Relative coordinates** eliminate a lot of tedious calculations. When using relative coordinates, you express a location with respect to the previous point entered. Thus, if you want to enter a point that is two units to the right, you can type R(2,0). This means +2 units in the X direction and 0 units in the Y direction from the previous point. This saves you the trouble of discovering the previous coordinate's X value, adding two to it, then entering the result as your new X coordinate. For relative coordinates, the parentheses are mandatory. The R alerts AutoSketch that you are providing relative coordinates and not an absolute point.
- **Polar coordinates** are also relative to the previous point. In AutoSketch, polar coordinates consist of a distance and an angle, surrounded by parentheses and preceded by the letter P. Polar coordinates are ideal for creating accurate angles. For instance, an equilateral triangle with 60-degree corners is simple to create using polar coordinates, but it is quite a trick without them. Zero degrees for polar coordinates is equal to the direction east on a compass. Ninety degrees is north, 180 degrees is west, and so on. Thus, to specify a point 60 degrees above the horizontal and three units away from the current point, you would enter P(3,60).

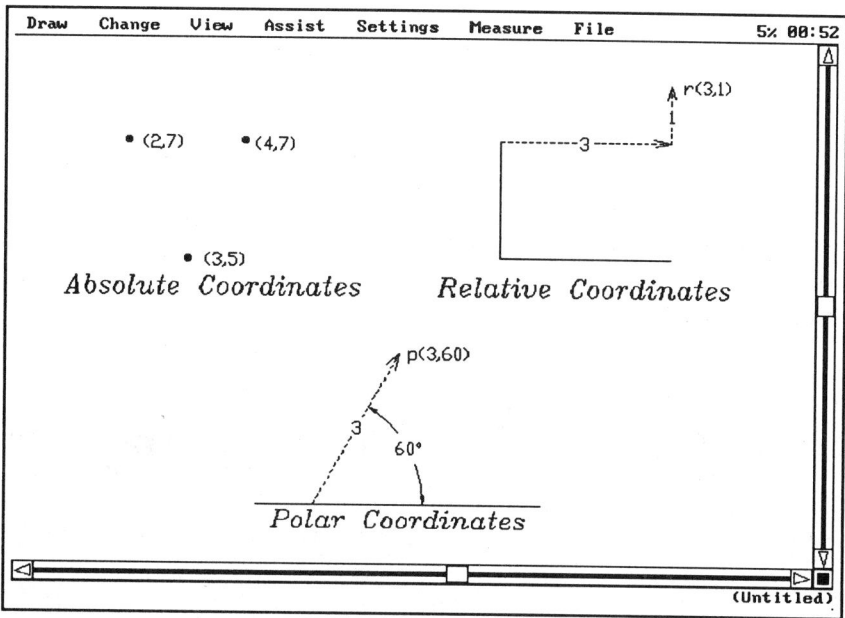

Absolute, Relative, and Polar Coordinates

Entering coordinates from the keyboard ensures accuracy. You will also find it convenient to use coordinate entry when a location is known, and you don't feel like hunting for it with the pointer. You can display a running indicator of the coordinates of your current pointer position at the bottom of the screen by selecting the Coords command from the Assist menu. When you are in the middle of a command, this mode will replace the memory meter and current time display at the upper right of the screen with the relative coordinates of your pointer to the last point you entered. This can aid in locating a relative point and save you from having to enter it from the keyboard in relative notation.

The coordinates that AutoSketch uses to express distances are measured in generic units. One AutoSketch unit can represent any one unit in any system of measurement: feet, inches, millimeters, centimeters, yards, or miles. Typically, this is one unit equal to one inch. Exceptions to this rule would be cases when you need to use a unit system other than English or architectural. You must decide what system of measurement is best for the particular drawing you are working on and remember what it represents. We give you an example of a very arbitrary unit relationship in Chapter 12.

You should select the smallest whole unit of measurement you need to describe the actual (full-scale) dimensions of the subject of your drawing. Your AutoSketch drawings should always be drawn full-scale.

For example, to draw the internal details of a watch one inch in diameter, you would let one unit represent one inch. You would have to enter distances in decimal fraction notation (.005 units equal .005 inches). Your drawing would be one *inch* in AutoSketch diameter, but only one *unit* in diameter. You would draw the watch in AutoSketch the same size as in real life, not larger or smaller as necessary when manually drawing on paper. You will learn later how to use AutoSketch's Plot and Print commands to make your actual hard copy drawing as physically large or as small as you need. By default, one AutoSketch unit will plot equal to one inch on paper. This can be changed, however.

To draw a larger object, such as an automobile, you should leave one unit equal to one inch, since that is the smallest whole unit you will deal with most of the time. Likewise, to draw the floor plan of a house (even though it is much larger than an automobile), you should use the default units relationship. You will often need to enter distances in terms of inches.

To help you remember the correlation between AutoSketch's internal units and the measurement system you have decided upon for your drawing, AutoSketch can be made to display its units in different formats on the screen:

- Decimal units express locations and distances as numbers followed by decimal fractions — for example, 3.89, 2.3456, or 1.000. This is the default. AutoSketch shows three places after the decimal point, but you can specify that AutoSketch display from zero to six decimal digits — from 1 to 1.123456. These settings affect display only. AutoSketch always uses maximum accuracy internally for keeping track of locations. Also, you are always free to enter coordinates with more or less than the currently displayed number of decimal places. If you enter more decimal places than can currently be displayed, then read back the position, you'll find that AutoSketch rounds off the number. If you increase the number of decimal places displayed, you'll find that the value you entered is intact.
- Architectural units are expressed as whole numbers of feet and inches, plus a fractional number of inches — for example, 4' 5-1/4", or 2'-0". If the coordinate or distance is less than one foot, only the inches and fractional inches are displayed. Fractional inches must have denominators that are powers of two: 2, 4, 8, 16, 32, or 64, up to 1024. Thus, you may enter 3' 1-3/32", but not 3' 1-1/3".

Each drawing can have its own method of measurement. The same AutoSketch unit can represent one inch or one mile; AutoSketch doesn't care. AutoSketch will automatically recognize the method you set up when you open the file. You select the format that you want AutoSketch to display coordinates and distances in with the Units command on the Settings menu. It will display the Units Display Format dialogue box, which you can use to make your selections for format and precision.

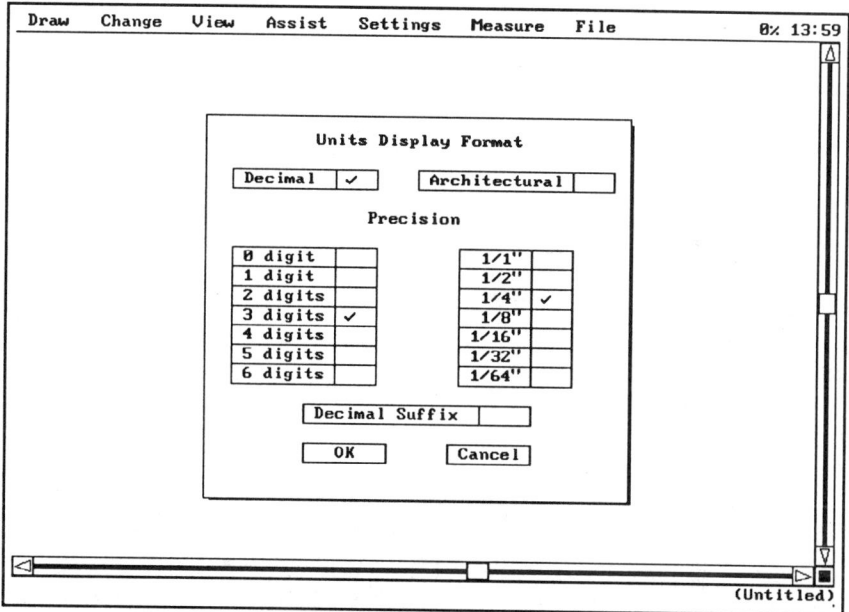

The Units Dialogue Box

If you elect for AutoSketch to use the decimal units format, you can also have AutoSketch add a three-character or less suffix to the numeric display. Thus, you can have AutoSketch show you coordinates like 4.5 mm, 10.375 yds, or 100.25 mi. AutoSketch's units haven't changed — only their display in a more meaningful form for you to work with has.

Obviously, decimal units are easier to enter in most cases. Even if you are working in architectural units, it is usually easier to type, say, 1.125 inches, than 1-1/8". And you can. AutoSketch will convert the distance you enter into the appropriate format, no matter what the current display format is. Any mental calculations you make as you go along will be much simpler in the decimal notation. The running coordinate display at the bottom of your screen will display in decimal units regardless of what unit display format you have selected.

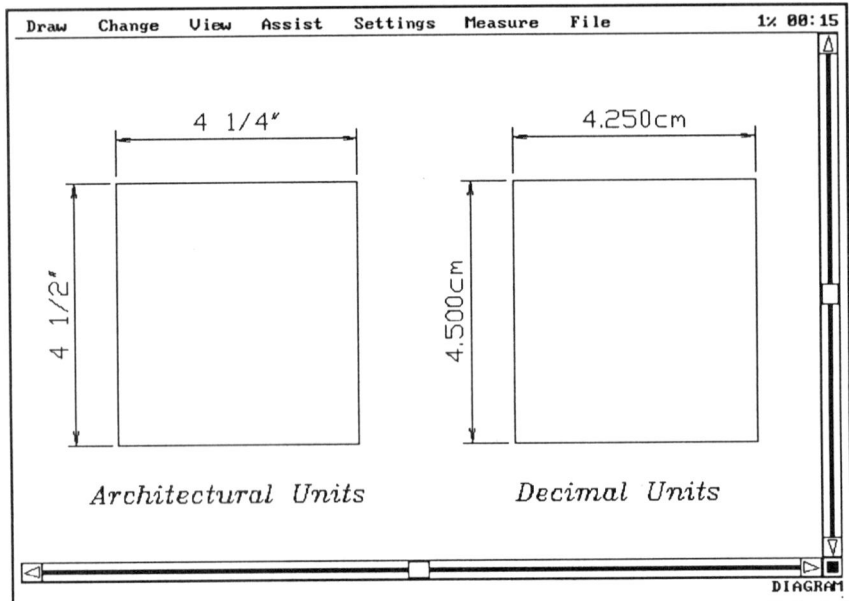

Decimal and Architectural Units

If you select Architectural Units for the display format, AutoSketch will "translate" its units into feet and inches notation so you won't have to. One unit will still equal one inch, but instead of having to calculate 186 inches, for example, when you mean 15′ 6″, you can enter the number directly and let AutoSketch sort it out.

After you have set up the units system for your drawings, you may discover that you then have a very small work space if you will be making a large drawing. AutoSketch can accommodate any size drawing you have in mind, but you will have to further adjust the way AutoSketch deals with the scale of your drawing. You will learn how to do this in Chapter 5, *Drawing Effects and Setup*. For now, let's push on to learning some more basics.

Files

What is a file? Many computer users go for months or years without ever grasping the concept. A *file* is a collection of information that the computer stores on a section of your disk — either a hard (fixed) disk, or a floppy disk. When you first save a file, an area is marked off on the disk and identified with the name given to the file. The saved information is written into this area.

You get the stored information back by loading the file. The computer goes to that named area of the disk and loads the information into its electronic main memory. Saving and loading functions are provided within virtually all commercial programs — and AutoSketch is no exception.

Files can contain various kinds of information. *Data* files can contain text from a word processor, facts and figures from a spreadsheet or database, or graphic drawing information from a graphics program such as AutoSketch. *Program* files — like the AutoSketch program, SKETCH.EXE — are like data files, but contain information that your computer interprets as instructions on how to do a particular job — for instance, processing a series of clicks from your keyboard and pointing device to create a detailed picture.

When you first start drawing in AutoSketch, your work is held in the computer's internal working memory — often referred to as RAM (Random Access Memory). This is also known as *volatile* memory, since its contents vanish instantly when your computer is shut off. AutoSketch drawings are created in volatile RAM memory, but must eventually be transferred to data files on your disk drive for more permanent storage.

All files have a *filename*. Under MS-DOS (or PC-DOS), filenames consist of up to eight letters or numbers, optionally followed by a period and up to three more letters or numbers. The last three characters are known as the *file extension*, and are usually used to denote the general type of the file. For example, program files always end in EXE or COM. AutoSketch drawing data files always have the extension SKD. This part of the filename is never shown within AutoSketch, but it distinguishes drawing files when you are working directly in DOS. (More detailed information on files, MS-DOS, and related mysteries is found in the appendix.)

Files are also identified by their location on a disk drive and in a *directory*. MS-DOS specifies disk drives by a single letter followed by a colon. By tradition, A: is always your first floppy disk drive, and C: is always the first hard disk. Individual disks can be further subdivided into directories, which let you separate files according to whatever categorization you wish. Programs usually are installed in their own directory; AutoSketch, by default, installs itself in a directory called SKETCH3 on drive C:.

When you want to retrieve a drawing that has been stored in a disk file, AutoSketch displays a dialogue box showing small preview images of the drawing files, called icons. You can use your pointer to select any of these, or you can select a different disk and directory, simply by clicking on them in the dialogue box with your pointer.

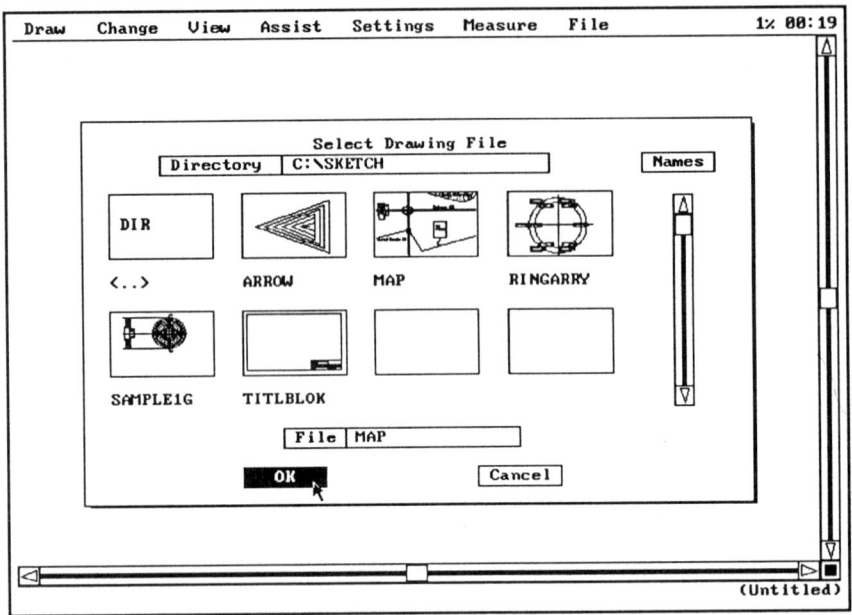

Retrieving a Saved Drawing

AutoSketch provides four main file functions (plus a handful of specialized conversion functions, which won't concern us until later). These file functions are:

- **New** — to clear any work from RAM memory and start a new drawing.
- **Open** — to retrieve a saved drawing file from disk.
- **Save** — to store the current drawing from memory to a previously named disk file.
- **Save As** — to store the current drawing in a file for the first time, or with a different name.

The simplest function is New. This prepares AutoSketch to begin a new drawing with a clean slate, erasing any previous work from working memory (but *not* from the disk). Whatever may be on the screen, and in the program's internal memory, is erased.

Saving a New File

Once you've created something you like on the AutoSketch screen, you'll want to transfer it to disk — to *save* it. The first time you save a drawing you need to give it a name, by which it can later be identified. The AutoSketch Save As command pops open a dialogue box asking you to type in a name for your drawing file. Later on you can use the quicker Save command and avoid the dialogue box; Save saves your work under the name you've already given. (If you try to save an as-yet-unnamed drawing, AutoSketch is cunning enough to automatically invoke the Save As function and force you to provide a name.)

When doing large copies or moves, or when inserting big parts into complex drawings, you may run out of memory. Keep an eye on the AutoSketch memory use indicator. If it's close to 100 percent, save your drawing before attempting any massive changes. If you do run out of memory, your command may not finish.

You may wonder why a separate Save As function is needed. It allows you to save the *same* drawing, under *different* names. Why? As you work, you'll often reach plateaus where something difficult or important is finally accomplished to your satisfaction. At this point, you should save the drawing to ensure that your efforts cannot be ruined by some unforeseen disaster — such as a sudden blown fuse, or the cat chewing on a power cord. Using Save As you can go even further, saving a series of snapshots of your work-in-progress. If you ever discover that you've somehow taken a wrong turn, you can always go back to one of the earlier saved versions and try again. (Later, we'll show how you can even grab portions of your earlier work and merge them with other drawings.)

Now, let's create a new drawing file named SCRATCH. This file will be used throughout the book as your scratch pad for experimenting with the various commands. You'll have to erase old work at times to make room for new experiments, but we'll get to that later.

Remember that if the far right of the prompt line reads (Untitled), the current drawing has not yet been saved.

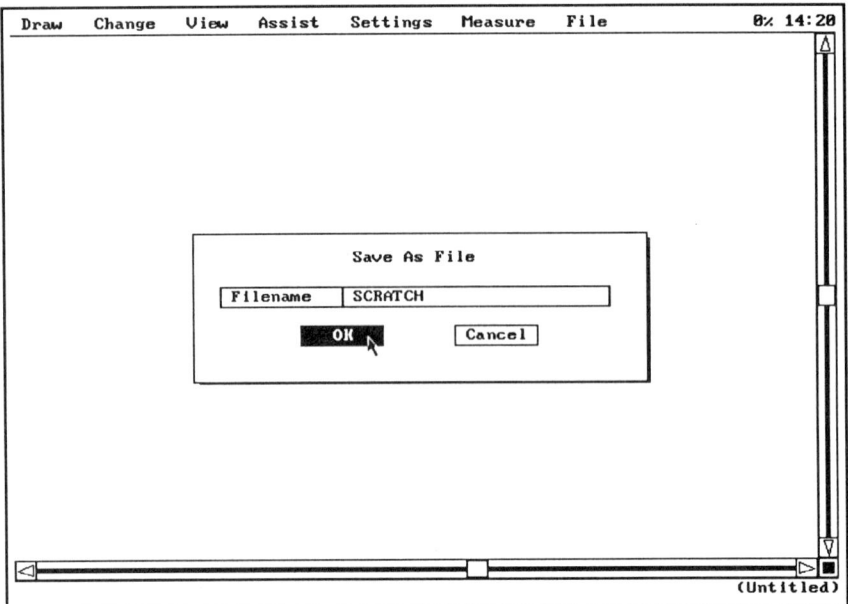

The Save As Dialogue Box

Saving a New File

Pull down **File** Select **Save As**	Click in or highlight the box to the right of Filename with your pointer.
Filename: **SCRATCH**	Type SCRATCH in the Filename box.
Click **OK**	Click the OK box to the right of the filename.
Click **OK**	Closes the dialogue box and saves the file.

Saving an Existing File

Next, save the same file again. This requires a different command than Save As, since the file already exists. Saving an existing file creates a new copy of your drawing on disk that includes any changes you made since the last time you saved it. The old copy of your drawing is given a new extension to its name (BAK), and this becomes your backup copy. Now the far right of the prompt line contains the existing name of the file you are using — SCRATCH.

Saving an Existing File

Pull down **File** Select **Save**	The file is saved.

Get in the habit of using the Save and/or Save As commands often. You should also make frequent backup copies of your drawings on separate disks. (This simple procedure is covered in the appendix.) Remember, until it's saved, your drawing is fragile and transitory. Even after the drawing is stored on disk, it can still be destroyed as easily as it was saved. Keeping multiple copies of everything is your only real protection.

Opening a File

Use the Open command to get your file (or any existing file) back once it's been saved. (Think of it as opening a file folder and looking inside.)

When the Open command is selected, a large dialogue box — titled Select Drawing File — will open up in the middle of the screen. The most direct method of telling AutoSketch what file to open is to highlight or click on the File box at the bottom of the Open dialogue box. Type in the filename of the drawing you want to edit, then press <ENTER> or click on the OK box at the side of the File box.

If you don't happen to recall the name of the file, or if you simply don't feel like typing it in by hand, you can pick it out using the pointer. The Open dialogue box shows you the available drawing files, either as a simple list of filenames, or as icons. To select a file, click on the box containing its icon. AutoSketch will place the drawing's name in the File box. Click on the OK button at the bottom of the dialogue box, and AutoSketch will load the drawing file.

You can select between the two types of file listings by clicking on the Names/Icons box at the upper right of the dialogue box. You'll generally want to use the more powerful icon display, as it gives you an idea of the actual appearance of each drawing before you open it. It's much easier to use than trying to remember what filenames like FIG1 or PLAN91 might have meant when you first created them.

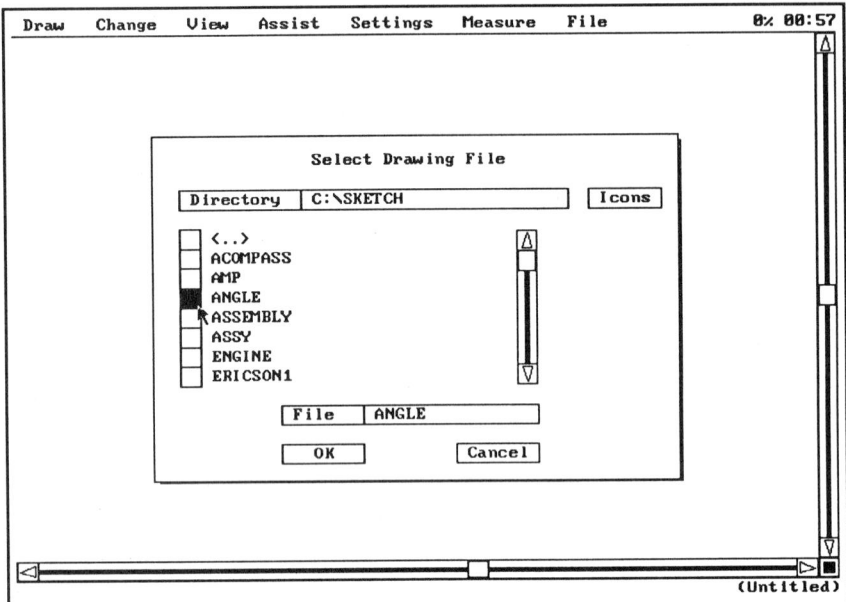

Opening a File With Name Display

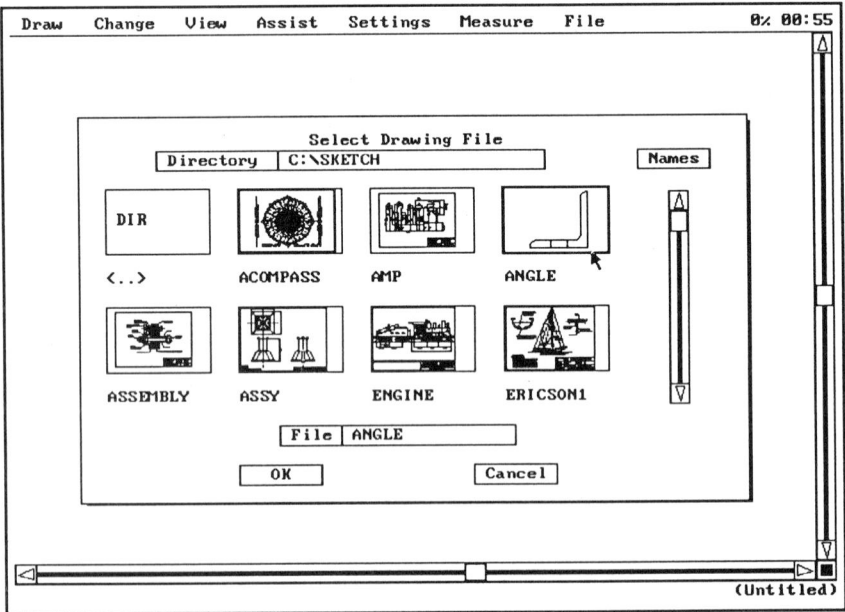

Opening a File With Icon Display

Whichever type of display you choose, AutoSketch always shows you the first eight files (or subdirectories), along with a vertical scroll bar at the right. To see more of the available file icons or names, click on the lower portion of the scroll bar, or on the arrow at the bottom of the bar. To return to earlier parts of the list, click on the upper part of the bar, or on the arrow at the top of the bar.

Icons shown in the Select Drawing File dialogue box reflect the view of a drawing just before it was last saved. You can alter the view (by zooming in on significant details, for example) to create more easily identifiable icons. This can be valuable with files you intend to store for long periods of time. You will also notice that drawings created in versions of AutoSketch prior to version 3.0 can be loaded into version 3.0, but will not show icons until they've been opened and saved at least once in version 3.0.

Opening a File

Pull down **File** Select **Open**   Use pointer.

Choose a file to open by typing in its name or by picking a name or icon from the list.

Select **File**
File: **SCRATCH**   Type SCRATCH as the filename.

Or you can click on the scroll bar to scroll through the file list.
Then click on the box next to the file you want.

Click **OK**   The file will now open.

Drawings may be opened from more than one directory on a hard disk, or from various floppy disks — wherever they've been saved. If the file you want is not in the current directory, you'll need to specify the drive and/or directory first, then the filename.

You can open a subdirectory of your current directory just as you would open an individual drawing file, by clicking on the box adjacent to its name in the names listing or on its icon box in the icons listing. Directory names are distinguished from drawing filenames by being enclosed in angle brackets <>; directory icons are blank except for the label DIR.

If the directory isn't displayed in the file list or icon display, the most direct method of specifying a new directory is to click on the wide Directory box at the top of the Open dialogue box, and type in the new directory *path*. (See the appendix for more information on DOS path names.) Then press the <ENTER> key, or click on the OK box at the right end of the Directory box.

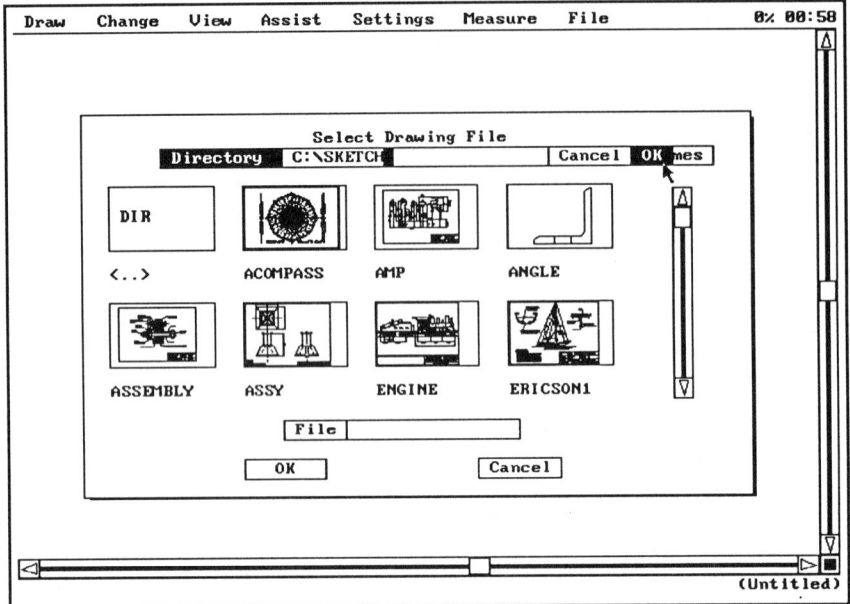

Selecting a Directory

Dealing with large numbers of files requires some forethought, especially when first setting up your disks. Throughout this book, we'll assume that you're saving all your files in the current (SKETCH) directory on your hard disk, or on the current floppy disk. (See the appendix for hints on using DOS directories to manage many files.)

Quitting

One final File command to become familiar with is Quit. Don't simply turn off your computer when you are done with your AutoSketch session. Quit is your recommended route back to the MS-DOS operating system. Get in the habit of always departing AutoSketch with the Quit command. This way AutoSketch will prevent you from accidentally abandoning a modified drawing and losing your changes.

Quitting AutoSketch

```
Pull down File Select Quit        Quit the drawing.
```

If your current drawing has been modified since it was last saved, AutoSketch asks if you want to save or discard the changes, or cancel the Quit command and continue drawing.

File Practice

OPEN. Use the Open command to retrieve some of the AutoSketch example drawings that came with the program. Load AutoSketch from its directory on your hard disk. If you've used the INSTALL program on the master AutoSketch disk, the example drawings will be in the same directory with the program itself. The example filenames or icons should thus be immediately visible in the Open dialogue box. Click on the one you want to try, then click on OK at the bottom of the dialogue box. Some of the example files are quite large and complex and may take several minutes to load depending on the speed of your computer. Be patient and don't panic if your computer seems to be hung up!

SAVE. Try using Save As to save one of the example drawings under a new name. Then open it to verify that it is the same as the original only with a different name. Also, if you have any AutoSketch version 2.0 drawings, you can load and save each one to create an AutoSketch version 3.0 icon.

FILENAMES. Experiment with filenames. What happens if you use more than eight characters? What characters *cannot* be used in filenames?

As you probably discovered, most punctuation and some characters, such as +, cannot be used. Also, filenames are limited to eight characters. We recommend that you stick to normal alphabetic and numeric characters and the - (hyphen).

Summary

In this chapter, we've laid a foundation that should serve you throughout all your work with AutoSketch. You should now be familiar with the overall layout of the AutoSketch screen display and the techniques you use to communicate with the program — the AutoSketch *user interface*. You've seen a few examples of how locations can be specified either directly with the pointer or by entering Cartesian coordinates. And, finally, you should have acquired at least a general feel for the way AutoSketch uses disk files to store your work. You should now be prepared to create your first drawing.

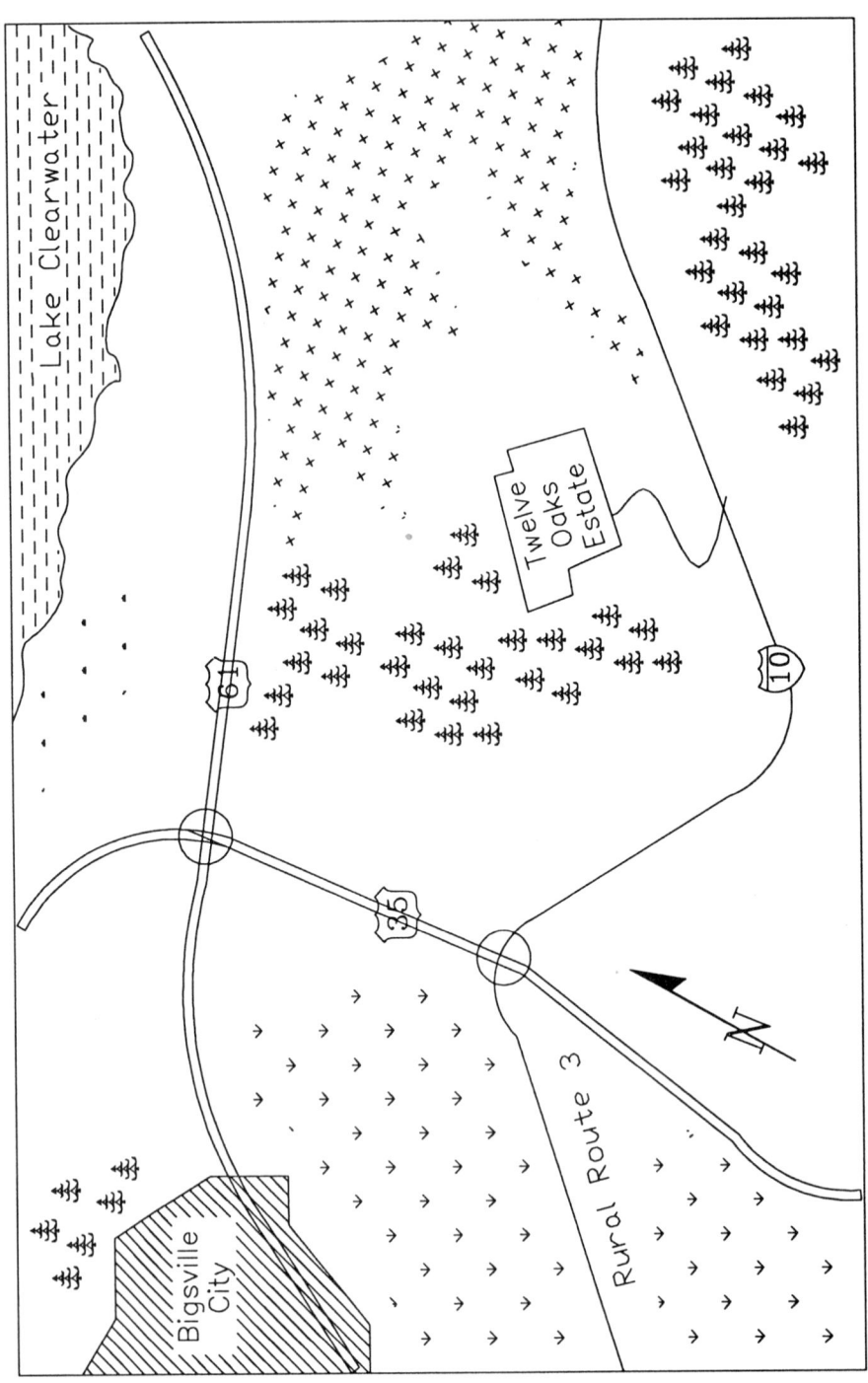

The Completed Map

Chapter 2

Drawing Fundamentals

AutoSketch drawings can be thought of as collections of specific drawing *objects*. These objects are created by AutoSketch commands, stored in AutoSketch drawing files, and can be manipulated by AutoSketch editing commands. No matter how complex the image is on your screen, you can always reach in and grab individual objects.

The simplest objects of all are *points*. More complex objects are lines, four-sided boxes, many-sided polygons, circles, arcs, curves, and text.

Object orientation is the key to how AutoSketch handles all basic drawing tasks. As far as AutoSketch is concerned, a line, box, or circle is a single object — not multiple dots (pixels) as is the case with many other graphics programs. No matter what size or shape the object, it is still just one AutoSketch object. There is never any need to specify all of the points that might be needed to trace the outline of the object.

The objectives in this chapter are to create simple drawing objects using the basic drawing commands and to combine these simple elements into useful pictures. Most of this chapter will be concerned with the Draw menu, which has commands for making all the primary objects.

It is important to remember that in the early chapters you should not be too concerned with accuracy. In the beginning, your main objective is to learn how to use the various commands and features. AutoSketch provides a variety of tools that will help you make accurate drawings. These tools will be discussed in succeeding chapters.

Points

The point is the fundamental element of all geometry. It is also the fundamental element of an AutoSketch drawing.

In AutoSketch, as in classic geometry, a point is a location in space. It has no size, only location. Although points in AutoSketch do show up on the screen as little dots, and they do appear on plots, their *location* is more important than their appearance. Since they have no real size, you don't have to allow for the thickness of the dots themselves when creating very precise drawings.

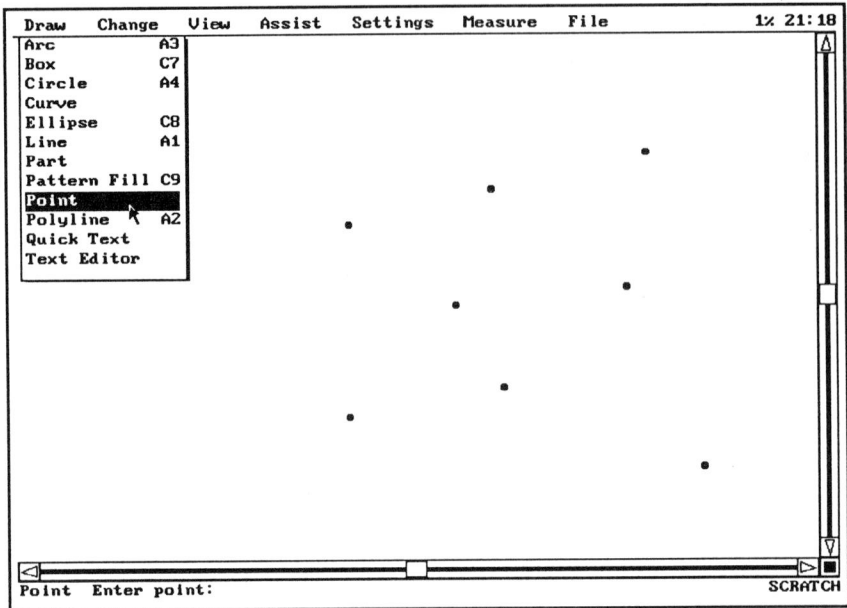

Points on the AutoSketch Screen

Creating Points

Pull down **File** Select **Open**	Open the existing SCRATCH file.
Pull down **Draw** Select **Point**	
Enter point: **5,7**	Type the coordinates.
Enter point:	Pick a point or type coordinates.
Enter point:	Pick another point.
Enter point:	Pick as many points as you desire.

As mentioned in Chapter 1, you'll find that the Point command automatically repeats, allowing you to enter as many points as you like. Also, remember that points can be entered either by indicating their location on the screen with your pointing device, or by typing in precise coordinates from the keyboard.

For simply locating the coordinates of a point without producing an object, see *Point* in Chapter 10, *Technical Drawing Aids*.

Lines

As you begin to add more complex objects to your drawing, the importance of the humble point becomes more apparent. Lines (in fact, almost all other AutoSketch drawing elements) are created by selecting a drawing command, then specifying a number of points telling AutoSketch where to position the desired object. When you select the Line command, AutoSketch will prompt you for two endpoints.

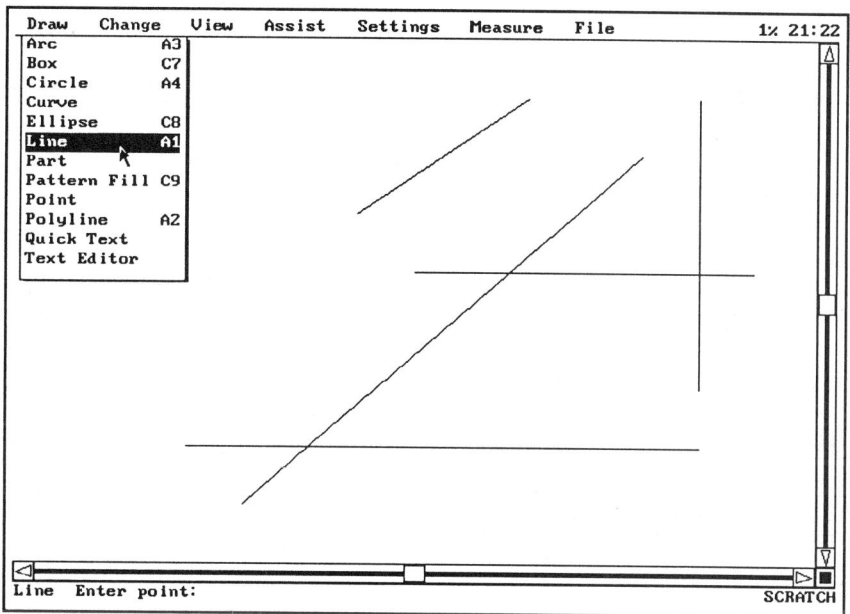

Lines on the AutoSketch Screen

Creating a Line

```
Pull down Draw Select Line
Enter point:                    Pick line starting point.
To point:                       Pick line ending point.
Enter point:                    Pick a point.
To point:                       Pick a point.
```

Continue to enter points until you feel comfortable with the way the Line command works. Try executing the Line command with <ALT-F1>.

You will notice that as you move the arrow pointer across the screen, a rubberband line follows the pointer. This rubberband continually shows where the actual line will fall if you release the pointer button at any given moment. The rubberband is used by most commands.

You should begin to see the advantages of the various forms of command entry. The pointing device lets you position lines using a rubberband display; you actually see the line as a building block that you can drop into place wherever you want. Coordinate entry, on the other hand, lets you locate the line much more precisely — but without the comfort of a continuous visual indication of what's happening. Both methods have their place.

For commands related to Line, see *Polyline* below, and *Linetype* and *Color* in Chapter 5, *Drawing Effects and Setup*.

Undo and Redo

Although you have probably made it this far without incident, eventually you will need to correct a mistake. AutoSketch gives you an easy way to recover from errors: the Undo command. If you aren't happy with how something turns out, you can immediately undo it and try again. It's easy enough to make a slip while trying to add a detail to a drawing, but with Undo, mistakes are easy to reverse. The only editing command that Undo can't undo is itself. To undo an Undo, you use the special command Redo.

Undo and Redo

```
Pull down Change Select Undo      The last line disappears — undone.
Pull down Change Select Undo      The next to last line disappears.
Pull down Change Select Redo      The next to last line reappears.
```

Using Undo you can step *backward* through the commands you've issued, retreating as far as you like, eventually dismantling your drawing entirely. Using Redo you can come back again, moving *forward* through the same sequence of commands you used in creating the drawing. Or, by cycling back and forth between Undo and Redo, you can make your last drawing change come and go quickly on the screen to help you decide whether you want to keep it or not.

AutoSketch allows you to use <F1> and <F2> to invoke these two commands, making them particularly convenient. Once you get accustomed to these keyboard shortcuts, there's little need to pull down the Change menu in order to undo. However, the menu does give you one useful bit of information — if there is nothing to undo, or redo, the respective option word is "greyed out" on the menu.

Undo and Redo work equally well with any of the Draw or Edit commands. However, if you save a file, don't expect to be able to "unsave" it by hitting <F1>. Also, if you save a file and then recall it, you won't be able to undo anything. That is, the Undo and Redo commands affect only the current editing session.

AutoSketch keeps a sequential record of all the commands you've used in the current editing session in a special Undo file on disk named $$UNDO.$AS. When you edit another drawing or quit AutoSketch, the program automatically deletes the Undo file and creates a new, empty Undo file.

If you undo, then perform some other drawing action, you cannot go back and redo. You must redo a command *immediately* or not at all. You can undo at any time, but in order to undo some past drawing action you'll also be forced to undo everything you've done since then — possibly dismantling a substantial chunk of work. Thus it's better to undo immediately as well.

One other, small thing about Undo. Notice that if you undo a drawing command, AutoSketch will take you out of command mode. For instance, if you're drawing repeated points, then undo one of them, you'll have to go back to the Draw menu and reselect the Point command if you wish to continue entering points.

Erase

When you select Erase, AutoSketch changes your arrow pointer to the hand pointer. You can then erase objects either singly or in groups. If you select single objects, they are erased immediately upon selection.

➥ *TIP: This action is similar to AutoCAD's ERASE command with the AUTO selection method, as opposed to AutoCAD's default selection method, which allows you to build selection sets one object at a time. The selection set is then erased by pressing the <ENTER> key whether the selection set contains one object or many.*

Erasing Objects

```
Pull down Change Select Erase
Select object:                    Place pointer on an object and click the button.
Select object:                    Erase more objects if you desire.
Select object:                    Click in clear space, near some objects.
```

Now, as you drag left you see a dotted Crosses box.
Drag right for a solid Window.

```
Crosses/window corner:            Drag left to cross some objects, then pick.
Select object:                    Place pointer to left and above an object
                                  and click.
Crosses/window corner:            Drag right, windowing some objects, and click.
Select object:
```

Since Undo is often used to remove things inadvertently done to your drawing, it may be tempting to think that Erase and Undo are rather similar. Actually, these two functions differ in a very fundamental way. You can undo things only in the order you originally drew them, but you can erase anything. Furthermore, if you undo an Erase command, you actually *put back* whatever you've removed.

Remember the power of object orientation. Don't be afraid to experiment — you'll always be able to back up using Undo. Draw any and all construction lines that might help you as you go. You can always remove them using Erase. All this may seem obvious now, as you sit with this book open on your desk, but it's up to you to apply the techniques we can only tell you about.

Boxes

A *box* is one of the easiest complex objects to create. Not only is it rather useful in a wide variety of drawing situations, but it can be conveniently specified using only two points for two diagonally opposite corners.

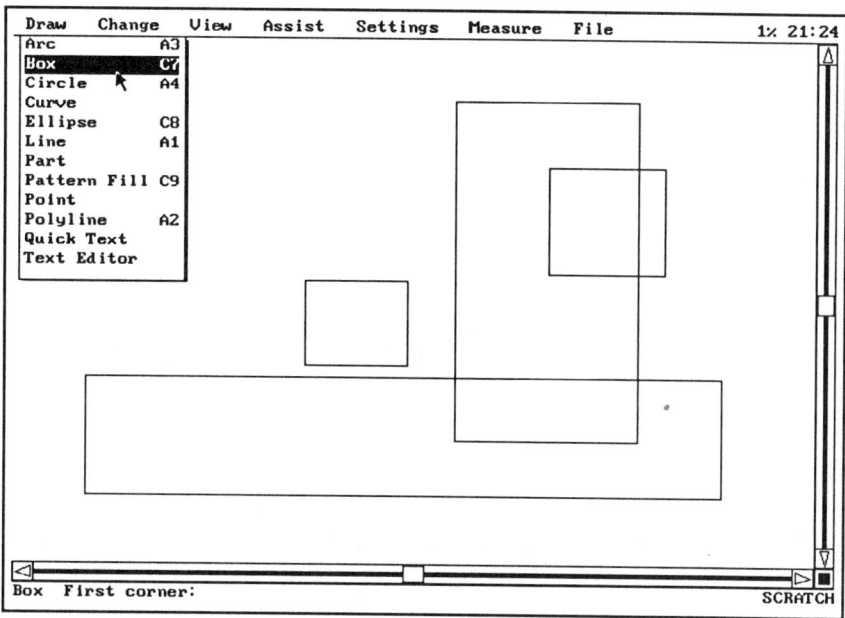

Boxes on the AutoSketch Screen

Creating a Box

```
Pull down Draw Select Box
First corner:                    Pick lower left corner.
Second corner:                   Pick upper right to create a box.
```

Continue making boxes if you desire.

Actually, the term box is used in AutoSketch to mean what rectangle means in geometry. An AutoSketch box can be perfectly square, but it doesn't have to be. However, opposite sides will always be parallel, and all the corners will be right angles. (In the next section you'll see a command that bypasses this limitation.)

Note that a box created using the Box command is *not* the same as a similar shape created with four lines, although it looks the same on the screen. All four lines of a box in AutoSketch comprise a *single* drawing entity. This will become significant when you start to use the editing commands.

Polylines

A *polyline* is an object composed of line and/or arc segments connected end-to-end. Just like a box, a polyline in AutoSketch is a *single* drawing entity. If you close the end of the last segment with the start of the first, a polyline can enclose a polygon. For example, a closed polyline made from three line segments forms a triangle.

Obviously, you can create polygons by using the AutoSketch Line command repeatedly — but the Polyline command is much easier to use. It also has other advantages; for example, you can alter the width of the polyline, an option not provided for any other type of line in AutoSketch.

➥ *NOTE: Prior to version 3.0, the Polyline command was called Polygon. Aside from the name change, the basic command functions exactly the same way in all versions. The ability to alter width is available only with Polyline, starting in AutoSketch version 3.0.*

Drawing a polyline is just like drawing a series of lines using the Line command, except that as you finish each line segment you are immediately ready to draw another. Thus, there will always be a rubberband line from your last-entered point to the arrow pointer.

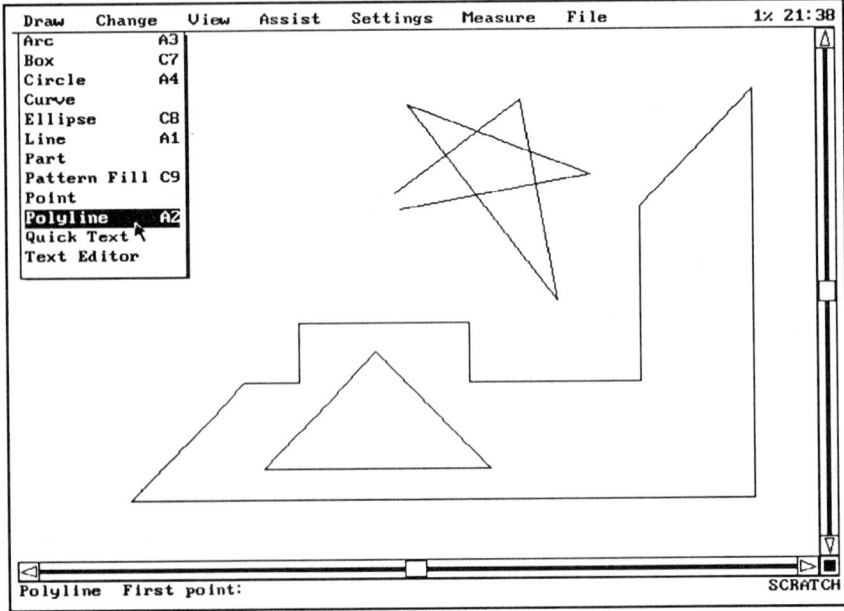

Close the Polyline by Double-Clicking

Creating a Polyline

```
Pull down Draw Select Polyline
First point:                    Pick.
To point:                       Pick another point.
To point:                       Pick or enter as many points as desired.
To point:                       Close it by picking a point on top of the first one,
                                or end it by picking two points on top of each other by
                                clicking twice without moving the pointer.
```
The prompt changes back to "Polyline First point:" when the polyline is completed.

Note that even if you are entering polyline points using keyboard coordinates, AutoSketch will still display a rubberband from your last entered point to the tip of the arrow pointer. If you continue to use the keyboard, just ignore this line. Moving the pointer to a vacant area of the screen can help you to keep the rubberband clear of the actual lines you are entering.

To terminate a polyline construction, you can either re-enter your starting point or just click twice when entering the last point. You can also end a polyline by selecting another command or the same command again. When using the keyboard, type the last set of coordinates twice, or retype the coordinates for the first point on the polyline.

For additional options for the Polyline command, see *Polyline Arcs* below and *Line Weight* in Chapter 9, *Technical Drawing Tools*.

Circles

Remember, AutoSketch does not merely draw images on your monitor screen. It actually creates and stores them mathematically. The circle is a good example of this system at work. A circle is difficult to draw freehand, yet is easily entered in AutoSketch with just two points: the center and any one point on the circumference.

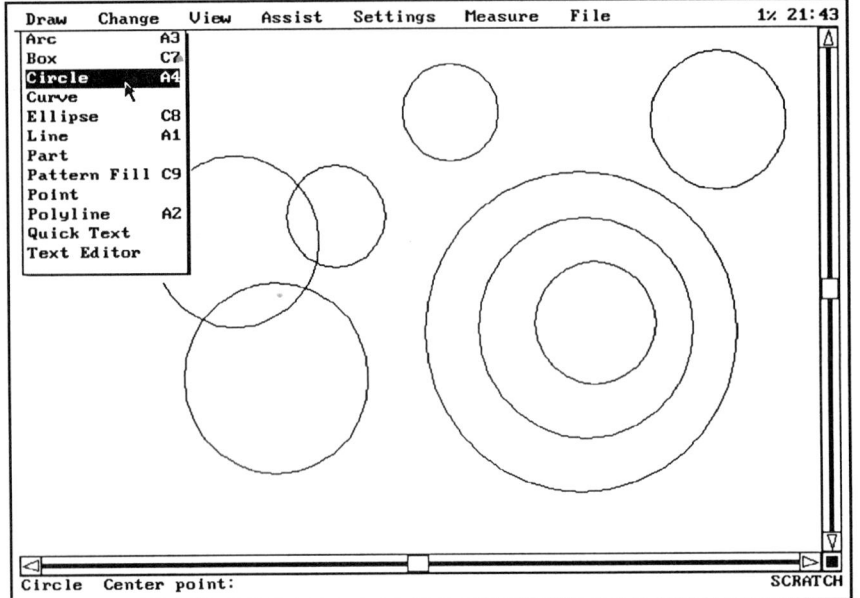

Circles on the AutoSketch Screen

Creating a Circle

```
Pull down Draw Select Circle
Center point                        Pick a point.
Point on circle:                    Pick point that will be the radius.
Center point                        Pick a point.
Point on circle: R(2,0)             Enter a 2-unit radius at 0 degrees.
Center point                        Draw a few more circles.
```

If you wish to draw a circle of a given size, notice that the distance between your two circle points represents the *radius* of the circle. Internally, AutoSketch stores a circle as one point and a radius, but you must use polar or relative coordinates to enter a radius. You can eyeball this distance using the pointer. To be more accurate, you can use the keyboard to enter coordinates. If you do use the keyboard, use polar or relative coordinates. With relative coordinates, be sure to use a 0 for either the X or the Y distance; then you can simply set the other of these two values equal to the desired radius.

Aligning a circle with other drawing elements can require considerable care. Most often, the center of a circle is a known point established by other elements within the drawing. In such cases, polar or relative coordinate entry will give you excellent accuracy.

Ellipses

Often, you'll want not a true circle, but an ellipse. In fact, ellipses are useful not just for elliptical objects; a circle, when seen in an isometric view, appears as an ellipse.

➥ *NOTE: While version 3.0 of AutoSketch has powerful ellipse drawing capabilities, earlier versions lack this command. Another good reason to update your copy! If you are still using version 2.0 or earlier, you can approximate an ellipse by using the Curve command, covered later in this chapter.*

Obviously, a circle has only one radius, which remains constant whichever direction you measure from center to circumference. An ellipse requires more complicated specification. AutoSketch gives you three different methods for entering ellipse dimensions.

The default technique for drawing an ellipse is deliberately similar to that for drawing a circle. You choose the Ellipse command from the Draw menu, and AutoSketch prompts you to enter the center point of the ellipse. You then specify the lengths of the two axes of the ellipse. You can place either the long axis or the short axis first, and you can specify the two axes at any angle. However, AutoSketch will ignore the angle of the second axis, using only the length of the axis line and automatically applying it at 90 degrees to the first one.

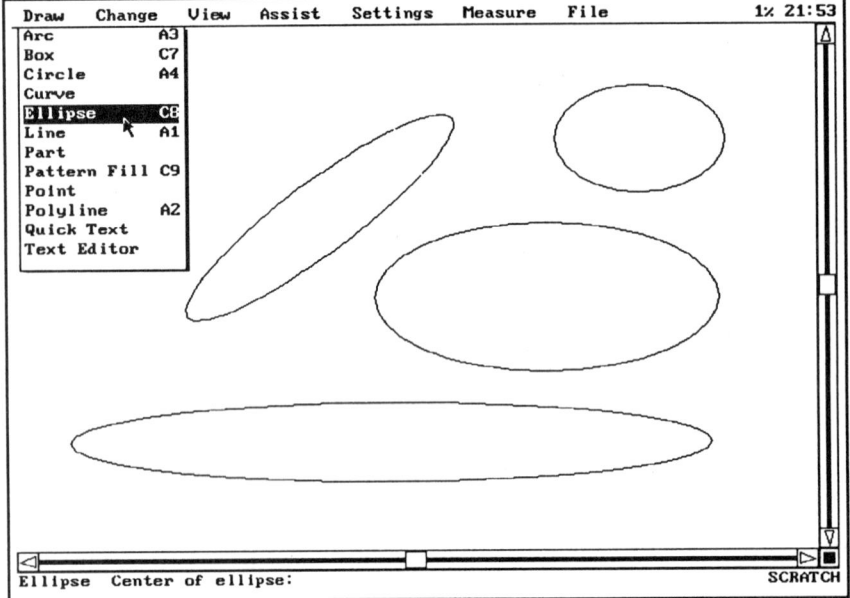

Ellipses on the AutoSketch Screen

Creating an Ellipse

```
Pull down Draw Select Ellipse
Center of ellipse:          Pick a point.
Axis endpoint:              Draw one rubberband radius.
Other axis distance:        Draw a second rubberband radius.
```

A rubberband ellipse is visible as you do this. Try rotating the rubberband radius, noticing that the angle is not important, only the length.

```
Center of ellipse:          Draw a few more ellipses.
```

AutoSketch lets you specify ellipses in two other ways. You choose the ellipse drawing method you want by means of the Ellipse command on the Settings menu. This displays a simple dialogue box listing the three ellipse input options. Click in the check box next to the desired drawing method. The active drawing method is indicated by a check mark. The default method, described above, is called "Center and Both Axes." If you change ellipse methods while the Ellipse command is repeating, you'll have to reselect the Ellipse command to activate the new method.

The second technique for drawing ellipses, "Axis and Planar Rotation," is particularly useful for isometric drawing. It allows you to create an ellipse by rotating a circle "into" your screen. You specify the first ellipse radius just as with the default drawing method. AutoSketch then displays a rubberband circle, and asks for a rotation angle. If you drew your radius line horizontally, imagine tilting the rubberband circle back into the screen. At an angle of 90 degrees, you see the circle edge-on, as a single line.

You'll probably find it easiest to enter the rotation angle directly from the keyboard, using polar coordinates. However, AutoSketch also allows you to use the pointer to position a rubberband line, indicating the desired angle visually.

The third technique for ellipse drawing is called "Two Foci and Point." This method is based on the classic method of drawing an ellipse with a piece of string and two push pins. The pins define the focus points. To draw the ellipse, loop the string around the pins, then trace all the way around in a circular motion while holding the string taut. Geometrically speaking, an ellipse is a path traced out such that the *total* of the distances from the two focus points to any point on the path is always constant.

AutoSketch will show you this in rubberband form. You are prompted to enter first one focus point, then the other. Then specify any point on the ellipse itself.

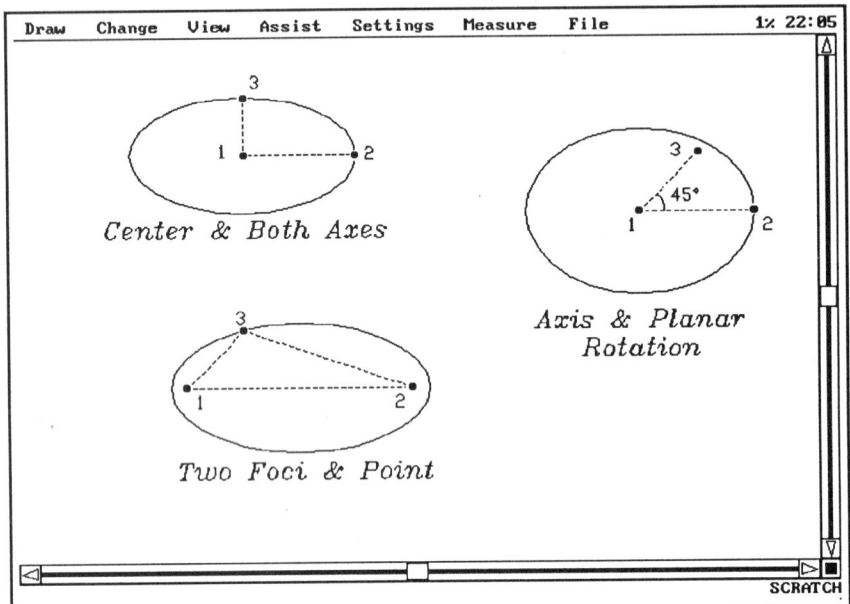

Alternative Methods for Ellipse Drawing

Alternate Methods for Creating an Ellipse

Pull down **Settings** Select **Ellipse**	A dialogue box appears in the center of the screen.
Select Axis and Planar Rotation Click OK	Click on the box next to the option. Closes the dialogue box.
Pull down **Draw** Select **Ellipse** Center of ellipse: Axis endpoint: Rotation around major axis:	Now you are in the Ellipse command. Pick a point. Draw one rubberband radius. Move the rubberband line to indicate the desired rotation angle. A rubberband ellipse is visible as you do this.

Try moving the pointer to show angles of 45 and 90 degrees, noticing what happens to the rubberband ellipse.

Enter **P(1,45)**	The ellipse is fixed in place.
Pull down **Settings** Select **Ellipse** Select Two Foci and Point Pull down **Draw** Select **Ellipse** First focus of ellipse: Second focus: Point on ellipse:	Click on the box next to the third option. The new input format setting takes effect. Pick a point. A rubberband line follows the pointer. Rubberband lines follow the pointer, connecting it to the two focus points.

A rubberband ellipse is also shown. Pick a point to finish the ellipse.

```
First focus of ellipse:
```
Try drawing a few more ellipses.

You may find it easier to get a really accurate ellipse if you use keyboard coordinates to designate the horizontal and vertical axes. Then use the Rotate command to turn it to exactly the angle you need.

➡ *TIP: AutoCAD lets you create ellipses in two out of the same three ways as AutoSketch. The first AutoSketch method, Center and Both Axes, is equivalent to AutoCAD's ELLIPSE command and its Axis endpoint 1 / Axis endpoint 2 / Other axis distance options. The second AutoSketch ellipse method, Axis and Planar Rotation, is the same as AutoCAD's ELLIPSE command with the Axis endpoint 1 / Axis endpoint 2 / Rotation options. AutoSketch's third method, Two Foci and Point, does not have an equivalent method in AutoCAD. Of course, AutoCAD also provides additional ellipse construction options that AutoSketch does not.*

Arcs

An arc is a portion of a circle. The Arc command is a shortcut for what you could otherwise accomplish by creating a complete circle and then cutting away the unwanted portion. Even though there is less of it, an arc takes more points to specify than a full circle. AutoSketch locates an arc by its two endpoints plus a third point on the arc itself.

As you select the second arc endpoint, a rubberband joins the arrow pointer to the first point. You can then dynamically size an arc passing through the second point as the pointer is moved.

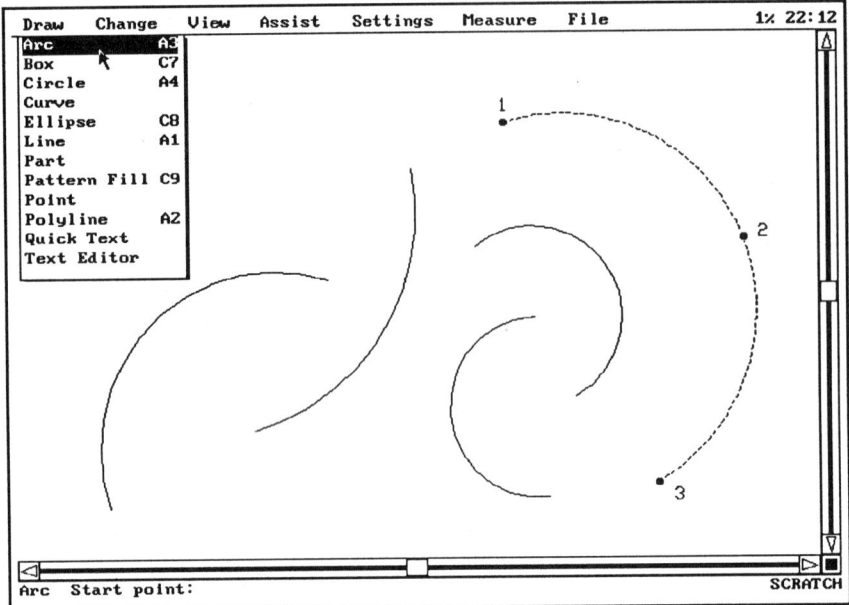

Arcs on the AutoSketch Screen

Creating an Arc

```
Pull down Draw Select Arc
Start point:            Pick starting point of the arc.
Point on arc:           Pick a point anywhere on the arc.
                        The rubberband arc curves through this point.
End point:              Pick endpoint of the arc.
Start point:            Draw some more arcs.
```

Bear in mind that if you choose three arc points that are exactly in line with each other, the arc will come out looking like a straight line. Also, the only way to get an arc that's a portion of an *ellipse* is to draw a full ellipse and break away the unwanted section. (We'll look at the Break command in Chapter 7.)

Polyline Arcs

The Polyline command allows you to mix arc segments with line segments, making it the most versatile drawing tool available in AutoSketch.

Polyline Arcs 2-17

➥ *NOTE: This capability was added only with AutoSketch version 3.0. In earlier versions, you can mix straight segments and arcs only by separately creating polygon or line segments and arc segments.*

As you draw a polyline, you can switch between drawing arc segments and line segments by selecting the special Arc Mode command on the Assist menu, or by pressing <CTRL-F1>. Polyline arc segments are drawn in exactly the same way as with the Arc command. Your last polyline point is assumed to be the starting point of the arc, and you are then asked to enter a point on the arc and an endpoint. This doesn't interrupt the current polyline.

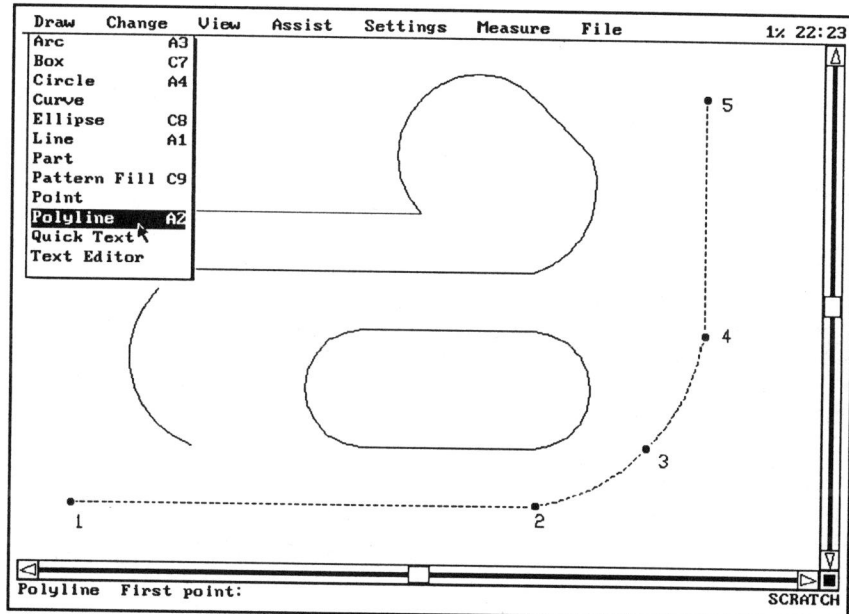

Polylines on the AutoSketch Screen

Creating a Polyline Arc

```
Pull down Draw Select Polyline
First point:                         Pick starting point for the polyline.
To point:                            Pick next point on polyline.
Pull down Assist Select Arc Mode     Switch to arc drawing.
Point on arc:                        Pick a point along the arc.
                                     The rubberband arc curves around this point.
Arc segment endpoint:                Pick endpoint of the arc.
Point on arc:                        Draw some more arc segments.
```

| `Pull down Assist Select Arc Mode` | Switch back to line drawing. |

Continue drawing segments. Double-click a point to end polyline.

Note that you can terminate the polyline while in either Line or Arc mode. However, you can't do this by placing two arc *midpoints* on top of each other, only start points. If you try to double up a midpoint, AutoSketch will warn you that your "Arc segment contains coincident or colinear points." This is in contrast to the Arc drawing mode, which will allow you to place any of the arc points on top of each other, or in a straight line with each other.

Note also that the Arc Mode command acts as a *toggle* switch. The current mode remains in force until you deliberately change it, even if you quit polyline drawing and then later start again. Of course, each time you start up AutoSketch afresh, you'll always begin in Line mode.

Curves

When you want a more complex curve (neither circular nor elliptical), the Curve tool allows you to approximate the desired shape. When drawing with Curve, you pick a series of points and AutoSketch then creates a smoothly curved line to fit around them.

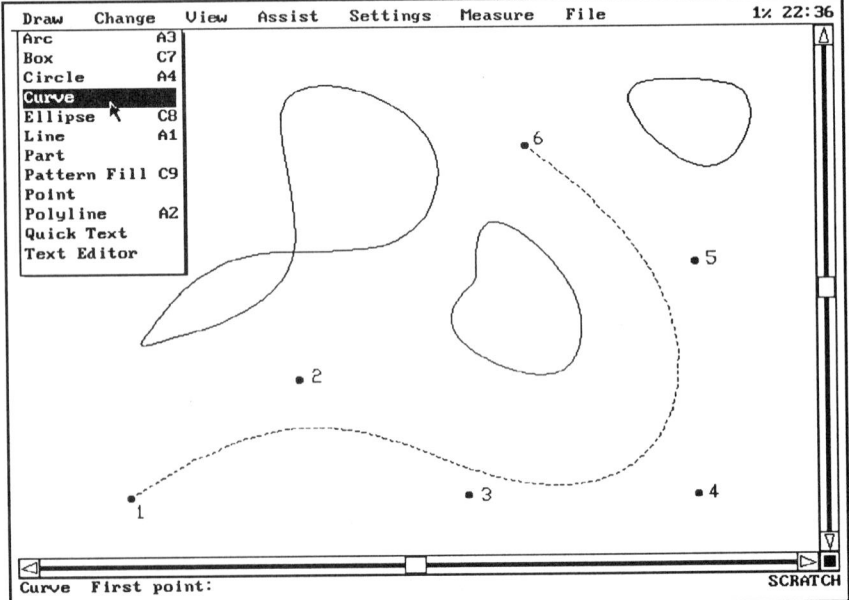

Curves on the AutoSketch Screen

Creating a Curve

```
Pull down Draw Select Curve
First point:                Pick a starting point.
To point:                   Pick a curve control point.
To point:                   Pick as many points as needed to rough out the desired curve.
To point:                   To end and see the curve, enter final point twice, or select a
                            new command, and the curve is smoothed.
```

Technically, the actual construction involved in creating a curve is called a "B-spline," which is a slick mathematical method of generating a smooth curve by specifying separate control points. Think of the points as "pulling" on the line to bend it into a curve.

AutoSketch refers to its curves in terms of straight lines between successive control points, and calculates a spline to fit them. The straight lines are the framework for the curve. All curve frames in your drawing can be toggled on to be visible, or off to be hidden, by means of the Frame command on the Assist menu. Switching the frames *on* can make working with curves easier. It's a necessity when you come to editing curves with the tools in the AutoSketch Change menu. For more on curves and frames, see Chapter 6, *Advanced Drawing Tools*.

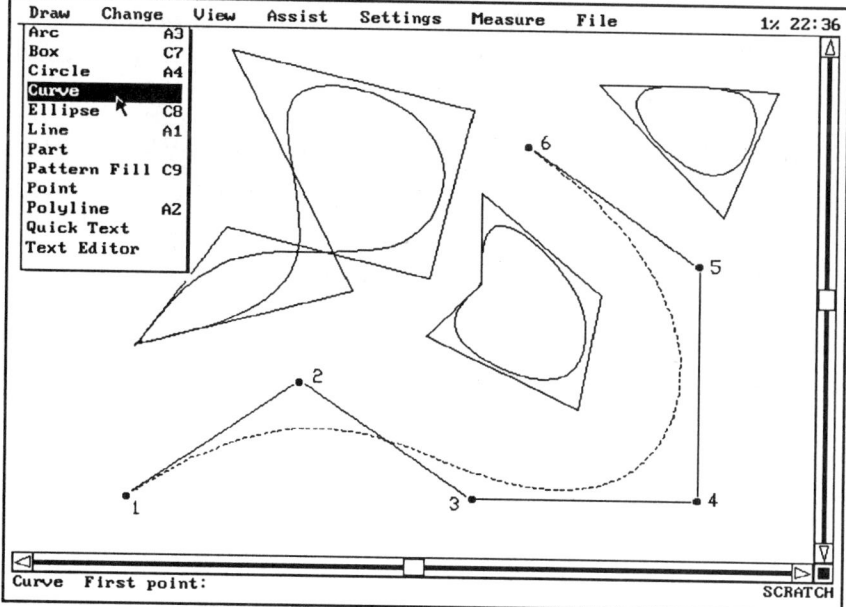

Toggle the Curve Frame On

Pull down **Assist** Select **Frame**	Toggle Frame on.
Toggle Frame back off.	

You may wonder where you need to enter control points in order to produce any particular curved shape, since a curve doesn't pass through its control points. There's a bit of artistry involved here. Points *pull* the curve toward themselves. The pull increases if you use more points, or increase the angle or distance between them. You can rough-in relatively unimportant parts of the curve with just a few points, and tighten up the significant sections by taking the time to place lots of points in a small area.

You can alter the shape of a curve after it's drawn by means of the Stretch command on the Change menu. Unfortunately, you can only move the existing control points, without deleting any or adding any new ones.

Like polylines, curves are considered to be single drawing elements for most editing operations. Keep in mind that no single curve may contain more than 200 control points.

➥ *TIP: In AutoCAD, a B-spline curve is made with the PLINE command with the Spline curve option. By default, AutoCAD creates a cubic B-spline curve that is the same as an AutoSketch curve. AutoCAD can also create quadratic B-spline curves if the SPLINETYPE system variable is changed from 6 (cubic) to 5. The two curve types appear similar, but a quadratic B-spline curve more closely follows control points than a cubic curve does. AutoCAD does not, however, allow you to display the curve's frame during editing as AutoSketch does. Instead, you must invoke the PEDIT command with the Decurve option to convert the curve back into its original straight PLINE segments. The Edit vertex option may then be used to move the curve's control points about, and the Spline option reapplied.*

Text

AutoSketch allows you to add text to your drawings. Text is handled just like simple geometric objects. Each line of text is treated as a single drawing element attached to an origin point.

Starting with version 3.0, AutoSketch provides two methods of adding text. The Quick Text command works like the Text command found in earlier versions, although there are now more options for controlling the appearance of the text. The Text Editor command is new in version 3.0, and allows multi-line blocks of text to be conveniently entered, edited, and even imported from ASCII files you create separately with a word processor or text editor.

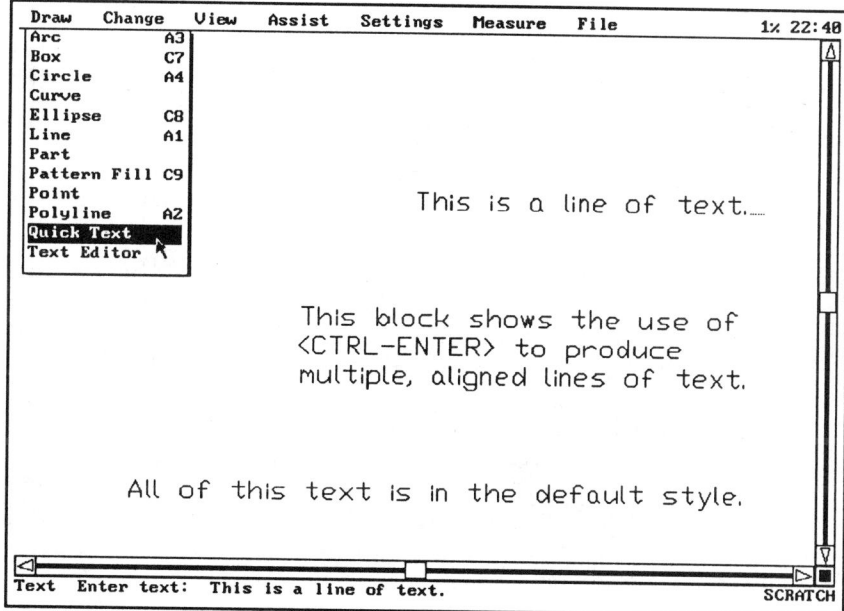

Adding Quick Text to a Drawing

Creating Quick Text

```
Pull down Draw Select Quick Text              Pick a starting point.
Enter point:
Enter text: Drawing in AutoSketch             Type desired text, and press <ENTER>.
```

Characters appear on the drawing as well as on the prompt line. You can easily enter multiple lines. Clicking the pointer button or typing <CTRL-J> or <CTRL-ENTER> will move the cursor down so that you can continue typing text on the next line. However, the two lines will become separate drawing elements.

Multiple lines entered using the Text Editor will appear as a single drawing object. The text editor is simply a dialogue box with a large empty area in which you can type your text. A number of editing commands are available along the bottom of the box; these will be discussed in Chapter 3.

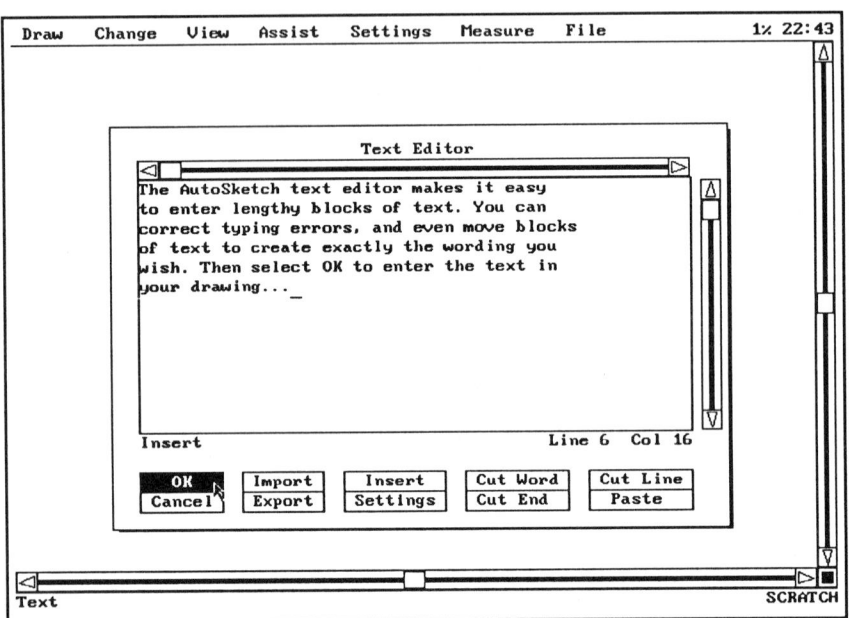

Entering Text in the Text Editor

Creating Text Using the Text Editor

```
Pull down Draw Select Text Editor
Enter point:                              Pick a starting point. The Text Editor dialogue
                                          box appears in the middle of the screen.
This is the first line of text.           Type desired text, and press <ENTER>.
And here's another line.                  Type another line of text.
Click OK                                  Click on OK to finish.
Enter point:                              Your text appears in the drawing.
```

A number of special text characters are available. These are turned on or off by means of special sequences of characters that you enter within your text. These sequences begin with a double percent sign (%%). The valid sequences and the effects they control are shown in the table below. The first time you enter a sequence turns the effect on; entering the same sequence again turns the effect off.

A Table of Special Text Characters	
%%o	overscore on/off
%%u	underscore on/off
%%d	the degrees symbol
%%p	the "plus-or-minus" tolerance symbol
%%c	the diameter symbol
%%%	the percent sign

As you type, the multiple percent signs will appear normally, either in the drawing or in the editor box. However, when you click the pointer or hit the <ENTER> key — or click on OK in the editor — the percent signs will vanish, and the specified effect or symbol will appear. The effects can be combined in any way you wish.

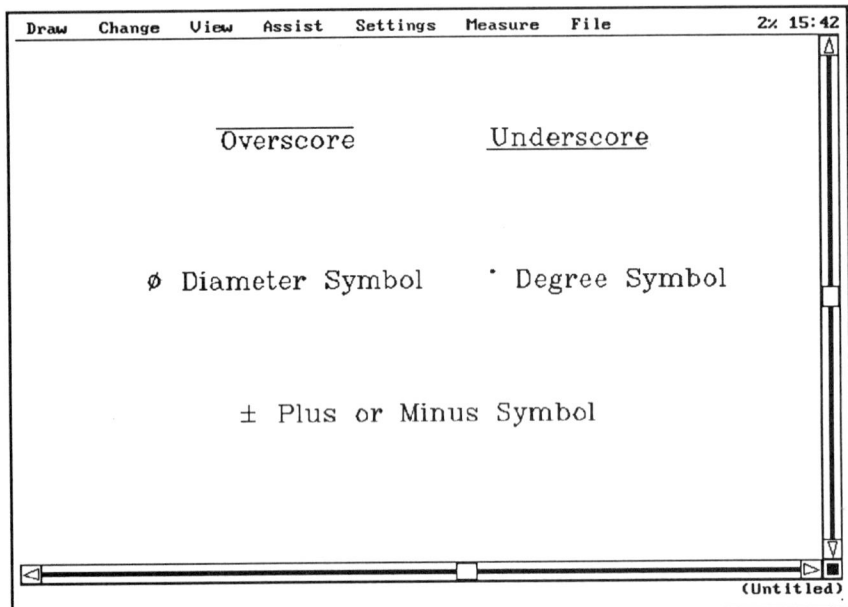

Special Text Characters

Starting with version 2.0, AutoSketch can also create text in various typestyles. We'll deal with some of the possibilities in the next chapter.

➥ *TIP: The AutoCAD DTEXT command performs identically to the AutoSketch Quick Text command, including character editing. The special text characters that begin with double percent signs (%%) are also equivalent. The AutoSketch Quick Text command should not, however, be confused with the AutoCAD QTEXT, or "quick text" command. AutoCAD's QTEXT command displays text in a drawing as simple rectangles that approximate the dimensional extents of the text entities they represent. This can be helpful to reduce display redraw and regeneration times. The AutoSketch Text Editor command does not yet have a corresponding command in AutoCAD as of Release 10.*

Command Practice

Before you try the Map Drawing Exercise, you can practice and try alternatives with the commands you have learned.

NEW. Begin a new drawing to use for the practice exercises. Use the New option from the File menu. Save the file as SCRATCH.

POINT. Use your pointing device to place some points on the screen in an arrangement that suggests a simple shape (a square, for example). Notice the difficulty of aligning the four corners accurately so that the square doesn't come out lopsided. Then try entering the following series of coordinate pairs: **1,1 3,1 3,3 1,3**. Compare your "freehand" square with this one. Consider the time it took to create both and the precision with which they appear on screen.

POINT. Try using the keyboard to enter very large coordinate values. They'll go way out in space, but AutoSketch has no objections. You just won't be able to see the results for now.

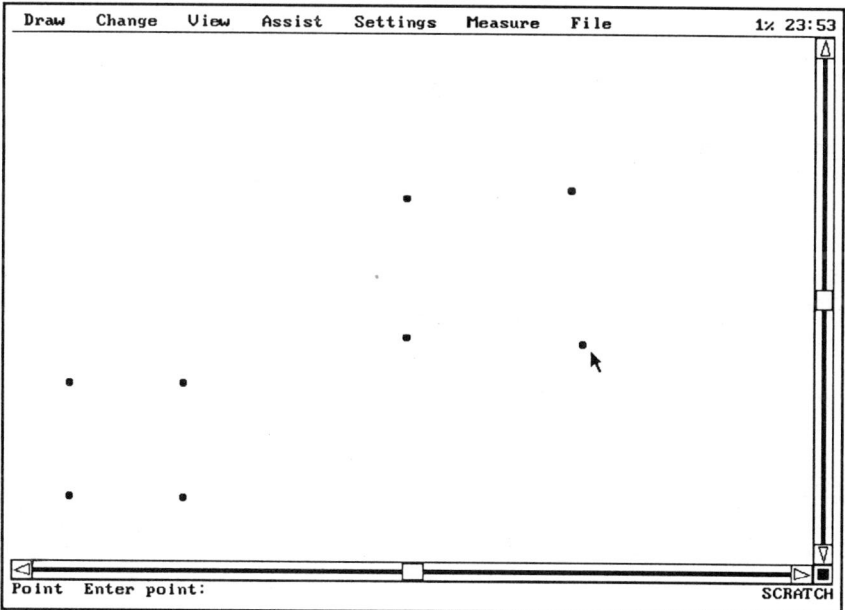

Practice With Points

LINE. Try creating a *continuous* line from multiple line segments. Notice that you have to begin each new line from exactly the same point you ended the last. Practice "double-clicking" your pointing device to simultaneously end a line and start a new one. Alternatively, try creating continuous lines by entering coordinates, re-entering the ending coordinate of each line as the starting coordinate of its successor.

LINE. Try creating some simple shapes using the Line command. For instance, create a square both freehand and using the same sequence of coordinates used in the Point Practice exercise (**1,1 3,1 3,3 1,3**). Remember, you have to double-click to start the next line on the same point as the endpoint of the last line. Try some other shapes. What relative coordinates might you use for an equilateral triangle?

ERASE, UNDO, REDO. Try undoing the last few commands, then redoing them back again. Then try to erase the first element you drew.

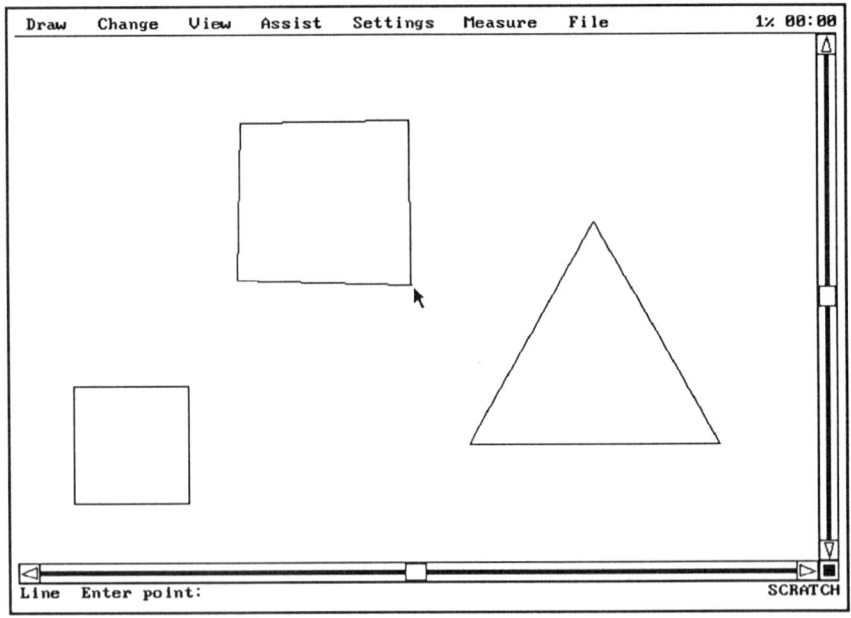

Practice With Lines

BOX. Create a box using the pointing device. Create a second box using the more accurate keyboard coordinate entry method. Use relative coordinates for the second point.

BOX. Create the same square described in the above LINE practice — first, freehand using the pointer, then using the coordinates. Notice that you now only need to enter two (diagonal) coordinates.

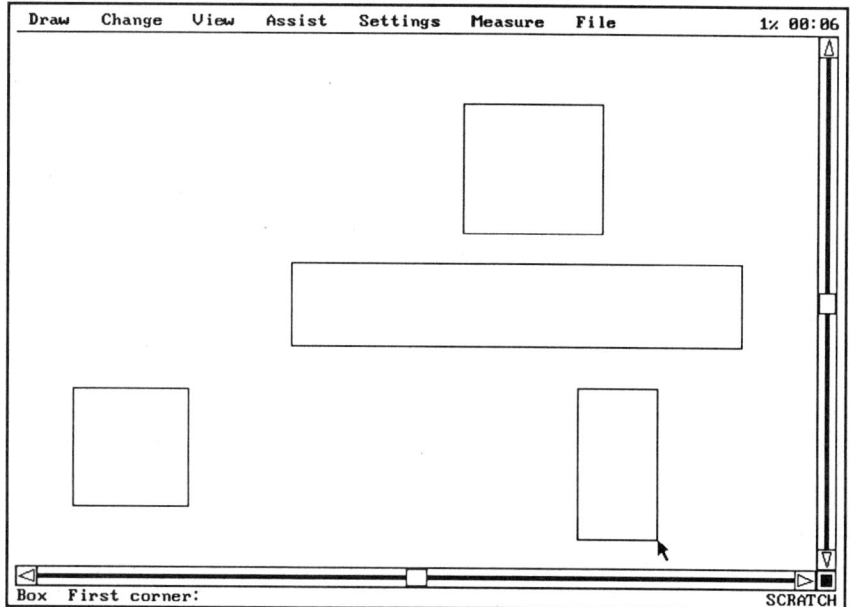

Drawing Some Boxes

POLYLINE. You've already tried drawing a square using absolute coordinates. Now try it using relative coordinates. Using the Polyline (or Polygon, for AutoSketch version 2.0) command, draw a square of three units on a side beginning at the (absolute) point (1,1). Notice that you'll need to switch to negative relative X and Y values as you come around the top of the square.

POLYLINE. Try the same exercise, using polar coordinates. (Obviously, the key angles are 0, 90, 180 and 270 degrees.) Notice that you can keep re-entering the same distance for each side.

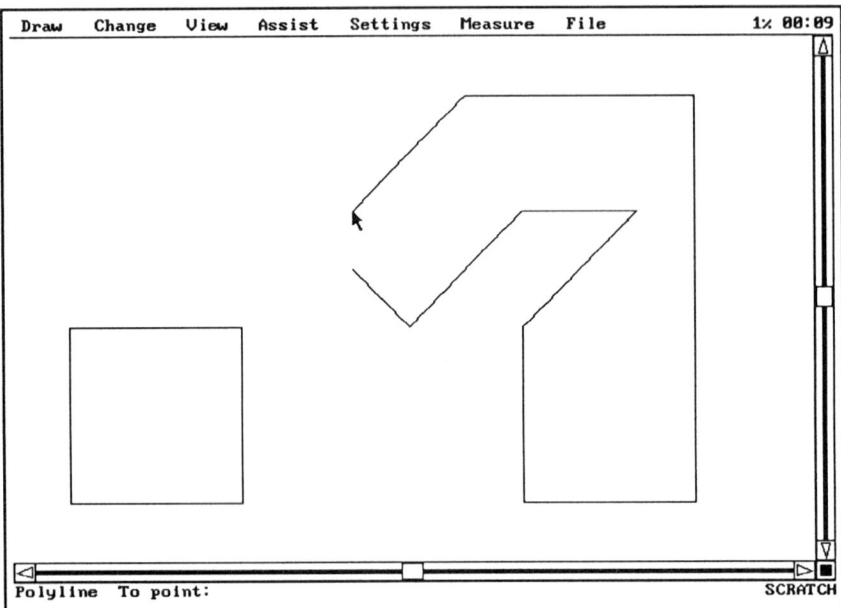

A Box Is a Polygon

POLYLINE. Try switching into Arc mode to create a racetrack shape. Draw a straight line, then a semicircular arc, then another straight line parallel to the first, then another circular arc to close the shape. (Keyboard coordinates will let you do the job accurately. What coordinates do you need for points on the two end arcs? Hint: to make it easy, pick a point half the distance between the two parallel lines, and the same amount past their ends; this is the midpoint of the arc.)

CIRCLE. Try to recreate the three-circle designs in the following illustration. The lower, interlocking pattern is particularly tricky. (Notice that two of the circles have the same X-coordinate at their center. Finding the third center requires a bit of elementary geometry. This third coordinate is not "integral" — that is, it does not fall on an even numerical location. AutoSketch allows you to enter fractional coordinates with up to seven decimal places.)

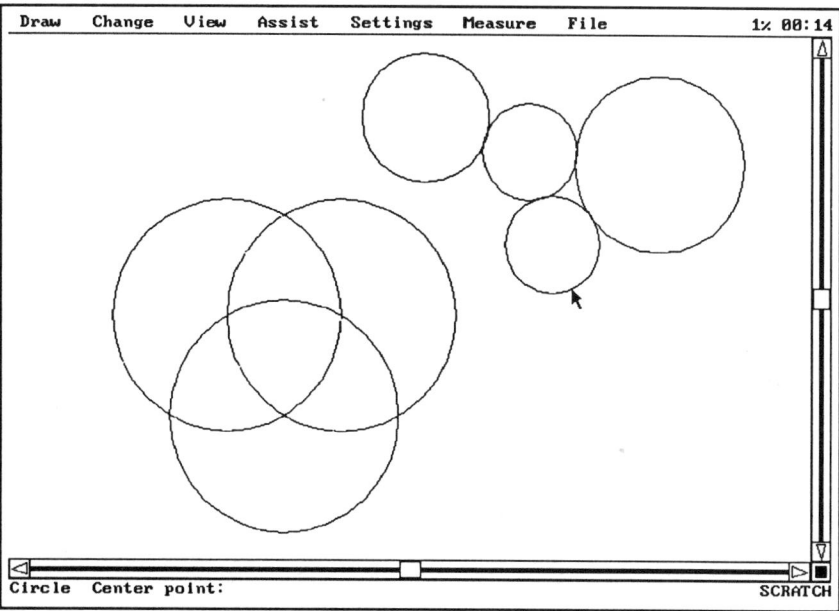

Practice With Circles

ELLIPSE. Try drawing ellipses using all three methods: Center and Both Axes, Axis and Planar Rotation, and Two Foci and Point. Get a feel for the differences between them.

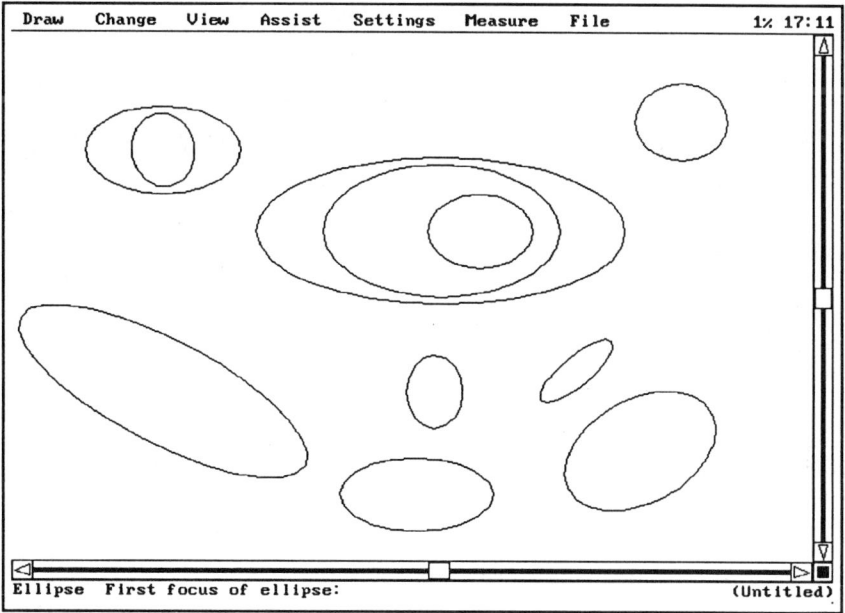

Practice With Ellipses

ARC. Create some arcs using whatever mixture of pointer moves and keyboard coordinates you like. Try to create a circle using two Arc commands.

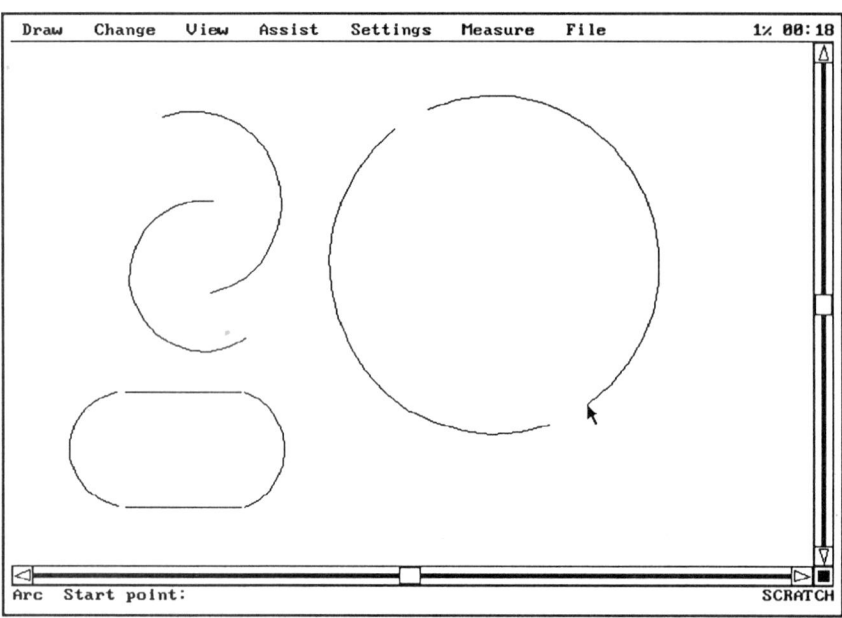

Draw a Circle With Two Arcs

CURVE. Turn Frame on. Try drawing something like a face, roughing in the features with straight lines, then complete the curve and watch as your picture is magically smoothed out.

CURVE. To get a feel for the "pull" exerted by control points, try laying a curve out using four control points in a simple rectangular arrangement. Surprise! The rectangle becomes an ellipse when you close the points. Next try the same thing but using one, two, three, or four extra points — first along one side of the construction rectangle, then bunched together near a corner, and notice what happens to the curve.

TEXT. Try entering a line of text, using the Quick Text command. Also try entering several lines of text, clicking your pointer or pressing <CTRL-J> or <CTRL-ENTER> to move down. Now enter several lines using the Text Editor. You may find you prefer one method over the other; both have their benefits.

Try entering some underlined text. How about an underlined percent sign? (Note that AutoSketch can sort out a large number of special text characters all at once.) Try entering a longer passage of text in the Text Editor, mixing in a variety of special effects as you go.

ERASE. By now, your drawing is probably pretty cluttered. Use Erase (if you haven't already!) to clean things up a bit. Try erasing some text; see if you can get the hang of where to select it. (AutoSketch uses an invisible baseline to position text, similar to the frame used for curves.)

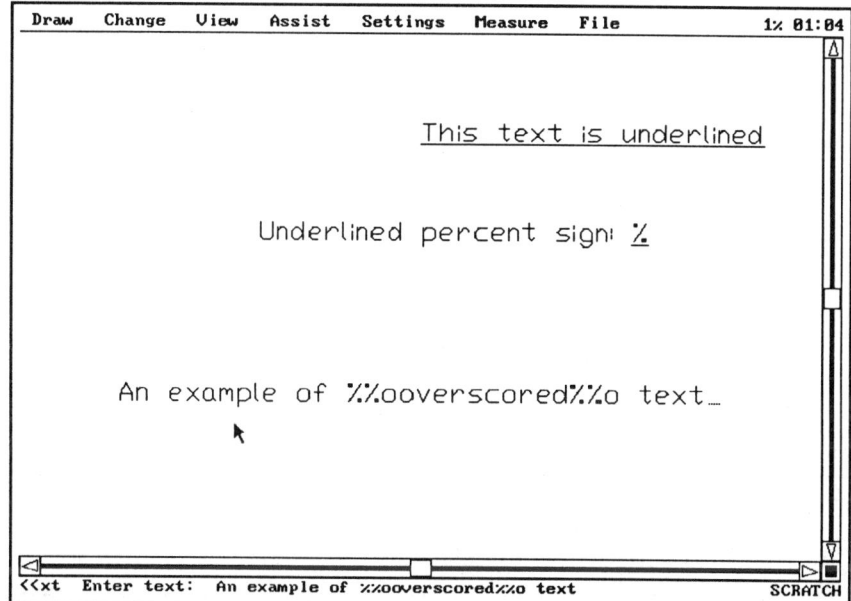

Use of Special Text Characters

Map Drawing

Now it's time to put what you've learned to use. This exercise will show you how to create a simple map: something that you might whip up, say, to show some friends how to get to your country cottage. Unlike a real map that is drawn to scale and is suitable for measuring distances, this drawing is like one you would sketch on scratch paper. You won't be drawing it to scale, so don't be too concerned about accuracy. Just try to get accustomed to using the commands.

In later chapters, we'll come back to this map and show you how you can use AutoSketch to refine it into a professional-looking drawing. You'll also find easier ways to create many of the elements of the map. However, the beauty of AutoSketch is that you don't have to know much about the program in order to turn out a useful piece of work.

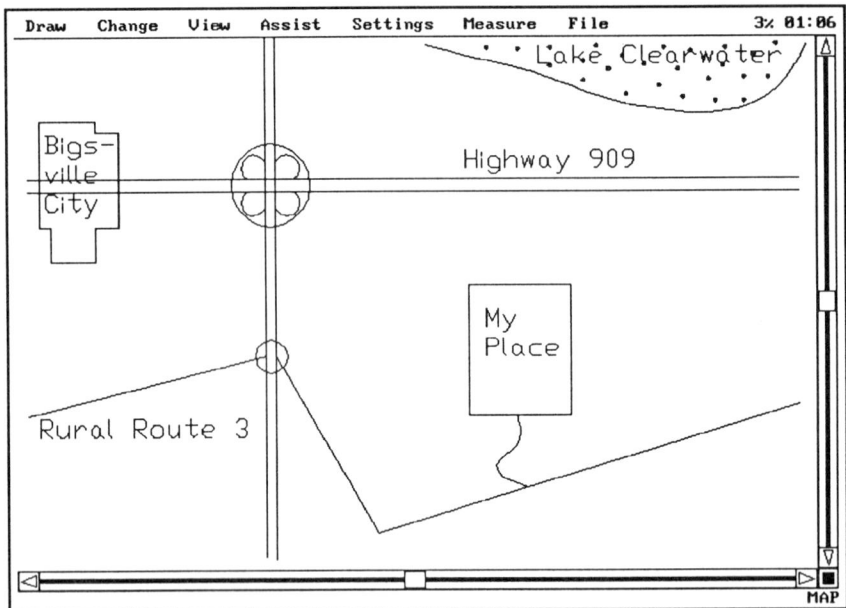

The Map

First, use the Point command repeatedly until you have a bunch of dots (representing water in a lake) across the top right edge of the screen. For a highway, use two long horizontal lines very close together, about two-thirds of the way up from the bottom of the screen. Draw another with a similar pair of vertical lines, about one-third of the way in from the left edge of the screen. At this point, your drawing should resemble the next illustration.

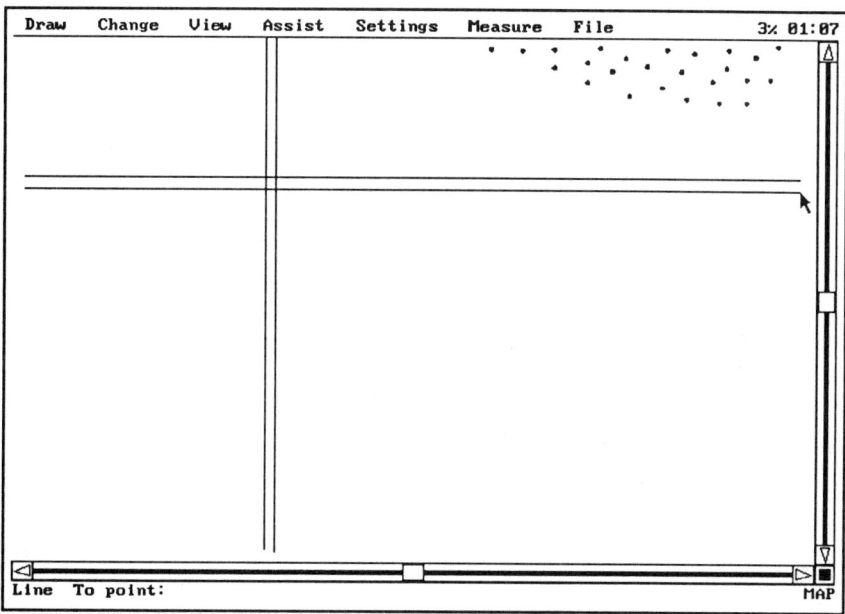

The Highway Lines

Map Drawing Exercise

Pull down **File** Select **New**	Start a new drawing.
Pull down **File** Select **Save As**	
Filename **MAP**	Save the blank drawing under the name MAP.
Click **OK**	
Pull down **Draw** Select **Point**	
Enter point:	Pick somewhere in the right corner.
Enter point:	Continue adding points to form Lake Clearwater.
Pull down **Draw** Select **Line**	
Enter point:	Pick left end of the top horizontal line of highway 909.
To point:	Pick right end.
Enter point:	Pick right end of the bottom horizontal line.
To point:	Pick left end of the bottom horizontal line.
Enter point:	Pick top of the left vertical line.
To point:	Pick endpoint.
Enter point:	Pick top of right vertical line.
To point:	Pick endpoint.
Pull down **File** Select **Save**	Save the MAP file.

If your lines have any steps, or jaggies, in them, they aren't truly vertical or horizontal. You might want to try redoing them, taking care to eliminate all the jaggedness from the rubberband lines before you "fix" them in place. You can also use keyboard coordinates, taking care to make X or Y coordinates the same for the two ends of horizontal or vertical lines, respectively. Or use polar coordinates, with angles in exact multiples of 90 degrees.

Next draw your estate with a box roughly in the center of the big empty area at the bottom right of the screen. Follow this with a closed polyline representing a major city in the upper left corner. Then, add a zig-zag horizontal open polygon as a local back road, about one-fourth up from the bottom of the screen.

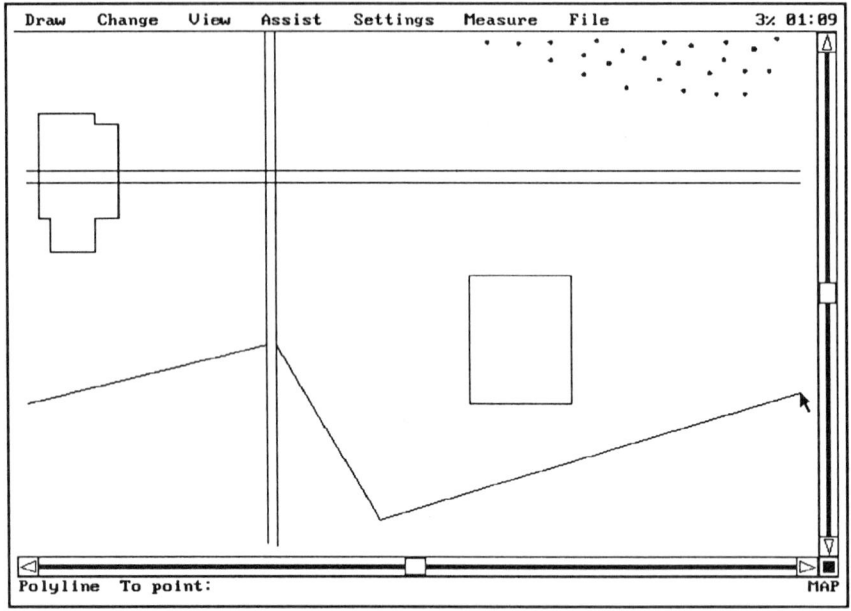

The Cities and Backroad Polylines

Pull down **Draw** Select **Box**	Pick points to make it about 1" square.
Pull down **Draw** Select **Polyline**	
First point:	Pick points for a random angular shape.
Close it, last point on the first.	
First point:	Draw a crooked line and double-click to end.
Pull down **File** Select **Save**	Save the MAP file.

You won't need a lot of circles. You can draw two small ones (representing small towns). Put one around the spot where the two double line highways intersect and another smaller one where the crooked "backroad" polygon crosses the vertical double line highway. To finish up the highways, try putting in a cloverleaf interchange. Put four arcs in the crossroads, emphasizing the intersection. (This is a tricky one — in Chapter 6 we'll see a way to get these kinds of things to match up exactly.)

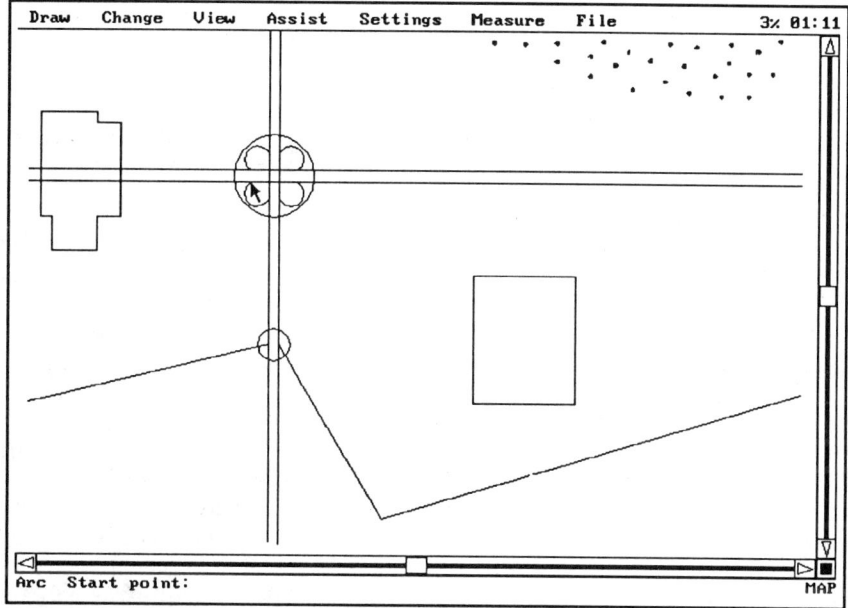

The Cloverleaf Arcs

```
Pull down Draw Select Circle
Center point:                      Pick top circle center point.
Point on circle:                   Pick circle radius.
Center point:                      Pick bottom circle center point.
Point on circle:                   Pick circle radius.
Pull down Draw Select Arc
Start point:                       Pick on a line, near an intersection.
Point on arc:                      Pick further out, 45 degrees from intersection.
End point:                         Drag to other line and pick.
Point on arc:                      Repeat for the other three arcs.
Pull down File Select Save         Save MAP file.
```

You just need three more things to finish up the map for this chapter. Place a curve across the upper right edge of the screen, enclosing the points you started off with. The curve and those points represent Lake Clearwater in our simple map. Connect your estate to the local backwoods access road. Use a nice "S" curve from the right side of the box down to the crooked line across the lower part of the screen. This leaves the last crucial step in building our map — the labels.

Pull down **Draw** Select **Curve**	
First point:	Contain the points with a gentle curve.
To point:	Pick several control points.
To point:	Double-click to end.
First point:	Connect the box to the crooked line.
To point:	Exaggerate the zig-zag to make an "S" curve.
Pull down **Draw** Select **Quick Text**	
Enter point:	Pick at left, in the BIG CITY.
Enter text: **Bigsville City** <ENTER>	Type "Bigsville<CTRL-ENTER>City" and <ENTER>.
Enter point:	Pick above the horizontal superhighway.
Enter text: **Highway 909** <ENTERN>	Type and <ENTER>.
Enter point:	Pick in the body of water.
Enter point: **Lake Clearwater**	
Enter point:	Pick a point along the backroad.
Enter text: **Rural Route 3** <ENTER>	Type and <ENTER>.
Enter point:	Pick within your property.
Enter text: **My place** <ENTER>	Type and <ENTER>.
Pull down **File** Select **Save**	Save latest changes.
Pull down **File** Select **Quit**	Get out of AutoSketch.

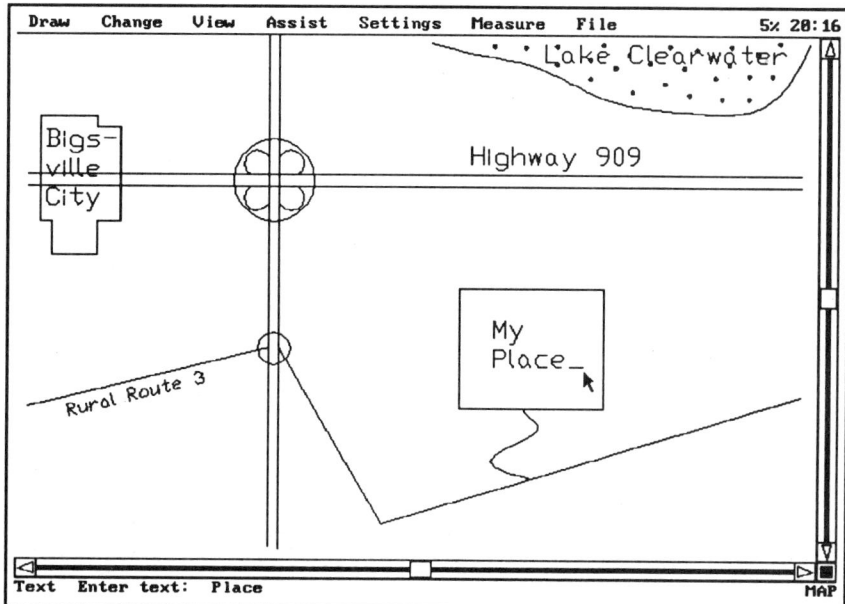

The Map So Far, With Text

Summary

What you've seen in this chapter has been true to its title: drawing fundamentals. You should now be at least roughly acquainted with all the major AutoSketch drawing commands: Point, Line, Box, Polyline, Circle, Ellipse, Arc, and Curve. Each command creates one type of drawing object, and you can build up just about any conceivable drawing using these objects. In addition to these simple drawing commands, you've also seen two commands that allow you to add text to your drawing: Quick Text for fast text entry directly on the drawing screen, and the Text Editor for creating larger blocks of text.

You've had a chance to experiment with the all-important Undo and Redo commands. When all else fails, Undo can be a life-saver. The Erase command is almost as essential. The drawing commands allow you to create various geometric objects; Erase lets you remove them.

Now that you've seen how to create AutoSketch drawing objects, you can move on and look at the powerful editing tools that allow you to modify them. That's the subject of our next chapter.

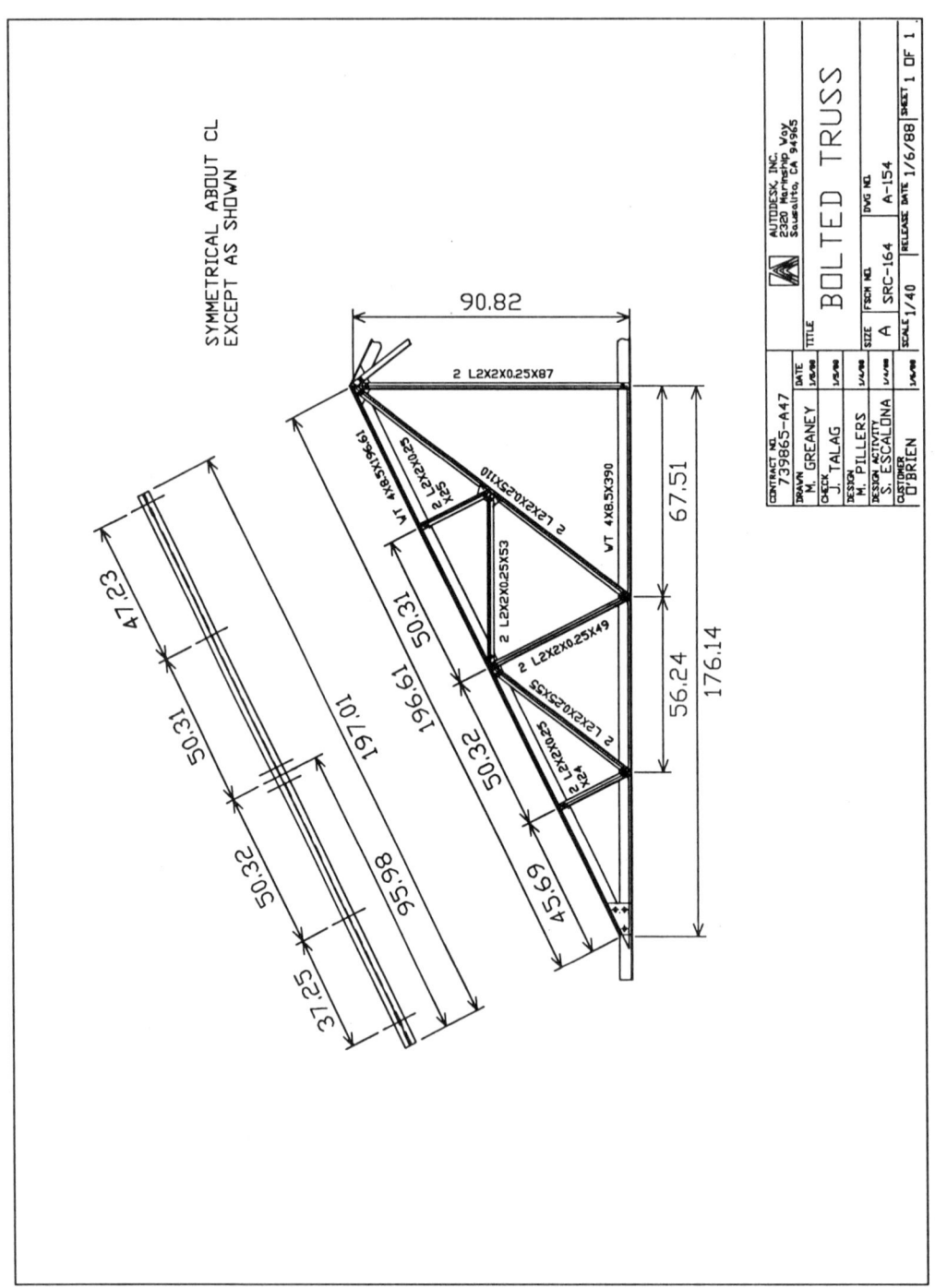

Bolted Truss, Courtesy of Autodesk, Inc.

Chapter 3

Basic Editing

Now that you've seen how to get some simple stuff up on the screen, you can begin to experiment with the *real* power of AutoSketch. Using commands from the Change menu, you'll see how the elements of a drawing can be shifted, copied, erased, and distorted in various ways.

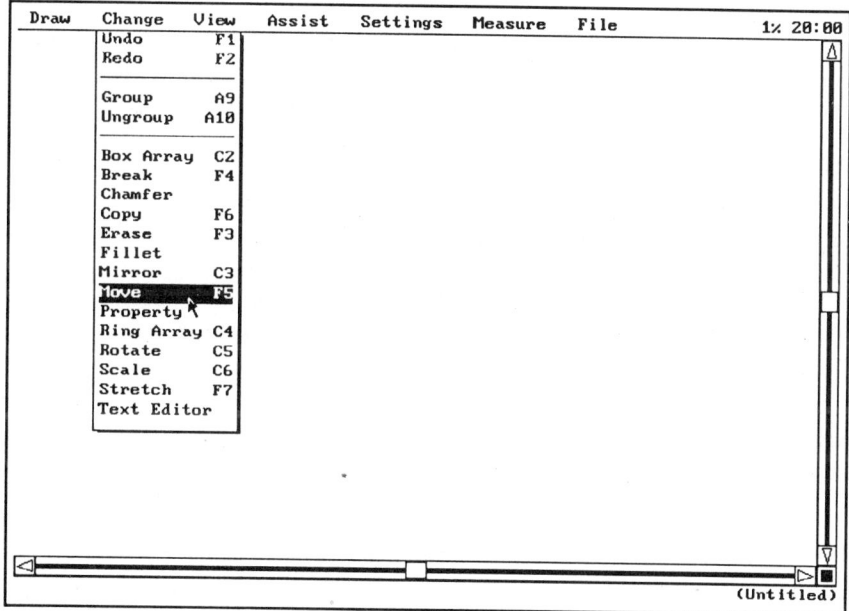

The Change Menu

The advantage of drawing with a computer, rather than an old-fashioned implement such as a pencil or Rapidograph pen, is that what appears on your screen is infinitely malleable. Nothing needs to be permanent; anything can be altered, any time.

We've already belabored the point that AutoSketch uses compact mathematical representations of drawing objects internally. AutoSketch isn't concerned with which dots on your screen are black or white. Whenever you want to see a picture, AutoSketch recalculates and redraws your picture rather than simply restoring a remembered pixel image to the screen. In this chapter you'll begin to see why this is important.

AutoSketch lets you alter any element within your picture in various ways. To begin with, you can move it, copy it, erase it, stretch it out of shape, scale it to uniformly change its size, mirror or reverse it, and rotate it. In Chapter 7, *Advanced Editing Tools*, we'll see some even more advanced possibilities: for example, cutting individual objects apart, or multiplying them into arrays.

Let's put some basic objects on the screen in order to practice the editing commands. By now, your SCRATCH file is probably becoming fairly crowded. Therefore, start a new drawing and then save it using the Save As command under the name SCRATCH. This will give you a new SCRATCH file that has a clear screen. Then use the various Draw commands (Line, Circle, Arc, Box, and Polyline) to make your screen resemble the following illustration. Use this as the basis for performing the editing exercises.

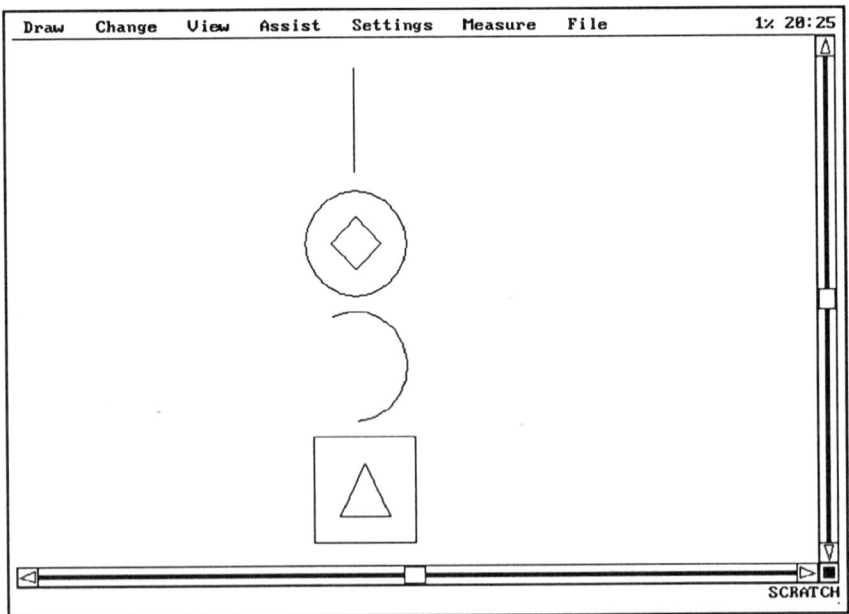

Draw These Objects

Setting Up the SCRATCH File

```
Pull down File Select Open            Open the SCRATCH file.
Pull down File Select New             The screen is cleared.
Pull down File Select Save As
File: SCRATCH                         SCRATCH file is recreated.
Pull down Draw Select Line
Enter point:                          Draw a line.
Pull down Draw Select Circle
Center point:                         Draw a circle.
Pull down Draw Select Arc
Start point:                          Draw an arc.
Pull down Draw Select Box
First corner:                         Draw a box.
Pull down Draw Select Polyline
First point:                          Pick a point.
```

Continue to pick the points required to complete the appropriate shape. Use Polyline again to draw both the triangle and the diamond.

Move

There's no great mystery to the Move command. AutoSketch lets you grab what you wish, and move it anywhere. The biggest trick is in the grabbing action itself.

Using the hand pointer, you can pick any single object on the screen. However, this can be tricky once your picture starts to get complicated. Often a better method is to use the Crosses/window box selector. The following exercise lets you try out all three methods.

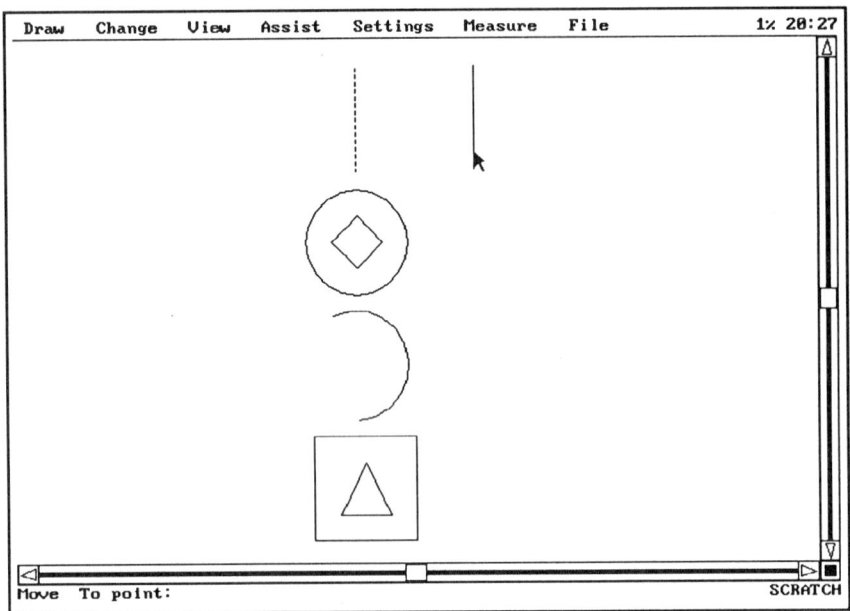

Move the Line

Moving a Drawing Element

First, try moving a single line.
Pull down **Change** Select **Move**   Activates Move.
Select object: Select the line.
From point: Select reference point.
To point: Pick a new location.
Pull down **Change** Select Undo   Undo last operation to put the line back.

Now, try to pull the diamond out of the circle, using a Window box.
Press <F5>   Activates Move.
Select object: Pick point within lower left of circle.
Crosses/window corner: Use Window to surround all of diamond *only*.
From point: Select reference point.
To point: Pick new location.

Finally, select both the box and the triangle with a Crosses box.
Select object: Pick point at the upper right side of the box.
Crosses/window corner: Drag left, enclose part of box and triangle.
From point: Select reference point.
To point: Pick new location.
Select object: <F1>   Select Undo, and repeat to undo all move operations.

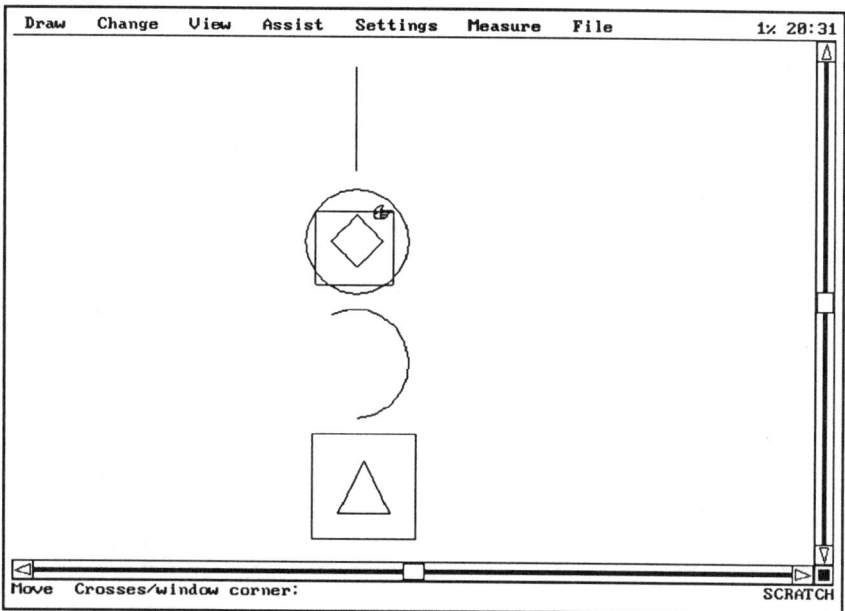

Moving the Diamond, With a Window

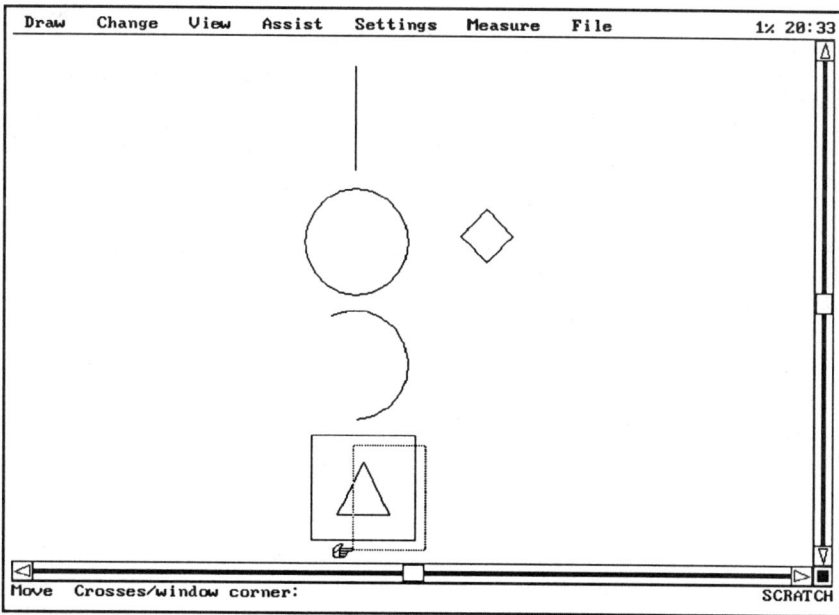

Crossing Selects the Box and Triangle

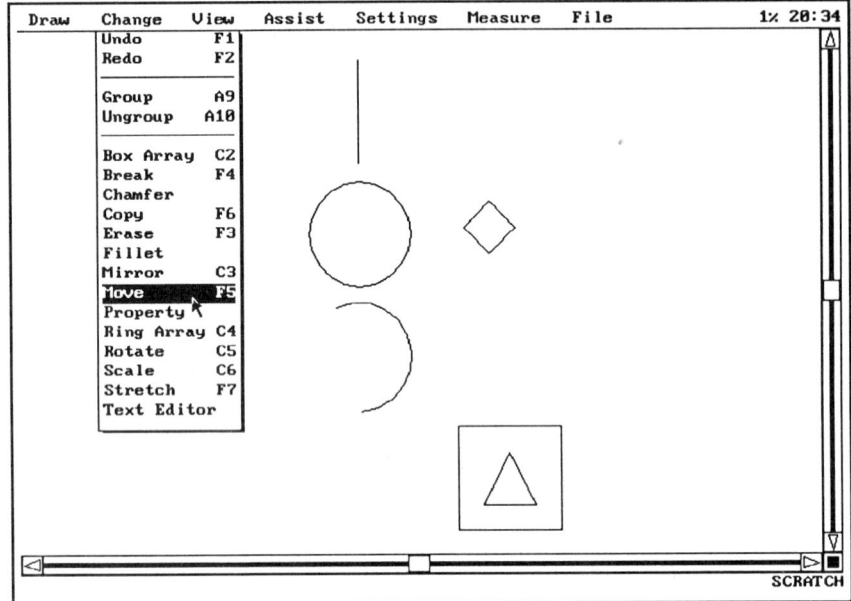

All Moved

Once you've selected an object or group of objects to move, AutoSketch asks you to pick a base reference point for the object or group. All objects will move relative to this base point. When you move the pointer, an outline of the selected items will have attached itself to your pointer. Like the rubberband lines presented by the Box or Circle commands, the outline image lets you accurately pick the new location for the objects you wish to move.

Picking an appropriate base point makes it much easier to move an object to its new location accurately. If there's a point on the object that you wish to locate precisely, pick that point as the base point. For example, to connect one end of a line to some other object on the screen, place the base point at the end of the line. If you wanted to place a line endpoint one drawing unit away from a reference point, you could pick the base point one drawing unit away from the line endpoint, then drag your pointer directly to the reference point.

When you move a curve object, you'll see a rubberband image not of the curve itself, but of its normally invisible *frame*. This may make it more difficult to position a curve accurately. The frame is always used by AutoSketch internally to locate the curve. Therefore, to select a curve for editing, you'll need to select the frame rather than the visible, and usually smaller, curve. Surrounding the curve with a large Crosses/window box is the easiest way to ensure that it is selected.

Copy

The Copy command is virtually identical to the Move command, except for one detail. As with Move, you select an object (or group of objects), then drag the outline version into a new location. Unlike Move, Copy leaves the original where it was. Try copying the line and the arc.

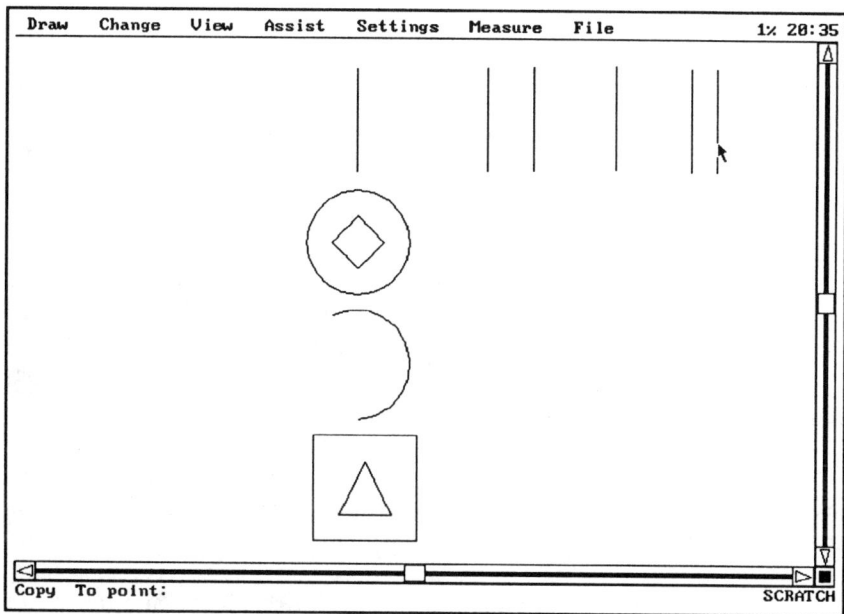

The Copied Line

Copying a Drawing Element

Copy the line a few times across the top of the screen.

Pull down **Change** Select **Copy**	Activates Copy.
Select object:	Select the line.
From point:	Pick reference point.
To point:	Pick copy location.

Now, copy the arc, using keyboard coordinates.

Pull down **Change** Select **Erase**	Erase one of the lines.
Press **<F6>**	Activates Copy.
Select object:	Select the arc.
From point:	Pick reference point.
To point: **R(2,0)**	Relative coordinates.

Use Undo to clean up.

Pull down **Change** Select **Undo**	Or <F1> to undo all the copies.

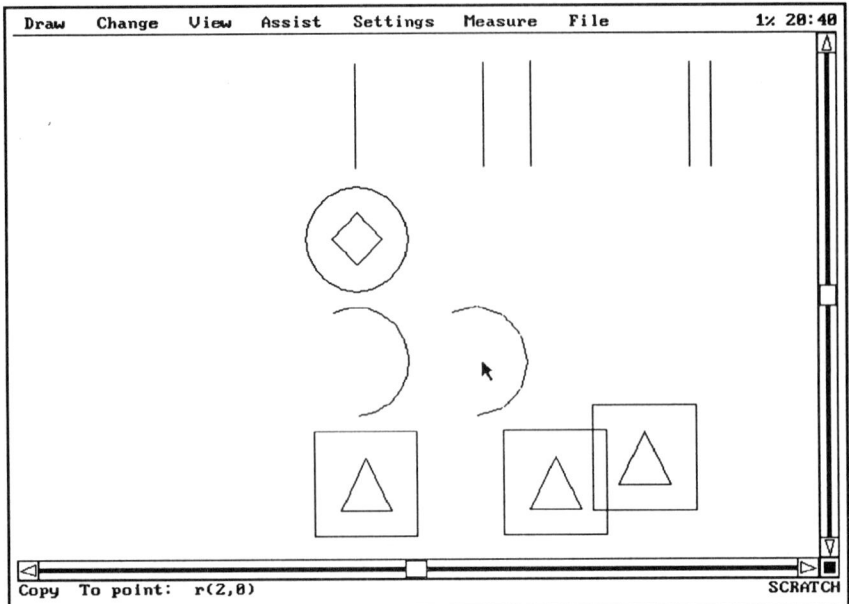

Copy Some More Objects

Obviously, Copy can be very useful when you have a drawing containing many identical objects, like the resistors in an electronic schematic or the windows on a house.

Copy can also be handy for doing quick-and-dirty experimentation on your drawing. For instance, if you want to modify an existing object, copy it several times and use the copies as guinea pigs to try out various ways of altering the original. This is often an easier (and safer) way to do a tricky bit of drawing than simply forging straight ahead and relying on Undo. Experimenting on a copy lets you try a complete sequence of modifications before you make up your mind about the results. You can create several "scratch" versions of an element, then move or copy the one you like best into position on your final drawing.

To create evenly spaced patterns of duplicate objects, see *Arrays* in Chapter 9, *Technical Drawing Tools*.

Rotate

Rotate is a fairly specialized command. However, it can be very useful for positioning an object or multiple copies of an object at very precise angles. You can specify rotations in increments of one degree.

An outline image shows the appearance of the object as you rotate it. Also, an indicator appears at the right-hand end of the prompt line (Angle: 0). The indicator changes as the pointer is moved, showing the current angle. A rubberband line from the pointer to the center of rotation defines the angle of rotation. When this line is horizontal and to the right of the center point, the angle is zero. From this position, the angle can be increased by pulling the rubberband line around the center point in a counterclockwise direction. The length of the rubberband line is irrelevant. If you wish to specify an angle by entering a second point from the keyboard, use polar coordinates. Again, the distance coordinate is irrelevant. Let's rotate the SCRATCH drawing line.

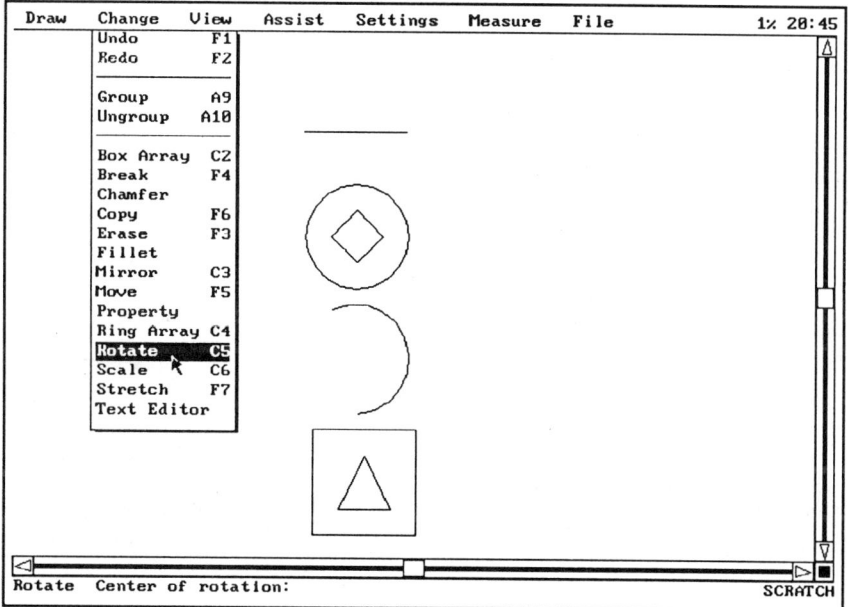

The Rotated Line

Rotating a Drawing Element

```
Pull down Change Select Rotate
Select object:                Select the line.
Center of rotation:           Middle of the line.
Second point: P(1,90)         Use polar coordinates to rotate 90 degrees.
Select object:                Select the arc.
Center of rotation:           Pick near the center of the arc.
Second point:                 Rotate about 45 degrees by moving your pointer back and
                              forth, then select a point.
```

Use Crosses/window to rotate a few more of the objects.

Select objects: <F1>   Undo the rotations.

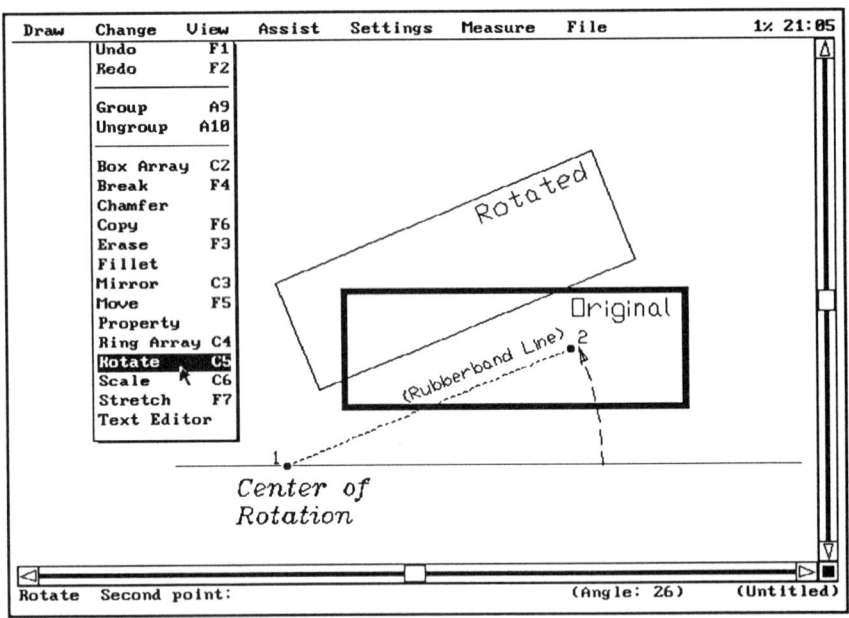

More Rotations

The trickiest thing about Rotate is placing the center of rotation. This is not necessarily the same as the visual center of an object. If you place the center point off to one side of an object, the object will swing across the screen as well as rotating — as though it were attached to the rim of a wheel.

Since the precise center of many objects can be difficult to locate, you may have to use the Move or Copy commands to correct any unwanted movement of the objects you rotate. Off-center rotations can sometimes be very useful, provided you are willing to do a bit of geometry beforehand.

For accuracy, you can enter the second rotation point by means of polar coordinates instead of rotating with the pointer. The distance coordinate can have any value at all. The angle coordinate specifies the amount of rotation. Many complex objects, such as gears, propellers, or star shapes, can be created by combining accurate rotations with use of the Copy command. Also see *Ring Arrays* in Chapter 9, *Technical Drawing Tools*.

By the way, if you are using the pointer to rotate a rectangular object, you can tell quite accurately when the sides are truly vertical or horizontal by noting when they lose their jaggy appearance. Moving the lines only slightly off horizontal or vertical will put at least one kink in them, owing to the finite resolution of your computer screen.

You can rotate in perfect 90-degree increments by enabling the Ortho mode, as described in Chapter 6, *Advanced Drawing Tools*.

Mirror

Mirror works like Copy — it creates a new object on the screen, duplicating the selected original. As you might expect, with Mirror the new object is a mirror image of the original.

Once you've selected the object to mirror, AutoSketch asks you for two points: a base point and one other. These two points create a rubberband line on the mirror's "surface" where you will see the reflection.

To help you even further, AutoSketch also displays an outline of the reflection itself, shifting it around as you decide where to place the second point in your mirror line. Mirror can be forced to create orthogonal copies of your objects by enabling Ortho mode, described in Chapter 6, *Advanced Drawing Tools*. For now, let's experiment with mirroring the arc and some text.

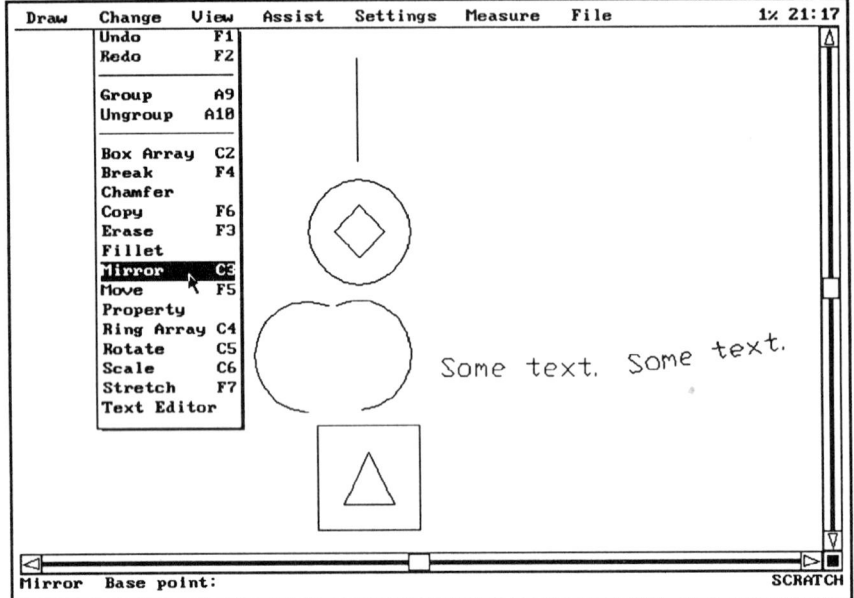

Mirror the Arc

Mirroring a Drawing Element

```
Pull down Change Select Mirror
Select object:                  Select the arc.
Base point:                     Select a point to act as one end of the mirror line.
Second point:                   Move your pointer to position the reflected image, then
                                select a point as the other end of the mirror line.
```

Mirror some more objects. Type some text and mirror it.

```
Select object:                  If desired, select more objects.
```

When you're done, undo all the Mirror commands.

```
Select objects: <F1>            Select Undo repeatedly to undo all the mirroring.
```

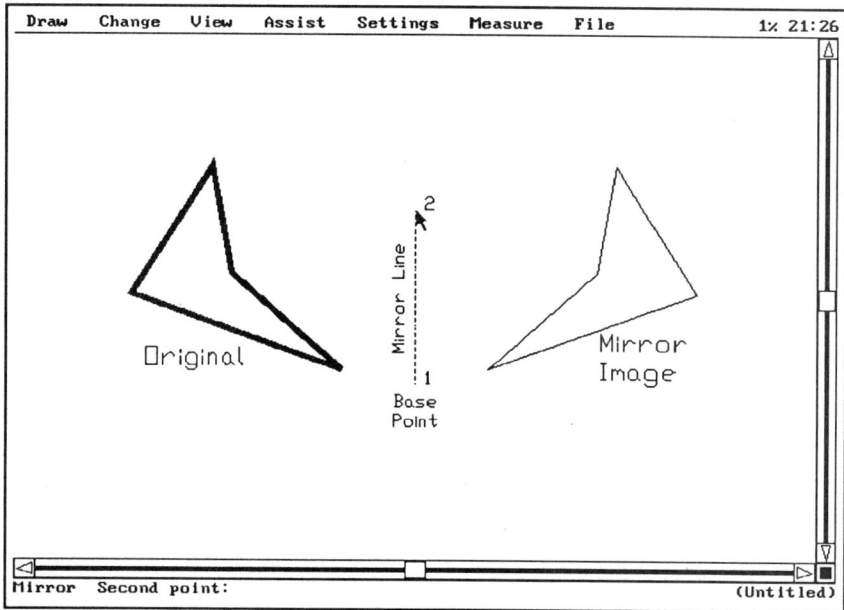

Mirrored Text

The Mirror command will not reverse text. When you mirror text, you are actually only reflecting the invisible baseline on which the characters are situated. Mirror creates a new baseline, but AutoSketch then uses it as a location on which to draw an exact copy of the original text.

Scale

The Scale command lets you change the size of objects in your drawing. After selecting the object(s) to scale, you are prompted to select a base point for reference. It is the one point that remains fixed as the object is resized. Therefore, if you want your scaled object to remain connected to some other drawing element, pick the attachment point as the base point. If you want it to remain centered in its previous location, pick the center of the original. If you only need to resize a portion of an object, see the Stretch command below.

A rubberband then stretches out from the base point. The longer you stretch this line, the bigger the outline image will get. The angle at which you extend the rubberband line is irrelevant. An indicator on the prompt line gives you a constant reading of the scale factor. When the outline reaches the desired scale, click the pointing device and the object will be rescaled. Try it.

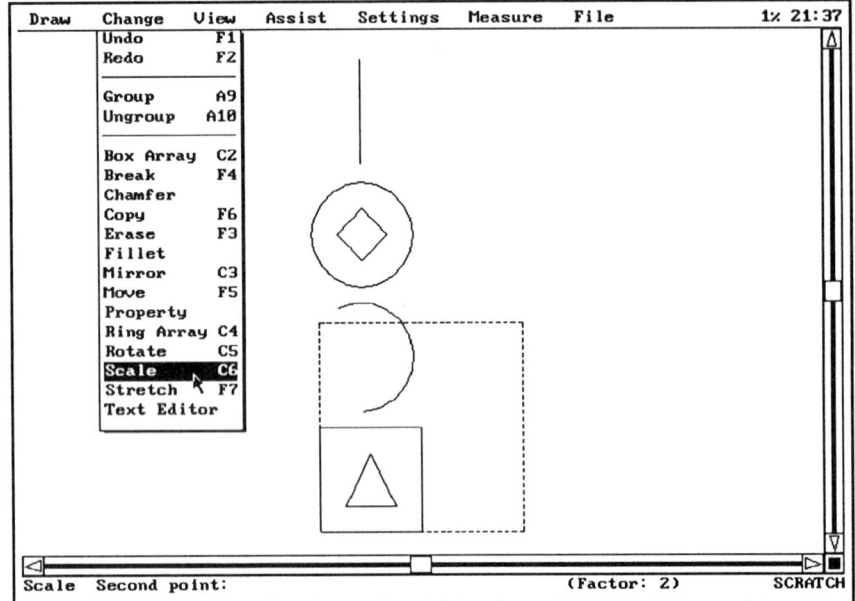

Scale the Box

Scaling a Drawing Element

```
Pull down Change Select Scale
Select object:              Select the box.
```

Select the box either directly or using the Crosses/window box.

```
Base point:                 Pick reference point.
Second point:               Drag, then pick when scale factor reads 2.
Select object:              If desired, select another object.
```

Scale some more objects. Try using various base point locations. Then undo it all.

You might think that relative coordinates could be used to enter an exact scale factor. Unfortunately, using keyboard coordinates with Scale probably won't give you the size changes you expect. For example, entering the second point as R(2,0) gives a scale factor not of 2, but of 2.2. It's usually easier to move the pointer slowly and watch the scale factor reading closely.

➥ *TIP: If you also use AutoCAD, don't confuse object scale dragging in AutoSketch with the AutoCAD SCALE command's Reference option. Reference lets you show AutoCAD the "before and after" sizes of the objects you want to scale either by dragging or relative coordinate input. While providing a relative coordinate for the second point of the Reference option's New length option will result in an accurate respective scale, it is not the same as AutoSketch's scaling method.*

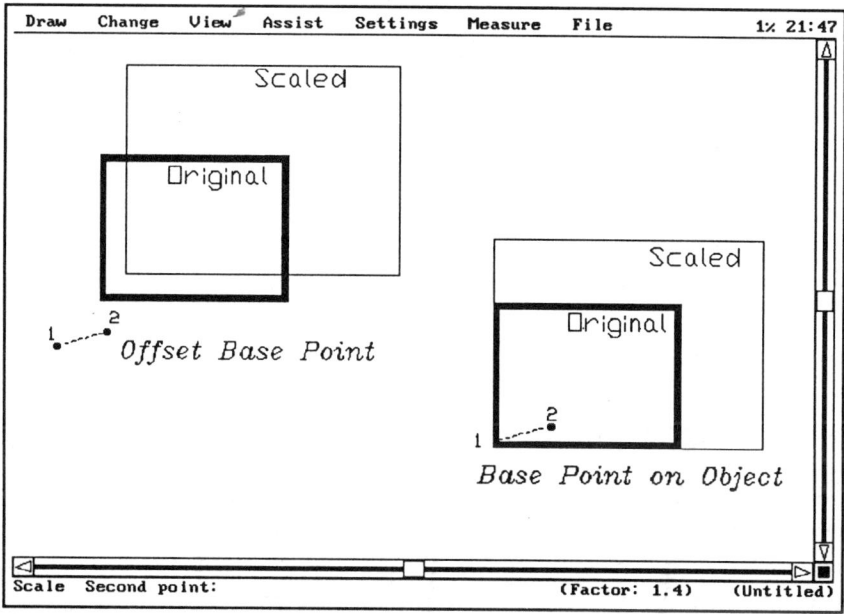

Use Scale Some More

Stretch

Stretch is perhaps the most powerful of all the Change commands. Scale allows you to change the size of objects that you've drawn, but Stretch lets you freely alter their shape.

The selection procedure for Stretch is slightly different from those of the other Change commands. Stretch automatically puts you into the Crosses/window selection mode. All object segment endpoints that are *within* the selection window are moved to the new location. Segment endpoints *outside* the window remain fixed, and lines *crossing* the window are stretched between any new endpoints. Also, in order to be selected for stretching, curves must have their frames made visible, using the Frame command on the Assist menu, as described in Chapter 6, *Advanced Drawing Tools*.

Beyond this, the function is straightforward. The Stretch base prompt needn't be answered with a point on the object to be stretched. Often, the ending stretch point is a point on another object. Rubberband lines show you exactly what's happening to your image, so you can simply stretch it like taffy. Unlike the Scale command, Stretch does respond the way you would expect to relative or polar coordinates. Try Stretch on the box. Then select a new file and discard your changes to clear the screen.

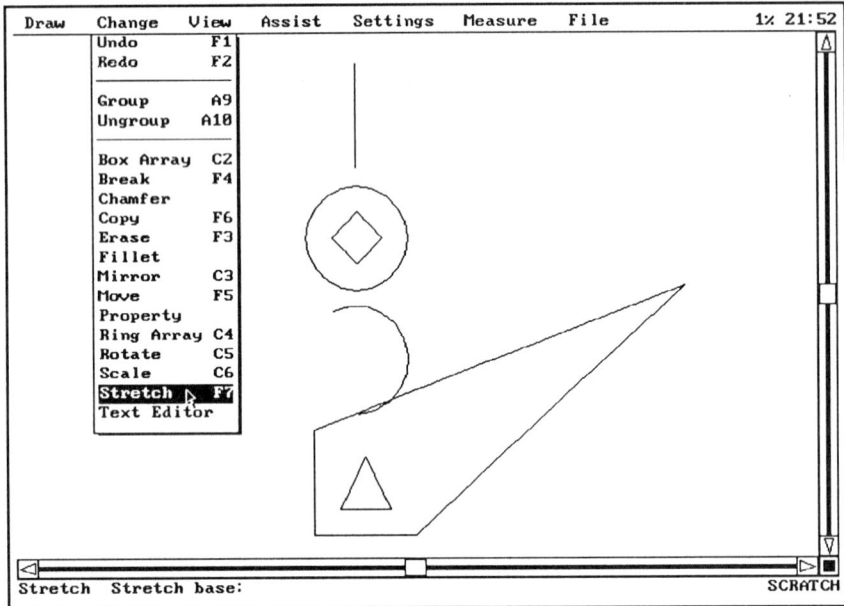

Stretching the Box Corner

Stretching a Drawing Element

```
Pull down Change Select Stretch
First corner:                        Select the box.
Crosses/window corner:               Use the Crosses/window box to surround one corner of
                                     the Box.
Stretch base:                        Select the corner of the Box as the point to stretch.
Stretch to:                          Select a point off to the right and up as the desired position.
First corner:                        If desired, select more objects.
```

Continue to practice using stretch.

```
Pull down File Select New
Click Discard                        Discard all changes.
```

Not all objects can be stretched. For example, points cannot be stretched into lines. If you attempt to stretch circles or ellipses, they will move, but not distort. If you don't include their centers in the Crosses/window box, they won't even move.

Text Editor

In Chapter 2 we looked at the Text Editor command on the Draw menu. But AutoSketch actually provides two Text Editor commands — one for entering text, the other for amending existing text. As you might expect, the latter is to be found on the Change menu. However, the two commands activate the same editor. The only difference is that the Change version allows you to select text from your drawing, rather than merely entering new text directly in the editor dialogue box.

➥ *NOTE: Versions of AutoSketch prior to 3 do not provide either of these Text Editor commands. Existing text cannot be altered, but must be replaced entirely.*

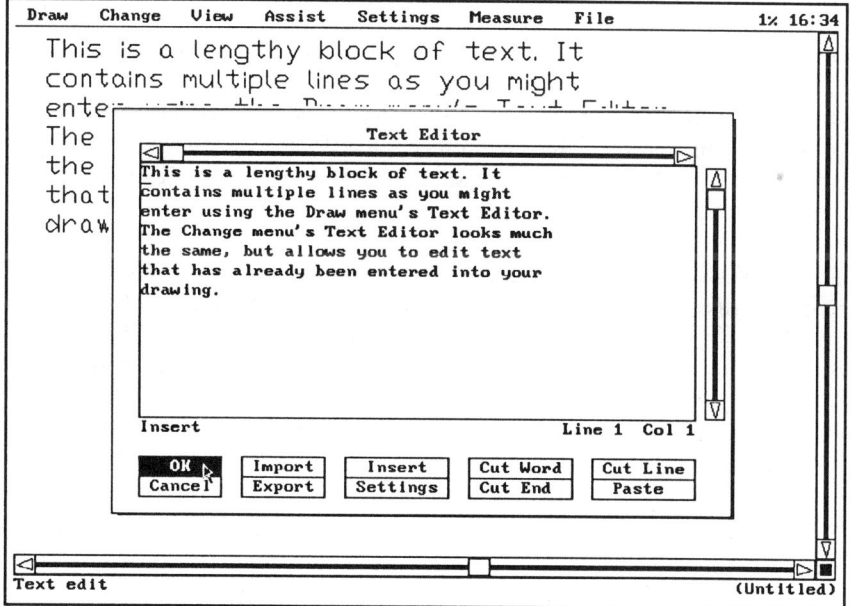

The Text Editor Dialogue Box

The Text Editor functions like the other Change commands. You select the command, and AutoSketch prompts you to select the object you wish to edit. When you select some text, the Text Editor dialogue box appears, with the text displayed in the editing window.

If you've worked with word processing software, the advanced Text Editor functions should be familiar. These functions are controlled by a series of command boxes across the bottom of the Text Editor dialogue box. An underline bar *cursor* indicates your current editing position within the text. You reposition the cursor by clicking at the desired text position with your pointer. A status line below the text window tells you the exact position of your cursor within the text, by row and column.

You can enter new text simply by typing it on the keyboard. By default, existing text is pushed ahead of the cursor. However, if you select Insert at the bottom of the dialogue box, an indicator at the bottom left of the text area changes from "Insert" to "Typeover," and the cursor changes from an underline bar to a block shape. Text typed now will overwrite existing text, letter for letter.

A series of commands also allows you to remove — or *cut* — selected text. You can remove a single word (Cut Word) or an entire text line (Cut Line). You can also remove all of the text from the current cursor position to the end of the text block (Cut End). To delete all of the text while in the editor, click at the start of the first word, and select Cut End. (Outside the editor, you could simply use the Erase command.)

Once cut, a piece of text can be re-inserted at a new location. Move the cursor to the desired location, and choose Paste at the bottom of the dialogue box. The cut text is inserted at the cursor position, pushing existing text ahead of it.

The "Insert" setting has no effect on Paste, which always pushes existing text ahead. Also, note that only the *last* piece of text cut is actually retained. That is, if you cut a word, then cut a second word, the first word is lost. When you paste, only the second word is inserted.

There are two other commands available in the Text Editor dialogue box: Import and Export. Import allows you to bring text in from a DOS text file, created by an outside text editing or word processing program. Export allows you to save an existing AutoSketch text block back to DOS as a text file.

AutoSketch likes its text files in pure ASCII format, with hard carriage returns at the end of each line, lines no longer than 256 characters, and blocks of text no larger than 2000 characters. If these terms are unfamiliar, be sure to use your word processor's non-document or unformatted mode to save text to be read into AutoSketch. You can also load text saved by AutoSketch.

The final command in the Text Editor dialogue box is Settings. This gives access to all the available text attribute controls: fonts, size, angle, and justification. These options can also be accessed directly from the Text selection on the Settings menu. They will be dealt with fully in Chapter 5, *Drawing Effects and Setup*.

Command Practice

Before you go on to the drawing exercises, you might find it worthwhile to practice with the commands covered in this chapter.

NEW. Use the File menu and select New to get a clean screen.

MOVE. Using the Draw menu, create a circle and a box, roughly equal in size. Move the circle so that it is tangent to the box on two sides. Notice that this is much easier than drawing the circle in this location (though not necessarily as accurate as detailed coordinate entry).

COPY. Draw a new circle, starting at coordinates (2,2), with radius 1. Copy the circle four times, placing the four copies in a square, with edges touching, using keyboard coordinates. The center of the circle is an ideal base point in this case.

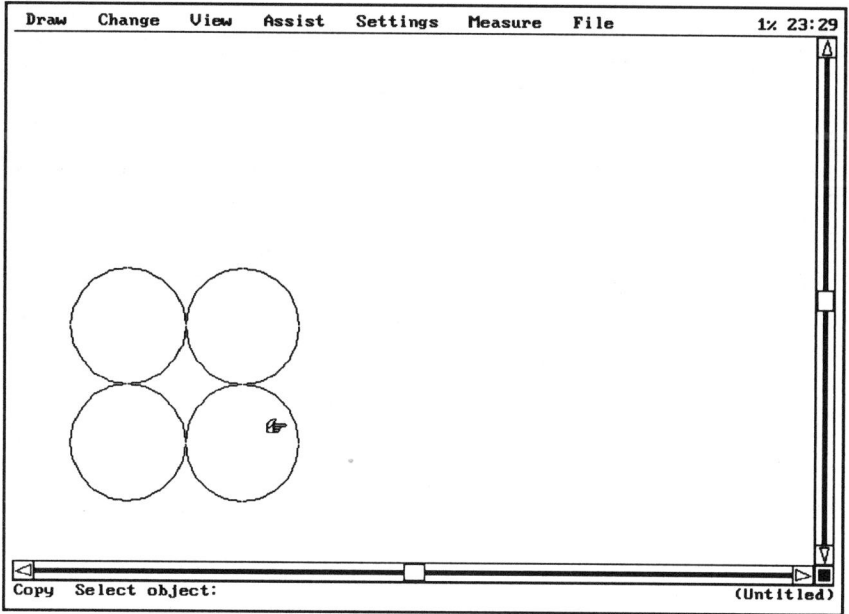

Copying the Circle

ROTATE. Draw a wide, short box. Use Rotate to turn it 90 degrees so that it becomes vertical. Try this once with a center point approximately in the center of the box, and once off to the side. Observe the motion of the box across the screen.

MIRROR. Use Mirror to reflect text and other entities at various angles. Experiment with trying to get accurate results. You'll find that you can't mirror the text upside down or backwards.

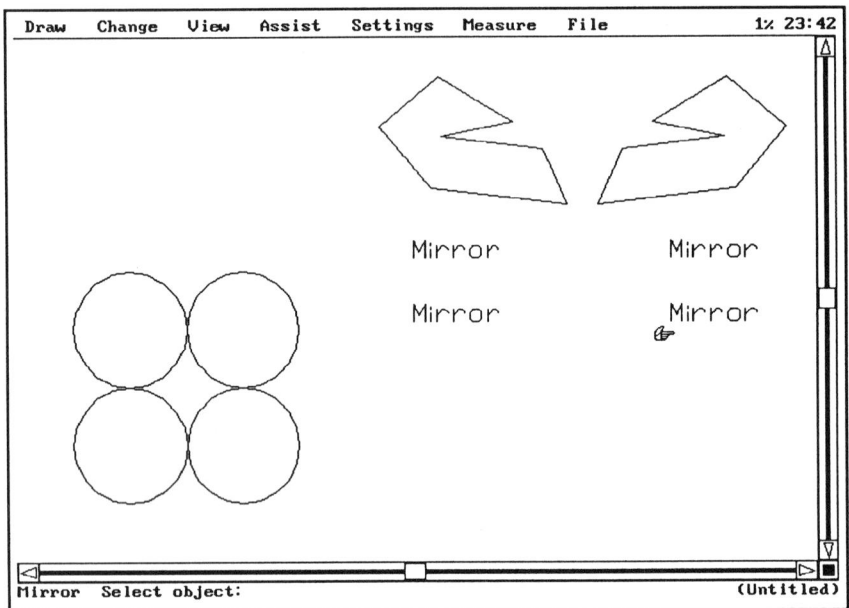

Mirror Practice

SCALE. Use Scale to change the size of one of the boxes. Do this first with the base point outside the box itself, then with the base point at one of the box's corners. How does the base point's position affect the location of the scaled box?

SCALE. Try using Scale on a circle. Then try it on some text.

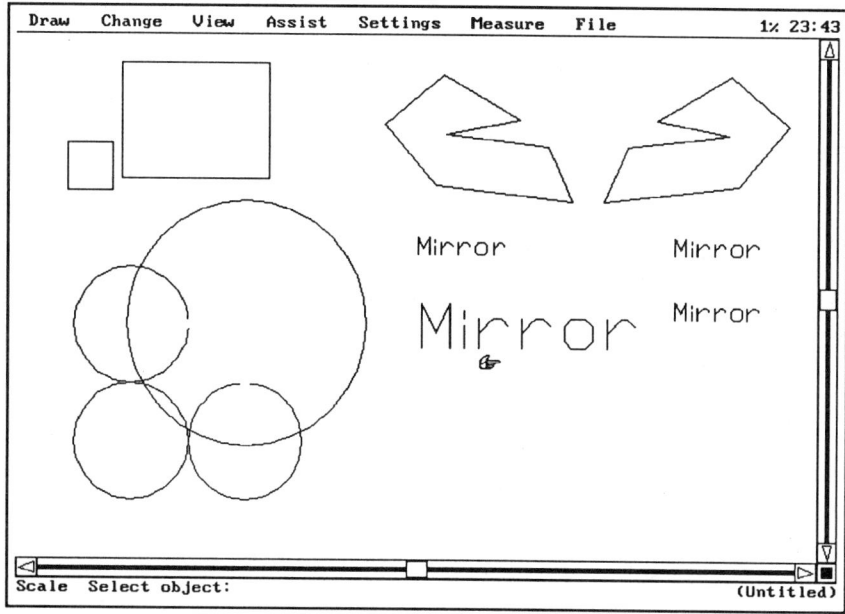

Scaling

STRETCH. Use the Polyline command to create an irregular four-sided polygon. Use Stretch on the corners to make it into a square. Use Stretch again on one whole side to turn it into an oblong rectangle. Then try turning the rectangle into a parallelogram.

STRETCH. Try using Stretch on some text.

STRETCH. Try using Stretch on a circle — first by including the center of the circle in the Crosses/window box, then by just including part of the circumference.

STRETCH. Draw a curve and try Stretch. Then try it with Frame on — which should make it much easier!

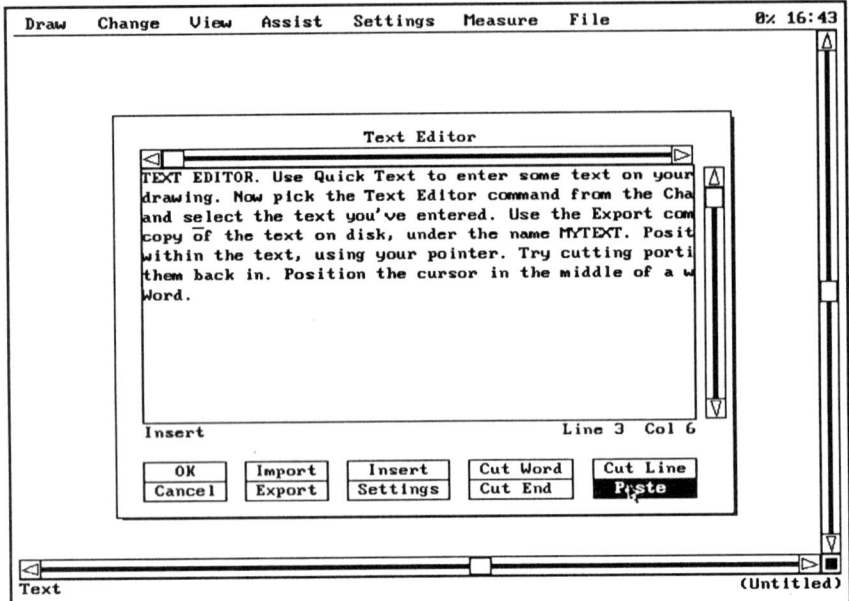

Stretching a Curve

TEXT EDITOR. Use Quick Text to enter some text on your practice drawing. Now pick the Text Editor command from the Change menu, and select the text you've entered. Use the Export command to save a copy of the text on disk, under the name MYTEXT. Position the cursor within the text, using your pointer. Try cutting portions out and pasting them back in. Position the cursor in the middle of a word, and select Cut Word.

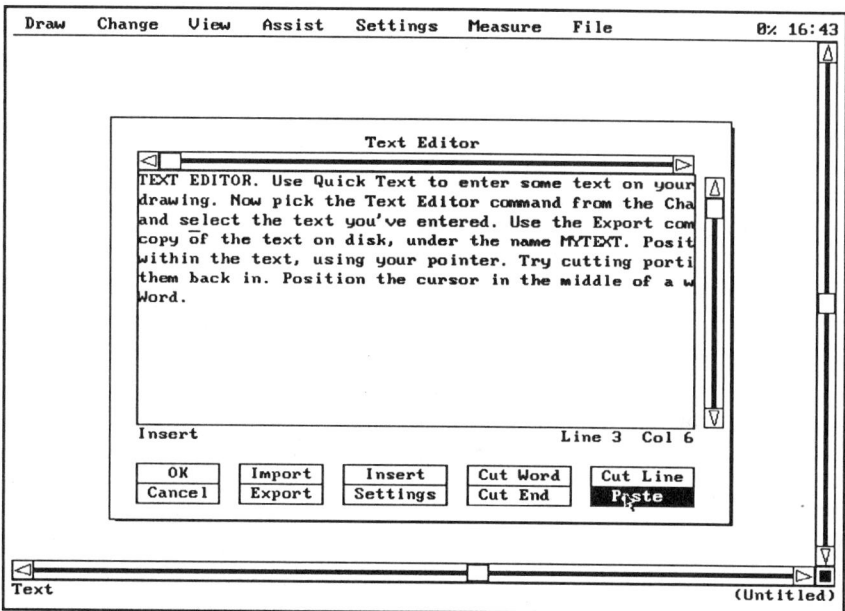

Working With the Text Editor

Place the cursor at the beginning of the text. Select Cut End. Now select Import, and enter your filename MYTEXT. You should be able to get your original text back. If you can handle a word processor, try quitting AutoSketch and reading in the MYTEXT file. Examine how the format of AutoSketch looks in your own word processor. That's how text should be formatted if you intend to import it into AutoSketch.

Map Drawing

It is time to start editing your map drawing. Put some woods around your country estate. Using Curve, create a flower-shaped swirl that can represent a tree as seen from overhead. Then use Copy to multiply this single tree into a little forest to the right of the estate.

Map Drawing Exercise

 If you have installed the IS DISK, you can open the MAP1 file. If you completed the map drawing exercises in Chapter 2, you can open your MAP drawing file instead.

 If you don't have the IS DISK, reopen your MAP drawing file and discard changes to your practice file.

```
Pull down Draw Select Curve          Use Curve to draw the tree.
First point:                         Select first point.
To point:                            Pick next point.
```

Pick as many points as needed to draw your tree.

```
Pull down Change Select Copy
Select object:                       Select the curve.
From point:                          Pick reference point.
To point:                            Pick copy location.
```

Copy as many trees as you want.

Suppose you wanted to add some detail to the box that represents your estate. Make a copy of the box in the blank area over at the left of the screen.

```
Select object:                       Select the "estate" box.
From point:                          Pick reference point.
To point:                            Copy to left side.
```

Put a label in the box that reads "Twelve Oaks Estate." If you like the new version better, how would you substitute it for the old one? Erase and Move should do the trick. Remember, you can always undo if things get messy.

```
Pull down Draw Select Quick Text
Enter point:                         Pick a point inside the box to the left.
Enter text: Twelve Oaks Estate       Type <Ctrl-ENTER> after each word.
Pull down Change Select Erase
Select object:                       Pick point below and to the left of old estate box.
Crosses/window corner:               Erase box and text.
Pull down Change Select Move
Select object:                       Pick point below and to the left of new estate box.
Crosses/window corner:               Select box and text.
From point:                          Pick reference point.
To point:                            Move to where the old estate was located.
```

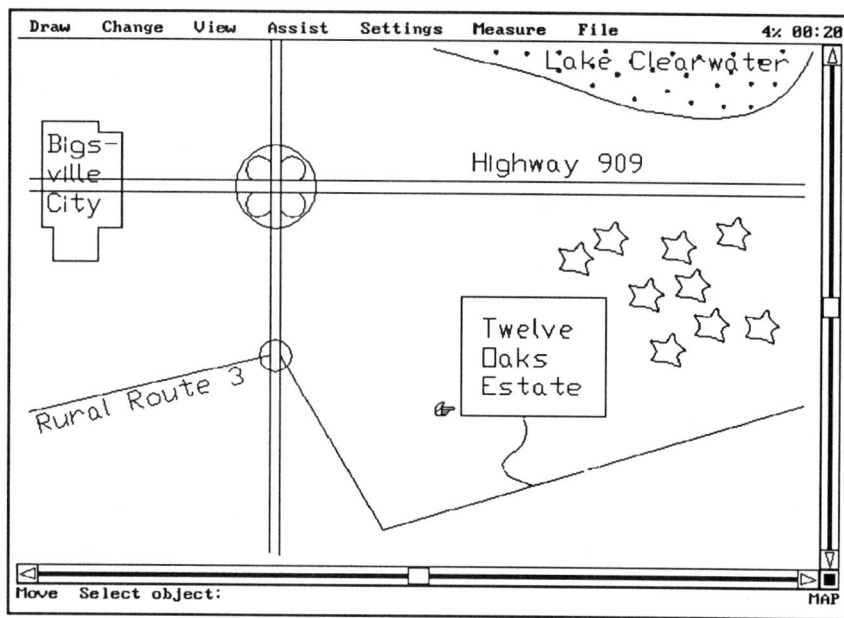

The Almost-Finished Map

Use Rotate to adjust the text label along the "backroad" so that the text lies parallel to the object it describes.

Pull down **Change** Select **Rotate**	
Select object:	Select "Rural Route 3" text.
Center of rotation:	Pick the middle of the word.
Second point:	Drag and pick the correct angle.

As a reward for getting this far, you can make your estate a bit bigger using the Scale command. Also, change the sizes of some of your trees to make the forest more realistic.

Pull down **Change** Select **Scale**	
Select object:	Select the estate.
Base point:	Pick the middle of the estate.
Second point:	Pick the appropriate scale.
Select object:	Select and scale some trees for variety.

You can adjust the sizes of some of the text labels, to make them more appropriate for what they refer to. For instance, "backroad" can have smaller lettering, the city larger lettering.

Use Stretch to adjust any loose details on your map. For instance, should the backroad run a bit more steeply northward at the right side of the drawing? Is the coastline of the lake just right? Remember that curve objects don't respond to Stretch; you'll need to toggle Frame on.

Pull down **Change** Select **Stretch**	Select an object.
First corner:	
Crosses/window corner:	Enclose some points.
Stretch base:	Pick the base point.
Stretch to:	Pick the desired position.
Pull down **Assist** Select **Frame**	Toggle Frame on.
Pull down **Change** Select **Stretch**	
First corner:	Surround a frame corner.
Crosses/window corner:	
Stretch base:	Pick the base point.
Stretch to:	Pick the desired position.
Pull down **File** Select **Quit**	Exit.
Select **Save**	When prompted, save changes to MAP.

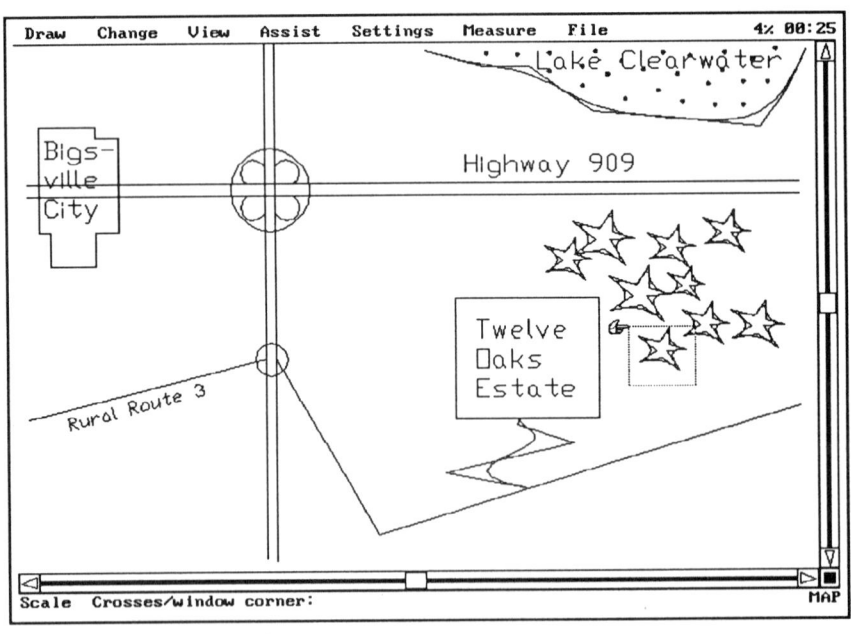

Map Exercise Completed

IS03SSEX.IMG

Summary

You should now have a grasp of all the fundamentals of creating and manipulating drawing objects in AutoSketch. You can draw circles, boxes, lines, and curves, and you can move them, copy them, or erase them. When you get down to it, that's all drawing is about.

However, AutoSketch provides you with a lot more than just the ability to draw crude objects on the screen. In the next chapter, we'll try out the various options AutoSketch gives you for viewing your drawing as it evolves. You can magnify sections and move the viewing area horizontally or vertically across a virtually infinite drawing surface. In subsequent chapters, we'll look at techniques that will refine both the accuracy and productivity of your drawing.

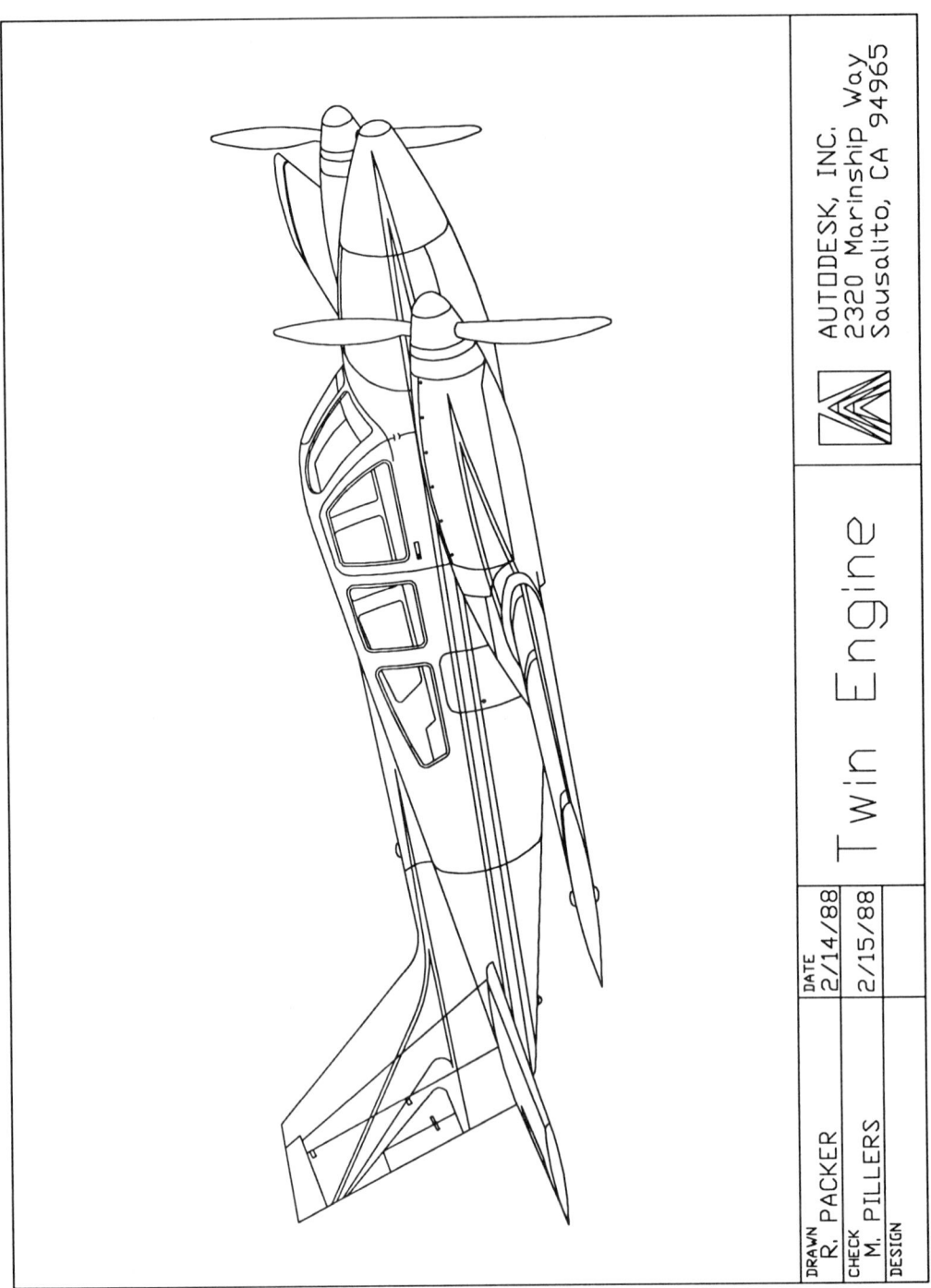

Twin Engine, Courtesy of Autodesk, Inc.

Chapter 4

Viewing Options

Now that you've examined all the basic drawing and editing functions, you can begin to look at some of the "accessory" capabilities of AutoSketch — those functions that make life easier and let you fully exploit the drawing power of the program.

Whether you are creating a new drawing or are viewing or editing an existing one, AutoSketch provides some convenient methods of exploring the drawing. Using commands from the View menu, you can magnify sections of the drawing to do detailed work, slide the drawing from side to side to view sections that may lie off the screen, or simply clean up the screen display when required.

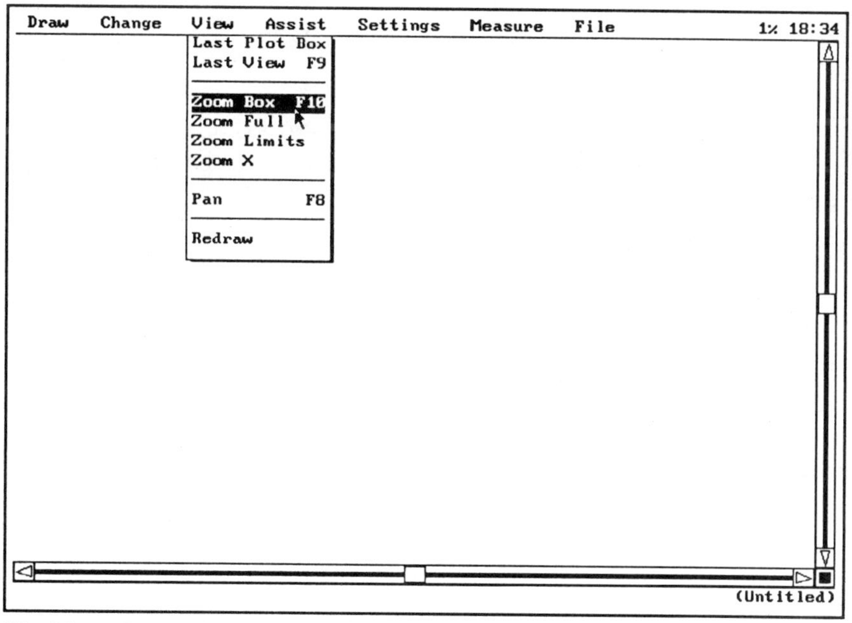

The View Menu

View control is yet another one of the benefits of AutoSketch's object-oriented approach. Because the program stores the drawing as a series of geometric entities, it can display a nearly infinite number of views of the same drawing information. The drawing can extend almost infinitely beyond the edges of your monitor screen, and it can have almost infinite detail beyond what can be displayed by the monitor's limited resolution. When you magnify a section of a drawing, the program redraws the image using its mathematical representation of the various drawing objects. Pixel-based *paint* programs, on the other hand, draw nothing more than the array of dots you see on the screen. If you magnify a pixel-based image, all you do is magnify the limited number of dots already visible.

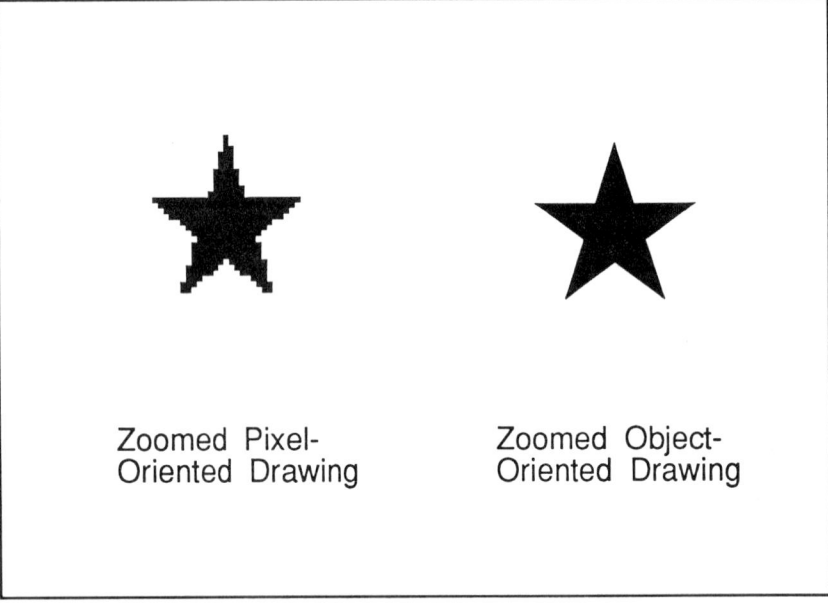

Magnifying Paint and Object Images

The most essential viewing control is *magnification*, accessed by various Zoom commands. AutoSketch provides four separate Zoom commands on the View menu. Each of these gives you a different method of telling AutoSketch how you wish to alter magnification. You can magnify any portion of a drawing almost infinitely, for very accurate work — or simply to get a clear view when things get cluttered.

If you magnify one section of a drawing so that it fills the screen, some of the rest of the drawing will be out of sight (off the edges of the screen). If you want to view an adjacent portion of the drawing, you don't have to zoom back out to the previous view, and then zoom back in on a new area. Instead, you can use the Pan command to scan the screen from side to side (like a viewing "window" onto your complete drawing) at any level of magnification.

It's important to note that any of the viewing commands described in this chapter can be used even while you are in the middle of a drawing or editing operation. For example, if you have just placed one end of a line and need more precision in placing the other end, you can use a zoom command to magnify the drawing, then carry on to finish the line.

When you save your drawing on disk, AutoSketch also saves all your current view settings, so that they are available in subsequent editing sessions with that drawing.

By the way, the terms "zoom" and "pan" are borrowed from cinematography. The zoom lens is a lens with variable magnification and allows the cameraman to enlarge whatever is being filmed. "Panning" means sweeping the camera from side to side, perhaps to scan the entire breadth of a scenic PANorama.

➥ *NOTE: The commands for moving around in your drawing are very straightforward, so this chapter omits the Practice and Drawing exercises, and uses the MAP drawing for the Reference Exercises.*

Zoom Box

Although it is not listed first on the View menu, Zoom Box is probably the most convenient of the zoom commands, and the one that you will use most frequently. Notice that it is the only zoom command on the menu that has a direct keyboard shortcut, the F10 key.

Zoom Box lets you visually select the portion of the picture you wish to magnify, or zoom in on. Using a selector box in this context is very natural, but unfortunately is possible only when zooming in; if you wish to shrink the view, that is, zoom out, there is no way to place a selector box around the area you wish to view, since it will be larger than the current screen. In order to zoom back out, you'll have to use one of the other View commands.

Let's go back to the MAP drawing and use the Zoom Box command to have a closer look at the circle that encloses the cloverleaf. Then, we'll try zooming in even closer on the interchange itself.

4-4 INSIDE AutoSketch

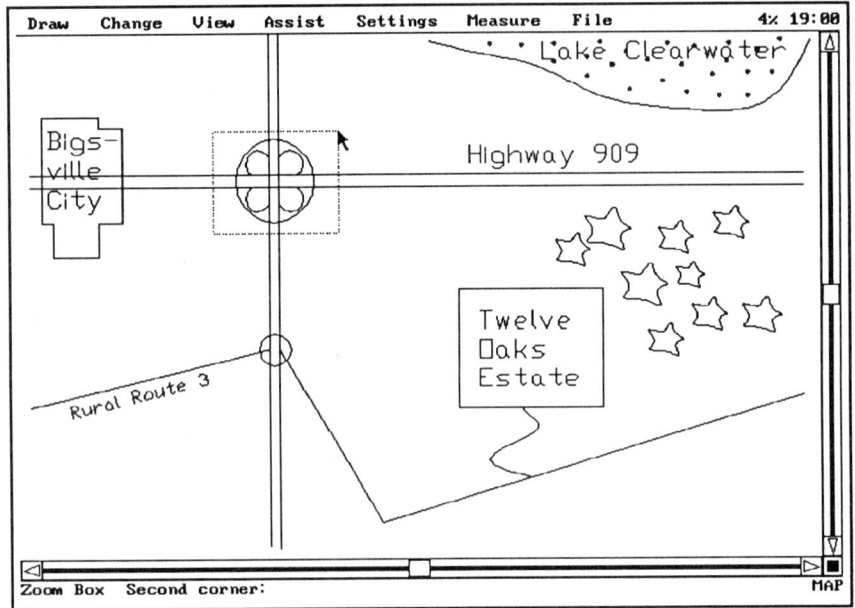

Zooming In on the Circle

Zoom Box

 Open the MAP2 drawing from the IS DISK or your MAP drawing from Chapter 3.

 Reopen or continue with the MAP file.

```
Pull down View Select Zoom Box
First corner:                    Pick below and left of circle.
Second corner:                   Enclose the circle. The view changes.
Press <F10>                      Activates Zoom Box.
First corner:                    Outside bottom left arc.
Second corner:                   Enclose the cloverleaf. The view changes.
```

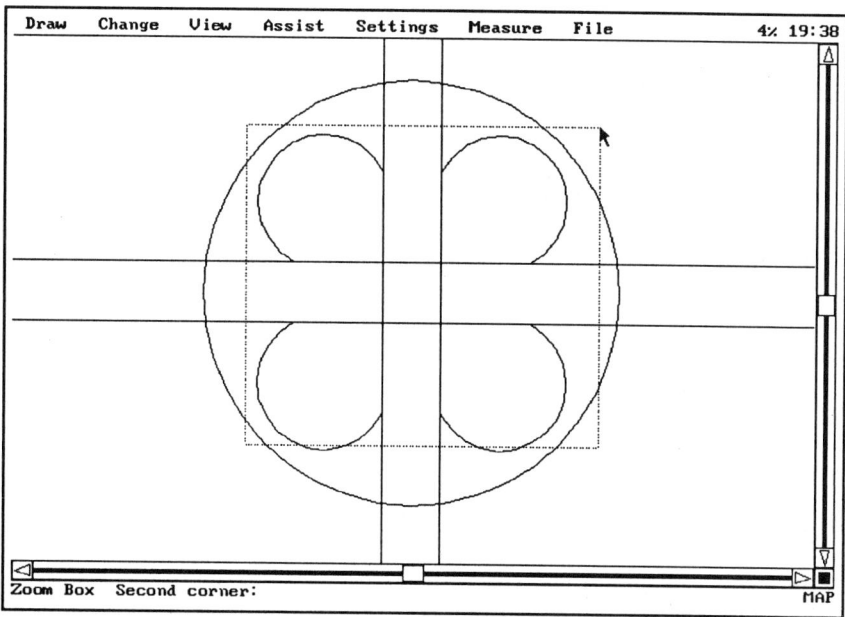
Zooming In on the Cloverleaf

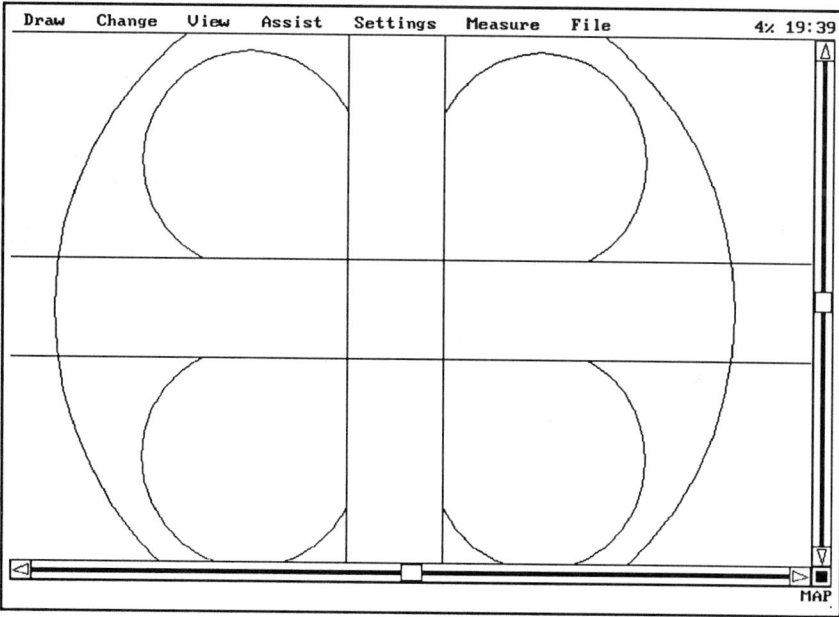
Zoomed In

While you are practicing moving around with the various Zoom commands, you may notice some imperfections in your drawing. You can try using some of the drawing and editing commands we've already discussed to clean up your work.

You are free to create a zoom box that has proportions very different from those of your screen. In such a case, the *smaller* zoom box dimension is centered within the visible screen, and the *longer* dimension fills the screen. For example, if you use a wide, short box, the width of the box will fill the screen horizontally after the zoom; the height of the box will be centered vertically.

➡ *TIP*: *AutoCAD's ZOOM command and Window option work the same as Zoom Box.*

Zoom X

The Zoom X command is not quite as convenient as the Zoom Box command, but it is more accurate. With Zoom X you specify a magnification factor relative to the current view. In this sense, Zoom X really is the most generic zoom command.

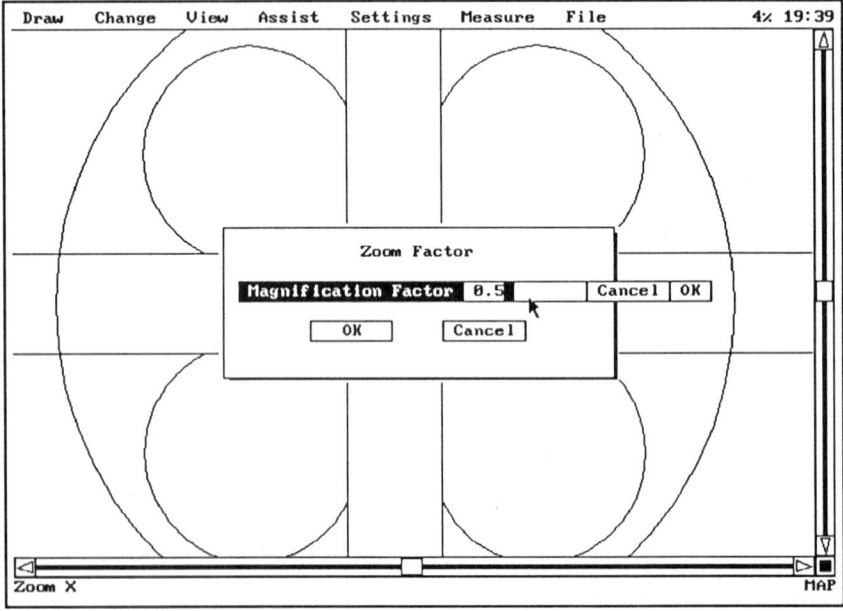

Selecting a Zoom Factor

Zoom X

```
Pull down View Select Zoom X
Click on the Magnification Factor text field
Magnification factor: .5
Click OK
```

The "Zoom factor" dialogue box appears.

Type in the desired factor.
Click on the main OK.

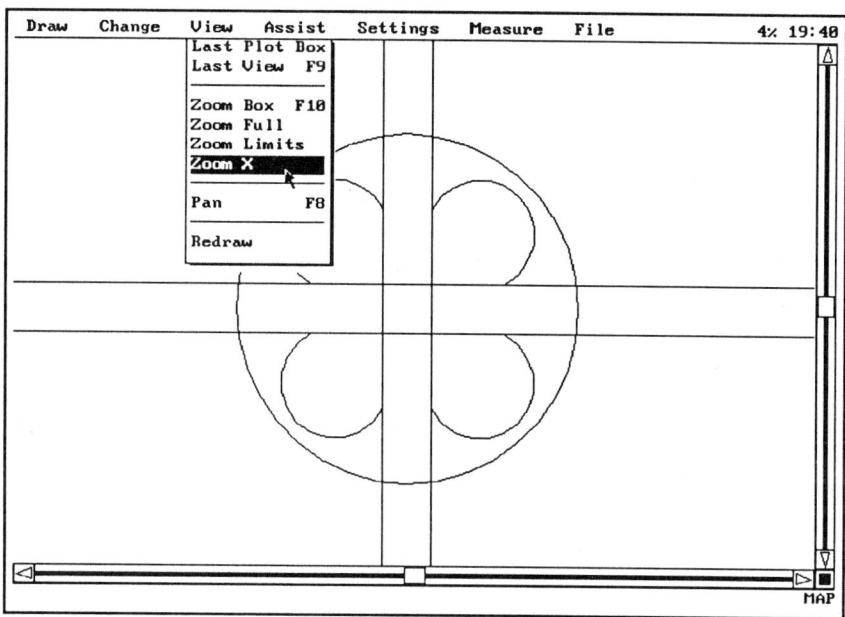

Zoom X With Factor 0.5

Note that fractional scale factors shrink the image. For example, a factor of 0.5 makes everything look half as big as before. Zoom factors greater than one magnify the image. A factor of two makes objects look twice as big on the screen.

There's no real limit to how large a zoom factor you can enter, although it is unlikely you would need to use into three-digit values — and negative scale factors are not allowed.

You can see that using the Zoom X command to zoom in and out precisely could require you to do a bit of math on-the-fly. For instance, suppose you zoom in by a factor of 3.5, then want to zoom back out by about half that amount. What factor would you enter? That's the reciprocal of 1.75 — one divided by 1.75, or approximately 0.571! Fortunately, it usually doesn't matter what your magnification is as long as you can see what you are working on.

Whatever factor you use with Zoom X, the center of the screen remains fixed. That is, whatever is dead center before you zoom will still be in the center afterward.

Zoom Full

AutoSketch zoom and pan commands let you create drawings of almost any size and shape. Zoom Full gives you the largest magnification that will still let all of your drawing entities be visible on the screen at once.

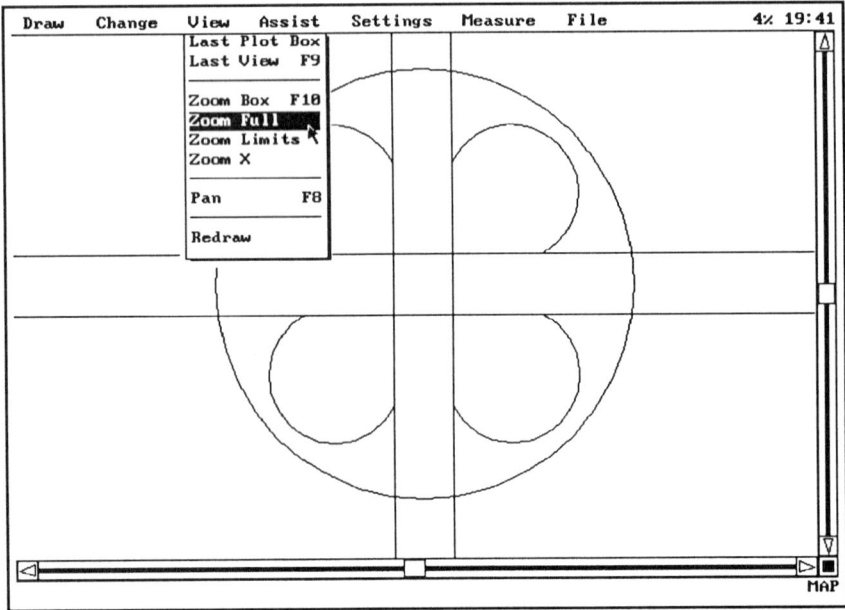

Select Zoom Full

Zoom Full

If you've made changes to your MAP drawing, save the file.

```
Pull down View Select Zoom Full
```

The view should zoom back out to the extents of the map.

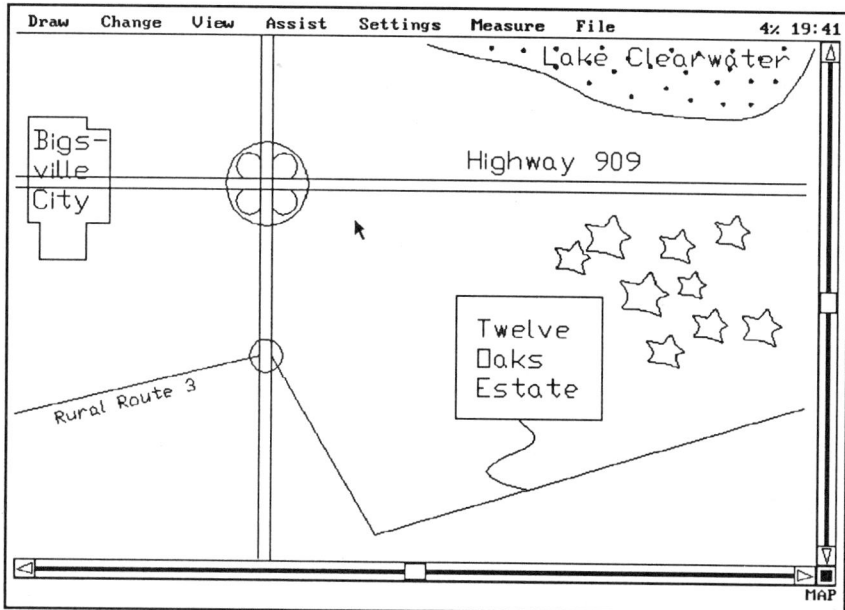

Now You See Everything

With a complex drawing, much of the fine detail will probably run together in the Zoom Full view, but you can at least get an idea of the overall layout. Of course, you might prefer to start by viewing the entire drawing area, and rough in some of the main features before zooming in to refine the details. The next command, Zoom Limits, lets you work this way.

➥ **TIP**: *AutoCAD's ZOOM command and Extents option work the same as Zoom Full.*

Zoom Limits

Zoom Limits returns you to the default magnification level. Think of the drawing *limits* as defining the edges of your sheet of electronic drawing paper within AutoSketch.

When you start a new drawing, AutoSketch shows you the entire sheet. You can use zoom commands to view a smaller section of the sheet — equivalent to using a magnifying glass on a paper drawing. Or you can extend the drawing limits — equivalent to switching to a larger sheet of paper — by means of the Limits command on the Settings menu. You can even use the Limits command to shrink the drawing area — equivalent to switching to a smaller sheet. (We'll look at the proper use of the Limits setting in Chapter 5.)

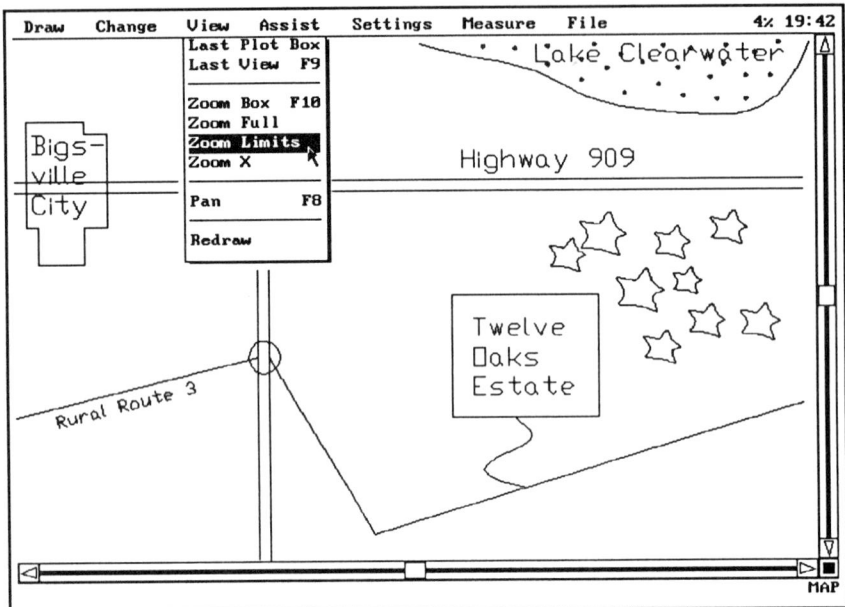

Selecting Zoom Limits

Zoom Limits

Pull down **View** Select **Zoom Box**   Zoom into a detail of the MAP drawing.
Pull down **View** Select **Zoom Limits**

The view should zoom back out to full sheet size.

The Zoom Limits command will always show you all of the drawing sheet. Zoom Full may zoom the drawing either in or out — whichever is needed just to fill the screen with what you've drawn so far. You can set up drawing limits as a convenient reference point to help you visualize your completed drawing. If your drawing happens to extend to the limits of the drawing area, Zoom Full and Zoom Limits will have the same effect.

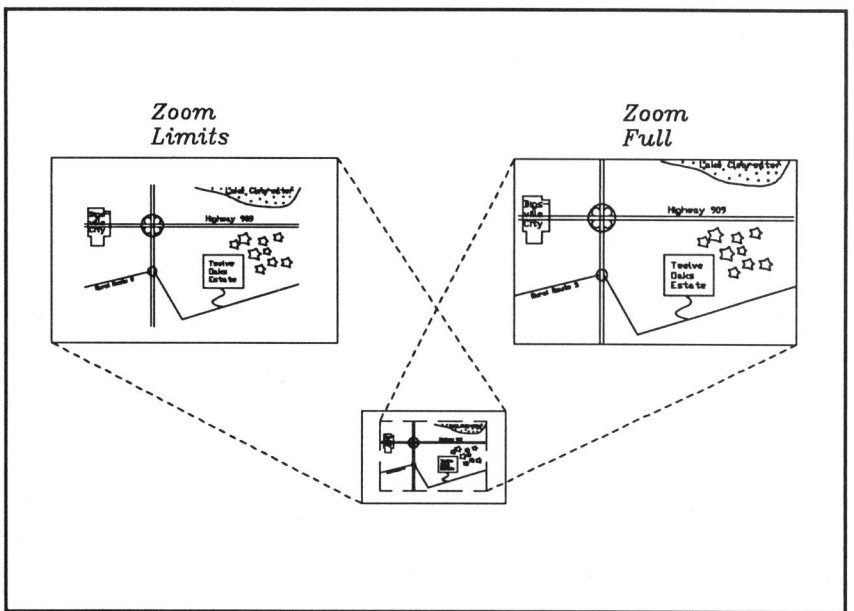

Zoom Full versus Zoom Limits

Both Zoom Full and Zoom Limits are useful as "escape" commands. If you find yourself buried deep in a complex drawing after repeatedly zooming in and out, you can always escape back — either to a view of all your work to date, or to an overview of your planned drawing area. This is great for getting your bearings.

Pan

Once you've zoomed in, you will often wish to look at parts of the drawing that are off the screen — preferably without going all the way back to the full or limits view. AutoSketch provides the Pan command to allow you to effectively slide the drawing past the "window" area that you can actually see on your screen. In this way you can bring into view elements that lie above, below, or to either side of the currently displayed area.

AutoSketch gives you two ways to move the viewing window: using the pointer to "grab" the drawing and shift it a given distance, or using the pointer to move the horizontal and vertical *scroll bars* located at the right side and bottom of the viewing screen.

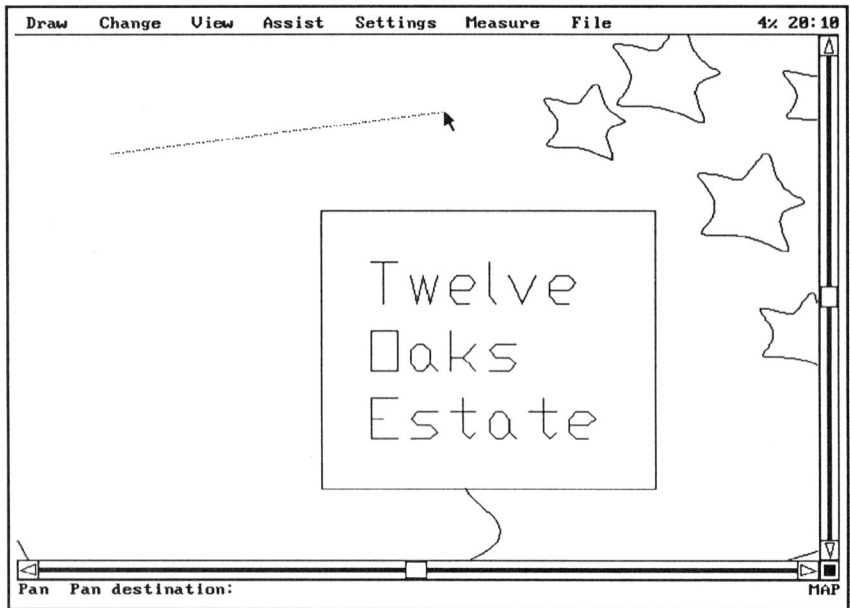

Using the Pan Command

Panning, Two-Point Method

```
Pull down View Select Limits        Return to the full default view.
Press <F10>                         Use Zoom Box to zoom in on Twelve Oaks Estate.
Pull down View Select Pan
Pan reference:                      Pick a point near the left edge of the screen.
```

A rubberband line follows the pointer. Keep this line horizontal by placing the second point at the same height as the first.

```
Pan destination:                    Pick a point an inch in from the right edge of the screen.
```

When the second point is selected, the screen is redrawn so that the reference point is displayed at the screen location chosen for the destination point.

```
Press <F8>                          Try reversing the pan by placing the points in the opposite order.
```

One advantage of the two-point method of panning is that it can be used with keyboard coordinate entry. Polar or relative coordinates are particularly handy for entering the destination point. Of course, you'll rarely need to pan with particular accuracy, and the pointer lets you pan more quickly. However, keyboard coordinates also let you pan farther than a single screen width, since the destination point need not be visible in the current view.

The two-point method of panning is particularly handy once you get familiar with the overall size and scale of a drawing. You can then estimate by how many units you need to pan in order to display a desired part of the drawing. The two-point method also gives you better control over the panning distance. The scroll bars are quicker but less predictable.

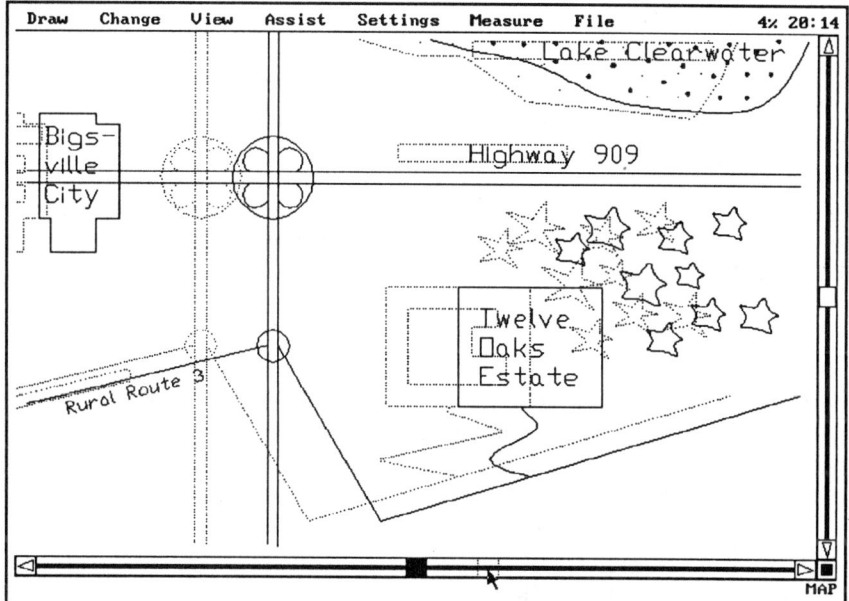

Using the Scroll Bars

Panning, Scroll Bar Method

```
Pull down View Select Zoom Full
Click on elevator box at bottom screen    An outline of the box moves along with the pointer;
                                          an outline of your drawing pans across the screen.
Move ghost image of elevator box          Position 1" to right of its original position.
Click on scroll bar to left of elevator box
```

Try doing a vertical scroll using the vertical scroll bar.

As explained in Chapter 1, the scroll bars actually give you a range of scrolling methods. You can click on the elevator box and drag it by any amount; you can click to the side of the elevator box to pan in half-screen steps; or you can click on the arrows to pan by quarter-screen steps.

The scroll bars permit only horizontal and vertical panning, while the two-point method allows diagonal panning as well. Still, the scroll bars are convenient; they are similar to the standard panning system used in other popular computing environments, such as Microsoft Windows, OS/2 Presentation Manager, or the Apple Macintosh. If you are already familiar with one of these environments, or plan to switch between AutoSketch and software that runs in one of them, you'll probably find the scroll bars very handy.

Last View

Last View is a shortcut that you can use in conjunction with the other View commands. AutoSketch always "remembers" the previous screen view. You can instantly recall this view, even if you're not sure how you got there in the first place. It's like an Undo for the viewing commands. The regular Undo command doesn't undo view changes.

Unlike Undo, Last View recalls only one previous view. You can use Last View to alternate between two views, but not to back up through a long succession of zoom commands. Last View can thus be used to keep two different views at your fingertips.

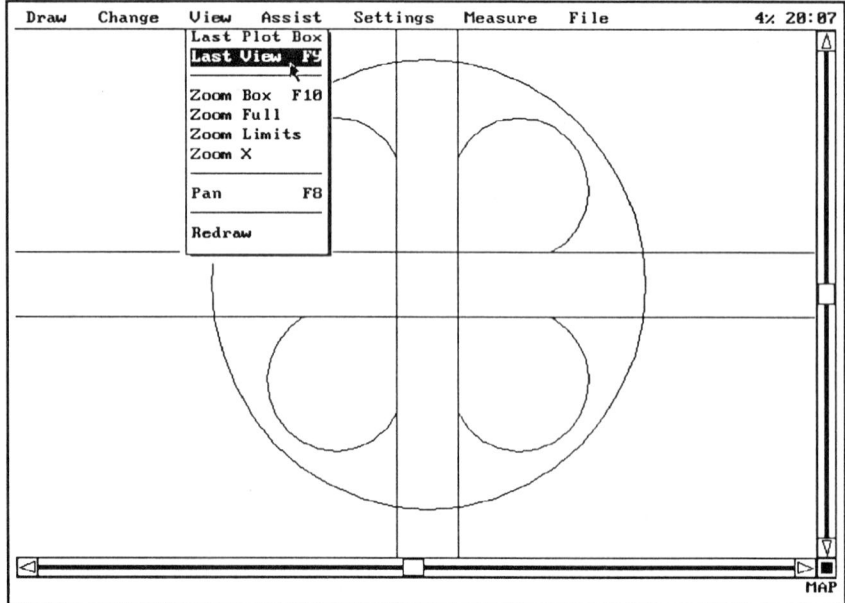

Selecting Last View

Last View

```
Pull down View Select Zoom Full        Return to original view.
Pull down View Select Zoom Box         Zoom in on the cloverleaf.
Pull down View Select Zoom Box         Zoom in still further.
Pull down View Select Last View        Use keyboard shortcut to move back one view.
Press <F9>                             Return to the most zoomed-in view.
```

Try alternating views by pressing <F9> repeatedly.

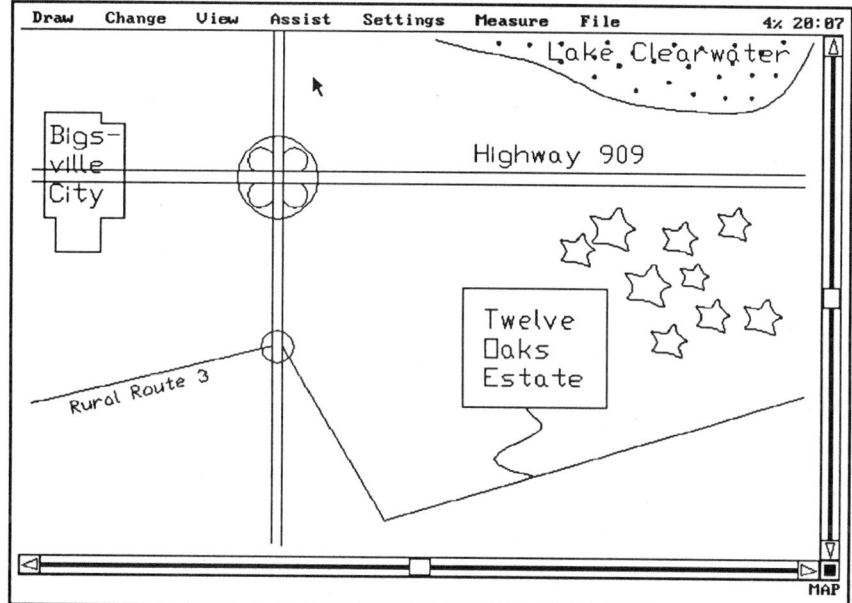

Back to Previous View

It is no coincidence that the Zoom Box and Last View commands are accessible using adjacent keys on the keyboard — <F10> and <F9>, respectively. Compare this to the use of <F1> and <F2> for Undo and Redo.

Just as it does not save your Undo status, AutoSketch also does not save Last View information with your drawing. When you reload a drawing, it will be at the zoom level you last saved it from — Last View will have no effect until you've changed zoom level at least once in the current drawing session.

➥ *TIP: AutoCAD's ZOOM command and Previous option work the same as Last View, except that Zoom Previous can scroll back through a series of zooms.*

Redraw

The Redraw command really doesn't do anything to change the current view. Rather, it simply recreates the view from stored information. This can be useful to clean up the display occasionally.

Redraw

```
Pull down View Select Redraw      The screen image is redrawn.
Click Redraw button               At the lower right corner of the screen.
```

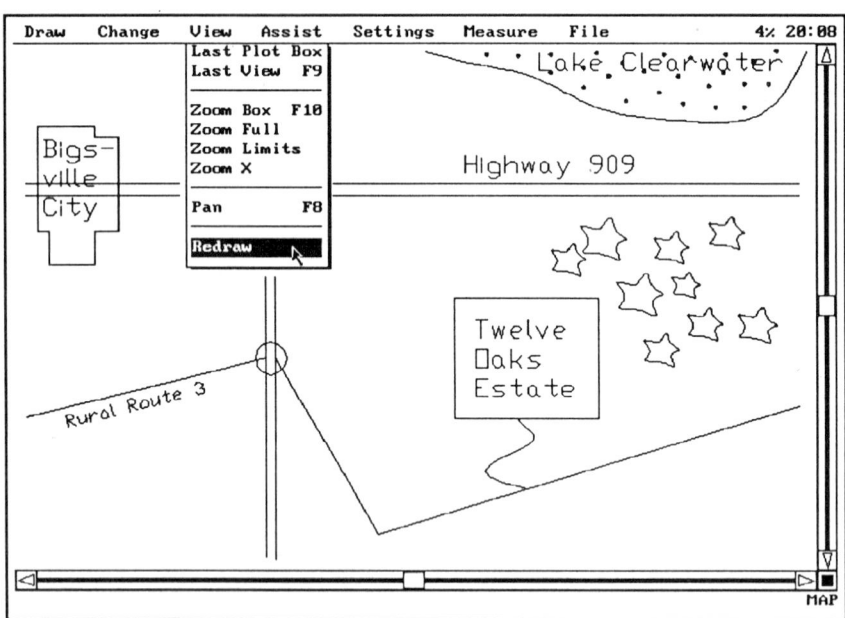

Selecting Redraw to Clean Up the Screen

You'll only need to use Redraw in a few situations. If you've been doing a lot of editing (especially moving and copying), your screen image may begin to deteriorate. Similarly, if you have displayed a reference grid (the Grid command is covered in Chapter 6) and then erased an object lying on the grid, you may find that some of the grid points are missing. Redraw causes AutoSketch to fully recreate the screen display, including the grid.

AutoSketch could redraw automatically, but this would cause it to pause frequently; instead, it lets you choose when you wish to tidy up. You can conveniently redraw any time you come to a natural pause in your work. (Also a good time to save your drawing!) Bear in mind that any change in view, using zoom or pan commands, also results in a complete redraw, so you'll probably need to use the Redraw command itself only if you've done a lot of work without changing the view.

Summary

The basic viewing commands covered in this chapter let you look at your drawing in a variety of ways. You can zoom in to magnify tiny details, or zoom out to get an overview of the complete layout. And you can pan at any angle, to view all of the drawing even while it's magnified to a size that's too large to fit on your screen.

In the next chapter, we'll move on to some of the more subtle viewing and setup controls. You'll see how to set up your drawing limits to make best use of the Zoom Limits command, and how to use drawing layers to speed up and organize your work. You'll also get a chance to dress up your work with colors and fancy line and text styles.

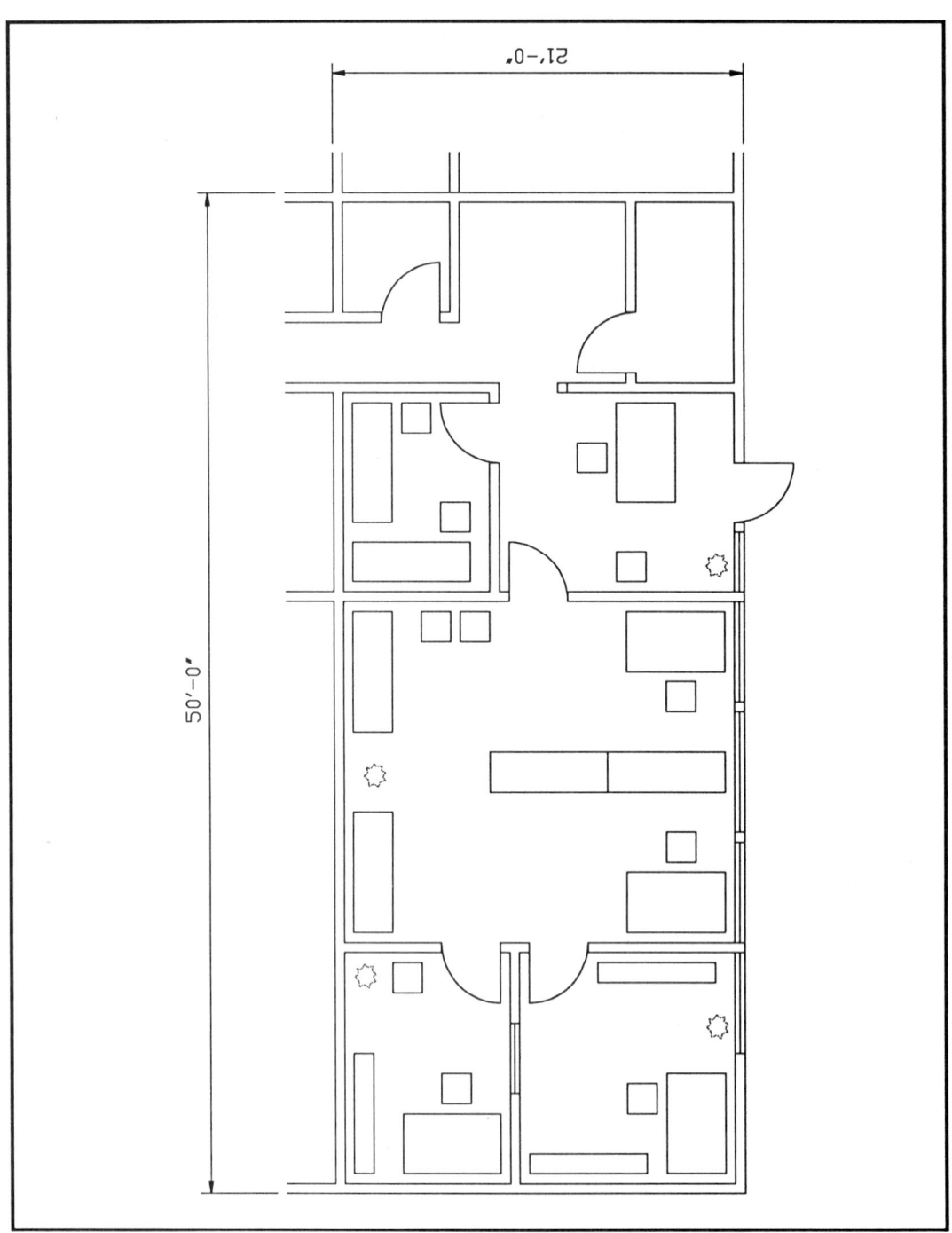

The Completed Space Plan Drawing

Chapter 5

Drawing Effects and Setup

So far, you've drawn in one color, using simple, solid lines. When you used text, it was square and unadorned. This is adequate for an amazing amount of work, but it's limiting in the long run. AutoSketch includes a set of commands that let you vary the look of your drawing elements.

In this chapter, you'll learn how to use some of the special effects available in AutoSketch to dress up your drawing and make its structure clearer.

The commands used in this chapter are located on the Change, Settings, and Measure menus.

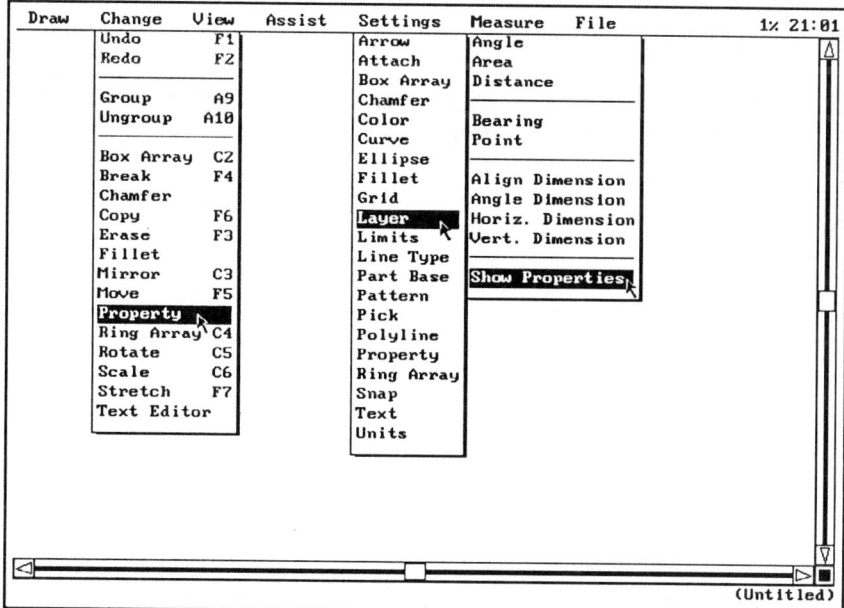

The Change, Settings, and Measure Menus

The Color command is an obvious one, but its use will depend greatly on what sort of display and plotter you are using. If you are working in monochrome, the Line Type command can often serve equally well to distinguish various parts of a drawing. Special line types are also very important in many types of engineering drawing.

Text settings are handy both in dressing up the appearance of text and in getting it to line up nicely with objects to which it refers.

The effect of the Limits setting is not immediately obvious. However, proper limits on the size of your electronic page help keep your work in perspective, so to speak. With a bit of effort, the Limits setting will help you draw in real-world coordinates. You can always specify a new set of limits at any time.

All these property settings are found on the AutoSketch Settings menu (most of which deals with much more advanced options). Two closely associated functions are tucked into the Change and Measure menus. The items you're going to look at in this chapter really deserve to be considered separately. They don't so much help you to *draw* (like the Settings commands in the next two chapters) as they help you to make your drawing clearer, more attractive, or both.

Color

The Color option on the Settings menu lets you set your current drawing color. Anything drawn after a change in Color setting will appear in the new color. Existing objects are unaffected by the Color setting; the color of existing objects must be altered with the Property command on the Change menu, as discussed later in this chapter.

When you choose the Color command, the Drawing Color dialogue box will display on the screen. Click your pointer on the small box opposite the color you want. The selected color's number will appear in the text box near the bottom of the dialogue box. Alternatively, you can click on the color number and enter a number from the keyboard. Let's open the SCRATCH file and turn all its objects red.

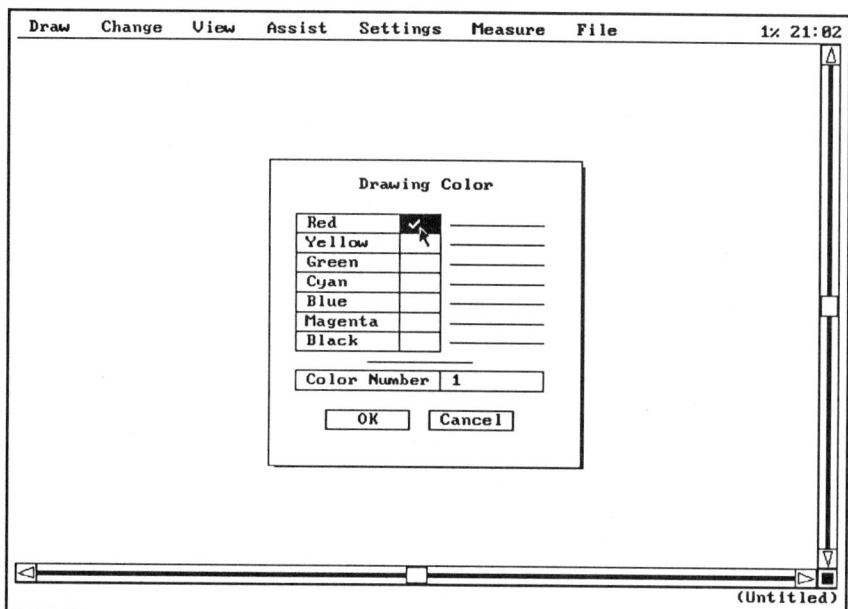

Selecting Color Red

Setting Object Color

```
Pull down File Select New          Open a new file.
Pull down Settings Select Color
Click Red
Click OK                            Set the color.
Pull down Draw Select Box           Draw a couple of objects in red.
```

Color can, of course, be used to "pretty up" an illustration. However, in technical work this is often not the primary consideration. A better, and perhaps more common, way of using color in design or drafting work is for coding various types of drawing elements.

For instance, if you are drawing a side view of a house, you might be eager to make the brickwork red, and the shrubbery green. However, if you are doing a cut-away view of some mechanical component, you could make metal parts black, plastic parts blue, wiring red, and text annotations green. Some of the color choices might run contrary to your artistic sensibilities, but they can make a complex design more comprehensible to someone else. Creative drawing is intended to amuse; technical drawing or drafting is intended to communicate.

You will often find that there are no "natural" colors to be used. In our map drawing, for instance, what color is a road? A city? And yet, it will almost always be helpful to code various elements of the drawing with color. For instance, text labels can benefit from being all one color — either bringing the text out, or causing it to be less obtrusive, or at least clearly differentiating the purely imaginary lines that make up the lettering from lines that represent actual physical objects.

```
Pull down Settings Select Color
Click Black                         Set color back to Black.
Click OK                            Set the color.
```

If you are using a color monitor, feel free to draw a few objects, change to another color, and draw some more objects. Those of you who are stuck with a monochrome monitor can also practice changing to the various colors even though they all look alike on the monochrome screen.

Even if you work on a monochrome screen, you may still wish to color code your drawings. With a pen plotter, your drawing can be plotted in color. You can also use color to plot varying line weights. AutoSketch's color numbers tell the plotter which pens to use. The plotter doesn't care if the "Red" pen really has red ink, or is a number 4 point to draw a fat black line.

On a monochrome display, you'll probably find it hard to keep track of which objects are what color, but later on you'll learn some extra commands that can help. If you work on a monochrome monitor and print on a single-color device such as a dot-matrix or laser printer, the Color command will be of little use.

The AutoSketch Pattern Fill command lets you create objects containing solid areas of color. These will be filled with the currently selected drawing color. The Pattern Fill command will be discussed in Chapter 9.

> *TIP: AutoCAD Release 9 uses a 16-color model; that is, there are a maximum of 16 valid color numbers. AutoCAD uses a 256-color model in Release 10 for compatibility with AutoShade. By contrast, AutoSketch is based on a 128-color model. You may need to make color adjustments if you will be exporting drawings to any of these other programs and you want to maintain your original colors.*

Line Type

Line Type is a good alternative to Color for clarifying a complex drawing, particularly if you are working on a monochrome monitor or planning to plot everything in a single pen color and width. For informal work, you can develop your own preference in line types. However, most types of technical drawing adhere to a strict coding system, so that specific line styles are always identified with certain types of drawing elements.

Most of the Settings commands bring up their own dialogue boxes, and Line Type is no exception. Selecting Line Type brings the Drawing Line Type dialogue box to the screen. Click the pointer in the small box next to the desired line type. A check mark will appear, marking your choice. After the appropriate line type has been selected, specify the scale by clicking on the Scale Factor box and then typing in the desired factor.

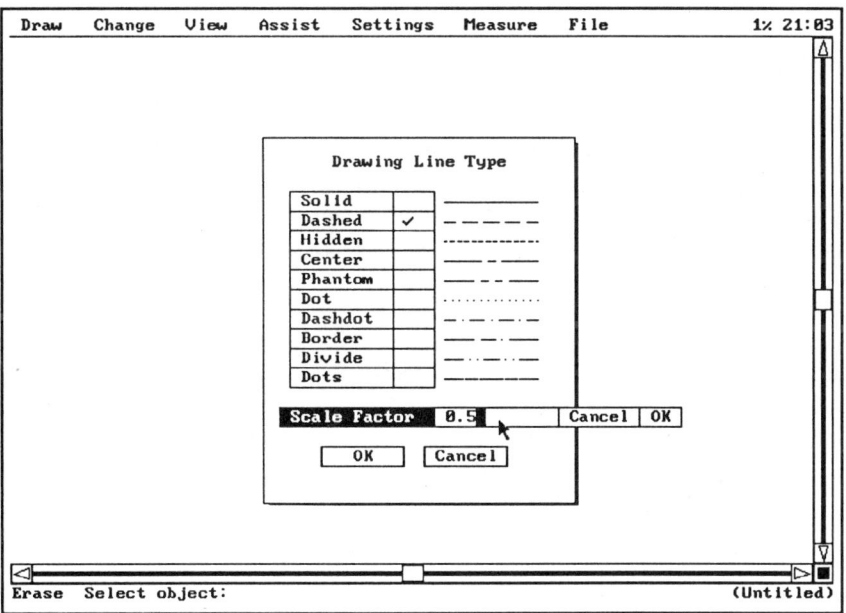

Setting Line Type Scale Factor

Setting Line Type and Line Scale

```
Pull down Settings Select Line Type
Click Dashed                              Select the Dashed style.
Scale Factor 0.5                          Enter a 0.5 scale factor.
Select OK                                 Click on the main OK box.
```

Draw some lines and circles. Change the line type and scale, and try drawing some more objects.

Pull down **Change** Select **Erase**	Erase the previous exercise.
Pull down **Settings** Select **Line Type**	
Click **Solid**	Set the style back to Solid.
Click **OK**	Click on the main OK box.

The use of certain line types is mandatory in engineering work where specific types of lines are always used to depict specific drawing elements. The names shown in the Drawing Line Type dialogue box reflect some of these drafting traditions. For instance, the short dashed line, Hidden, is used to represent lines that are hidden behind other parts of a component. The long-short-long dashed line, Center, is used to mark the centers of cylindrical shapes or circles.

The Scale Factor setting may seem a bit obscure, but it simply lets you change the spacing of dashed or dotted lines. If you want closely spaced dots or dashes, use a small setting. For wider spacing, use a larger setting. The default is 0.5; a value of zero reduces all line types to solid lines. Halving the scale factor will double the density of the line elements — giving you twice as many dashes or dots per drawing unit. Doubling the scale factor gives half as many dashes or dots. As you change scale factors, you can see the effect your changes will have in the sample line types shown in the dialogue box.

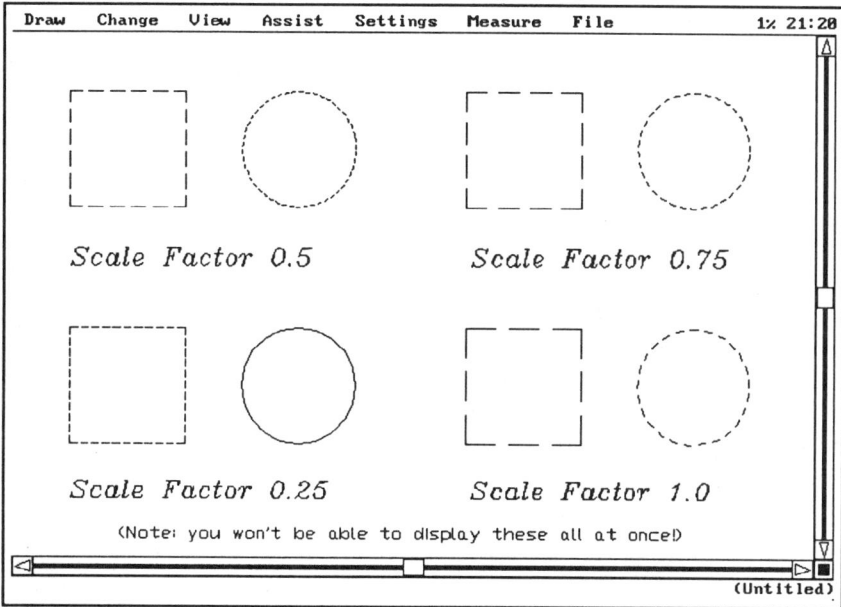

Effect of Scale Factor Setting

The main use of the Scale Factor option is to coordinate the plotted line type appearance with the drawing limits and plotting scale. Otherwise, you might find that the preset line types show up with awkward spacings — for instance, dotted lines with one dot at either side of the screen (or sheet) and nothing in between. If you were printing a section of your drawing magnified to twice the scale at which it was drawn, you would want to cut the scale factor in half.

A change in scale factor automatically affects all dotted or dashed lines in your drawing. This is in marked contrast to other settings such as Color or Line Type, which, when altered, affect only objects drawn from that moment on. Text, dimension markings, and wide polylines are not affected by the Line Type setting.

Text Effects

By default, AutoSketch uses a simple, fast-displaying text style. However, you'll often want to enter text at different sizes, at odd angles, or even in entirely different typefaces. You may want to emphasize certain words by italicizing them. The Text option on the Settings menu lets you accomplish these sorts of effects.

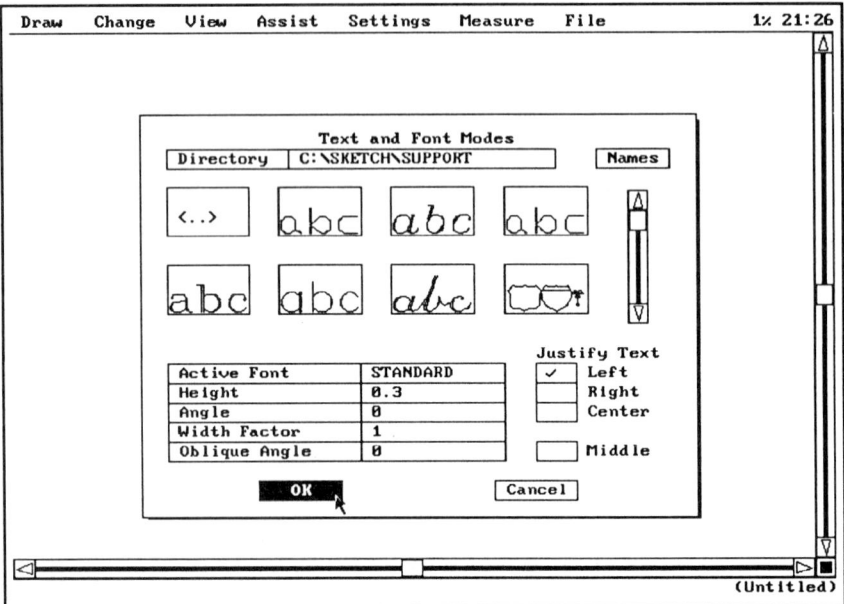

The Text Settings Dialogue Box

Text Size and Angle

Once you have selected the Text option, the Text and Font Modes dialogue box appears. You can then enter values for how you would like all subsequent text to appear. Note that any text effects you apply will not be transferred either into or out of the Text Editor. In other words, you cannot format text with italics, underlining, etc., in a word processor and import those effects.

Changing Text Settings

```
Pull down Settings Select Text
Height 0.75                      New height.
Angle 0                          Leave at 0, the default.
Width factor 1                   Leave at 1, the default.
Oblique angle 15                 For italicized text.
Click OK                         Click on the main OK box.
Pull down Draw Select Quick Text
```

Type a few words, then change some of the other options and type some more words.

The Height option changes the size of your text. A height value of 1.0 produces capital letters that are exactly one drawing unit high. The default height value of 0.3 produces text of a reasonable size at the default zoom magnification.

As with snap and grid settings, you'll find that the text width automatically defaults to match your Height setting. If you want narrower or wider text, use the Width Factor setting. A width factor of 1.0 is standard and produces text that is two-thirds as wide as it is high. A width factor of 0.5 produces very narrow text. Width factors larger than 1.0 stretch the letters sideways.

The Oblique Angle produces italics. A positive angle of about 15 degrees produces normal italic text. An angle of 30 degrees produces "intense" italics. Greater angles are likely to be useful only for special effects, and tend to be unreadable. Negative angles can be effective in special circumstances.

The Angle setting controls the angle of your lines of text on the screen. Thus, an angle of 45 degrees will produce text that climbs uphill as it extends toward the right of the screen. An angle of zero produces normal horizontal text.

Text Font

Starting with version 2.0, AutoSketch has also been able to work with more than one text style, or *font*. In addition to the standard text style, AutoSketch provides seven more styles in the form of disk files. Additional styles can readily be purchased; AutoSketch uses the same text files as its older brother, AutoCAD, which is well supported by this sort of accessory product.

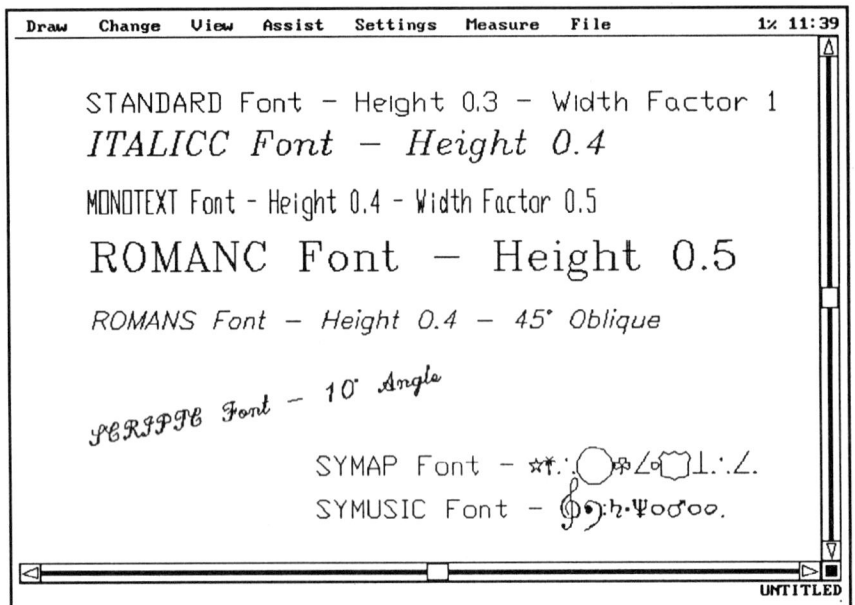

Various Text Settings

Changing Text Font

`Pull down `**`Settings`**` Select `**`Text`**

Make sure that icon text samples are displayed. If they are not, click on the Icons box.

`Click `**`ROMANC`**	Click on the first icon in the second row.
`Click `**`OK`**	Click on the main OK box.
`Pull down `**`Draw`**` Select `**`Quick Text`**	
`Enter point:`	Pick any point.
`Enter text: `**`A sample of ROMANC text.`**	Enter a sample of text on your drawing.
`Pull down `**`Settings`**` Select `**`Text`**	
`Active Font: `**`ITALICC`**	Click on the text box, and enter the font name.
`Click `**`OK`**	Click on the main OK box.

Enter some more text.
Try using different fonts with various Height, Width Factor, Angle, and Oblique Angle settings.

Like the Select Drawing File dialogue boxes in AutoSketch, the Text and Font Modes box lets you preview your choices as icons, if you wish. Select the Icons box to view icon samples of the available font files, and Names to change back again to a simple filename listing. You'll find that the Names listing appears slightly more quickly on your screen, while the Icons display is much more informative.

The fonts included with AutoSketch have been chosen for definite reasons. The STANDARD font gives the best compromise between simplicity and readability. MONOTEXT is very similar, but is not proportionally spaced; this allows columns of text to line up vertically, which can be important for tables and other structured layouts. The ITALICC font is a true italic, more elegant than a merely slanted version of some other font. The ROMANC and ROMANS fonts are your basic serif and sans-serif fonts, similar to those commonly used in publications or correspondence. SCRIPTC is an ornate font, best reserved for special occasions.

The SYMAP and SYMUSIC fonts actually consist not of alphabetic characters, but of special-purpose symbols, for use in mapmaking and music, respectively.

➥ *NOTE: Text fonts are handled somewhat differently in AutoSketch version 2.0. Version 2.0 allows up to seven fonts to be pre-loaded and then selected within the Text and Font Modes dialogue box. Version 3.0 does not require pre-loading. Aside from the need to load fonts in a separate step, however, the basic operation is the same.*

The term "font" within AutoSketch is actually somewhat erroneous. Wherever AutoSketch says "font," this refers to what a printer would call a *typeface*. This distinction could be disorienting to users accustomed to working in desktop publishing. However, the AutoSketch usage is consistent, so there's no real confusion once you adapt to the new nomenclature.

Text Justification

AutoSketch version 3.0 allows you to center or justify entire blocks of text. These help you create tidy-looking text annotations for your drawings.

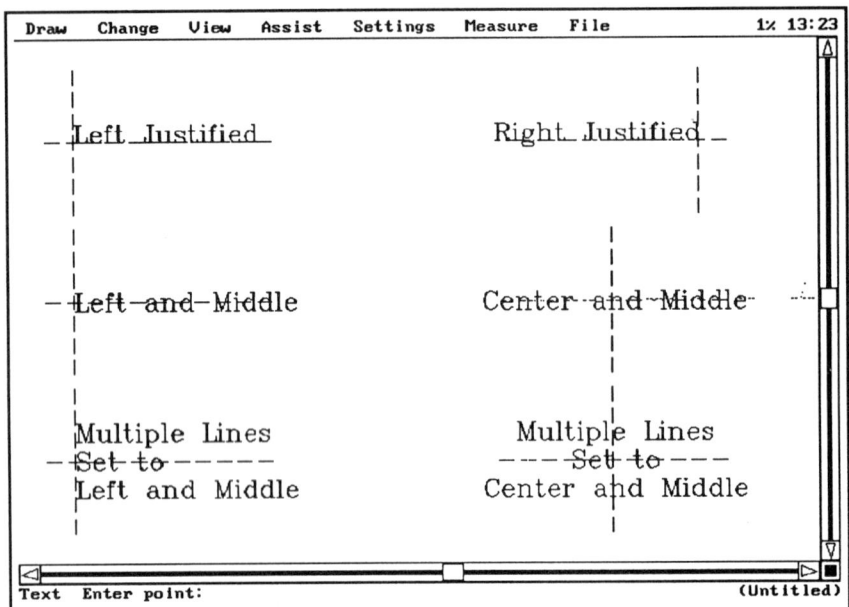

Effect of Text Justification Settings

Changing Text Justification

Pull down **Draw** Select **Line**	Draw a vertical reference line in the middle of the screen.
Pull down **Settings** Select **Text**	
Justify Text **Center**	Click the Center format box.
Click **OK**	Close dialogue box.
Pull down **Draw** Select **Quick Text**	
Enter point:	Pick a point near the top of the vertical reference line.
Enter text: **Centered <ENTER>**	Type a word or two, and press <ENTER>.

AutoSketch redraws the text, centering it on the base point.
Repeat the experiment, using each of the Justify Text settings.

The Middle format setting most visibly affects multi-line blocks of text that are entered via the text editor. All the lines will be vertically centered above and below the selected text base point. Thus, a three-line text block will have its middle line aligned with the base point, with the first line above it and the third line below it. With single lines, the effect of Middle justification is more subtle. Normally, AutoSketch vertically aligns the bottoms of characters on the chosen base point. With Middle set, characters are vertically centered on the base point, dropping the text down slightly.

➥ *TIP: Middle can be combined with Center to generate captions that are centered both horizontally and vertically. For instance, you could use these settings to center text within a box. You would need to place the text base point at the center of the box — but in later chapters we'll be discussing tools (such as Attach) that make this easy.*

Layers

The ability to work in layers is one of the greatest conveniences available in AutoSketch. For complicated drawings, layers help to keep it all under control.

The term layer should be taken literally. Envision working on a series of clear plastic sheets, overlaid on each other. AutoSketch gives you ten such layers. You can work on any of them, although the default is layer 1. You can switch from layer to layer at any time using the Layer command on the Settings menu. When you create an object, it is placed on the currently *active* layer.

When you select the Layer command, the Layer Status dialogue box appears. Click the Current box next to the desired active layer. Click the Visible boxes next to all the layers that you want visible on the display; check marks appear in all the selected boxes.

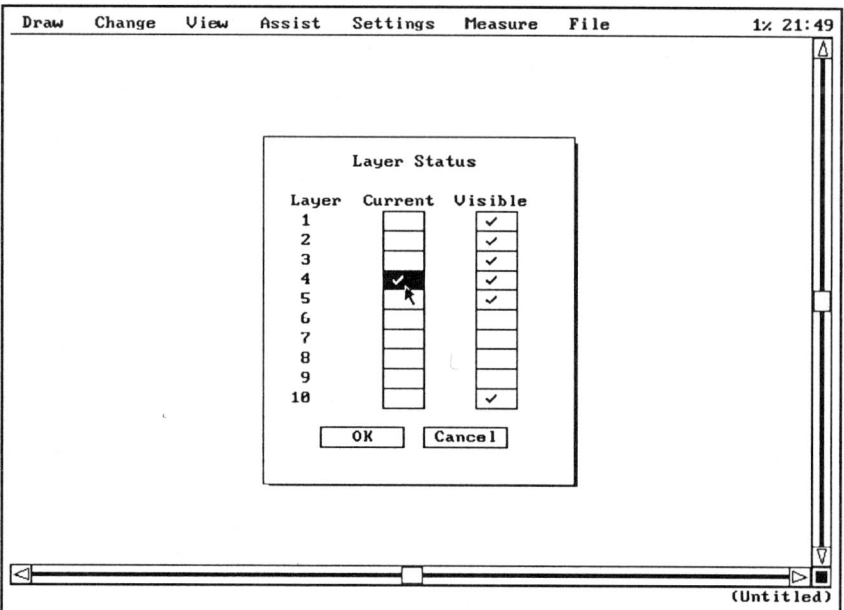

Setting a New Current Layer

Setting Active Drawing Layers

```
Pull down Settings Select Layer
Click 2                              Make layer 2 current.
Click 1                              Make layer 1 invisible.
Click OK                             Click main OK box.
```

Notice how the screen is now blank, as all your past work is on layer 1. Draw a few objects on layer 2.

```
Pull down Settings Select Layer
Click 1                              Make layer 1 current.
Click 1                              Make layer 1 visible.
Click 2                              Make layer 2 invisible.
Click OK                             Click main OK box.
```

Your current work disappears, and previous work reappears.

```
Pull down Settings Select Layer
Click 2                              Make layer 2 visible; leave layer 1 as is.
Click OK                             Click main OK box.
```

Work from both layers appears together.

The easiest way to tell what layer an object is on is to use the Show Properties command on the Measure menu. To check the layer of multiple objects, it may be quicker to make individual layers invisible, until the objects vanish from your screen.

You can change the layer of any object at any time with the Property command on the Change menu. This will be discussed in more depth later.

For now, the real question regarding layers is what do you *do* with them? As you get to know your way around AutoSketch, standardize various elements of your drawings. For instance, decide what drawing layers and colors to use for text and dimension lines, and stick to them religiously. There's nothing more annoying than getting lost in a random assortment of layers, so the sooner you can standardize, the less trouble you'll have. You can even use AutoSketch to create and print out a sheet listing your assignments of layers and colors.

The major advantage of this separation comes from the fact that layers can be individually switched on or off. When a layer is made invisible using the Layer Status dialogue box, objects on it disappear from view as though they'd never been. They won't display, they won't print out, and they are protected from being inadvertently altered by any of the Change commands (which will work on any visible object regardless of the layer it's on).

Suppose you've created a complex drawing. You could produce a much clearer view by switching your text layer *off*. You could even locate different sets of text labels on different layers. Thus you could easily produce, for example, a floor plan with just the wiring labeled, or with just the plumbing labeled, or with both the plumbing and wiring hidden away and just the walls visible. All of these views could be extracted from a single drawing.

Using layers you can essentially build a family of drawings, one on top of another. Elements of each related structure can be perfectly registered with those of the others. For instance, wiring can be made to follow the walls of a floor plan exactly. Later, you can independently display or print just the parts you want to view at the moment.

Of course, turning off layers that you don't currently need can also greatly speed up screen redraws in a complex drawing and make it easier to see what you're doing.

AutoSketch insists, reasonably enough, that you have at least one layer visible at all times, and exactly one active layer. When laying out complex drawings, bear in mind that AutoSketch provides only ten layers, whereas professional design programs such as Autodesk's own AutoCAD give you an unlimited number. You'll need to plan your drawing carefully to get the best use out of the available layers. This kind of planning pays off in many other ways, so it's really no extra burden.

Once you set comfortable standards, set up some blank prototype drawings, as described in the appendix. These drawings act as templates, letting you instantly restore your most commonly used AutoSketch settings in preparation for a new project. Many repeating elements — such as borders or titles — can be saved in a prototype file and will never have to be redone.

➥ *TIP: AutoCAD will also allow you to freeze, make, and assign color and line types to layers for better layer management.*

Show Properties

Any time you need information about how an object was created, the Show Properties command can help. It will not only tell you about the object's color or line type, it will also show you what *type* of object you're dealing with.

When you activate the Show Properties command and select an object, a dialogue box will appear on the screen, listing the object's type, layer, color, and line type.

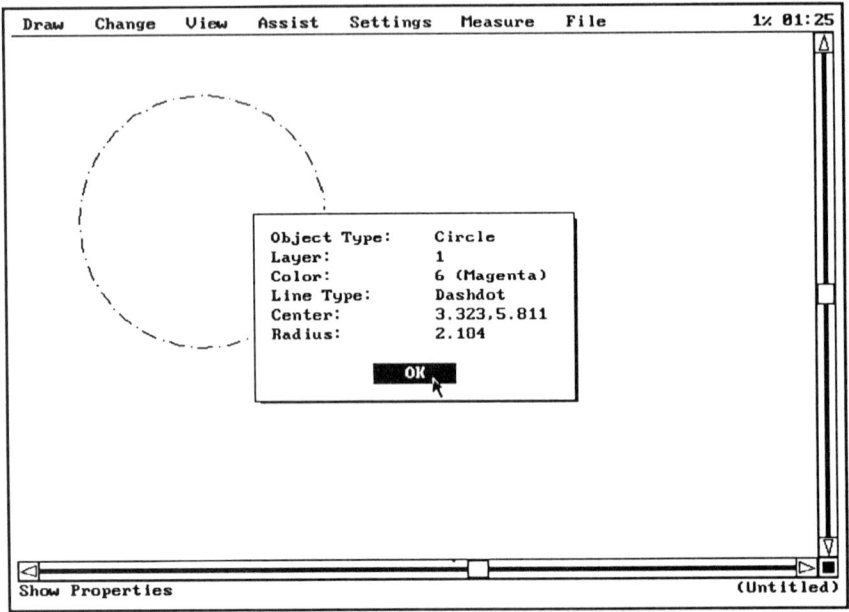

Checking an Object's Properties

The information provided by the Show Properties command can be very useful. For instance, suppose you see a rectangle on the screen. It could have been created as a box, or it could have been made up from a series of four line objects. If you're going to edit the drawing, the distinction could be significant.

Showing Object Properties

```
Pull down Settings Select Line Type
Click Dashdot                              Set a fancy line type.
Click OK
Pull down Settings Select Color
```

Click **Magenta**	Set a fancy color.
Click **OK**	
Pull down **Draw** Select **Circle**	Draw a dotted, magenta circle.
Pull down **Measure** Select **Show Properties**	
Select object:	Select the circle.

AutoSketch shows you all the circle's properties.

Click **OK**   Select the OK box.

Try some other objects, with different line and color settings.
Also, be sure to try Show Properties with some fancy text.

If you're working on a monochrome monitor, the Show Properties command will be your only means of double-checking color settings. It can also help if your line type scale or zoom factor is too small, and all lines look solid on the screen.

➥ *TIP: The AutoCAD LIST command is similar to Show Properties, yet it provides additional information such as 3D coordinates, area, and perimeter.*

Change Property

The Property command on the Settings menu and the Property command on the Change menu work hand-in-hand. The (Settings) Property command shows you the Change Property Modes dialogue box. The choices you make there will enable the changes that are possible through the (Change) Property command. The (Change) Property command allows you to reset the properties of a selected object to match its current settings. You'll recall that changes in color and line type (other than scale factor) affect only elements drawn subsequently. The only way to reset what you've *already* drawn is by using the (Change) Property command. Simply set the combination of properties you want from the (Settings) Property command, select the (Change) Property command, and then select the object(s) you wish to change. You can use the Crosses/window box to change large numbers of objects together.

The Change Property Modes dialogue box allows you to limit the specific properties affected by the (Change) Property command. By default, all property settings are enabled: color, layer, line type, and several others we haven't dealt with yet. Click your mouse on the box next to those modes you wish to remain *unchanged*; a check mark is shown next to those modes that *will* be changed.

5–18 INSIDE AutoSketch

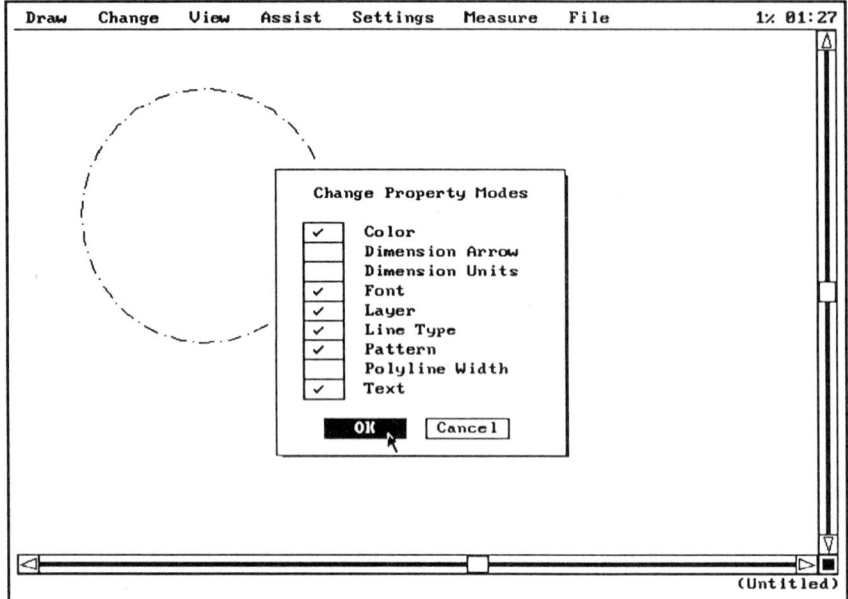

Changing an Object's Properties

➡ *NOTE: In early versions of AutoSketch, Text settings were unaffected by Change Property commands. Starting with version 2.0, however, all text properties can be changed.*

Changing Object Properties

Change your current line type, layer, and color settings.

```
Pull down Settings Select Property
Click Layer                              The check mark next to Layer disappears.
Click OK                                 Select the main OK.
Pull down Change Select Property
Select object:                           Select some objects.
```

Use the Show Properties command to confirm the changes.
Be sure to try Change Property on some text.

➡ *TIP: AutoCAD's CHANGE and CHPROP commands are similar to the Change Property command in AutoSketch.*

Drawing Limits

Setting the purely imaginary limits of a drawing may seem a fruitless use of your time, especially when you realize that AutoSketch permits you to draw just as far outside these limits as you like. However, the Limits setting can provide some very real benefits.

To begin with, adjusting your limits appropriately can make the Zoom Limits command much more useful. In this regard, you can think of the Limits setting as a way of "saving" a view of your entire drawing. There are a few advanced functions that work best when the limits are set to encompass all of the actual drawing. The Grid command, covered a bit later in the next chapter, is a good example.

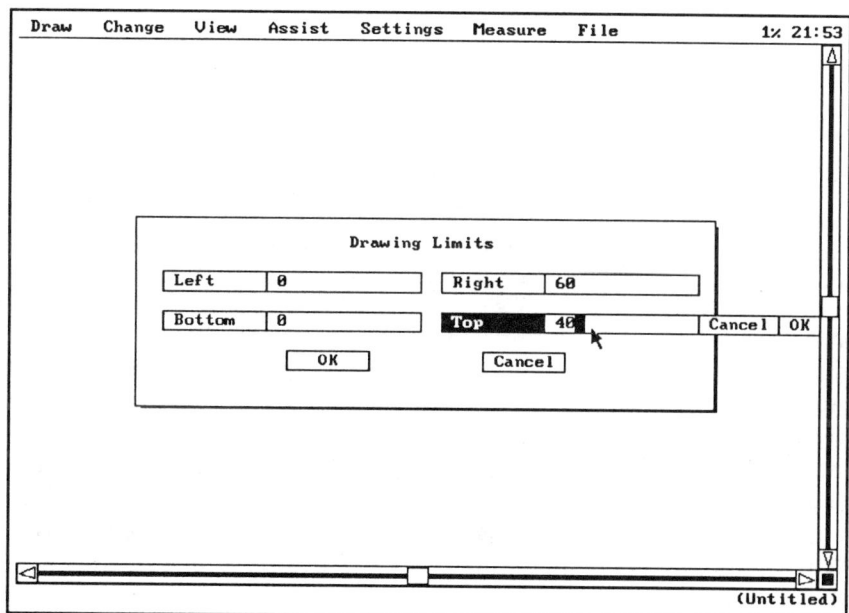

Setting Drawing Limits

Setting Drawing Limits

```
Pull down Settings Select Limits
Right 60                                 Change to 60 units.
Top 40                                   Change to 40 units.
Click OK                                 Click the main OK box.
Pull down View Select Zoom Limits
Pull down Settings Select Limits
Right 12                                 Change back to 12 units.
Top 9                                    Change back to 9 units.
```

```
Click OK                                      Click the main OK box.
Pull down View Select Zoom Limits
```

The most practical use of Limits is to set the electronic sheet size after the appropriate units and scale have been decided. Since AutoSketch can zoom in or out almost infinitely, there's no reason to constrain your work to the default units and display size. This means, whether you are drawing the space plan of a 30-foot by 60-foot office or a diagram of a microscopic integrated circuit, you can draw at full scale, zooming in and out as needed. The system of measurement you decide upon to equal each unit will determine the area of the drawing space you will need. Remember, each unit can represent any distance you want it to. You just shrink or expand your limits to accommodate the subject.

You also have to think in terms of scale for plotting. Once you have chosen a unit system, plotting scale, and sheet size, you will have enough information to set your limits.

If you do not intend to make a paper copy, your limits need only accommodate the overall size of the object being drawn. However, if you are planning on making a printed or plotted hard copy of your drawing, you should set your limits according to the paper size and scale.

It takes a little bit of planning and calculation to get everything worked out. Suppose you want to draw the above-mentioned floor plan with 1 AutoSketch unit equal to 1 inch, and you do not intend to make a hard copy. It would make perfect sense to set your Limits to 60' horizontally (what the AutoSketch dialogue box calls "right") and 40' vertically (referred to as "top"). Notice that the vertical dimension should be approximately two-thirds of the horizontal if you want the drawing area to roughly match the proportions of your display screen. Of course, this is not compulsory, and there's no harm in using a short, wide area or a tall, narrow one.

But what if you needed to make a hard copy of the space plan at a specified scale on a particular sheet size? What would you do?

If you know that your particular drawing is going to fit on a specific sheet size at a given scale, it is relatively easy to determine the limits. Simply take the hard copy sheet size and multiply it by the plotting scale. The result is the electronic paper size, which is equal to the limits. For example:

- If 1 unit = 1 inch and the scale is to be 1/4"=1'0", every inch of paper = 4'0".
- Thus, a 17" x 11" sheet represents 68' x 44', (since 17 x 4'= 68', and 11 x 4'= 44').
- Set the drawing limits to 68' x 44'.

But how would you determine the right scale factor if you knew the size of an object that had to fit on a certain paper size? This requires a little bit of trial and error.

- Determine the actual object size, for example 60' x 30'.
- Decide upon the paper size, for example 17" x 11".
- Test a scale. 17" x 11" paper at 1/2"=1'-0" can accommodate a 34' x 22' object.
- The scale is too large.
- Test a smaller scale. 17" x 11" paper at 1/4"=1'0" can accommodate a 68' x 44' object.
- This one should work.

Similarly, how would you determine the right sheet size if you knew the object size and the scale factor was already defined?

- Determine the actual object size: 60' x 30', for example.
- Determine the scale: 1/2"=1'0".
- Test a paper size. 1/2"=1'0" on a 17" x 11" sheet can hold an object of 34' x 22'.
- The paper size is too small.
- Test a larger paper size. 1/2"=1'0" scale on a 36" x 24" sheet can hold an object of 72' x 48'.
- This one should work.

We recommend putting 0,0 at the lower left corner of the limits and paper. However, you can also use the Limits setting to build in an offset from the normal (0,0) drawing origin. This could be valuable if you are measuring all your drawing distances against some external reference point. Positive left and bottom Limits settings will move the zero point away to the left and down, so that it is no longer within your drawing Limits. Negative values will include the (0,0) origin somewhere within your actual drawing area.

It's a good idea to set up a reasonable set of limits at the start of any drawing job, and to update them whenever the original values begin to seem inadequate.

➡ *TIP: To avoid confusing yourself, always do a Zoom Limits immediately after setting Limits. This lets you get your bearings. Also, if you have version 2.0, to avoid wasting large amounts of paper, be sure to check your plotting scale before you output the drawing. For more information on plotting, see Chapter 8, Getting Output. For Zoom Limits, see Chapter 4, Viewing Options.*

Command Practice

We suggest that you experiment a little with the commands that were just covered before going on to the drawing exercise. Use the File menu and select New to get a clean screen.

COLOR. Create a box. Note that the default color is black. Use the Color option from the Settings menu. Try each of the colors in turn, drawing a new object each time. Try entering random color numbers, and see what colors result.

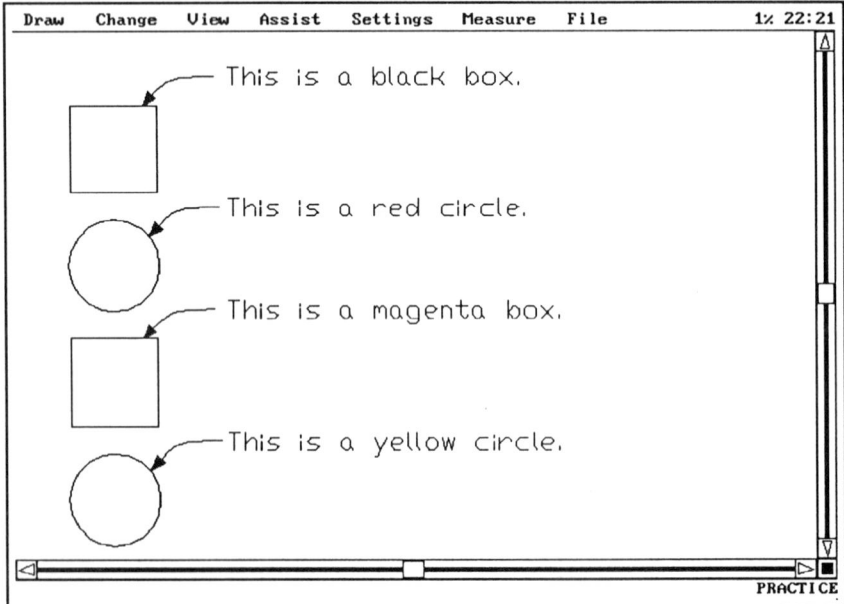

Changing Colors

LINE SCALE. Try setting some different scale factors. You'll find that extreme scale factors can do very strange things to your drawing.

TEXT SETTINGS. Type in some text, using different height values. Try using a value of 0.02, then zoom in to see if the text really does display that small. Then try a value of 2 or more.

TEXT SETTINGS. Try some different obliquing angles. Prove to yourself that angles of more than 30 degrees tend to look very peculiar (not to say illegible). Try negative angles.

TEXT SETTINGS. Use the baseline angle to print text at various angles. See if you can print some text upside-down.

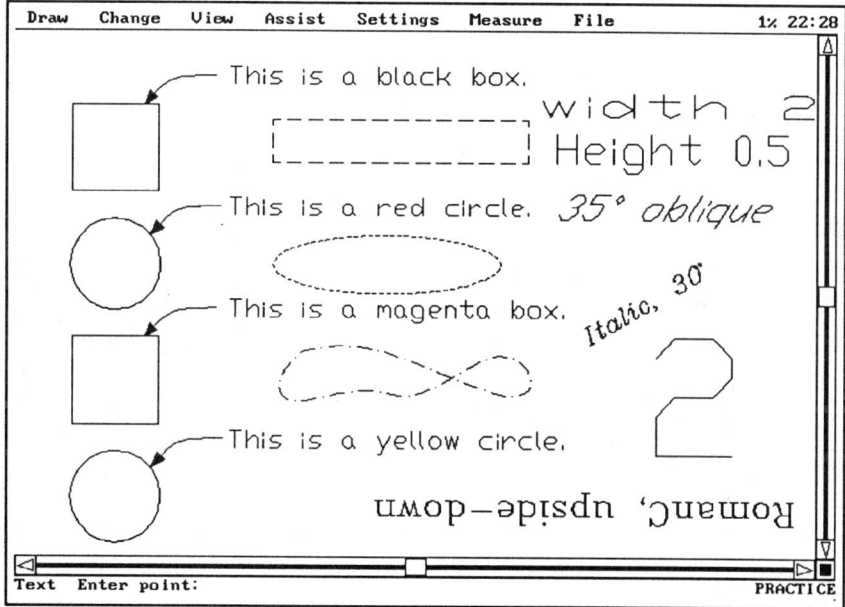

Text and Line Type Choices

LAYER. Set the current layer as 2, and make it invisible. Using the Property command on the Change menu, reset the layer of a circle. You'll find that it abruptly vanishes from the screen. Draw a new box; it appears normally. Then select Redraw from the View menu; the box disappears. Go back to the Property command on the Settings menu, and set layer 2 visibility back *on*. The circle and box reappear.

LAYER. Set the active layer to 1 again. Try to erase the circle. You'll find that making a layer inactive does nothing to protect it from modification. The only thing you *can't* do to inactive layers is to draw on them. To protect a layer, you *must* make it invisible.

CHANGE PROPERTY. Change the black box to red. That is, change the Color setting to red, then use the Property command to reset the box's color. Change its line type to dashed.

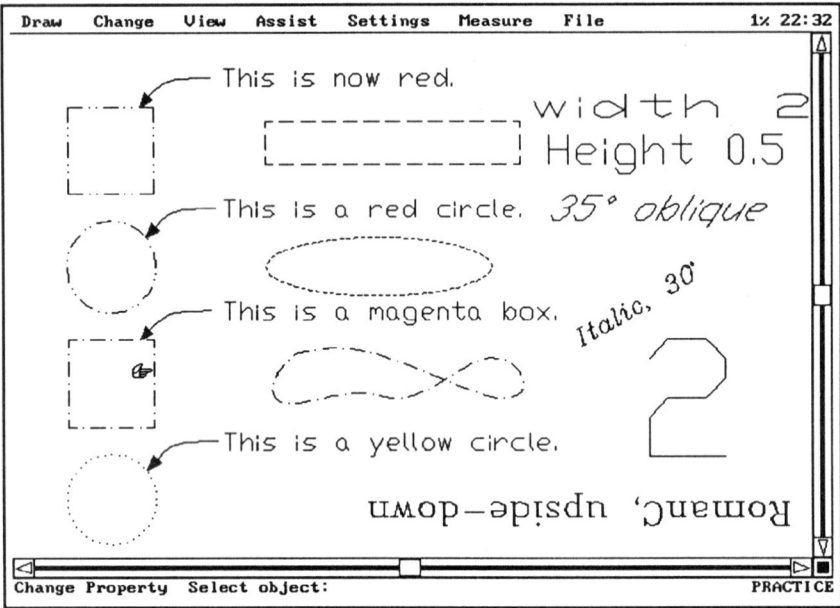

Changed Properties

Use the Show Properties command to check the values for the box. Pull down the Settings menu and enter some non-standard text values: say an obliquing angle of 45, a text angle of 135, and a height of 2. Enter some Quick Text, then use Show Properties to inspect it.

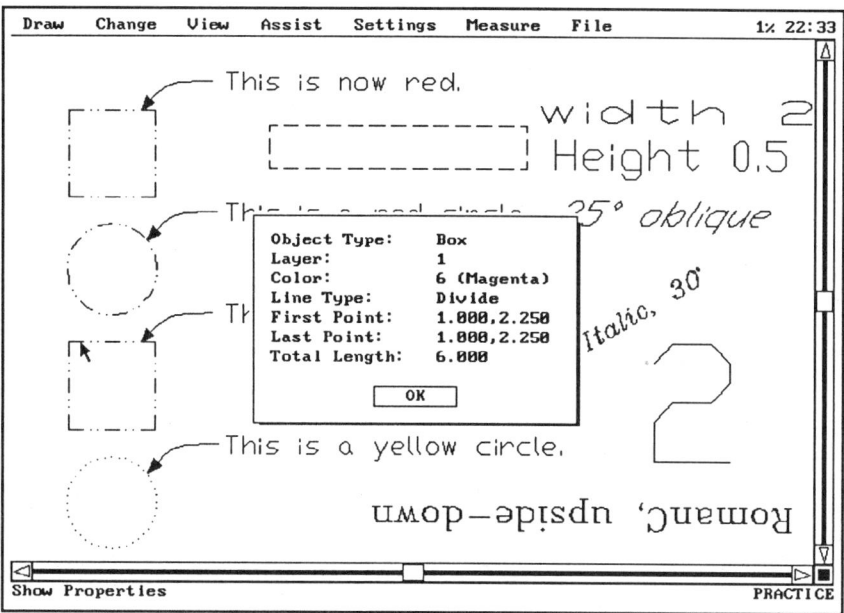

Showing Properties of the Magenta Box

Space Plan

In this section you will begin creating a simple floor plan, which can eventually be elaborated into a professional space plan. We'll be going about this task in a more organized fashion than in the previous examples. To start with, we'll create just the furniture for our plan. Unlike the MAP drawing, however, we will make this drawing in real-world size. In the next chapter we'll draw the plan itself. Then, in Chapter 7, we'll see how easily and flexibly AutoSketch allows you to combine the two.

This exercise is an introduction to one of the powerful ways in which AutoSketch allows you to structure your work. Elements that repeat throughout one or more drawings can be created separately, just as we are going to do with the simple furniture drawings for the space plan. These component drawings can then be brought in to the space plan using the Part command on the Draw menu. That way, you only draw each component once. We'll look at the Part command itself later in Chapter 7.

From here on, those of you who are using color monitors (or monochrome monitors and pen plotters) should change colors as noted.

5–26 INSIDE AutoSketch

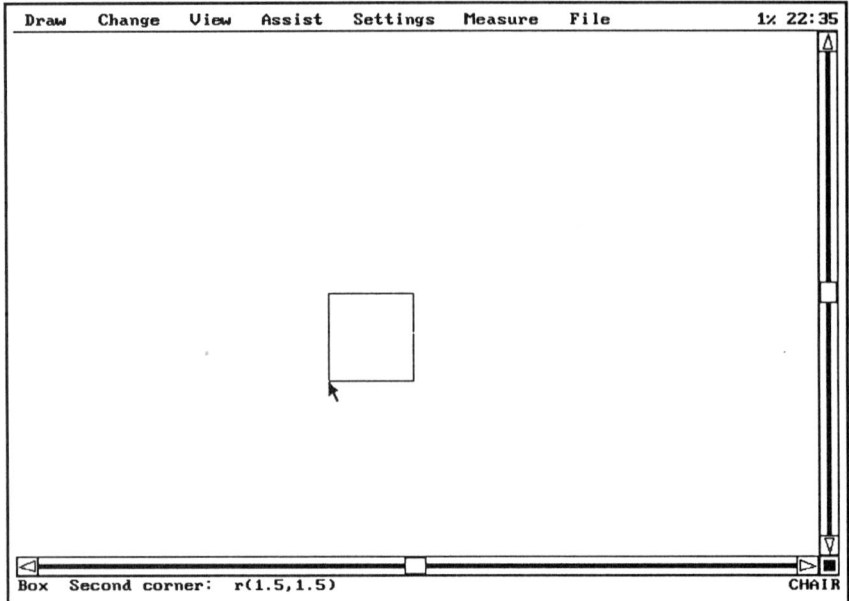

Drawing a Chair

Space Plan Drawing Exercise

```
Pull down File Select New              Prepare a clean slate.
Pull down File Select Save As
Filename CHAIR                         Save file as CHAIR.
Click OK
Pull down Settings Select Color
Click Magenta                          Change to magenta.
Click OK                               Pick the main OK.

Pull down Draw Select Box
First corner:                          Pick a point.
Second corner: R(18, 18)               18 inches square.
Pull down File Select Save             Save changes to CHAIR.
```

Next, start a new drawing and draw a plant. Set Color to green. Set Line Type to Dot, and the scale factor to 4.0. This value seems to give a pleasant sort of shaded effect, but you might need to vary the setting to get the best output from your own equipment.

First, draw a circle with an 18-inch diameter, for use as a reference. Then, using Curve, draw a frame shaped like a nine-pointed star within the circle. Then delete the circle. This should produce a rough representation of a potted plant. You can easily come up with a far more elaborate symbol, if you wish to take the time. Save the drawing under the name PLANT.

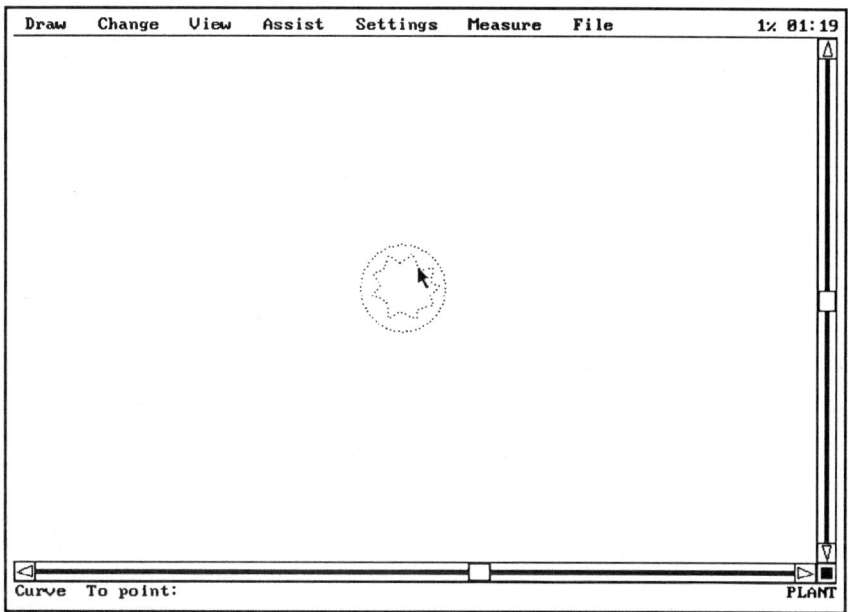

Using Curve to Draw a Plant

```
Pull down File Select New                    Start a new drawing.
Pull down File Select Save As
Filename PLANT                               Save file as PLANT.
Click OK                                     Click the main OK box.

Pull down Settings Select Color
Click Green                                  Change to green.
Click OK                                     Click the main OK box.

Pull down Settings Select Line Type
Click Dot                                    Change to dot.
Scale factor 4.0                             4.0 scale factor.
Click OK                                     Click the main OK box.

Pull down Draw Select Circle
Center point:                                Center of the screen.
Point on circle: R(9,0)                      18-inch diameter circle.
Pull down Draw Select Curve
First point:                                 On the circle.
To point:                                    Finish the plant.
```

```
Pull down Change Select Erase
Select object:                          Erase the circle.
Select Save                             Save changes to PLANT.
```

Open up a new drawing. Save as FLOOR. Now you will already have the drawing created when you want to call it up.

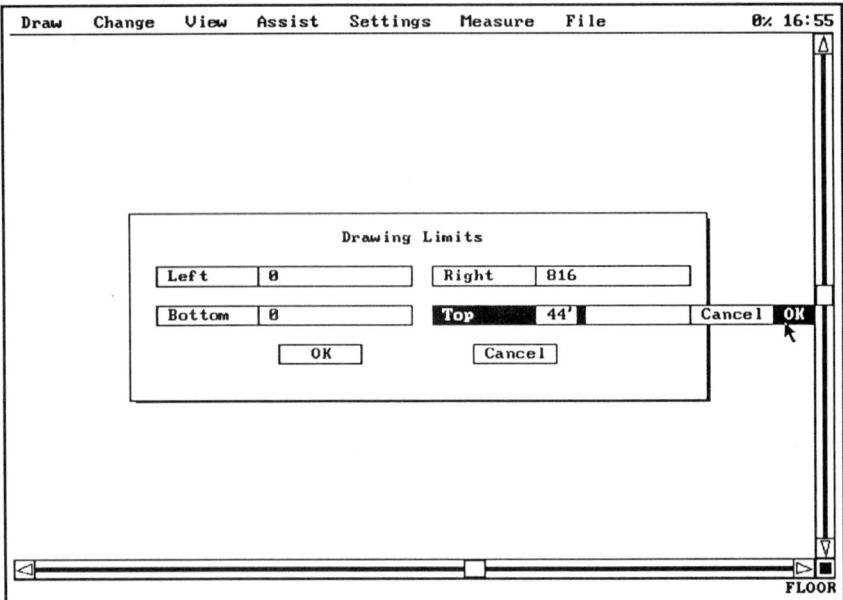

Setting Limits for the Space Plan

```
Pull down File Select New
Pull down File Select Save As
Filename FLOOR                          Save file as FLOOR.
Pull down Settings Select Limits
Right 68'                               AutoSketch converts it to 816 inches.
Top 44'                                 AutoSketch converts it to 528 inches.
Click OK
Pull down View Select Zoom Limits
Pull down File Select Save              Save the FLOOR drawing.
```

The limits are based on the fact that you will be drawing full scale, one drawing unit to one inch, to be plotted at 1/4"=1'0", on an 11"x17" sheet of paper. Saving an "empty" drawing ahead of time this way is a powerful AutoSketch technique, discussed more fully in Chapter 12. Even though you've drawn nothing, the FLOOR drawing retains all

Settings values. Once configured, FLOOR can serve as a time-saving starting point for many different drawings, each of which can be stored under a new name by means of the Save As command.

Summary

In this chapter we've covered some of the most sophisticated controls available in AutoSketch. Using appropriate color, line type, and text settings, you can make your drawings more attractive and more legible. Settings such as layers and limits help you to organize your work, and produce complex drawings to a proper scale.

In the next chapter, you will begin to apply some of the precision features of AutoSketch, including Snap and Grid. Using these, and the Part drawing functions covered in Chapter 7, you can continue to evolve the space plan example into a professional drawing.

PART TWO

Drawing Aids

This part allows you to progress beyond mere sketching into the realm of real technical drawing. It should also give you a feel for the relationships between the program's various commands. Although you can perform many drawing tasks without using any of these more advanced commands, mastering them will make your drawing jobs a lot easier.

This part is subdivided as follows:

- **Advanced Drawing Tools** introduces you to B-spline curves and commands to make your drawings accurate.
- **Advanced Editing Tools** shows you how to use the power of the computer to help you make bigger changes to your drawing fast.
- **Getting Output** covers the the process of extracting a hard copy of your drawing data from AutoSketch.

As you deal with AutoSketch at a more sophisticated level, you'll often be coordinating several drawing processes at once. The result is not only better-looking drawings, but also time well spent.

In this part, you're going to start a floor plan, or more correctly, the "space plan," of an office. The most important difference between the previous examples and this one will be precision. A space plan is a drawing that might be used by a facilities planner or by an office manager to plan office space usage. The same techniques introduced here will apply to most technical drawing applications.

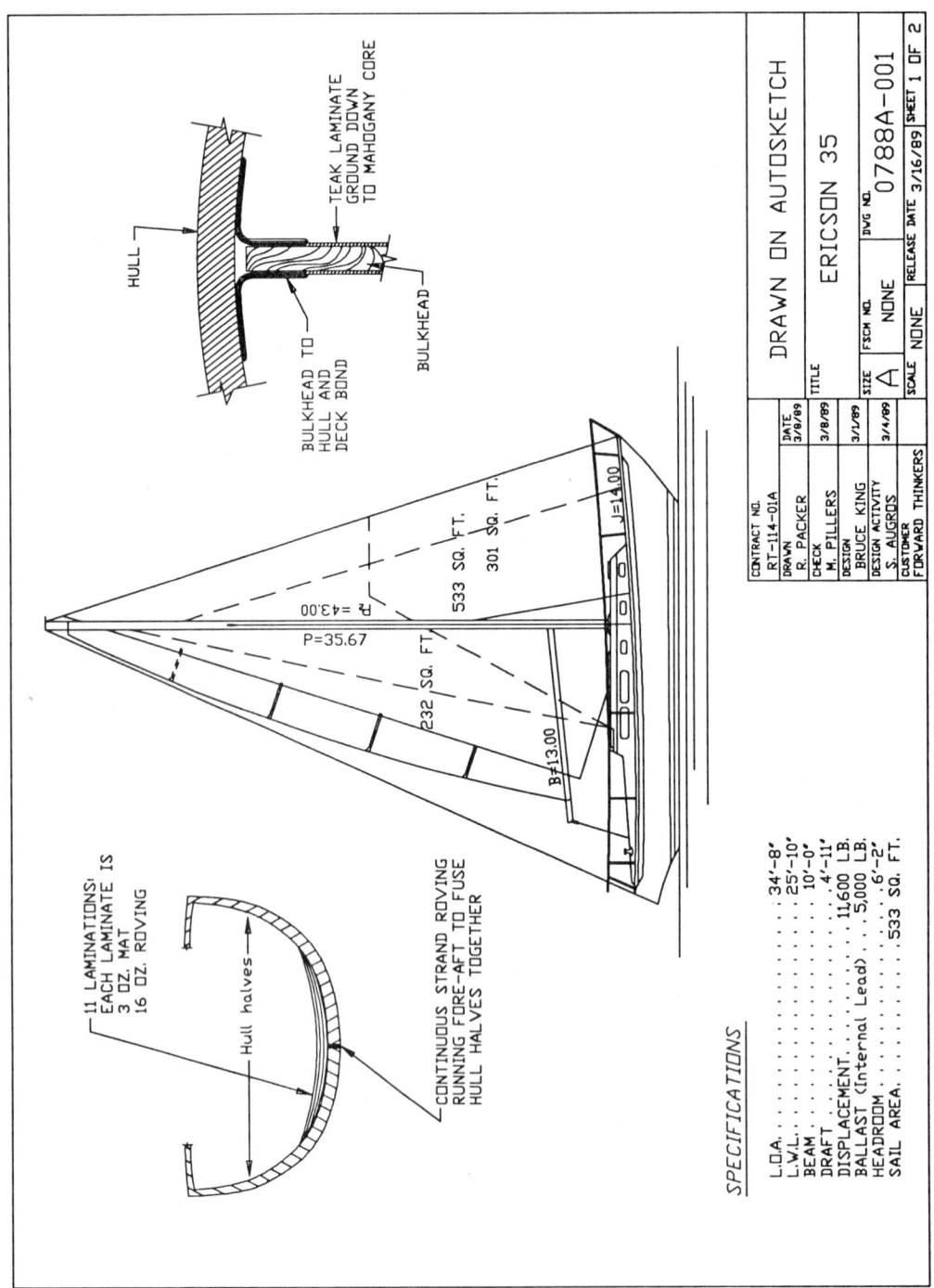

Ericson 35, Courtesy of Autodesk, Inc.

Chapter 6

Advanced Drawing Tools

As you explore the more advanced possibilities of AutoSketch, you will work chiefly with the Assist and Settings menus. However, you'll also be using the basic drawing commands you learned in Section One.

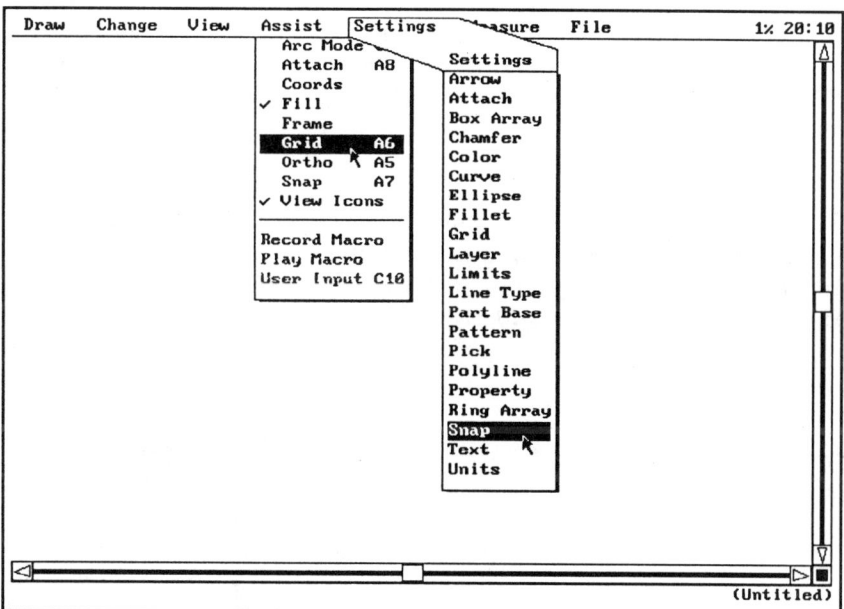

The Assist and Settings Menus

Most of the options on the Assist and Settings menus have a strong effect on drawing appearance and precision, but are not tied to any one drawing action. AutoSketch groups these support commands into two separate menus.

The Settings menu controls a number of drawing properties. These let you enhance your drawing with color or different line types, or help you organize your work into drawing layers. You have already dealt with these functions in the previous chapter. The other Settings items control the actions of Assist menu toggles.

The selections on the Assist menu toggle on and off several settings that help you to control the movement of the drawing pointer and how and where points are picked. These controls can help you simplify many common drawing tasks.

The Attach, Grid, and Snap settings are vital for production of accurate drawings. Without them, AutoSketch cannot draw accurately unless you constantly type in coordinates. When you pick points freely, AutoSketch rounds off the current pixel position of the pointer to arrive at a drawing coordinate. This chapter will show you how you can draw accurately with the pointer.

Curves

When AutoSketch draws a curve, it does so by fitting the curve between control points you enter. The Curve command on the Settings menu lets you control the precision of curves: the higher the curve setting, the smoother your curves will look. Lower curve values will speed up screen redraws and plots but produce rougher curves.

When you select Curve on the Settings menu, the Curve dialogue box appears. Enter the desired number of drawing segments, then click on the OK box. All existing curves will be redrawn using the new value. Any new curves you draw will also use this value.

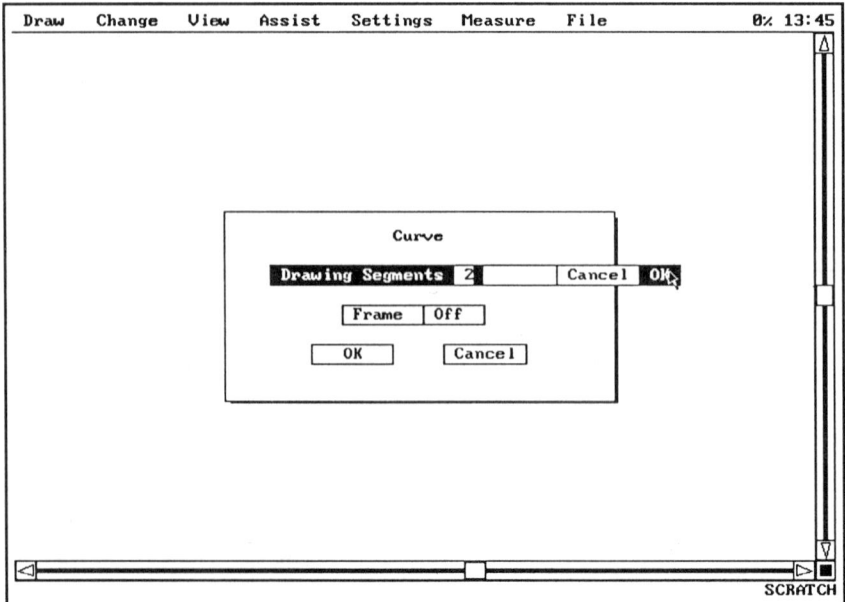

Setting the Curve Control Points

Setting Curve Segments

```
Pull down File Select New
Pull down File Select Save As
Filename: SCRATCH
```
Start a fresh drawing.

Save as SCRATCH.

```
Pull down Settings Select Curve
Drawing Segments: 2
Click OK
Pull down Draw Select Curve
First point:
To point:
```
Use 2 segments.
Click the OK box.

Pick a point.
Draw a curve. It looks terrible.

```
Pull down Settings Select Curve
Drawing Segments: 8
Click OK
```
Set back to 8.
Click the OK box. Does the curve look better?

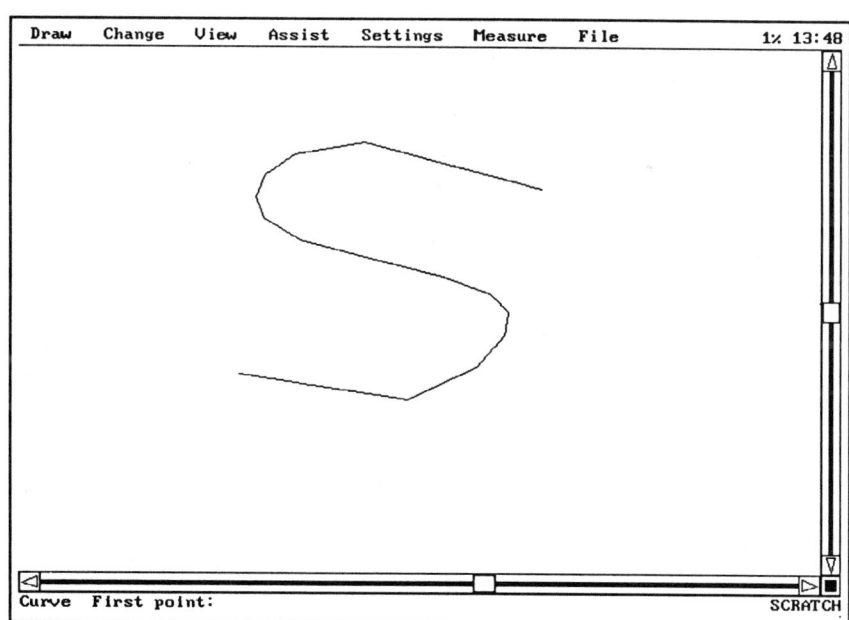

Curve With Drawing Segments at 2

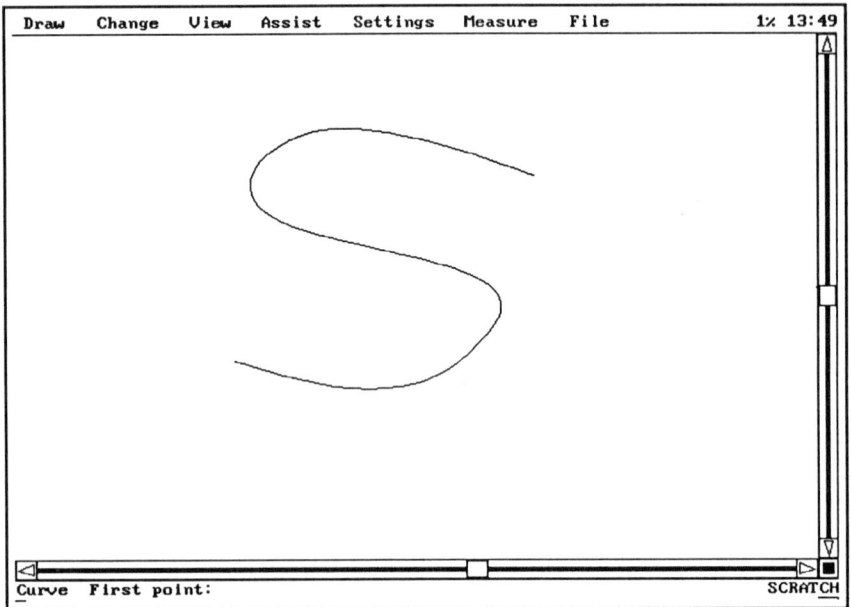

Curve With Drawing Segments Back at 8

If you are creating a large number of complex curves, especially on a relatively slow computer, you can set the curve setting to a low value before you begin work. This will speed up the responsiveness of AutoSketch and let you output trial plots more quickly. When you're ready to output your final drawing, you can reset the curve value to a higher level — eight or more. AutoSketch automatically redraws all curves whenever the curve setting is changed. How to draw curves is covered in Chapter 2, *Drawing Fundamentals*.

If you set an unrealistically high curve value, you may be waiting a long time while your curves are redrawn. A very high value such as 99 can make your computer seem to lock up for several minutes at a time. Don't panic — AutoSketch will catch up with you eventually. Obviously, it's best to avoid such high settings. You probably won't see much difference past the default setting of eight.

Frames

The Frame setting on the Assist menu is crucial for performing even simple curve work in AutoSketch. To select a curve, you must either enclose all of its invisible control points in a Crosses/window box or select its frame. With Frame toggled off, your pointer won't seem to grab the curve.

Toggling the Frame On

Setting Curve Frame

```
Pull down Assist Select Frame          Frame is now on.
Pull down Assist Select Frame          Frame turned back off.
```

For convenience, AutoSketch also lets you toggle Frame on or off from the Curve settings dialogue box, described in the previous section.

Setting Frame on will reveal the control points, connected by line segments. From then on, selecting the curve is merely a matter of selecting the frame, like any other object. In the next chapter, you'll see how you can further modify your curve by grabbing individual control points and using Stretch on them.

After you toggle Frame on, a tick mark will appear on the Assist menu next to the Frame option, and all the existing curves will display their construction frames.

Ortho Mode

The vast majority of lines you draw in AutoSketch — or on the back of a napkin — are vertical or horizontal. Such lines, always perpendicular to each other, are called *orthogonal* lines. They're so fundamental that AutoSketch has a special drawing mode to help you deal with them.

Setting Ortho mode on prevents you from drawing anything but true orthogonal lines. This can be quite a time-saver. Rather than constantly specifying angles of 90 degrees, you can draw freehand with complete confidence that everything will come out true. You could achieve the same results manually by using polar or relative coordinate entry; however, Ortho mode is usually easiest.

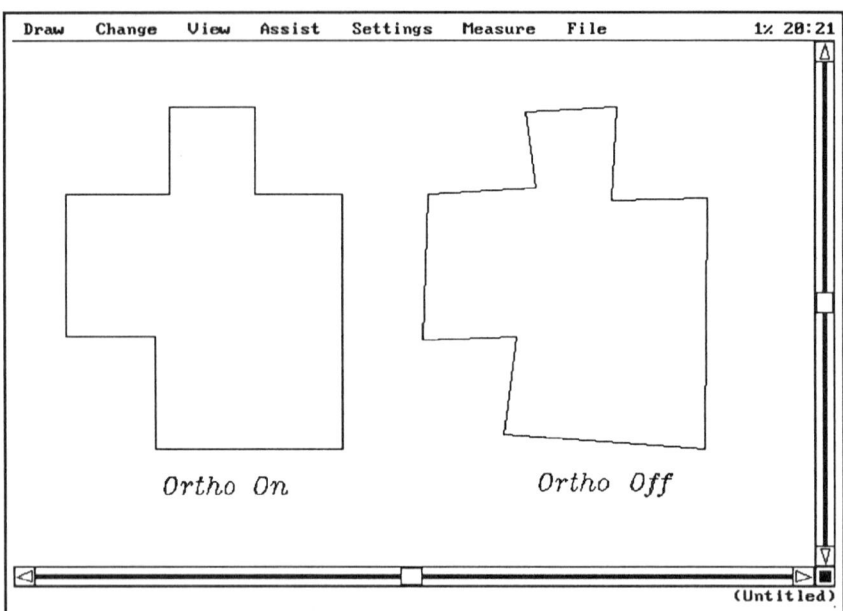

Drawing With Ortho On and Off

Setting Ortho Mode

```
Pull down Change Select Erase          Erase the curve.
Pull down Assist Select Ortho          Ortho is now on.
Pull down Draw   Select Polyline       Draw a simple shape. Try drawing diagonals.

Pull down Assist Select Ortho          Ortho is off.
Pull down Draw   Select Polyline       Try again to draw a perfect rectangle.
Pull down Assist Select Ortho          Ortho is back on.
```

After you select Ortho from the Assist menu, a check mark appears next to the Ortho option on the menu, indicating that the setting is on. This will only be apparent if the Assist menu is again pulled down after selecting Ortho. However, all rubberband lines will be constrained to vertical and horizontal, reminding you that Ortho is set.

➥ *TIP: You may find it tricky to close up a complex polyline with Ortho mode enabled. If you navigate your orthogonal lines so that the endpoint comes quite close to the start point, AutoSketch will automatically move the endpoint slightly so as to attach it to the start point. Unless you're careful, this may create a slightly angled line despite the Ortho setting. This automatic polyline-closing operates even if Attach mode is turned off. Attach is discussed fully later in this chapter.*

Grid Display

Grid is one of the simplest of AutoSketch functions. All it does is draw a grid of reference dots on the screen. These dots act as an aid to accuracy — especially when combined with Snap, discussed in the next section.

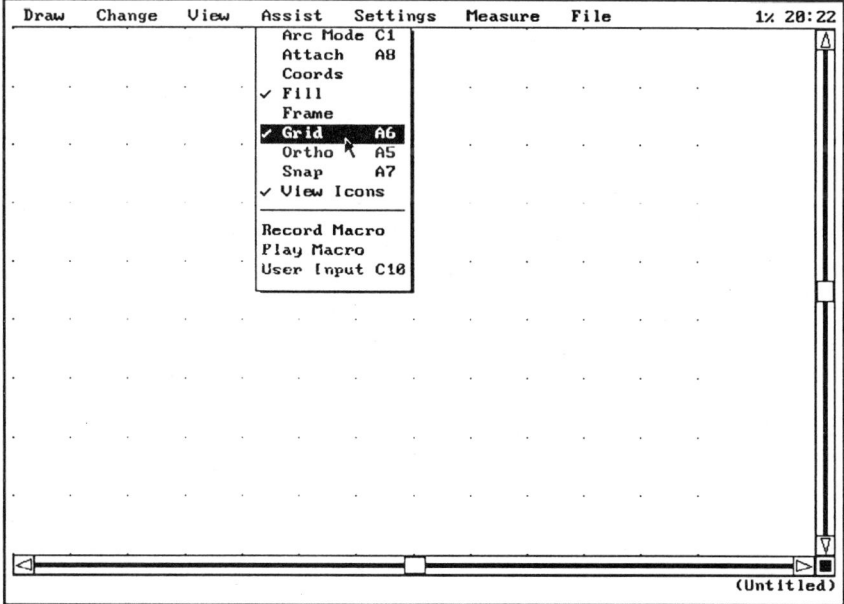

Turning the Grid On

Grid Display

Pull down **Change** Select **Erase**	Erase the rectangles.
Pull down **Assist** Select **Grid**	Grid is toggled on.

Selecting the Grid option on the Assist menu toggles Grid mode on or off. A check mark is shown on the Assist menu when Grid is set on.

Grid dots are never part of your drawing. Think of them as being on an eleventh drawing layer, which you can make visible, but which can never be active. The grid "layer" never contains anything but a grid of dots with a specified spacing. It acts like a reference sheet laid over your actual drawing.

Grid Spacing

Selecting the Grid option on the Settings menu brings up a dialogue box, allowing you to enter a numerical value for both horizontal (X) and vertical (Y) grid spacing.

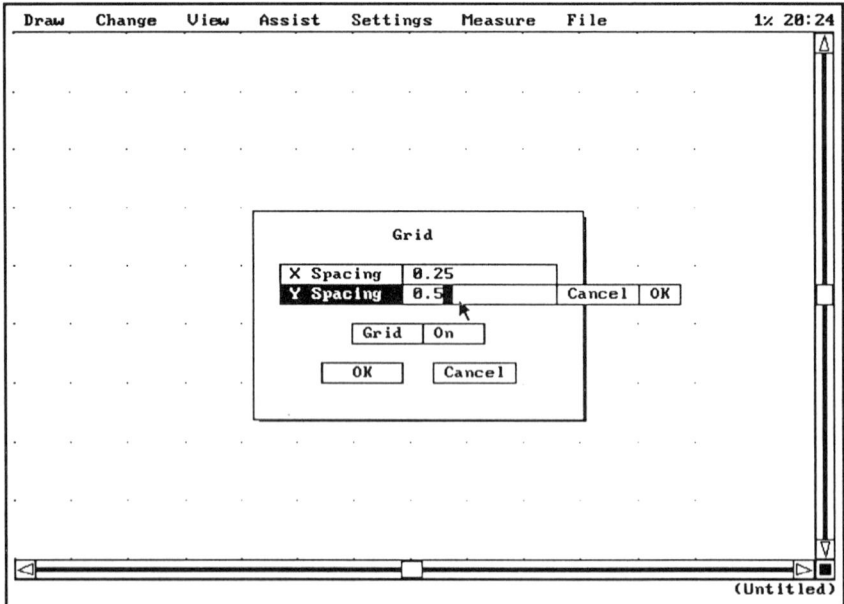

Changing the Grid Settings

Grid Spacing

```
Pull down Settings Select Grid
X spacing .25                    Horizontal spacing.
Y spacing .50                    Vertical spacing.
Click Grid                       Only if Grid is off.
Click OK                         Click the OK box.
                                 Grid changes to new spacing.
```

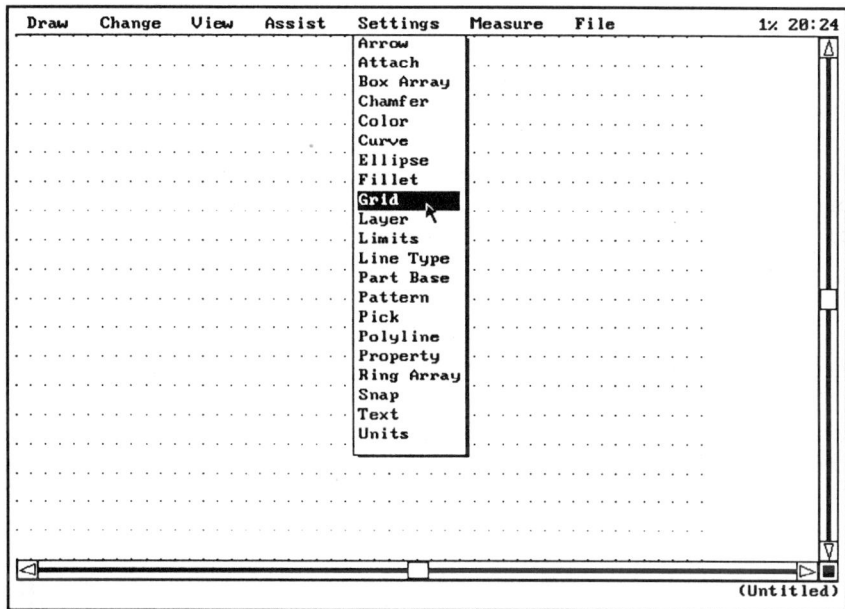

Grid With New Settings

When you set the X spacing, the Y spacing automatically changes to the same value. If you want different X and Y spacing, simply alter the Y value manually. Also, note that you can switch the grid on or off from this dialogue box. If you go back to the Assist menu, you'll see that the check mark appears regardless of which menu you use to turn the grid on. By default, Grid is set to 0, which causes the grid spacing to equal the current snap spacing. Snap mode is discussed later.

If you pick a very fine grid spacing — less than about 0.05 at the default zoom level on a VGA display — AutoSketch may display a dialogue box stating that the grid is too dense to display. In these cases, AutoSketch automatically turns Grid off. You'll have to pick a larger grid spacing and turn the grid back on.

If you are using a lower-resolution display, such as the CGA type, some of the grid spacings in the exercises may be too small to display. Substitute larger values whenever this happens. Try multiplying the given values by two or four until the grid displays.

Many technical drawings include multiple elements that must be evenly spaced. Examples would include the roads on a map, component parts on an electronic schematic, or the studs and joists in a house plan. For any such applications, you can set the grid to an appropriate size and use it as a visual guide. It can also be used as a visual indicator for Snap mode.

Snap Mode

Ortho and Grid are still not enough for precise drawing. Like Ortho, Snap mode limits the motion of your drawing pointer. Snap restricts all new drawing points to equally spaced points. This snap spacing defaults to 1 x 1, but can be reset to match your needs. Snap and Grid are completely independent. Snap controls point input; Grid is only a visual aid. Still, you should make the grid setting an even multiple of — if not actually equal to — the snap spacing.

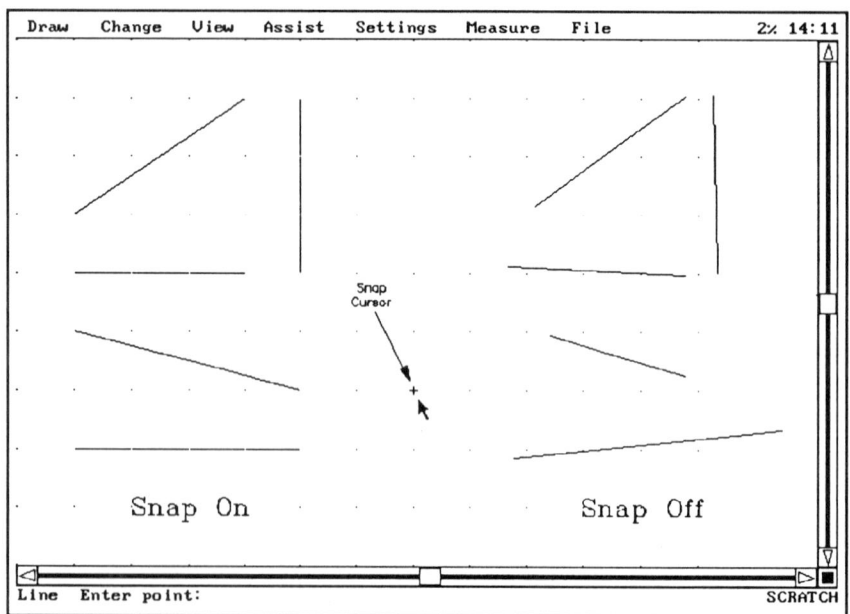

Objects Drawn With Snap On and With Snap Off

Snap Mode

```
Pull down Assist Select Ortho      Turn Ortho off.
Pull down Assist Select Snap       Activates Snap.
Pull down Draw Select Line         Draw a few lines.
Press <ALT-F7>                     Snap turned back off.
Pull down Draw Select Line         Draw a few more lines.
```

Do you see the difference?

```
Press <ALT-F7>                     Turn Snap back on.
```

When you're in Snap mode, the screen pointer can be moved as before, but a little cross-shaped Snap cursor hops around with it, showing the actual drawing point. With Snap on, you can pick points only on these snap points — unless you enter specific coordinates from the keyboard.

As with all of the Assist options, a check mark shows next to the Snap option.

Snap Spacing

Selecting the Snap option on the Settings menu brings up a dialogue box similar to the one provided for the Grid option, allowing you to enter numerical values for horizontal (X) and vertical (Y) snap spacing. You can also turn Snap on or off from this dialogue box.

As with the Grid option, if you go back to the Assist menu, you'll see that the check mark indicator appears regardless of which menu you use to turn Snap on. Also, as with Grid, when you set the Snap X spacing, the Y spacing automatically changes to the same value. If you want different X and Y spacing, you must alter the Y spacing yourself.

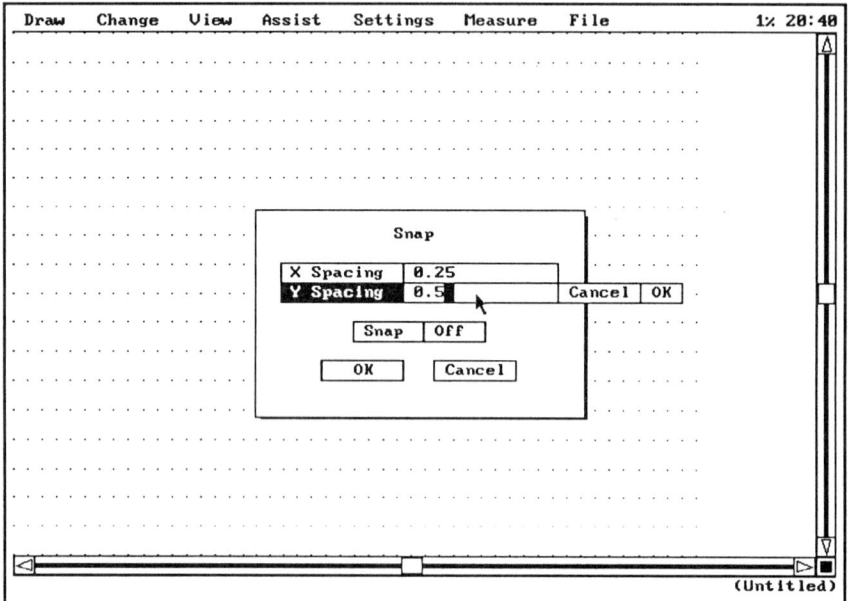

Changing the Snap Settings

Snap Spacing

```
Pull down Settings Select Snap
X spacing: .25                    Horizontal snap.
Y spacing: .50                    Vertical snap.
Click Snap                        Be sure Snap is on.
Click OK                          Draw some lines using the new snap settings.
                                  Snap changes to new values.
```

Snap is one of the most useful functions available in AutoSketch. You can use Snap to set the basic resolution of your drawing. With Snap set to 0.25, you will never create elements closer together than this distance. All other distances will be even multiples of the snap distance.

Snap helps you to achieve precision in your design by preventing you from creating lines other than in appropriate locations. Snap helps you to lay out many types of complex designs. For instance, an engineer creating circuit diagrams could use Snap to produce a clean arrangement of lines without ever having to worry about dimensions. An office space plan could be quickly laid out to the nearest foot using Snap. Even complex mechanical components tend to have as many dimensions as possible designed in even increments.

For accurate drawing, you should have Snap on most of the time. The only exceptions would be when picking points with Attach set, as described in the next section, or when using the Crosses/window box. Otherwise your work is only eyeball-accurate — defeating much of the value of AutoSketch.

Coordinating Snap and Grid

Get used to coordinating your Snap with Grid and Zoom so you always have an appropriate visual reference for the current level of detail being drawn.

For example, you may lay out a site plan with a Snap setting of 5' and a Grid setting of 20'. To add detail, you might zoom in and draw with a one-unit snap and five-unit grid. Adding some portions might require zooming even further and setting a 0.25 snap with a one-unit grid. You are always free to set the combination you need, but remember that picking points without Snap or Attach on is never truly accurate.

There is a particular combination of Snap and Grid that can be very useful if you're trying to create isometric drawings.

Isometric views are often used in technical applications to represent three-dimensional objects. An isometric drawing is much like an artistic or pictorial drawing, but the representation of perspective is simplified. An isometric has no vanishing point — that is, lines do not converge into the distance, the way we normally perceive them. The beauty of an isometric is that it is quite easy to draw. Lines that appear orthogonal in a normal, or plan, drawing will fall on 30-, 90- and 150-degree angles in an isometric.

To generate these angles easily, you need to set your Grid and Snap with an X to Y ratio of the square root of three to one ($\sqrt{3}:1$). For example, you could set the Grid X spacing to 1.732051, the Grid Y spacing to 1, Snap X to 0.1732051 and Snap Y to 0.1 units. This gives a Grid to Snap ratio of 10:1.

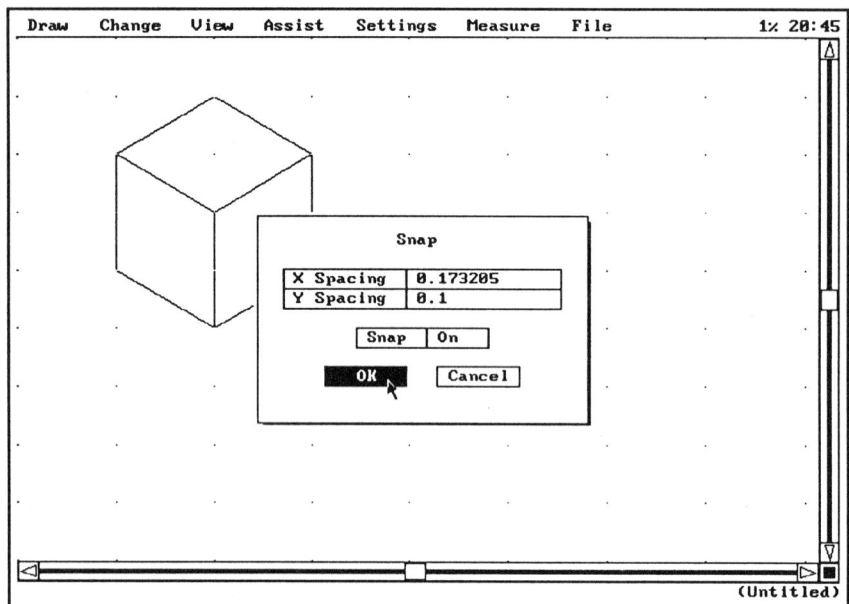

Cube Drawn With Isometric Snap Spacing

> **TIP**: *If you find yourself working in feet and inches a lot, you can similarly set up a very convenient combination of grid and snap. The key here is to use a grid to snap ratio of 1 to 12. In other words, if the Snap X and Y are set to one unit, and this represents one inch on the drawing, then you can set the Grid X and Y to 12 units, providing a visual guide to one-foot increments. If you're drawing an object more than a few inches in size, you'll also want to reset the drawing limits.*

Attach

Snap attracts your drawing pointer to precisely spaced points. Attach provides a variation on this basic theme, creating a sort of magnetic attraction between your drawing pointer and certain features of actual objects displayed on the screen.

As you went through the exercises in Section One, you may have wondered if there was an easy way to get polylines to close, or to get lines to join where they're supposed to. Attach solves these problems. Using Attach, you can place new points accurately with the drawing pointer, relative to existing objects rather than to uniformly spaced snap points.

The Attach option can be activated from either the Assist menu or from the Attach Mode dialogue box displayed by the Attach selection on the

Settings menu. Once Attach has been activated, the usual check mark will appear in the Assist menu next to the word Attach.

Attach will cause point coordinate entry to come from the nearest active attachment point. This may be disconcerting at first, particularly if you forget that Attach mode is enabled.

Setting Attach Modes

AutoSketch lets you select from a number of standard types of attachment points, including the ends of lines, the corners of boxes, or the centers of circles.

You can individually enable or disable attachment modes by selecting the Attach option on the Settings menu. The Attachment Modes dialogue box appears. Select the modes desired, bearing in mind that if you have too many active at once you may have trouble getting things to attach the way you want. Picking near an intersection of two lines, for instance, with both Intersect and End Point modes active may cause problems. For convenience, Attach can be set on or off from the Attach mode dialogue. When settings are complete, click on the OK box.

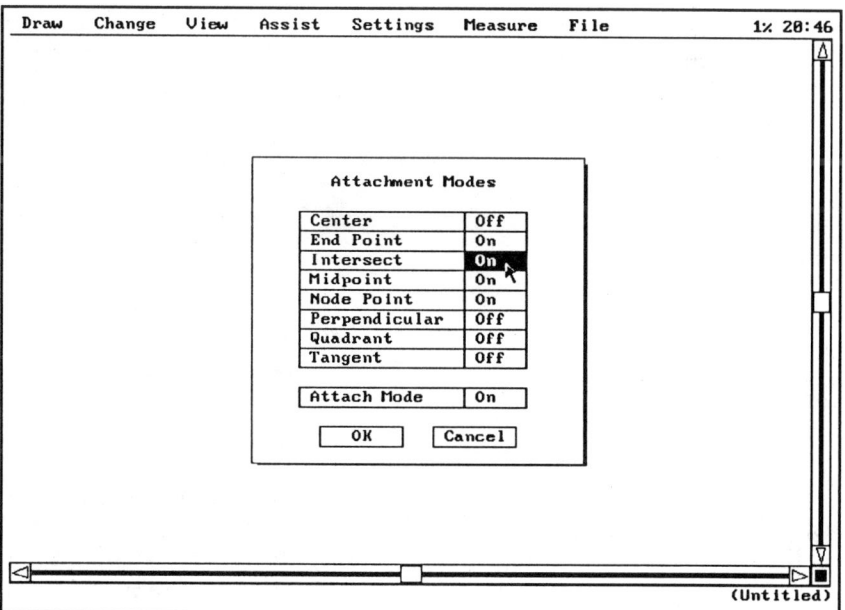

Setting Attach Modes

Setting Attach Modes

Pull down **Settings** Select **Attach**

Turn all modes off except for End Point.

Click **Attach Mode**	Be sure Attach is on.
Click **OK**	Select the OK box.
Pull down **Draw** Select **Line**	Try drawing some lines, end-to-end.

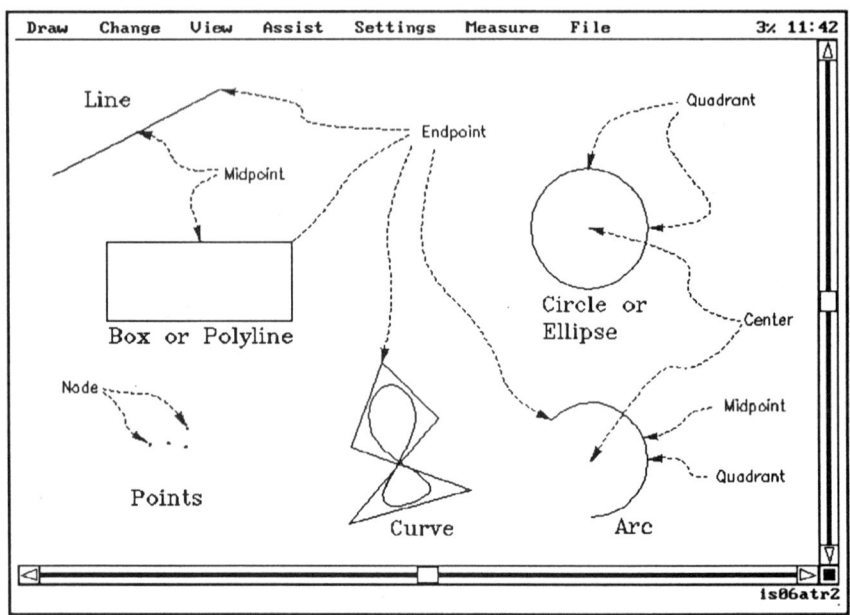

Entities and Their Attach Modes

Types of Attach Modes

Center mode is fairly straightforward, allowing you to attach to the center points of circles or arcs. This is the easiest way of finding the center of an existing circle! However, when you wish to attach to the center of a circle, remember that AutoSketch expects you to point at the visible circumference of the circle, rather than at or near the center itself. That is, if you set Center mode on and all the other modes off, then pick on a circle, your point will set itself in the center of that circle, no matter what part of the circle you selected. It is almost impossible to attach to the center of a circle if both Center and Quadrant modes are set on. Your points will inevitably attach themselves to the quadrants rather than the center. Therefore, when attaching to the center of a circle, be sure to set Quadrant off.

End Point lets you snap to the ends of existing lines, arcs, or polylines, or to the corners of a box.

Intersect is perhaps the single most powerful Attach mode. It allows you to attach objects to locations that are defined by the meeting of several AutoSketch objects. Also, by using the intersection of temporary construction lines or curves, you can locate a point that would otherwise be difficult to find. Once the point is attached to the intersection point, the construction lines can be removed with Erase.

The Midpoint Attach mode lets you place new points exactly in the middle of existing lines, curves, arcs, or the sides of boxes.

Node Point simply attaches to the nearest point. Though somewhat oddly named, this is one of the most useful settings, especially when used alone. You can carefully set points using the other Attach modes, then use just the Node Point mode in complete confidence that things will attach only at the points you've marked. Node Point will also snap to the ends of text baselines.

Perpendicular is a trickier mode to use, but it can be useful in certain circumstances. It guarantees that a line you draw will be perpendicular to the last object line selected. There are two ways to use this mode. To draw *toward* your perpendicular line, pick the first point, then pick a point on the object you wish to be perpendicular to. To draw *away* from your perpendicular line, pick a point on the line you wish to be perpendicular to, then select the second point elsewhere. The latter mode may be somewhat easier to use, as it constrains your rubberband line to be perpendicular to the selected object. You can thus see what you're doing.

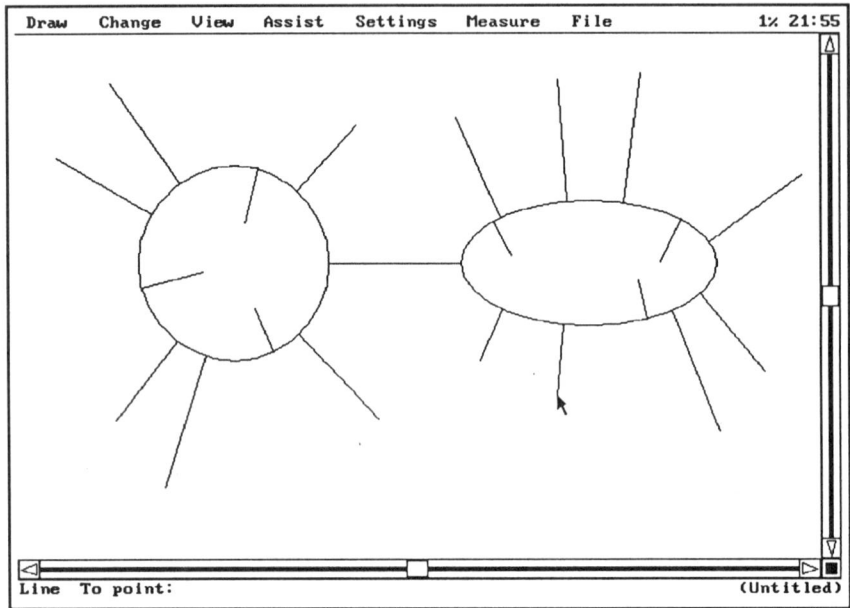

Perpendicular Attach Mode

Whichever way you work, toward or away, try to pick your points as close as possible to their precise location. That way, AutoSketch is more likely to pick the point you wanted.

Quadrant attaches to points set every 90 degrees around the circumference of a circle or arc — at the top, bottom, left, and right.

Tangent is probably the most specialized of the attach modes. It works only when connecting to circles, arcs, and ellipses. Like Perpendicular, Tangent mode can be used when drawing toward or away from the target curve. When drawing *toward* the curve, your lines will snap to the nearest point that will make them exactly tangent to the curve. When drawing *away* from the curve, you'll see a rubberband line attach to the curve. You can run this line around the entire circumference of the curve, and drop it into place as usual, by selecting the second point. The second point can even be on a second curve, in which case the "toward" behavior will apply in relation to that curve.

➥ *TIP: AutoCAD has the additional modes of Nearest, Insert, and Quick in its OSNAP mode, which is equivalent to AutoSketch's Attach. The Nearest mode simply finds the closest point on an object that is also nearest to the pointer. Insert mode attaches points to the insertion point of an AutoCAD block. Quick mode causes AutoCAD to stop searching for points after it finds the first one to satisfy a current mode.*

When drawing *away* from a curve, you'll find your tangent lines will stay pointed one way, clockwise or counterclockwise. To reverse them, move your pointer *inside* the curve or circle and back out on the other side of the tangent point.

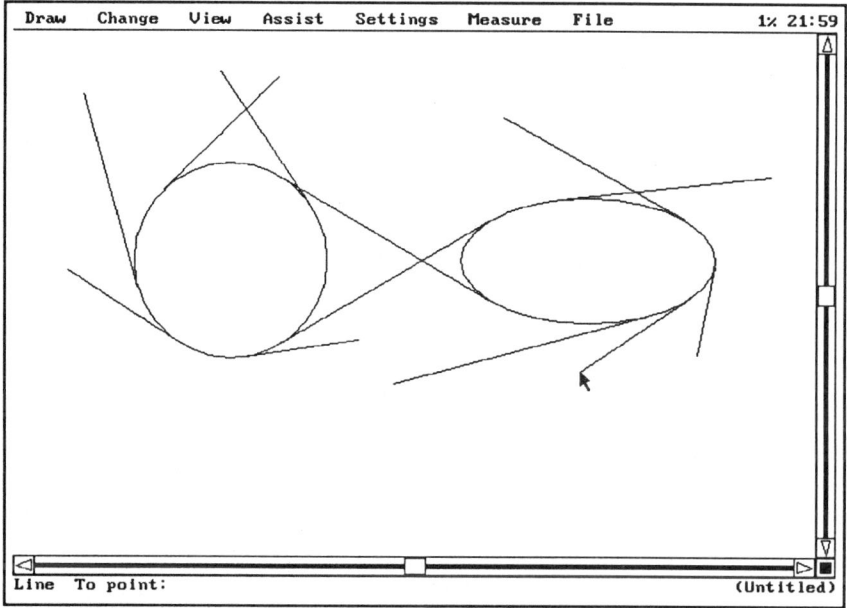

Tangent Attach Mode

In general, setting all but one of the modes off is a very effective way to ensure that attachment occurs exactly where you want it to. Always enable only the minimum number of Attach modes.

You may not want to have both Snap and Attach active at the same time when working on a crowded drawing. You may find AutoSketch picking very unexpected points!

You can avoid possible conflict by switching Snap and Attach on and off as required for each point. You can do this even in the middle of a complex drawing operation — for example, between points on a polyline, or after picking the center of a circle but before picking the point on the circumference. The keyboard shortcut toggles, <ALT-F7> for Snap and <ALT-F8> for Attach, are particularly convenient in this sort of situation. However, menu choices will also work.

Pick Spacing

Successfully picking objects for Attach and other commands depends on clicking your pointer close to the exact point AutoSketch needs. You can adjust the interval your pointer must be from an object with the Pick option on the Settings menu.

When you select Pick, the Pick Interval dialogue box appears. At this point, enter the desired pick distance expressed as a percentage of screen height, then click on the OK box.

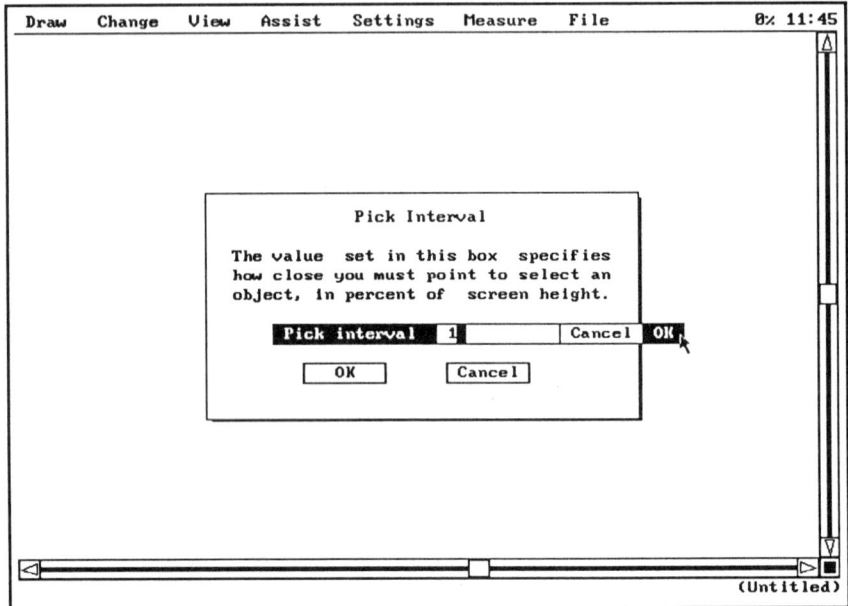

Setting the Pick Interval

Setting the Pick Spacing

```
Pull down Settings Select Pick
Pick interval: 1                    Leave it set to 1.
Click OK                            Click the OK box.
Pull down File Select Save
```

Think of Pick as the size of the net with which you catch points on the AutoSketch screen. Pick affects not only the Attach modes, but all object selection operations. For instance, when Move asks you to "Select object," Pick determines how close the pointer must be to an object when you click to select it.

Pick resolution is expressed in units of one percent of your screen height. This ensures that object selection will be successful within the same relative area around the cursor regardless of zoom level or the physical dimensions of your display. On a wider monitor screen, the same percentage setting will define a wider pick area. For example, if you have a 14-inch monitor, a one percent pick interval gives you a pick area just a bit larger than 1/8" square. On a 20-inch monitor, the pick area will be closer to 3/16" square. Since the area is always in proportion to the total size of the display, you shouldn't have to adjust Pick if you alternate between two different size monitors.

➡ *TIP: In AutoCAD, object selection area is adjusted with the APERTURE command and system variable for OSNAP mode, and the PICKBOX system variable for general object selection.*

Be careful not to set Pick too high, or attachment will be highly unpredictable. About five percent should be the largest pick interval you'll ever need.

For more on point selection, see Snap, Grid, and Ortho earlier in this chapter.

Command Practice

NEW. Select File, then New, to start with a clean screen.

CURVE/FRAME. Draw a curve and then try to move it. Next, set Frame on and try again. With Frame still on, try using Stretch to change the shape of your curve. Notice that you can stretch the frame, but you have to complete the stretch before you see the effect on your actual curve.

ORTHO. Set Ortho on. Select the Polyline command. See what kind of shapes you can create and what kind you cannot.

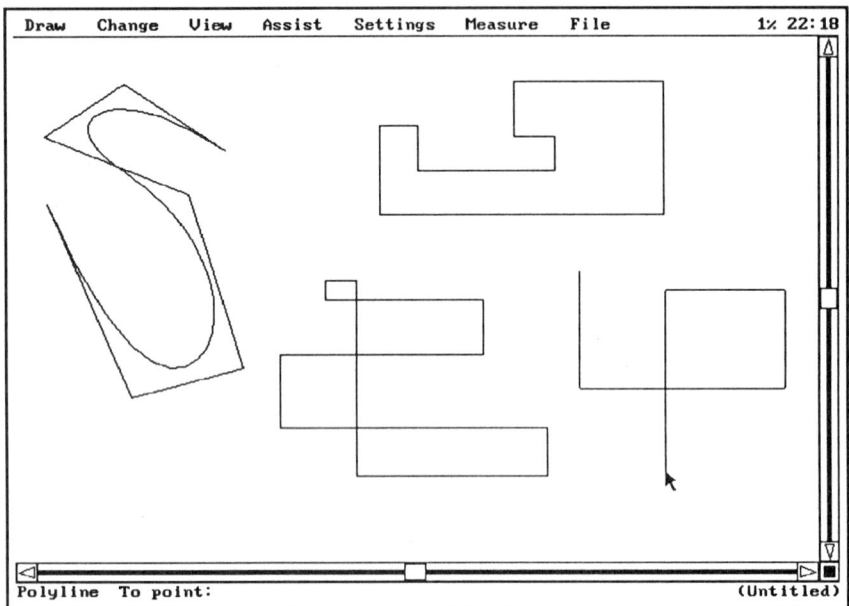

Drawing With Ortho On

SNAP/GRID. Set Grid on, with X and Y spacing both set to one unit. Set Snap on, with a spacing of 1.5 for both X and Y. Now try drawing a box so that all four corners lie on grid points. Try again, but with a Snap spacing of 1.35. Notice that snap points and grid points do not need to correspond at all.

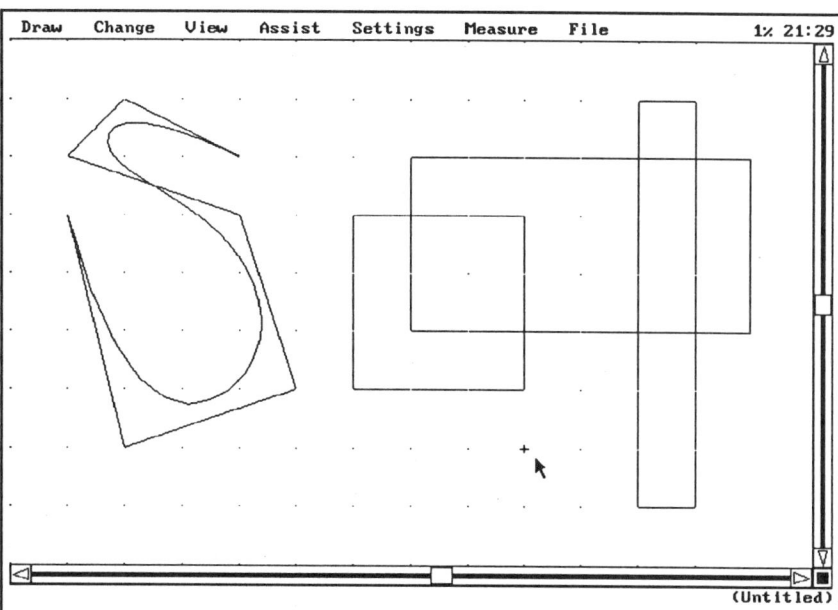

Drawing With Snap, Grid, and Ortho On

ATTACH/MOVE. A good way to get the feel of subtle commands such as Attach is to take them to the limit. Try creating two boxes, one at either side of the screen, then setting the pick interval to 50 percent or 100 percent (absurd values, which you'd never use in practice). Using Move and Attach in End Point mode, attach one box to the other at various locations. Note that the objects you try to move will have acquired a life of their own. Try successively smaller pick interval settings. You should find that the pick value doesn't have to be very large to be useful.

SETTINGS/ATTACH. Using the Settings menu, enable Attach mode, and set all of the Attach options off except for "Midpoint," and turn Attach on. Set Pick to five. Draw a box in the middle of the screen. Now try to split the box into quarters with lines so that it looks like a pane window. How might you divide a box into quarters using diagonal lines?

Space Plan

It's time to start setting up the FLOOR file for some real drawing. Open the FLOOR drawing, turn Snap, Grid, and Ortho mode on, and Attach off. Then, using Polyline with relative coordinates, draw the outer wall 50 feet wide by 21 feet high. Next, use the Move command to center it in the screen. After things are nicely centered, draw the inside of the wall 6 inches within the outer wall all the way around. Although this effectively draws two boxes, you should use the Polyline command instead of the Box command so you can later clean up the intersections of these units with intersecting interior walls.

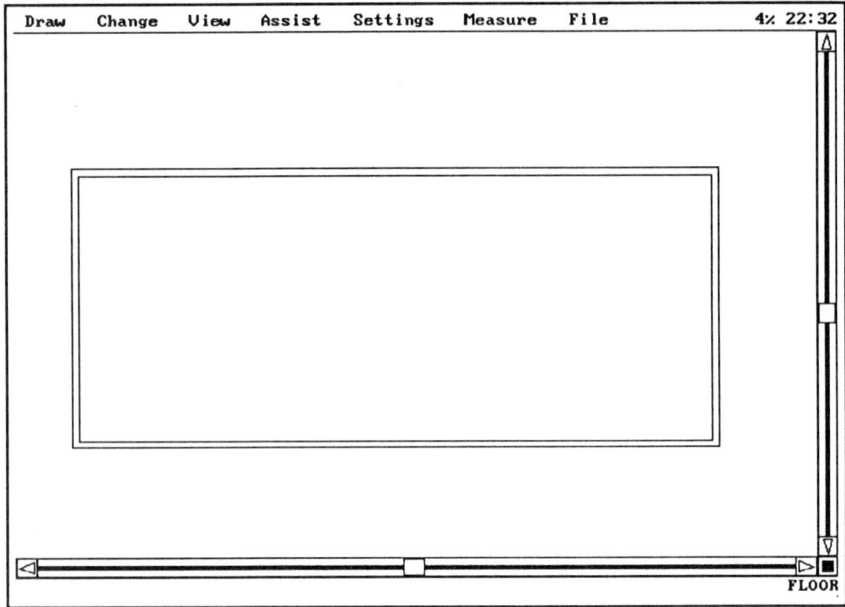

The Outline of the Space Plan

Space Plan Drawing Exercise

```
Pull down File Select Open
Filename: FLOOR                         Open the FLOOR file.
Pull down Settings Select Units
Click Architectural On
Click OK                                Click OK box.
X spacing 6
Y spacing 6
Click Snap On                           Turn Snap mode on.
Click OK

Pull down Settings Select Grid
X spacing 12                            Horizontal spacing.
Y spacing 12                            Vertical spacing.
Click Grid On                           Turn grid display on.
Click OK                                Click the OK box.
Pull down Assist Select Ortho           Turn Ortho on.

Pull down Draw Select Polyline
Enter point:                            Start in the lower left corner.
To point: R(50',0)                      Relative coordinates.
```

To point: **R(0,21')**	
To point: **R(-50',0)**	
To point: **R(0,-21')**	Finish the box.
Pull down **Change** Select **Move**	Center the box.
Pull down **Draw** Select **Polyline**	Draw the second box 6 inches inside the first box.

After drawing in the outer wall, continue to enter the inside walls as shown. Don't worry about precise dimensions — Snap will keep your plan accurate, although your own design can deviate from ours if you like.

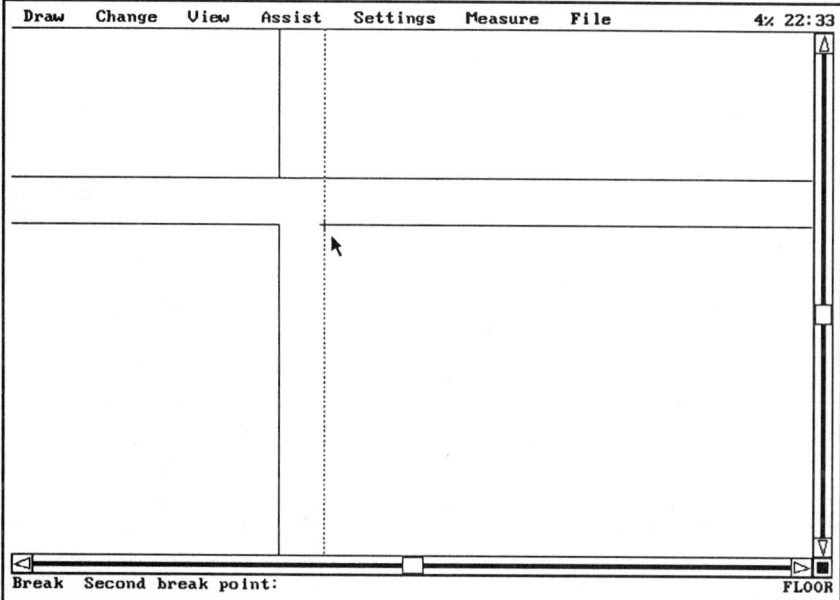

Breaking Away Excess Lines

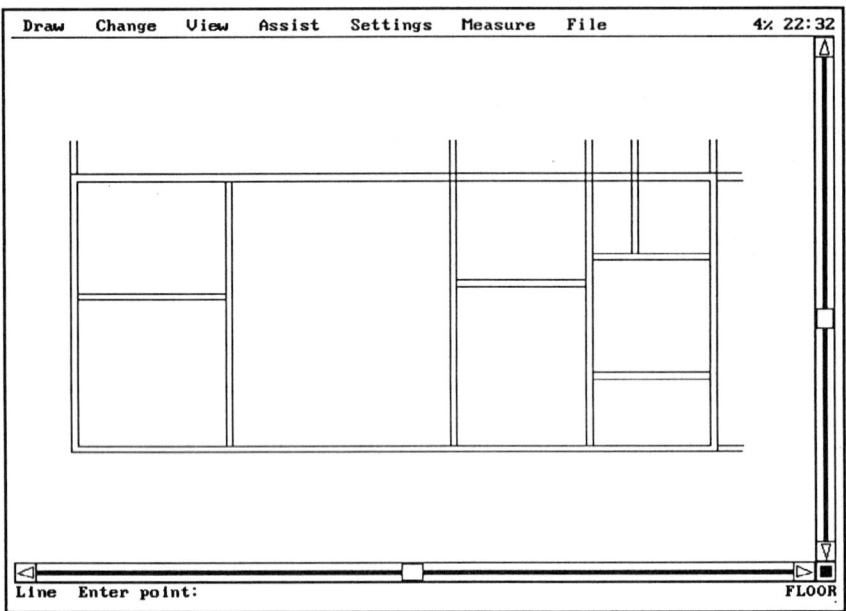

Draw the Walls

When you're done, save the file. In the next section, you'll be able to do some *really* interesting things with it.

```
Pull down Draw Select Line
First point:                          Draw the inner walls.

Pull down File Select Save            Save the file.
```

Summary

The tools covered in this chapter allow you to draw with absolute precision, without expending much more effort than you would for a freehand sketch. If you are drawing objects with a lot of right angles, you can use Ortho mode for both speed and accuracy. Objects that have a lot of equally spaced elements — for example floor plans, electronic schematics, street maps, and many others — become a "snap" to draw when you turn Snap and Grid on, with the appropriate spacing.

Accurate mating of objects or individual lines within a drawing can be assisted by Snap as well, provided that the desired attach points all lie on the snap grid. If the points do not fall on snap locations, then Attach can solve the problem. Attach also provides a few powerful capabilities of its own — such as the ability to find the midpoint of a line or the center of a circle.

In the next chapter, we'll look at some editing tools that let you modify, manipulate, and organize drawing objects in ways that can save many hours of drawing time.

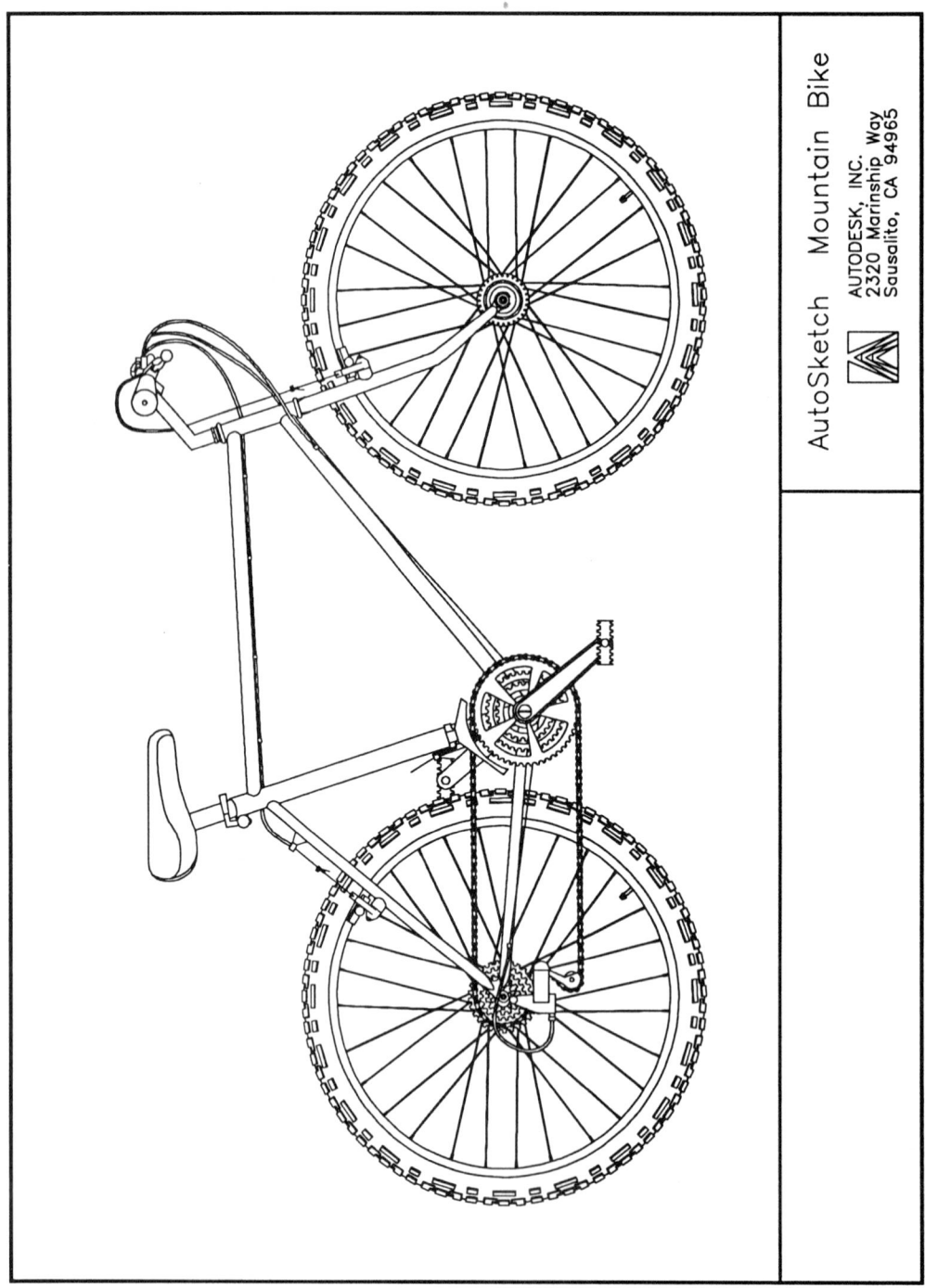

Mountain Bike, Courtesy of Autodesk, Inc.

Chapter 7

Advanced Editing Tools

Up until now, you have created and modified objects one at a time. In this chapter you'll see how to trim or break apart single objects, to combine multiple objects into groups that can be handled as conveniently as a single object, and to store entire collections of objects for re-use. The commands we'll be dealing with in this chapter are located on the Change and Settings menus.

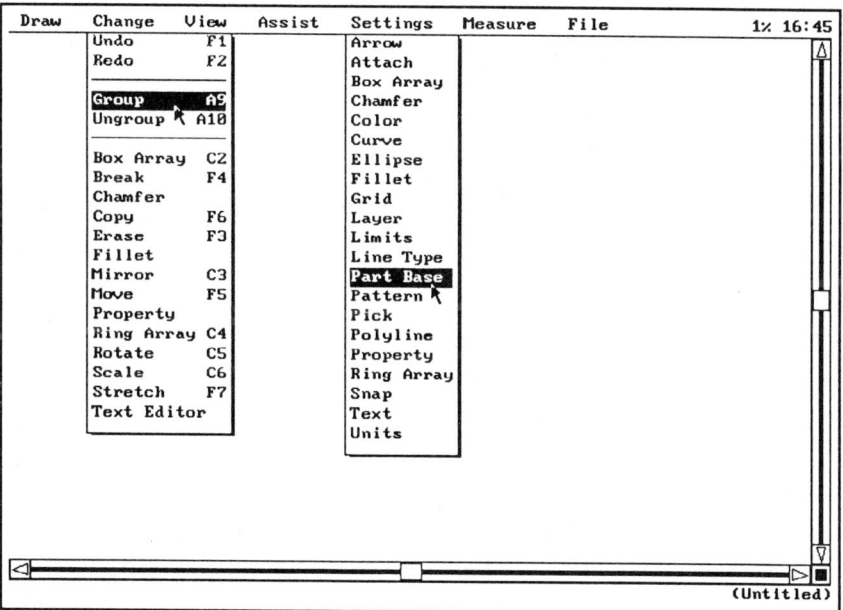

The Change and Settings Menus

By allowing you to transfer objects easily between drawings, these powerful AutoSketch commands free your drawings from the limits of any single workspace. They also free you from the need to recreate anything you've already drawn. Objects you use frequently can be filed away and recalled whenever they are required. As you work with AutoSketch, you can build up an extensive library of common parts of varying degrees of complexity. Big drawing jobs become as easy as snapping these "prefab" parts together.

Break

The Break command lets you literally break apart the fundamental AutoSketch drawing objects or cut away pieces of them.

There are two situations in which you use the Break command. First, you can use it to clean up unwanted sections of existing objects, such as line intersections and hidden lines. For instance, suppose you want to show a line passing behind an object on the screen. It's much easier to draw a line right through the object, then break away the middle, than it is to draw two separate lines stopping at the edges of the object (especially if you turn on Attach in Intersect mode).

Another situation would be to provide an alternate method for constructing objects. For instance, you could create an arc by first drawing a circle, then using Break to cut away the unwanted portion. Sometimes this is the easier method, simply because a circle is specified differently than an arc; you may know the points required to specify a circle, but not the points required for an arc.

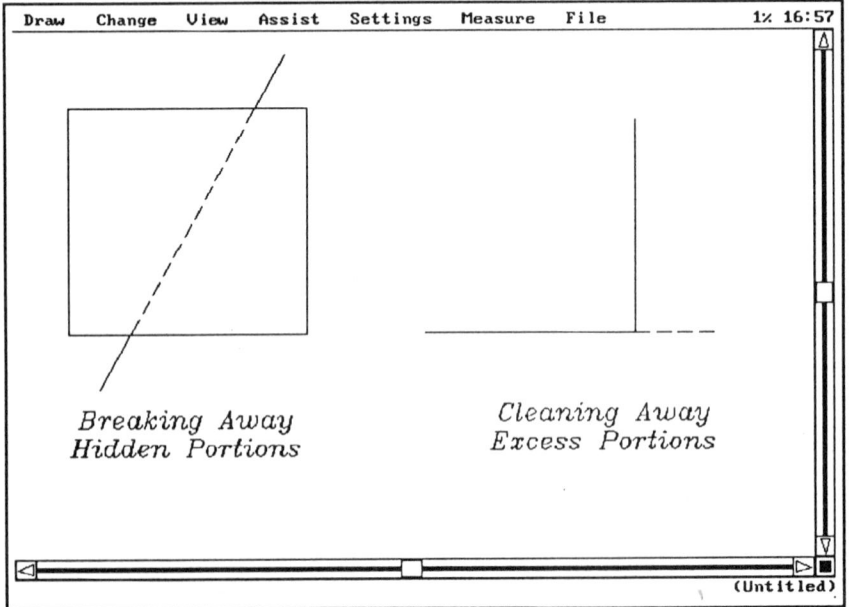

Two Uses of the Break Command

Activate the Break command by selecting Break from the Change menu, or by pressing <F4>. You'll be prompted to select an object. Once selected, the object is highlighted. You are then prompted to pick the break points. After the points are chosen, the portion of the selected object between the two break points is deleted, and the Break command repeats. Any remaining portions of the original object are now individual objects.

Breaking an Object

```
Pull down File Select Open                   Open the SCRATCH file.
File SCRATCH
Pull down Change Select Erase                Erase the screen.
```

Check to make sure Attach is turned off and Ortho is on.

```
Pull down Draw Select Line                   Draw a square, overlapping all corners.
Pull down Change Select Break                Activates Break.
Select object:                               Choose a line.
First break point:                           Pick a line endpoint.
Second break point:                          Pick at nearest intersection.
Pull down Settings Select Attach             Turn off all Attach modes, except Intersect.
Click Attach Mode                            Turn Attach Mode on.
Click OK                                     Close the dialogue box.
Select object:                               Clean up another corner.
```

Attach should help you get a perfectly clean corner.

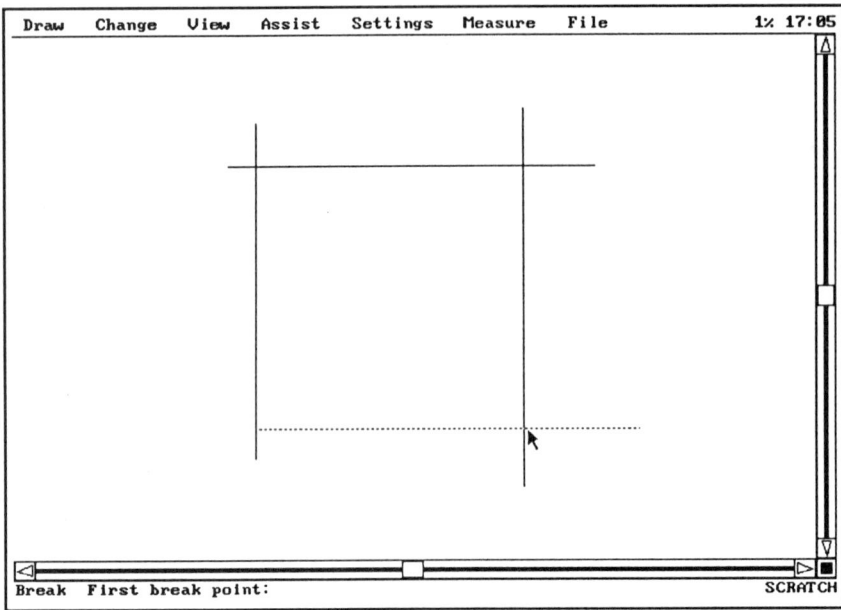

Using Break to Clean Up the Corners

In practice, you can quickly draw complex objects without regard to clean line intersections, and then go back in a magnified view and trim off the protruding ends using Break. You can also use the Stretch command to pull line ends back so that they meet up properly, but the Break command is usually more convenient.

➥ *TIP: To break off line ends quickly and accurately, pick the line to break and the first break point where you want the line to end. When prompted for the second break point, pick a point anywhere, past the end you wish to break off. AutoSketch will calculate the exact endpoint of the line as the second point. This avoids having to accurately pick the endpoint or use the Attach End Point mode.*

Note that when you break a closed curve, circle, or polygon, AutoSketch removes a section proceeding *counterclockwise* from the first break point to the second. Therefore, always pick your break points in that direction.

You may find that curves are difficult to break properly. You have to turn Frame display on from the Assist menu, and even then the results can be unpredictable. The trouble is that you don't actually break the curve itself, but the frame. The two open ends of the frame on either side of the break become new control points for the curve, changing its shape. You can create two new curves to simulate the broken larger curve by tracing over the larger curve and then erasing it.

Group

The Group command allows you to create your own complex objects. Just as a box is one object and not four separate lines, grouped objects are always recognized as a single entity. If you were working on a machine design, for example, you might create a drawing of an angle bracket bolt and a nut. You could group these and then easily copy them into place wherever you need them.

To group objects together, select the Group command, then select the objects to be grouped — either by clicking on them one at a time, or by using a Crosses/window box. Objects highlight as they are selected to indicate that they are included in the group.

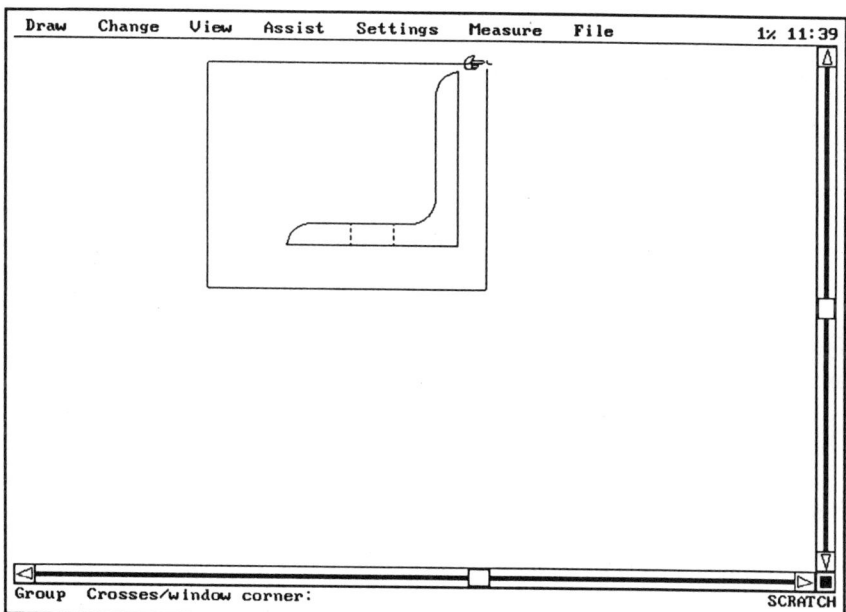

Selecting Lines to be Grouped

Grouping a Set of Objects

Pull down **Change** Select **Erase**	Erase the screen.
Pull down **Settings** Select **Snap**	Set Snap to .125 and turn it on.
Pull down **Draw** Select **Polyline**	Draw the angle bracket's visible lines.
Pull down **Settings** Select **Line Type**	Set Line Type to hidden.

```
Pull down Draw Select Line           Draw the hidden lines for the bolt hole.
Pull down Change Select Group        Activates Group.
Select object:                       Use Crosses/window.
Crosses/window corner:               Enclose all the lines.
Pull down Change Select Move
Select object:                       Pick one of the lines. The whole bracket is selected.
From point:                          Move the angle bracket so the lower right corner is
                                     at point 8,3.
```

The Group command behaves a little bit differently from other AutoSketch commands in that it doesn't actually complete what it's doing until you select another command. While Group is active, objects are continually added to the current group. You must actually select another command, or even select the Group command again, in order to complete a group. You can be sure you've closed a group off when the highlighted objects display normally.

Groups can include up to 1000 separate objects. Attempting to group more than 1000 objects will pop up a dialogue box stating that you have "Too many items in group." However, a group counts as a single object when included in a larger group. Therefore, should this ever come up, you can get around the 1000-object limitation by first building up a series of subgroups. You may run out of memory, though.

You can "nest" groups up to eight levels deep — that is, create a group within a group within a group... You get the idea.

The Group command can be used as a convenient shortcut for editing multiple objects on the fly. Sets of objects that have been grouped behave like a single object. You can select a group by pointing at any element within it. The entire group can be moved or copied as a unit. You can change the entire group's properties, such as color or line type, with a single command. You can even group several existing groups into a bigger group.

Grouping objects can also be an excellent way to prepare drawings for storage and re-use (as you'll see when dealing with the Part command).

There are several limitations on what you can do to a group of objects. You cannot break an object within a group. If you use the Measure menu's Show Properties command on any portion of a group, the properties dialogue box will indicate only that the object type is a group.

➡ *NOTE: Prior to version 3 of AutoSketch, none of the Attach modes would work when selecting members of a group. Also, Stretch would not work on grouped objects. These limitations no longer apply in the latest release of the program.*

Ungroup

Fortunately, if you need to edit objects within a group, you can always ungroup them. The Ungroup command restores all members of a group to their original form.

If you need to ungroup a nested group, remember that you'll need to ungroup once for each level. Each use of Ungroup will remove only the uppermost level of grouping. Subgroups will still have to be subsequently selected and ungrouped individually.

➥ *TIP: The AutoCAD BLOCK command is used to group objects into what AutoCAD calls blocks. AutoCAD blocks may also contain non-graphical information such as sizes, text, and prices. An insertion point is required, however, similar to that discussed in Part Base below. To ungroup AutoCAD blocks, the EXPLODE command is used. Once a block is created, it becomes like an AutoSketch group or part. However, AutoCAD blocks may be inserted many times in the current drawing without having to repeatedly load them from disk as with an AutoSketch Part, discussed below.*

Parts

Combine the concept of the group with the AutoSketch file system to get an idea of what the part commands are all about. Using Parts, you can combine drawings by inserting an existing drawing into the one you're working on.

There are actually three separate commands that control the use of parts in AutoSketch: Part on the Draw menu inserts an existing part file; Part Clip on the File menu conveniently creates a part file; and Part Base on the Settings menu allows you to specify the reference point by which the part will be located.

Actually, you've already created numerous parts, since any AutoSketch drawing file can be treated as a part. However, proper use of parts requires some planning. Drawings you plan to insert as parts should be prepared by setting their Part Base, by grouping their component objects, and by organizing the objects with the layers as you want them to appear in later drawings. You'll also want to ensure that the scale of the part matches that of the drawings into which it is to be inserted.

There are no practical limitations on how complex a part can be. You might create and combine standardized drawings and title blocks organized by layers and stored as separate parts.

Bolts, nuts, threads, and other details are needed many times in many different mechanical designs. Electronic schematic drawings are made up of many standard symbols representing components such as transistors, resistors, and integrated chips. All these elements could be made up once and then stored away as parts for speedy insertion into each new drawing. Complete libraries of parts can be built up in this way.

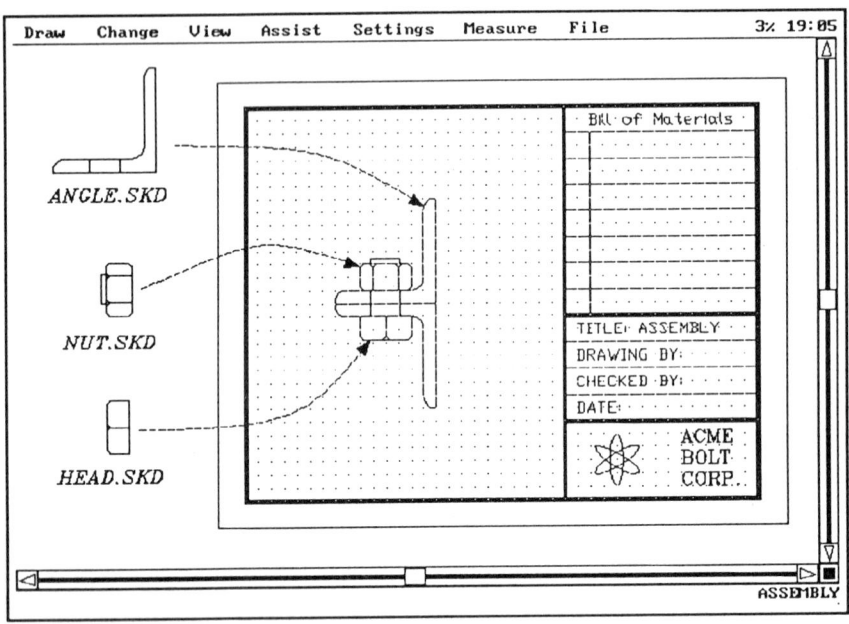

Example of Combining Parts to Create a Drawing

You should group the elements of a drawing that are to be used later as a part. This is not mandatory. However, you'll probably want to treat these objects as a unit once they are inserted in the new drawing. You can always ungroup them if need be.

There are some pre-made part libraries available commercially that are compatible with AutoSketch. In fact, Autodesk offers 24 different symbol libraries for architectural, engineering, electronics, and business administration applications. Each library contains an average of 150 symbols drawn to industry standards and scale. These cost a bit of extra money, but can be a great time-saver. Contact Autodesk at (800) 223-2521 (from the U.S. or Canada) for more information.

➥ *TIP: AutoCAD's answer to creating part files is the WBLOCK command. It can create a part file from selected entities, or export a previously created block. AutoCAD symbol libraries, like its drawing files, are not compatible with AutoSketch.*

Part Clip

The Part Clip command on the File menu provides a more focused means of creating part files. It allows you to save specified portions of your current drawing to a new file.

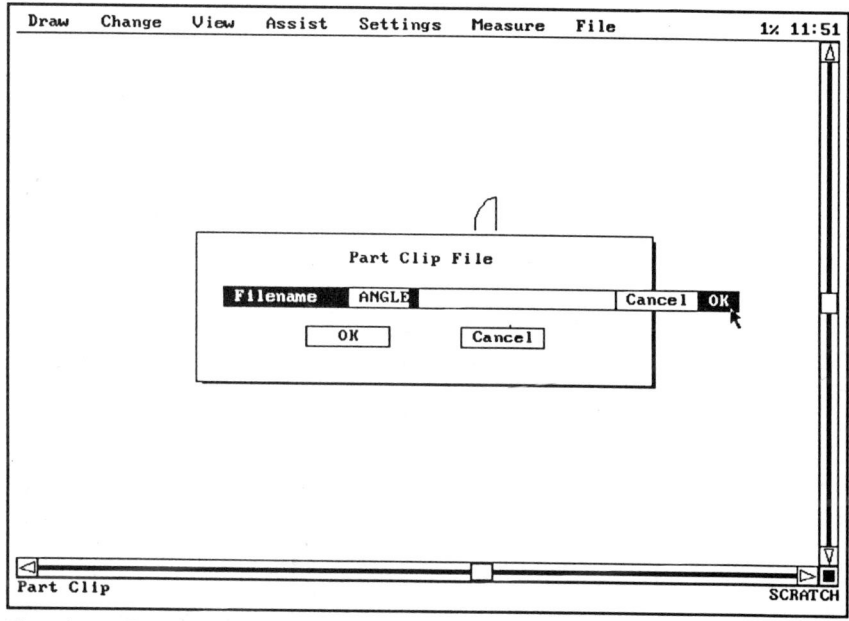

Creating a Part File

Creating a Part File

```
Pull down File Select Part Clip
Filename ANGLE                      Type ANGLE as the name of the part file.
Click OK                            Close the dialogue box.
Insertion base:                     Select the lower right corner of the bracket.
Select object:                      Select the angle bracket.
```

The entire angle bracket is highlighted.
Select any command to complete the part.

Your disk drive should access momentarily as the part is saved.

Part Clip functions like the Group command. It allows you to select more and more objects and terminates only when you select another menu command.

Part Base

Whenever an object is inserted into a drawing, it attaches itself temporarily to your cursor by its base point. You are then free to drag the part into position before you place it. The Part Base command controls where this point is and how you specify it. It is used primarily to set the base point for the current drawing, which will be inserted into another drawing later.

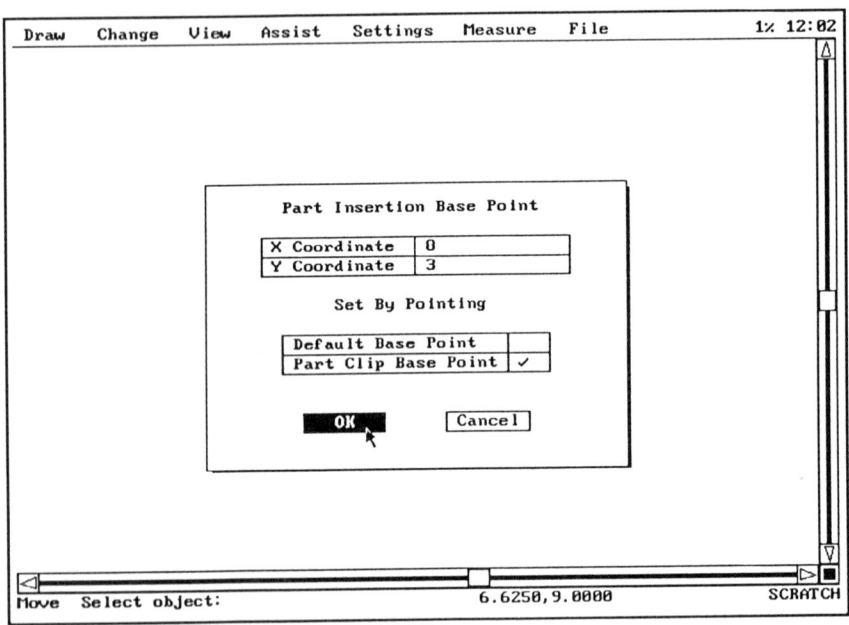

The Part Base Dialogue Box

Setting Part Base

```
Pull down Settings Select Part Base    The Part Insertion Base Point dialogue box appears.
X Coordinate 8                          Type in 8 as the X Coordinate.
Y Coordinate 3                          Type in 3 as the Y Coordinate.
Click OK                                Close the dialogue box.
```

If you don't provide a different base point, the base point will default to the drawing's (0,0) origin point, perhaps leaving the object itself floating quite a distance away from the pointer when you try to insert it. There's no harm in this, and when making parts such as standardized title blocks, the origin makes a useful base point, since these parts will always align the same way in relation to the drawing page. With (0,0) as a base point, you can use parts as though they were extra drawing layers, since they will all align perfectly on top of one another the way true layers do. With smaller parts, however, you will more often want to set a reference on the object itself.

Part Base lets you set the base point either by entering coordinates or by pointing. When you select the Part Base command, you are presented with the Part Insertion Base Point dialogue box. Here, you can enter coordinates to change the current drawing's base point. If checked, the Default Base Point option lets you point to the coordinates at the new base point. The Part Clip Base Point option controls whether you will be prompted to show AutoSketch the base point for any part files you make from the current drawing with the Part Clip command or whether they will have the origin as their base point also. The Part Clip Base Point option is checked by default since you probably won't want all your parts based at the current drawing's origin.

➥ *TIP: If you create a part and insert it later into a drawing only to find out that it would work better with a different base point, you can recreate the part with a copy in your current drawing by pointing out the new base point. AutoSketch will warn you that the file already exists. If you elect to replace it, the new base point will be in effect the next time you insert the part. If you need to change many parts, however, it may be easier to load each one as a drawing and use Part Base to change the default.*

The easiest way to ensure an accurate base point is to use Attach or Snap. Alternatively, if the coordinates of the attachment point are known, they can be entered manually.

➥ *TIP: The AutoCAD BASE command would be used to set the default insertion point in an AutoCAD drawing.*

Inserting a Part

When you choose the Part command on the Draw menu, the Select Part File dialogue box appears. It is almost identical to the Select Drawing File dialogue box for the File Open command. As usual, files can be selected by name, by icon, or by selecting the File box and typing in the file name. When you've chosen a part file and clicked OK, the part will appear, highlighted and attached to the drawing pointer. Drag the part to its final destination, and click the pointer to fix it in place.

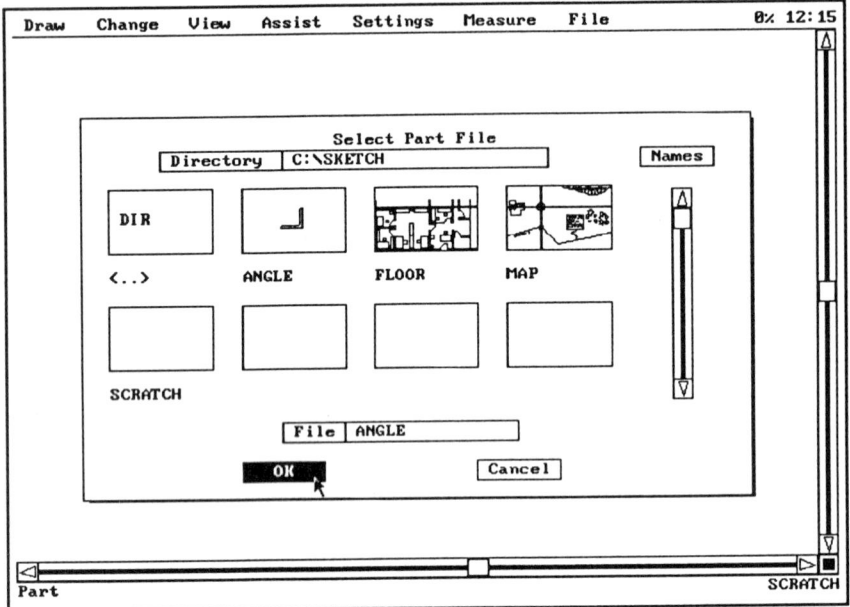

Selecting a Part File for Insertion

Inserting a Part

Pull down **Change** Select **Erase**	Erase everything.
Pull down **Draw** Select **Part**	Insert the part.
File: **ANGLE**	Select the ANGLE file.
Click **OK**	Click OK box. The part appears, highlighted.
To point:	Pick a point. The part is inserted into the drawing.

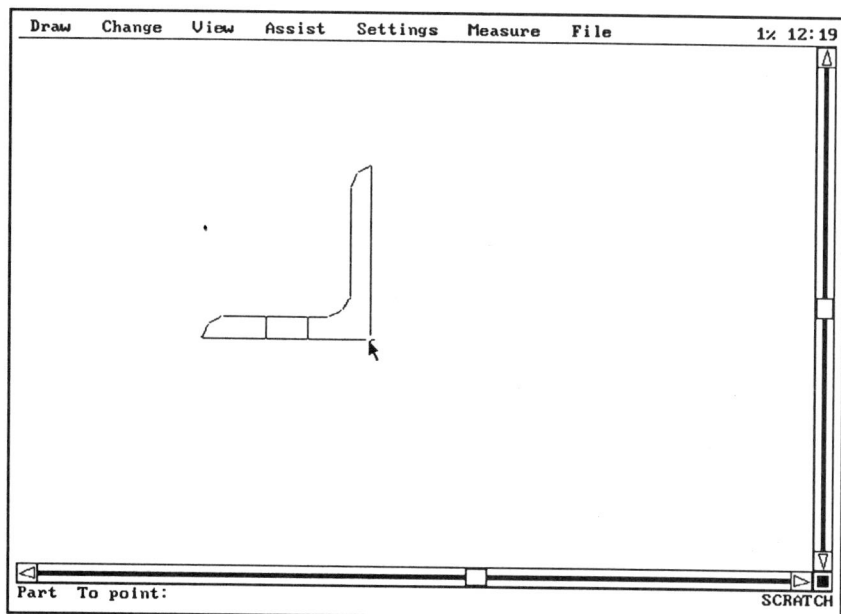

Inserting a Part Into a Drawing

The Part command inserts the part file exactly as it was drawn, with all of its properties intact except for Grid and Snap settings.. This includes the layer properties it was drawn with. No matter what your current drawing layer, the part will end up on the same layer it was on when you last saved it. You'll need to use the Property command on the Change menu if you wish to locate the part on any other layer. A better alternative might be to define certain layering conventions for all your drawings. For instance, you might put all text on layer 4, and all physical objects on layer 1. If you adhere to these conventions at all times, you can be certain that your parts will coordinate consistently.

➥ *TIP: For AutoCAD owners, the INSERT command is used to make a duplicate of a saved part called a block. If an AutoCAD block has been used in the drawing at least once already, it need not be loaded from disk. AutoCAD also provides flexibility in allowing the user to independently scale and rotate blocks as they are inserted.*

Try making your current drawing into a part and then inserting it into itself.

Macros

One of the most advanced features in AutoSketch is its macro capability. A macro is essentially a small program that can automate repetitive or complex operations within another program — such as AutoSketch. Fortunately, you don't need to know a thing about programming to use AutoSketch macros. You can simply tell AutoSketch to remember a series of actions as you perform them. After that, AutoSketch can repeat the actions exactly, like a player piano.

There are five commands that control the creation and use of macros. On the Assist menu you'll find the Record Macro command, which stores a series of actions as a macro, and the Play Macro command, which plays back the stored actions. There's also a special-purpose command, User Input, which we'll deal with a little further along. On the File menu you'll find the Make Macro and Read Macro commands, which allow you to store your current macro to a disk file and read back a previously stored macro from a disk file.

If you wish to push AutoSketch to its limits, you'll find that stored AutoSketch macro files work like a genuine programming language. Macros are stored as standard text files and are composed of simple English-like commands. It's not all that difficult to create advanced macros that can accomplish all sorts of difficult jobs quickly and easily. You can use pre-recorded macros as a starting point for further elaboration, or build your own macros entirely from scratch. You will probably wish to use a text editor or word processor separately from AutoSketch, although it is possible to use the AutoSketch Text Editor command for this purpose.

Recording a Macro

Creating a macro is easy. Select the Record Macro command and perform the actions you wish to store. Then pull down Assist once more. You'll find that the Record Macro command has been replaced with End Macro. When you select End Macro, AutoSketch records what you just did.

Macros 7-15

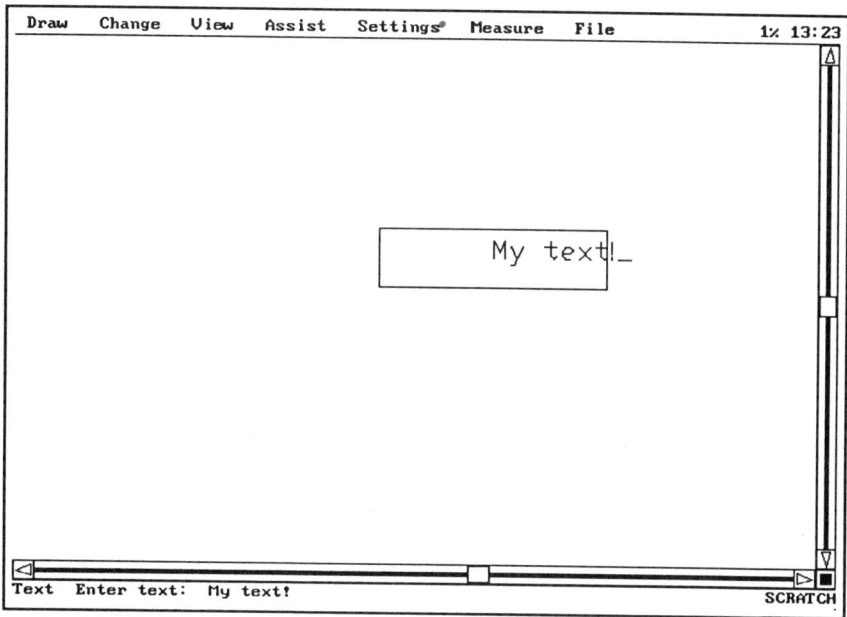

Recording a Macro

Recording a Macro

```
Pull down Settings Select Line Type      Set Line Type to solid.
Pull down Change Select Erase            Erase everything.
Pull down Assist Select Record Macro     Start macro recording mode.
```

All actions from now until you select End Macro will be stored.

```
Pull down Draw Select Box
First corner: <CTRL-F10>                 Press <CTRL-F10>, then pick a corner point.
Second corner: R(4,1)                    Enter relative coordinate to complete box.
Pull down Settings Select Text           Click Left Justify mode, then Center Justify, then
                                         Middle Justify.
Click OK                                 Close the dialogue box.
Pull down Draw Select Quick Text
Enter point: R(-2,-0.5)                  Enter relative coordinate.
Enter text: <CTRL-F10>My text!<ENTER>    Press <CTRL-F10>, then type "My text!"
                                         and <ENTER>.
Pull down Settings Select Text           Turn off Middle Justify mode.
Pull down Assist Select End Macro        End macro recording mode.
```

The macro you just made will create a four-by-one unit box with some text centered in it. Note that you press <CTRL-F10> or select User Input from the Assist menu. You must select User Input before entering any value or point that may be different each time you run the macro. Thus, the relative coordinate R(4,1) is repeated verbatim each time the macro is run. Where you typed in "My text!," you will be able to enter any text you like when you play back the macro.

Notice also the tricky use of dialogue boxes. The macro remembers only that you clicked on each box; because the box acts as a toggle, this may either enable or disable the specified mode. We had you select Left Justify first, in order to clear Center Justify — just in case it is already enabled when the macro is run. Then you can select Center Justify, confident that you are in fact enabling that mode. There's no similar work-around for Middle Justify. Our macro blithely assumes that Middle Justify is originally turned off. If you run this macro with Middle Justify already enabled, your text will not be middle justified within the box.

Obviously, relative coordinates are an absolute godsend when creating macros. They allow your macro to operate independently of the starting position. You will frequently want to structure your macros this way: start with a <CTRL-F10> (User Input) point, then proceed with relative coordinates.

It can take some practice to get the knack of recording a faultless macro. There's a strong tendency to get stage fright and enter erroneous keyboard or pointer actions. There's no going back if you slip up; in most cases you'll just have to select End Macro and try again. So take your time. It helps if you really shift yourself mentally into slow-motion while recording. AutoSketch will play back your macro at high speed, regardless of how long you took to record it. It's a bit like using a telephone with an auto-redial function. You still have to be careful not to dial the wrong number!

Playing Back a Macro

Once you've recorded a macro, the Play Macro command will no longer be greyed out on the Assist menu. To play back the currently stored macro, simply select Play Macro.

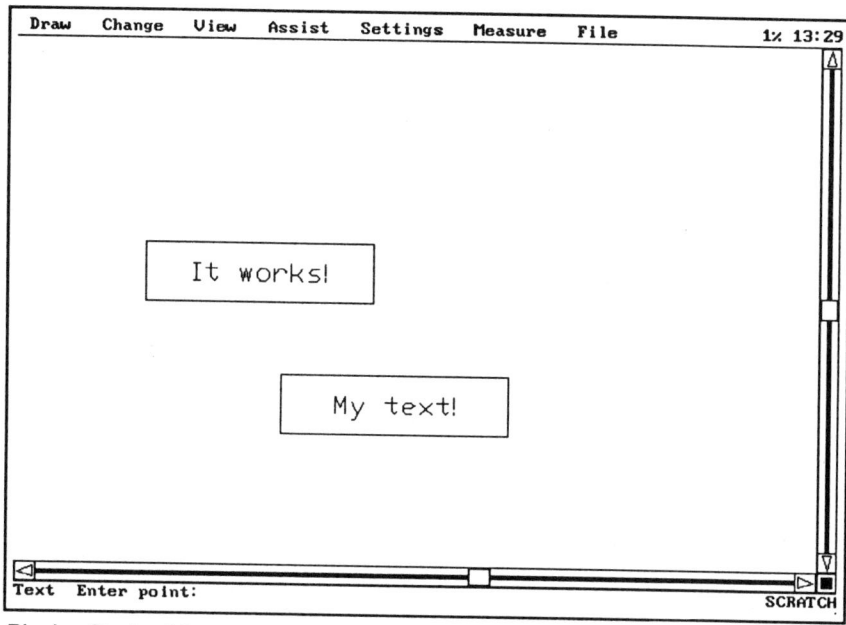
Playing Back a Macro

Playing a Macro

Pull down **Assist** Select **Play Macro**	Run the macro.
First corner:	Pick a point. The box appears.
Enter text: **It works!**	Type in some new text.

The text is centered in your box.

Depending on how fast your computer runs, you should barely see the individual recorded commands flash by. You will definitely see the text settings dialogue box flash up on the screen. You can cancel a macro while it is playing back by pressing <CTRL-C> — that is, by holding the <CTRL> key while you press <C> on the keyboard.

You can automate many repetitive drawings using part files. However, when a part requires some modification each time, a macro may work better. Parts are always recalled exactly as they were created, whereas macros can pause and ask for specific information that satisfies unique circumstances. For example, the above example macro lets you create a box around any text; a part file would always have exactly the same text it started with.

Saving and Loading Macros

Assuming that your macro works as you'd like it to, you'll probably want to save it for re-use. The procedure is just like that for saving a drawing file.

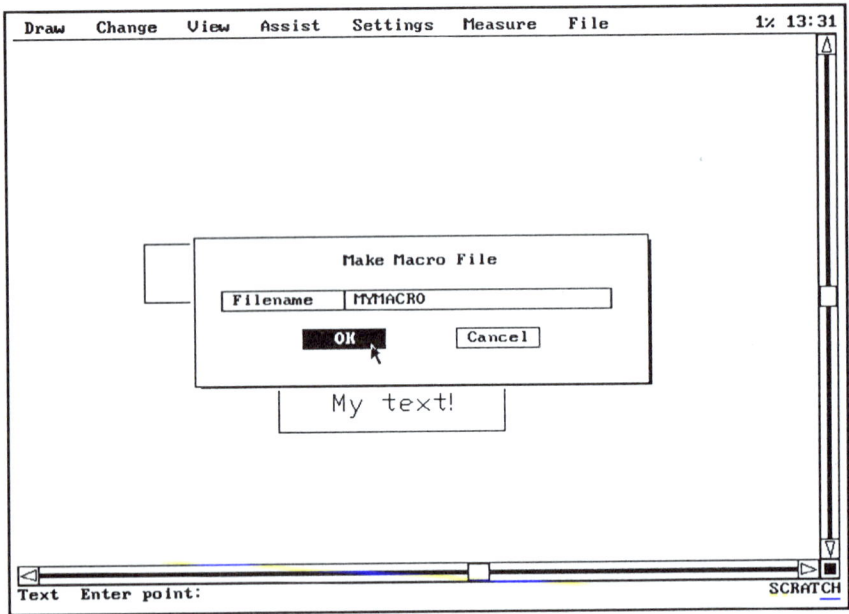

Saving a Macro

Saving and Recalling a Macro

Pull down **File** Select **Make Macro**	The Make Macro File dialogue box appears.
Filename **MYMACRO**	Type in a name.
Click **OK**	Close the dialogue box, and your macro is saved.
Pull down **File** Select **Read Macro**	Pick MYMACRO from the Select Macro File dialogue box.
Pull down **Assist** Select **Play Macro**	Your box text macro should run as before.

By default, the Make Macro File dialogue box offers to save your macro using the same name as your drawing. Thus, in the above exercise, you should see SCRATCH in the dialogue box. You can use this if you wish; however, if you expect to have more than one macro assigned to any one drawing, you will need to modify this name, or successive macros will overwrite each other. You could end up saving a new macro file over the top of one that you'll need later. If you use the drawing filename for your macros, you should at least add a number: for example, SKETCH1, SKETCH2, and so on.

A better naming convention is to try to give your macros descriptive names like BOXTEXT1 or NUT&BOLT to help you identify their purpose when you are in other drawings. Bear in mind you've only got eight characters to work with.

AutoSketch uses the filename SKETCH to save each macro when it is recorded. By using Read Macro to load SKETCH, you can always retrieve the last recorded macro.

If you find at some point that both the Make Macro and Read Macro commands are greyed out on the menu, even though you know there's a valid macro loaded in AutoSketch, check to make sure that the macro isn't *running*. You can't load or save macros until the current macro ends or is terminated by a <CTRL-C>.

Editing a Macro

There's nothing mysterious about the way macros work. Each action you make while recording a macro is stored as a text command. When you use Make Macro, these commands are saved in a standard ASCII text file. You can edit this file using any text editor or a word processor in non-document or unformatted mode. You can modify the stored commands, delete them, or add new ones.

Here's the complete text of the macro you just created:

```
MENU "Draw","Box"
ASK USER
STRING R(4,1)\013
MENU "Settings","Text"
PICK 39 13
PICK 39 15
PICK 39 17
PICK 12 19
MENU "Draw","Quick Text"
STRING R(-2,-0.5)\013
ASK USER
MENU "Settings","Text"
PICK 39 17
PICK 12 19
```

You could load this file, MYMACRO.MCR, into your text editor and make various kinds of changes. For example, you might want to make the box bigger. The following example describes how you could do this. If you aren't experienced with a text editor, you needn't try this now.

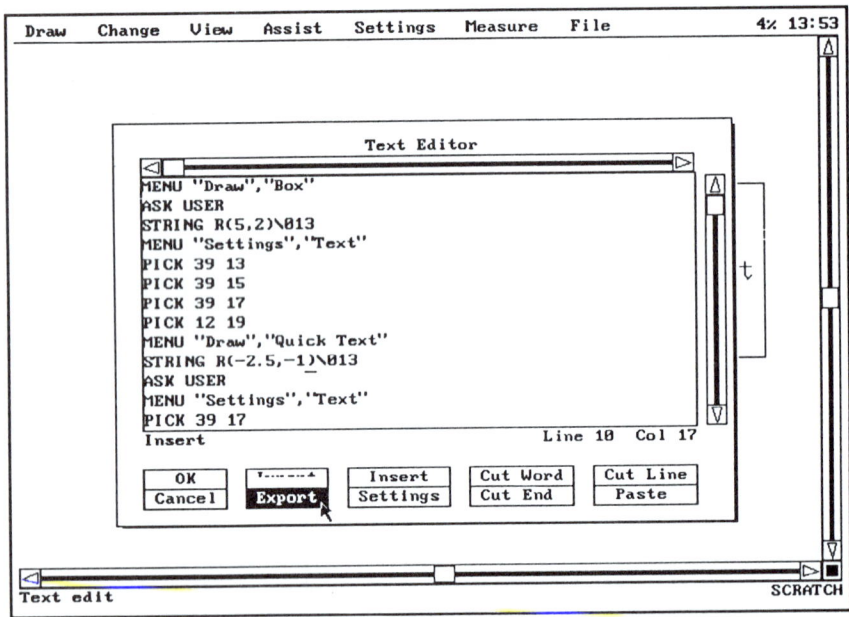

Editing a Macro

Editing a Macro

`Pull down `**`File`**` Select `**`Quit`**   Get out of AutoSketch.

Run your favorite text editor, and load MYMACRO.MCR.

Alternatively, use the AutoSketch Text Editor as follows.

`Pull down `**`Draw`**` Select `**`Text Editor`**
`Enter point:`   Pick any point.
`Click `**`Import`**   Select the Import option.
`Filename `**`MYMACRO.MCR`**   Enter name of file and click OK.
`STRING R(5,2)\013`   Change the (4,1) in the third line of the program to (5,2).
`STRING R(-2.5,-1)\013`   Change the next-to-last line to read as shown.

Save the file, preferably under a new name, such as NEWMACRO.

```
Click Export                    Select the Export option.
Filename NEWMACRO.MCR           Enter the new name and select OK.
Click Cancel                    Select Cancel in the text editor dialogue box to avoid entering
                                the macro text into your drawing.
```

If you used your own text editor, run AutoSketch again.

```
Pull down File Select Read Macro    Pick NEWMACRO from the Select Macro File
                                    dialogue box.
Pull down Assist Select Play Macro  The box text macro runs, but with a bigger box.
```

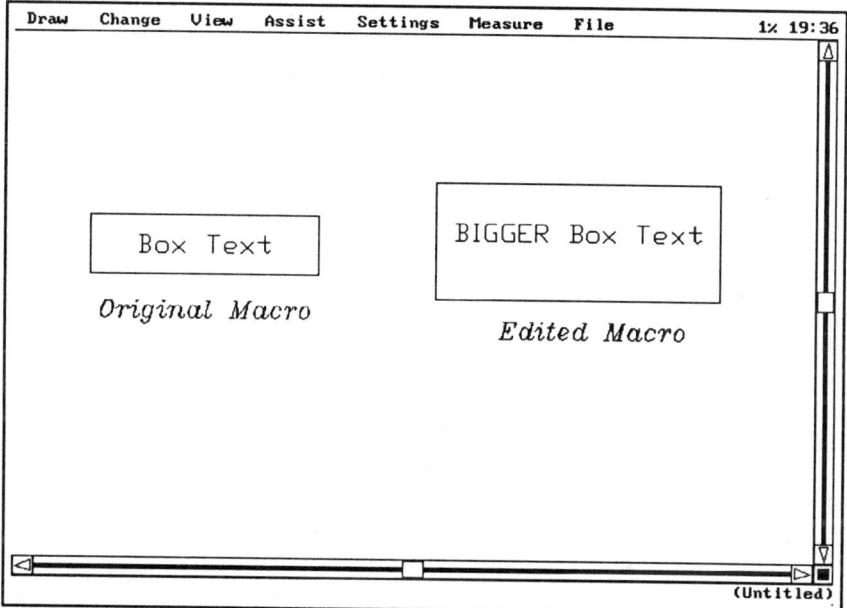

Two Versions of the Box Text Macro

There are only nine AutoSketch macro commands in all, so this new "language" is not a hard one to master. However, as with all programming, you have to be careful not to introduce extra text or formatting codes that will be incomprehensible to AutoSketch. Doing so could prevent your macro from working, cause it to behave unpredictably, or even crash your computer, losing whatever work you did since last saving your drawing. If you've never been exposed to programming at all, we recommend you go slowly and carefully, and experiment on scratch drawing files that you wouldn't mind losing in the event of an accident.

A good rule, demonstrated above, is to avoid changing anything you don't understand. Thus, in line three, we changed the relative coordinate values, without disturbing the "\013" (the ASCII code for <ENTER>).

In Chapter 12, we'll come back to the idea of writing your own macros and offer some suggested applications for this very powerful technique. (A complete listing of macro commands can be found in Appendix C of your AutoSketch Reference Manual. For convenience, a brief list is also included in the appendix of this book.)

➡ *TIP: AutoCAD does not have a capability for recording macros like AutoSketch. However, macro instructions can be placed in an AutoCAD memo file, making AutoCAD's user interface very customizable. AutoCAD also includes the extremely powerful AutoLISP programming language that lets users create their own commands.*

Command Practice

Before you move on to the drawing exercise, complete the practice exercises that deal with the commands covered in this chapter.

NEW. Pull down File, select the New option, and discard SCRATCH.

BREAK. Draw a circle. Then draw a box so that it overlies one side of the circle. Set Attach, with Intersect mode. Now use Break to cut away the section of the circle that lies within the box so that the box appears to be in front of the circle. Note carefully which direction you have to go from first break point to second. If you do it wrong, don't panic — hit <F1> to undo, and try again.

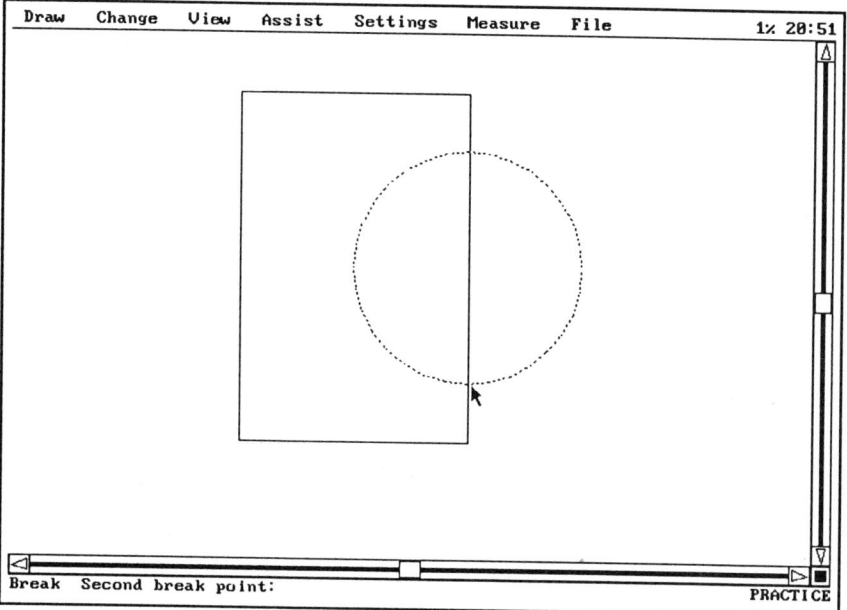

Breaking the Circle

GROUP. Use the Group command to group the two objects together. Now use Move to shift the objects around the screen. You'll find that they move as one.

BREAK/GROUP. Try to break the grouped arc now.

PART INSERTION. Now insert the ANGLE part. This part was given a specific base point and its insertion point will correspond to the base point.

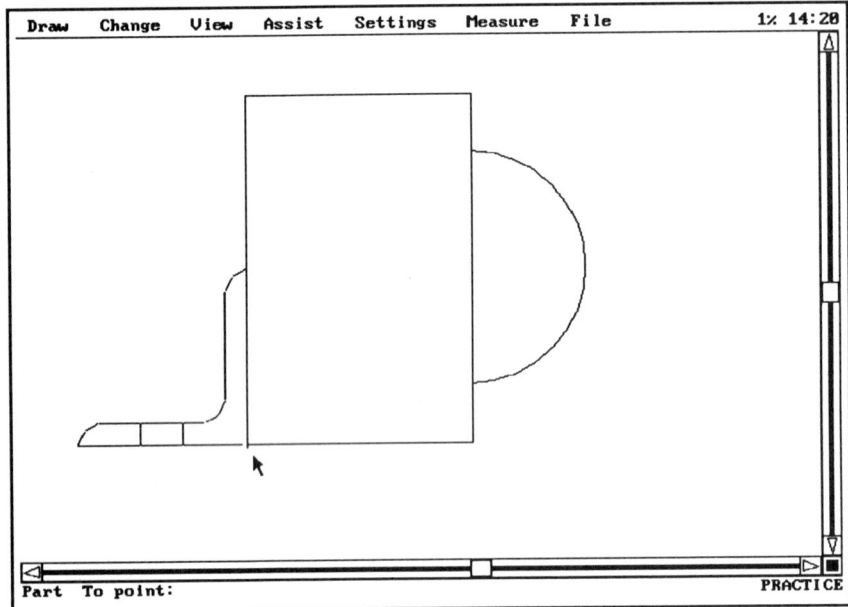

Insert the ANGLE Drawing

UNGROUP. Select Ungroup from the Change menu. Ungroup the original block and erase the arc. After a part has been inserted and it is a group, you can still change it. To change a grouped object, all you have to do is ungroup the object. If there are nested groups, you may have to ungroup until every nested group is undone.

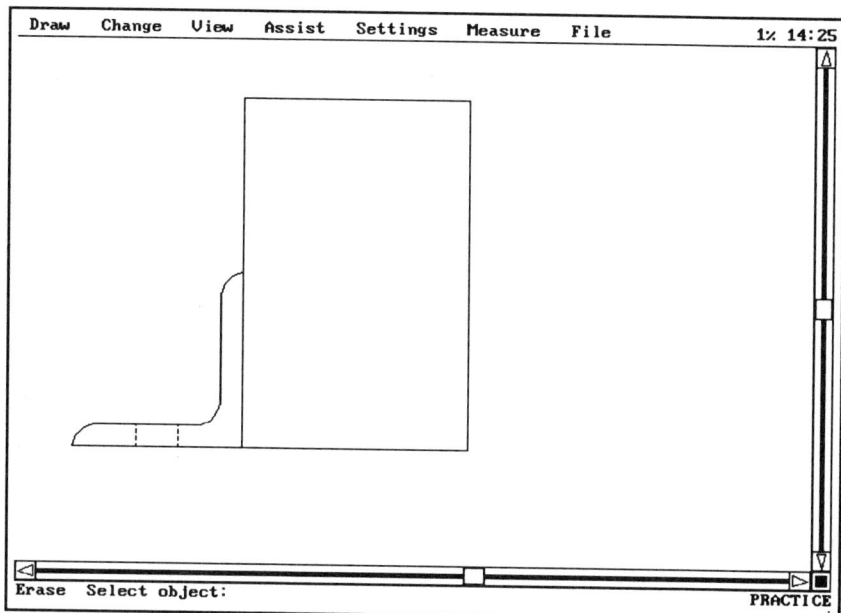
Ungroup and Erase the Arc

MACRO. Try to create a macro that will double the scale of any selected object. Enable Record Macro, then press <CTRL-F10> before selecting an object. You can use R(0,0) as the base point, making it the same as the selection point. When asked for a second point, enter "R(1.8,0)", which will just double the scale. Then select End Macro. Notice that a relative distance for the second point of 1 actually makes the scaled object 1.1 times the size of the original (a discrepancy in AutoSketch); hence the use of 1.8 to double the size.

Space Plan

In this set of drawing exercises, you are going to make a few more parts to be inserted into your space plan. You will also update your PLANT and CHAIR drawings so that they too can be inserted properly.

The goal of these exercises is to produce a drawing that resembles the following illustration.

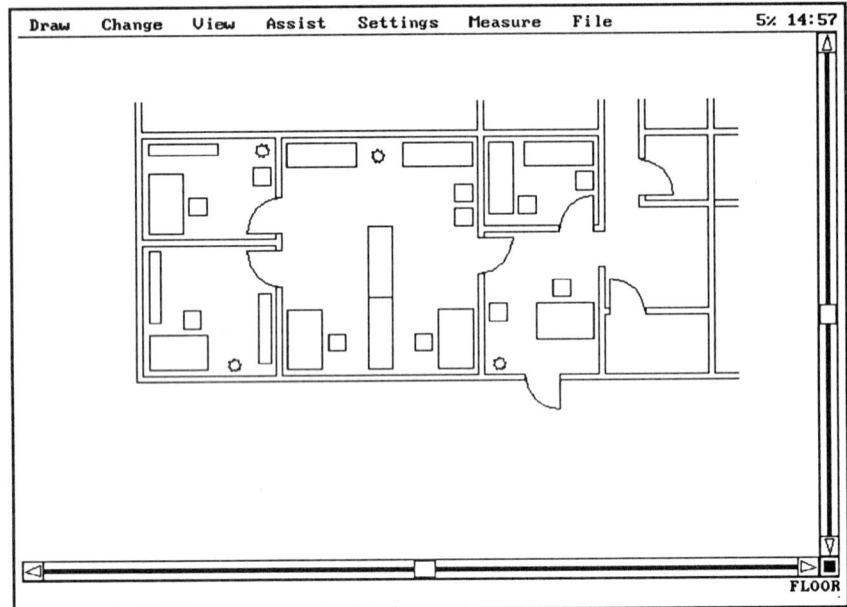

Finished Parts Inserted into FLOOR Plan

You will create several new furniture parts, then update the base points of the existing PLANT and CHAIR. These parts will then be inserted into the FLOOR drawing that you will clean up with Break. First, create the new parts:

Space Plan Drawing Exercise

`Pull down `**`File`**` Select `**`New`**	Discard SCRATCH or your practice work.
`Pull down `**`Draw`**` Select `**`Box`**	Draw a 3'x5' rectangle.
`Pull down `**`Settings`**` Select `**`Part Base`**	
`Click `**`Default Base Point`**	Use this option.
`Insertion base:`	Pick the middle of a long side.
`Pull down `**`File`**` Select `**`Save As`**	Save as DESK.
`Pull down `**`File`**` Select `**`New`**	Start a new drawing.
`Pull down `**`Draw`**` Select `**`Box`**	Draw a 2'x6' rectangle.
`Pull down `**`Settings`**` Select `**`Part Base`**	
`Click `**`Default Base Point`**	Use this option.
`Insertion base:`	Middle of a long side.
`Pull down `**`File`**` Select `**`Save As`**	Save as TABLE.
`Pull down `**`File`**` Select `**`New`**	Start a new drawing.
`Pull down `**`Draw`**` Select `**`Box`**	Draw a 1'x6' rectangle.
`Pull down `**`Settings`**` Select `**`Part Base`**	
`Click `**`Default Base Point`**	Use this option.

Insertion base:	Middle of a long side.
Pull down **File** Select **Save As**	Save as SHELF.

Open the PLANT and CHAIR drawings you made in Chapter 5, give each a part base, and save.

Next, make a DOOR symbol complete with swing arc. Using Attach, Snap, and Grid, draw a temporary 36-inch horizontal line, then a perpendicular line at the same length from the right end. Next, place the center of a circle at the intersection of the two lines, and the second point (the circumference point) at the endpoint of the vertical line. Now break the circle from the endpoint of the horizontal line to where it intersects the vertical line. This should break away everything but the arc you want. Now clean up by using Erase to get rid of the horizontal construction line.

When you finish drawing the door, give it a part base and make it a group.

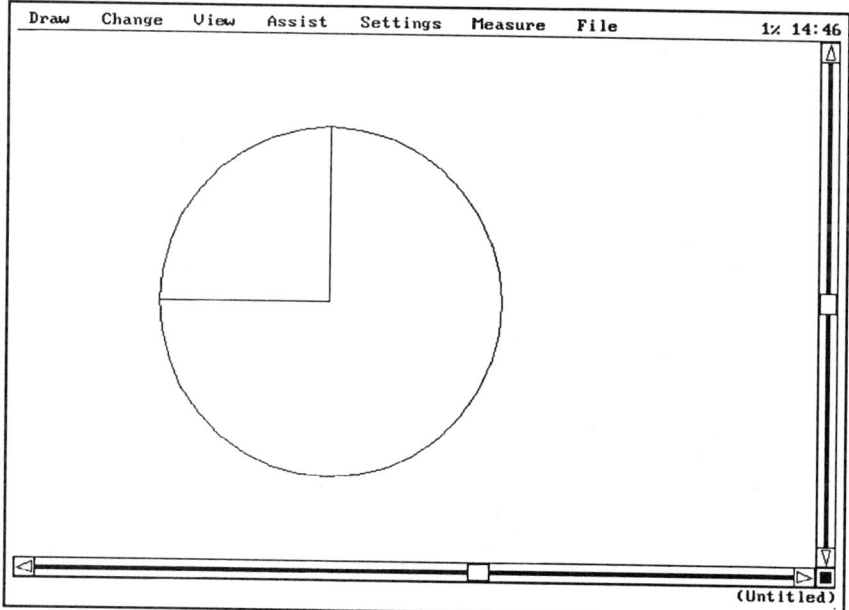

Draw a Circle and Two Lines

Pull down **File** Select **New**	Start a new file.
Pull down **Assist** Select **Attach**	Turn on.
Pull down **Assist** Select **Snap**	Turn Snap on.

Pull down **Assist** Select **Grid**	Turn Grid on.
Pull down **Draw** Select **Line**	36-inch horizontal line. 36-inch vertical line.
Pull down **Draw** Select **Circle**	
Center point:	Pick the intersection.
Point on circle:	36-inch radius.
Pull down **Change** Select **Break**	Break the circle.
Pull down **Change** Select **Erase**	Erase the horizontal line.
Pull down **Settings** Select **Part Base**	
Click **Default Base Point**	Use this option.
Insertion base:	Endpoint of vertical line.
Pull down **Change** Select **Group**	Group the door.
Pull down **File** Select **Save As**	Save new DOOR file.

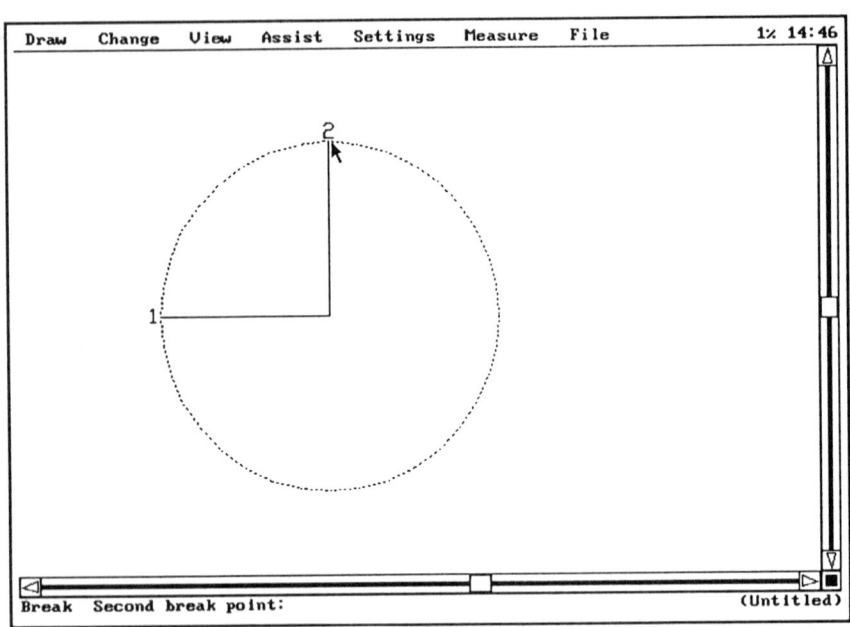

Break From 1 to 2 and Erase the Horizontal Line

➡ *TIP: Using temporary construction lines is a very powerful technique made possible by the easy deletions available in AutoSketch. Professional draftsmen often use them to lay out a drawing. Always feel free to use extra lines to make life easy for yourself and to improve accuracy. Use separate layers for complex constructions.*

After you finish updating and creating parts, the next step in completing your space plan will be to use Break and Zoom to clean up any remaining intersections where the walls join. Then insert your various parts in the space plan.

 Open the FLOOR1 drawing file from the IS DISK.

 Open the FLOOR drawing file.

Pull down **Settings** Select **Attach**	Disable all but Intersect mode, turn Attach on.
Pull down **View** Select **Zoom Box**	Zoom in on the intersection of two walls.
Pull down **Change** Select **Break**	Clean up the intersection.
Press **<F9>**	Zoom back to original view.
Press **<F10>**	Zoom in on each of the other intersections.
Pull down **Change** Select **Break**	Clean up all of the intersections.

Using the Part command, pull in the various parts that have been created — PLANT, CHAIR, DESK, TABLE, and SHELF. Locate each one somewhere in the drawing. The exact insertion points are not critical. Decorate your plan to your own taste. Place all the parts on layer 2, to keep them separate from the walls.

You should be able to use the Change commands to easily manipulate the doors and furniture around the space plan. Use Move, Copy, and Rotate to put all the parts into their correct locations. Refer to the illustration for possible part locations.

Once the parts are placed, use Zoom and Break again to break the walls where the doors have been added.

Pull down **Assist** Select **Ortho**	Turn off Ortho.
Pull down **Settings** Select **Layer**	Set the current layer to 2.

Ensure that layers 1 and 2 are both visible.

Pull down **Draw** Select **Part**	Insert each of the parts.
Pull down **Change** Select **Copy**	Copy each part until you have enough.
Pull down **Change** Select **Move**	Move the parts to their proposed locations.
Pull down **Change** Select **Rotate**	Rotate any part that needs it.
Pull down **View** Select **Zoom Box**	Zoom in on a door.
Pull down **Change** Select **Break**	Break the wall segments out of the door.
Pull down **View** Select **Pan**	Move around the drawing to each door.

```
Pull down Change Select Break          Break the wall lines out of all doors.
Pull down File Select Save             Save the file.
```

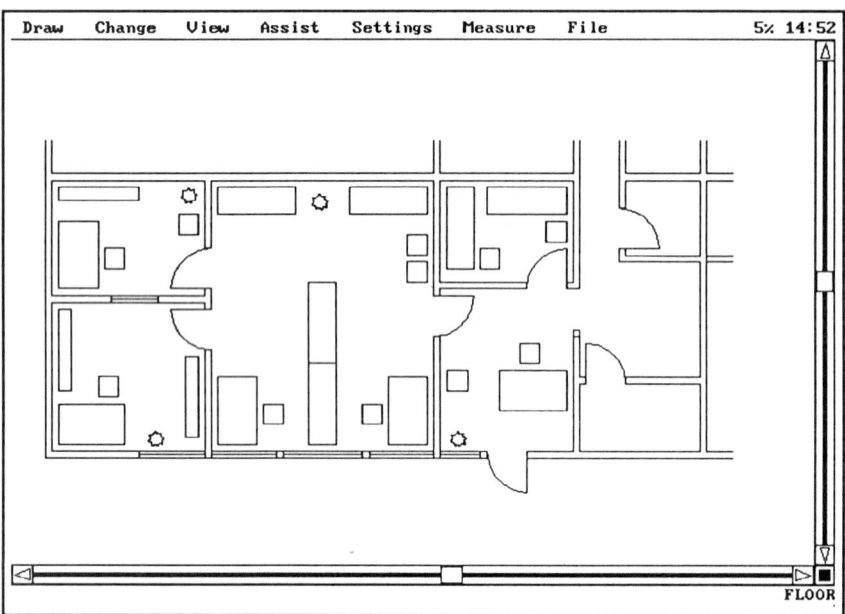

The Finished Space Plan

If you want to dress up the plan some more, make some windows, and insert them as shown in the illustration.

Summary

In this chapter, we've looked at several loosely related features. The Break and Group commands are roughly opposite, allowing you to break apart fundamental objects or build up complex compound objects, respectively.

The Group command works naturally with the part commands, since parts should usually be grouped before they are saved for reuse. Parts are one of the most powerful features available in AutoSketch, allowing you to save pieces of your drawings that can later be reused. Many standard items can be stored as parts: electronic components, mechanical components, title blocks, and many others. The part commands also allow you to merge complete drawings, since any drawing can be treated as a part and read into another by means of the Draw Part command.

AutoSketch macros are handy for automating simple, repetitive drawing tasks. They can accept user input during playback, and can even be written and edited like real programs.

You have now seen almost all of the drawing and editing commands available in AutoSketch. In the next chapter, we'll look at the various options available for plotting and printing your work.

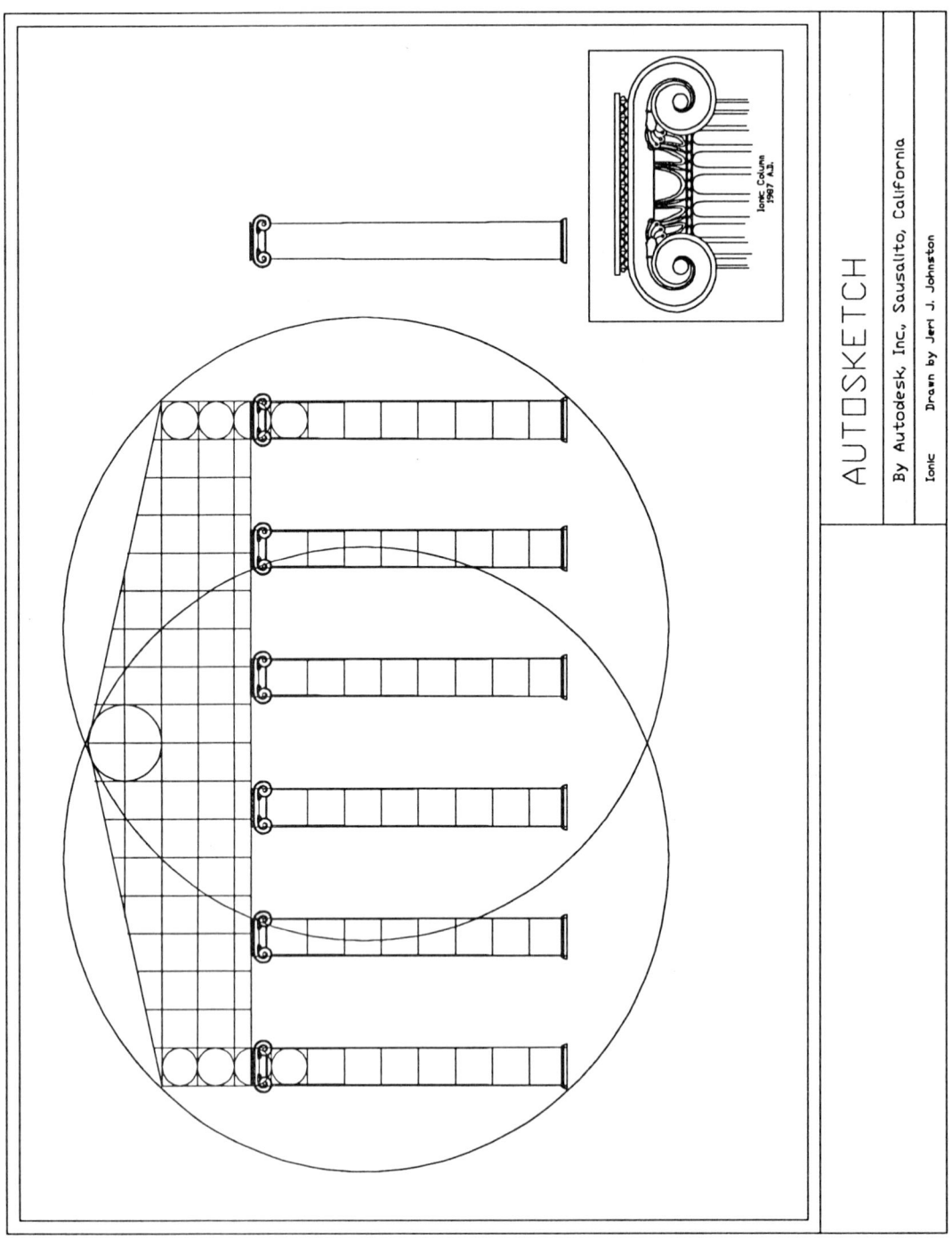

Ionic Columns, Courtesy of Autodesk, Inc.

Chapter 8

Getting Output

The final goal of your drawing efforts is to get an image on paper. AutoSketch makes this fairly effortless with default settings for paper size and drawing scale. It also provides considerable flexibility in customizing your output on the final page. You need to have a general awareness of the entire printing process, even if you plan to use the simple defaults.

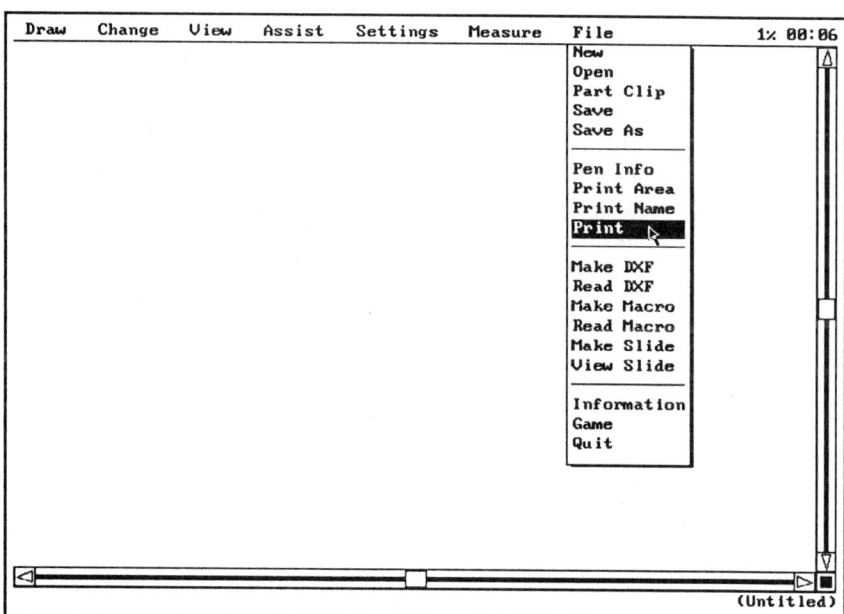

The File Menu

The output commands are located on the File menu. There is some logic behind this; printing is an action that generally involves your entire drawing file. There are four commands that control printing or plotting: one command to actually start plotting, and three commands to set up various options. These will appear on the menu as either Print or Plot commands, depending on whether you have installed AutoSketch for a printer or a plotter.

If you've configured AutoSketch using printer option 1 — "No printer/plotter" — the Plot options will be greyed out on the menu. If you've configured for the wrong printer or plotter, or the wrong communications port, AutoSketch may "freeze" or "lock up." If this happens, type <ALT-CRASH>, that is, hold down the <ALT> key while you type CRASH. AutoSketch will terminate and you can reconfigure AutoSketch before trying again.

Throughout this chapter, we'll follow the convention used by the AutoSketch manual and refer to Plot commands and plotting. If you have a printer, mentally substitute Print and printing.

The kind of output results you can expect will vary considerably depending on the kind of output device you are using. Some criteria for selecting an appropriate printer or plotter are mentioned in the appendix.

Plot

Selecting Plot does just that — it plots (or prints) the drawing. In most cases, you should first set up your output options, using the Plot Area command. However, AutoSketch includes default settings that allow you to select Plot without any preliminaries. The many Plot Area options can be a bit daunting at first, so it's handy to be able to at least get some quick trial output.

Let's try this first. Later on, once you've set your own Plot Area options, the Plot command will use them, rather than its own defaults — allowing you to control plotting much more accurately.

Plotting a Drawing

 Open the MAP2 file from the IS DISK or reopen your MAP file.

 Open your MAP file.

```
Pull down File Select Plot                    And it plots!
```

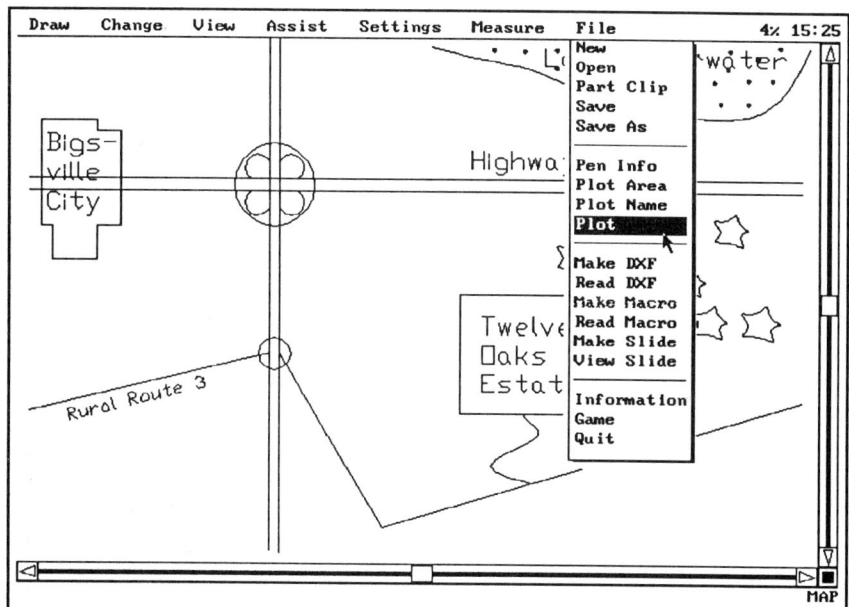

Plotting a Drawing

Using Plot without first setting the Plot Area options is roughly equivalent to using the Plot Extents option in the Plot Area dialogue box, as explained in the next section. Your hardcopy will not be plotted at any predetermined scale, nor will it necessarily be arranged to make the best use of the printer or plotter page. However, you can at least be sure that all of the visible objects in your drawing will make it onto the paper.

Objects on invisible layers never plot. This gives you a lot of control over your output. Just be sure that unwanted layers are invisible, and the desired layers are visible, before selecting Plot.

When you plot, it is also very important to be aware of the status of your output hardware. Before selecting Plot, always ensure that your output device is ready to receive data. Otherwise, nothing much will happen. You may get a warning box from AutoSketch reporting:

```
Cannot plot or print this drawing.
(The disk may be full or the
printer or plotter may not be
properly connected.)
```

Click on OK to get rid of this box, enable your plotter or printer, and try again.

You may also get the same warning if your disk is actually full and you have configured AutoSketch to plot to a file. (This is particularly likely on a floppy disk system.) Your AutoSketch manual points out the correct use of the MS-DOS SET command to ensure that the temporary plot file is written to your data disk — presumably the one with the most available space.

If you are using a dot matrix printer, you may find that printouts can take quite a while to print. Carefully chosen Print Area settings can help. With both dot matrix and laser printers, you are limited to standard sizes of paper. You'll have to use the Print Area options to either change the printing scale or print large drawings in sections that can later be pieced together.

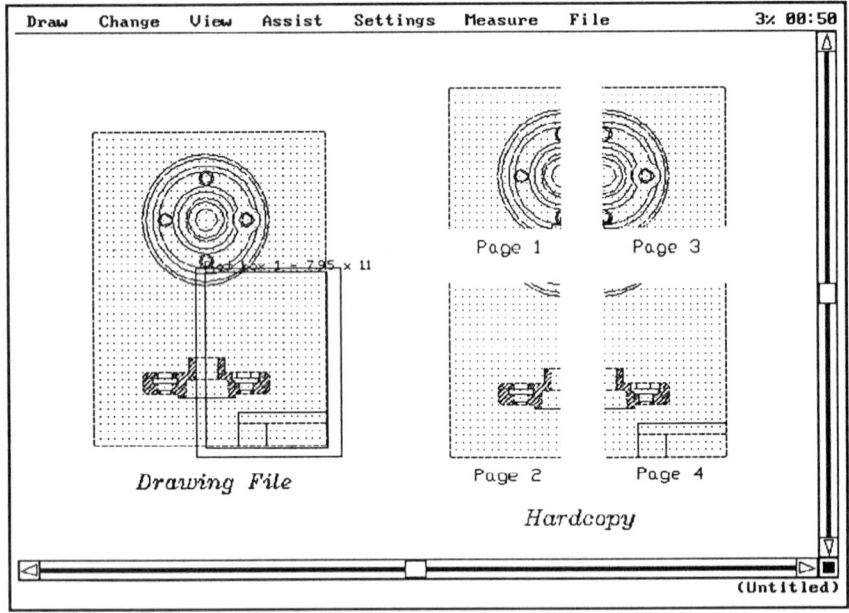

Printing in Sections

Plot Area

Plot Area is the major AutoSketch output control. It doesn't actually plot anything, but it does provide most of the control over how your drawing will plot. Using this command you can set up the size, orientations, and scale of the plotted image, and even crop out smaller portions of the image to plot by themselves.

AutoSketch provides an elegant visual system to help you arrange your drawing on the final plotted sheet. When you've finished selecting Plot Area options, AutoSketch adds a *plot box* to your drawing. A plot box looks like a regular AutoSketch box, but includes a text annotation at the top, stating that it is plot box number X (where X will be 1 for the first plot box, and increments each time you set up a new plot box), and giving its dimensions. You can set up different plot boxes for the same drawing, allowing you to plot different areas of the drawing, or at various scales.

The plot box is not really part of the drawing; it never plots out. What it does is represent an outline of your eventual plotted sheet, superimposed on your AutoSketch drawing.

➥ *NOTE: The X and Y plot size values shown under Plot Box Settings will be equal to the effective plotting area of your output device. Since most devices can't plot all the way to the edge of a sheet, the sizes will be somewhat less than the paper size you select.*

When you select the Plot Area command, you'll be faced with a dialogue box containing a hefty number of options. To use AutoSketch's visual system to verify correct plot area and scale, you must have Create Plot Box turned on (the default) before you click on OK to close the dialogue box. If you want to place just a part of your drawing on the page, you should also turn on Create Clip Box.

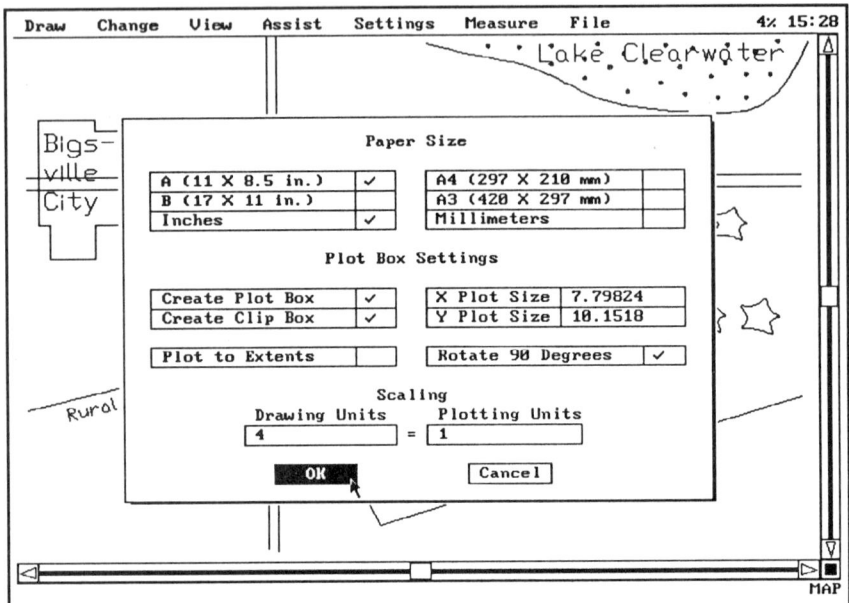

The Plot Area Dialogue Box

Setting Plot Area

```
Pull down File Select Plot Area
Drawing units 4                         4 drawing units.
Plotting units 1                        Leave set to 1.
Select Rotate 90 Degrees                Turn on.
Select Create Plot Box                  Leave on.
Select Create Clip Box                  Turn on.
Click OK                                Click the OK box.
```

If you select the Plot to Extents box, AutoSketch will create a plot box that surrounds all the objects in your drawing. The effect is similar to that of using Plot without first setting any Plot Area options at all, as we saw in the previous section. However, Plot to Extents has the advantage that it does place an actual plot box on your drawing, giving you a starting point that you can adjust, if you wish.

Plot to Extents will produce a plot at the largest possible scale that will include your entire drawing. If you need accurately scaled plots, you must set up the scaling options and plot box yourself. Plot to Extents does not guarantee that your drawing will be particularly well arranged on the sheet. However, it does guarantee that all parts of the drawing will show up — except, of course, for objects located on invisible layers.

Depending on your output device and selected paper size, the AutoSketch plot box will appear either tall and narrow (portrait mode) or short and wide (landscape mode). If the default orientation of the box doesn't match the proportions of what you've drawn, you may want to select the Rotate 90 Degrees option from the Plot Area dialogue box. This will effectively rotate the drawing in relation to the printed or plotted page.

For accuracy, you should manually specify how many drawing units will correspond to how many plotting units. For instance, if you've drawn the space plan of an office, you may want to set 48 drawing units to be equal to one plotting unit. For example, if you've created your drawing using one unit to equal one inch, and you want the plot to be at 1/4" = 1'0" scale, use 48 drawing units to one plotting unit. Select and enter appropriate scale factors in the Drawing Units and/or Plotting Units boxes. Note that if you've selected Architectural units display, the dialogue box converts your input to feet and inches. For more information on units, see Chapter 1, *Getting Started*.

If you've turned on the Plot Box and Clip Box options, you'll see the new plot box and an Accept/Modify dialogue box when you click on OK. Your drawing will automatically zoom to allow you to see these boxes. You can select Modify to go back to the Plot Area dialogue box, or Accept to return to your drawing. The screen will return to its previous zoom level. If you can't see the plot or clip boxes, you can use the Last Plot Box option on the View menu to automatically zoom to the extents of the last plot box. This is the same view you saw when the Accept/Modify dialogue box appeared. If the plot box is too large to be seen, you can also use Zoom Full. If it's too small, look for its lower left corner at the left and bottom coordinates specified in the Drawing Limits dialogue box of the Limits Command, since it is always anchored there.

Unless you specifically set the Scaling option in the dialogue box, the plot box is drawn with a default scale of one drawing unit to one plotting unit. (If you select millimeters, it will be one mm per unit.)

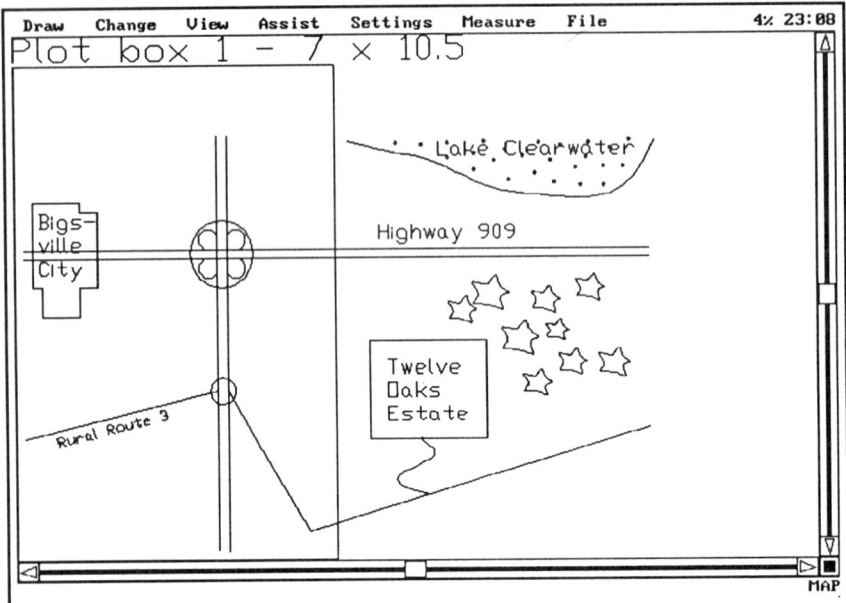

Zooming to Last Plot Box

Plot and Clip Boxes

The plot box shows the area of your plotted sheet in relation to your drawing.

The clip box shows the portion of your drawing that will actually plot. Any portions of the drawing outside the clip box will not be plotted. Portions outside the clip box but within the plot box will be left blank on the plotted (or printed) sheet. By default the clip box appears somewhat smaller than the plot box, and is centered within it. The border between the clip box and the plot box provides a margin around your plotted sheet.

Each time you use Plot Area, you'll produce another set of plot and/or clip boxes. This allows multiple plot settings to be stored in a drawing. However, only one set of plot/clip boxes can be visible when you select Plot. Either erase any spare boxes, or move them to an invisible layer. If you want to examine the Plot Area settings of the last plot box, execute the Plot Area command again. Be sure to exit the dialogue box by selecting Cancel. Clicking on OK will make a duplicate plot box.

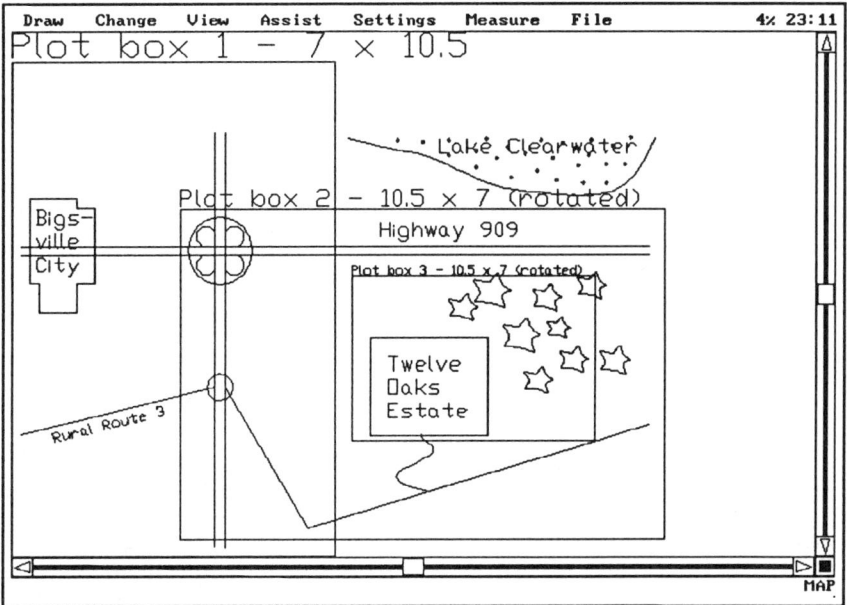

Multiple Plot Boxes

To sum up: use the plot box to set the final size of your output in relation to the paper you are using. Use the clip box to cut away any portions of the drawing that would fall within the plot box area, but you don't want plotted. The plot box performs overall scaling of the plot; the clip box does cropping or trimming of unwanted areas. You'll always use the plot box, but you may find yourself using the clip box only rarely. That is why the plot box setting always defaults to on, while the clip box defaults to off.

Some further settings can be made from within the Plot Area dialogue box. The actual size of your paper can be specified using the Paper Size section of the dialogue box. You can either select one of the preset sizes, or set a size manually using the X Plot Size and Y Plot Size measurements. These can be specified either in inches or millimeters, depending on the setting of the two corresponding boxes.

If you switch from one type of units to another, the existing X and Y Plot Size settings will automatically be converted to the new units. Your actual output will stay the same size. However, it will no longer be correctly scaled. In other words, one inch would suddenly represent one millimeter, rather than 25.4 millimeters.

Editing Plot and Clip Boxes

Only what is inside the plot box will plot. You can manipulate the plot box using normal Change commands, effectively positioning your drawing on this simulated sheet.

Editing the Plot and Clip Boxes

```
Pull down View   Select Zoom Full
Pull down Change Select Move              Move the clip box.
Pull down Change Select Stretch           Stretch the plot box.
Pull down Change Select Scale             Rescale the plot box.
Pull down Change Select Undo              Undo the Stretch and Scale changes.
```

You could, for example, place the plot box so that half your drawing sticks out on the left. This would be useful if you wanted to plot half the drawing at twice the scale. However, even if you specified accurate scaling, bear in mind that if you visually stretch the plot box, your output would not be scaled as precisely as if you had manually set the scale. Thus, if you use Stretch or Scale to enlarge the plot box, you are effectively shrinking the plotted drawing. If you shrink the box, you are enlarging the plot. Although it's the plot box that changes size on the screen, the piece of paper it represents will remain the same size, so it's your drawing that will be sized instead. Even if you use Stretch on the plot box, its proportions will always stay the same, always accurately representing the proportions of your actual plotter or printer page.

Pen Info

Unless you are using a pen plotter or a printer with color capability, you can ignore this command entirely. If you are using a multi-pen plotter, you have the option of deciding which color in your drawing will be plotted by which pen. This lets you adjust the plot so that the colors in your drawing correspond to the pens you have installed on the plotter. Of course, you can also use this function to change colors so that the plotted colors are quite different from those on the screen.

Setting Pen Info

```
Pull down File Select Pen Info
Click OK
```
                                      Select the pen for each color.
                                      Select the OK box.

The Pen Speed option allows you to slow down plotting for any pens that have particularly delicate drawing characteristics. Generally speaking, finer pens can plot faster than broad pens, so AutoSketch lets you set pen speeds individually in a single plot. Refer to the pen manufacturer's recommendations in selecting an initial pen speed. With some experimentation you may find that you can increase the pen speed without affecting plot quality. This will also depend on the quality of paper you are using.

When you select the Pen Info command, the Pen Specifications dialogue box will appear. Select the desired pen number and pen speed for each color by clicking on the appropriate numbers in the Pen Number and Pen Speed columns. The number of pens available will vary depending on the output device you selected when installing AutoSketch. When you've made all of your selections, click on the OK box.

If you do not have AutoSketch configured for a multi-pen plotter, you won't be able to select colors for each pen within the Pen Info command. However, Pen Info will still allow you to set your pen speed. Of course, if you're using something other than a multi-pen plotter, the pen speed settings will have no effect.

If you need to use multiple pens to achieve different colors or widths in a single-pen plotter, group objects of different colors to different layers, and plot with only one layer visible at a time. Once each layer's plot has finished, turn the layers that were just plotted off, turn another layer on, change pens, and plot again without disturbing the paper.

Plot Name

AutoSketch also allows you to plot to a file on disk. It treats this file exactly as though it were a plotter or printer, saving all of the data and commands it would have sent to a device. This file can then be sent to the same type of plotter or printer at a later time or at a different location, even if AutoSketch isn't available. For example, if you install for an Epson printer, with printing to a file enabled, then the file you create will print correctly only on a computer system equipped with an Epson printer. Of course, if you have the opportunity to use several different output devices, perhaps attached to several different computers, you can reconfigure AutoSketch as many times as necessary and create plot files that will be compatible with each.

However, because it is prepared for the plotter or printer, the plot file cannot be brought back into AutoSketch. It is essentially a snapshot of your drawing — exactly as the hardcopy itself would have been if you had plotted directly to paper rather than to disk.

There are many uses for this capability. For example, your copy of AutoSketch might be installed on your computer at home, while your plotter is attached to a system at the office. AutoSketch gives you a way of bridging the gap. Using the Plot Name function, you can create a plot file that you can easily transfer from your home system to the office system for plotting.

The Plot Name command lets you save up a number of plot files, which could then be sent over a network and plotted by someone else, or perhaps spooled in one batch to the plotter at some time when it might otherwise not be in use — for example, after normal working hours. You can use the MS-DOS COPY command to move the plot file(s) to a floppy disk to be plotted elsewhere.

Setting Plot Name

```
Pull down File Select Plot Name
Filename MAPPLOT1                    Enter plot filename.
Click OK                             Click the OK box.
```

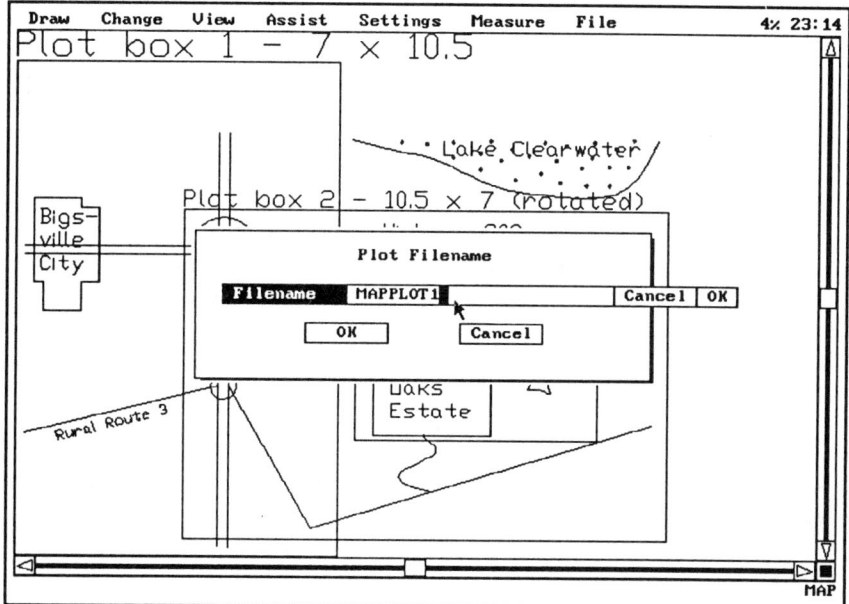

The Plot Filename Dialogue Box

Plot Name only works if you've made a special provision when installing or configuring AutoSketch. If you want to use the Plot Name function, the first step is to configure AutoSketch correctly. To reconfigure AutoSketch, either use DOS to delete the SKETCH.CFG file from your AutoSketch directory, or start AutoSketch using the /R or -R option by typing the command SKETCH /R or SKETCH -R on the DOS command line. When asked to specify a plotter, select the model that you will be using even if it isn't attached to the computer on which you are currently running AutoSketch. Then, when asked to specify the connection for your plotting device, pick option 4 — File.

Once configured, AutoSketch will run normally. When you're ready to plot, you can first use the Plot Name command to supply a name for the plot file, or simply select Plot. If you haven't previously specified a filename, you'll get the same Plot Filename dialogue box you'd get with Plot Name. Once you've provided a name using either method, instead of trying to send the plot output to an actual printer or plotter, AutoSketch stores the information in your named file. For instructions on maintaining multiple AutoSketch configurations, see the appendix or the *AutoSketch Installation Guide*.

When the plot file has been copied into the computer that has the plotting device attached, use the DOS COPY command to send the file to your output device. With most types of printers or plotters (attached to the parallel port), the following command should print the file:

`C:>COPY YOURFILE.PLT PRN: /B`

Of course, you should substitute the actual plot file name for YOURFILE. Note that you must include the PLT file extension that is automatically attached by AutoSketch to the eight-character file name.

If your output device is attached to a serial port rather than the parallel port, you'll need to consult your DOS manual concerning the use of the MODE command to properly configure the serial port. Some plotters require handshaking to communicate effectively with your computer. The DOS PRINT command may work in some cases, or you can consult a good AutoCAD dealer for a spooler program that can "talk" to your plotter.

➥ *TIP: Within AutoCAD, all the output options discussed in this chapter are controlled through the two commands PLOT and PRPLOT. In addition to plot sizing, scaling, area, pen colors, and plot files, AutoCAD can substitute line types, adjust for pen widths, and remove hidden lines in 3D drawings.*

Command Practice

Here are a few practice exercises that you might find helpful.

PLOT. Without further ado, simply select Plot and see what happens. If AutoSketch and your computer hardware are set up correctly, you should get a reasonable printout of the map, although chances are that it won't be properly centered on the page.

PLOT AREA. Use Zoom Box to magnify the big city. Select the Plot Area command, set Plot Box and Clip Box both on, and select Plot to Extents. Choose Accept from the Accept/Modify dialogue box. Zoom to Last Plot Box, then try adjusting both plot and clip boxes using the Scale, Stretch, and Move commands. When using the Stretch command on a plot box or clip box, you can only choose one box corner at a time. For the MAP drawing, you'll need to rotate the plot box. If you try using the Rotate command, it won't work. You have to set rotation from the Plot Area dialogue box.

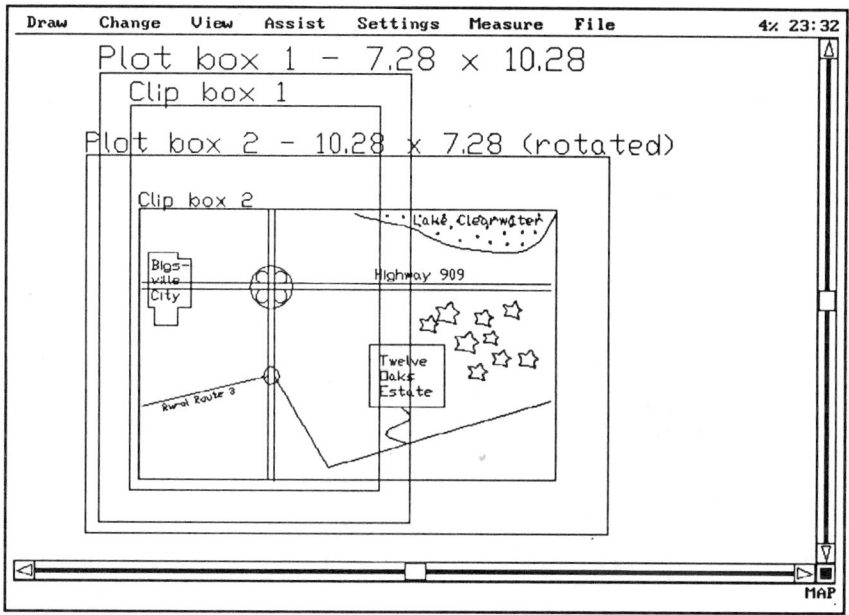

Setting the Plot and Clip Boxes

PLOT AREA. Select Plot Area again, and set Plot Box, Clip Box, and Rotate 90 Degrees on. You'll notice that a second set of boxes appears on your drawing, marked "Plot box 2" and "Clip box 2." Adjust the clip and plot boxes using the Stretch command.

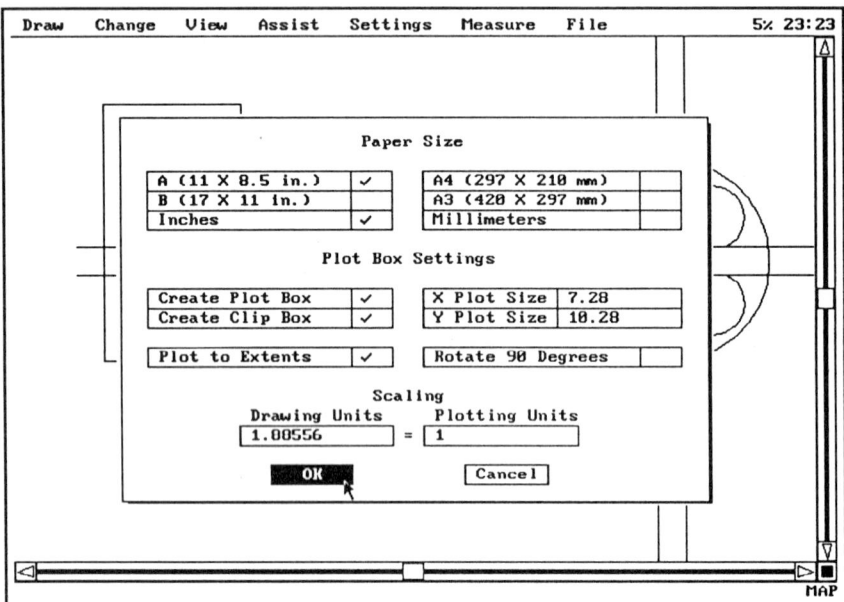

Rotated Plot Box

ERASE. Erase both the first and second clip boxes and first plot box. Be sure to save the modifications to the MAP drawing. Then pull down File and select New.

PLOT. Before you do much output, it's a good idea to experiment a bit with simple jobs. You'll see the results more quickly, and you may also save some paper. Try creating a handful of simple objects — the usual box, circle, and polygon combinations. Set up your Plot Area and Pen Info options. Now plot.

PLOT. Try a few different scaling and clipping setups. Also, try making your clip box larger than your plot box. Does this affect the output? Try "blowing up" a small section of your sample drawing to fill the page, or clipping away most of a drawing so only one detail prints in the middle of the page. Finally (if you're working with a plotter), try some variations on pen color assignments and speeds.

PLOT. Try loading and printing some of the sample drawings that came with your AutoSketch package.

Space Plan

Open the FLOOR drawing and plot it. Set up Pen Info if you are using a multi-pen plotter.

Use Plot Area to set Drawing Units to 48 and Plotting Units to one. Since you drew your space plan with a real scale, one unit being equal to one inch, this will yield a plotted drawing with a scale of 1/4" = 1'0". Set Plot Box on and Clip Box off. Be sure to rotate the plot box 90 degrees. Use only the Move command to relocate the plot box so that it surrounds your space plan.

If you've installed AutoSketch to plot to a file, you can take this opportunity to define a plot name for your FLOOR file, and plot it to a file.

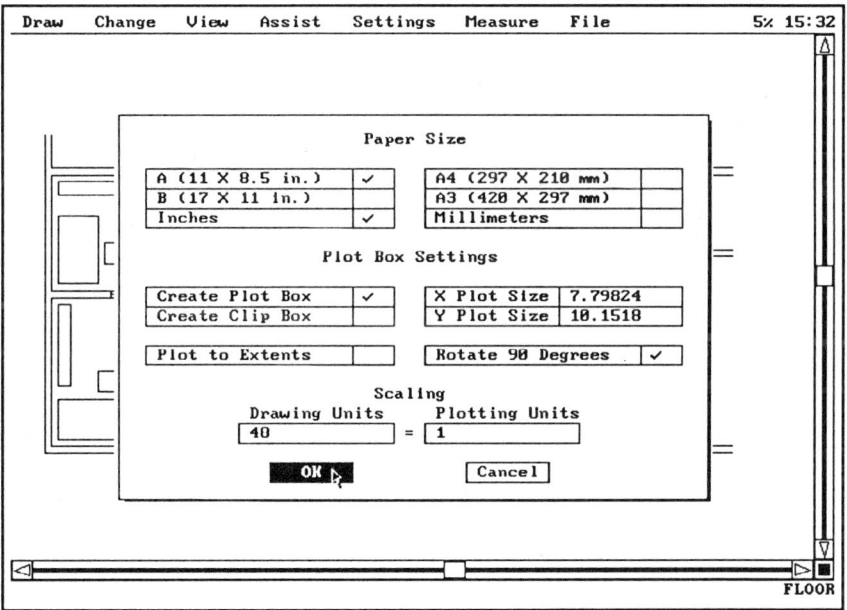

Setting the Plot Area Parameters

Space Plan Drawing Exercise

 Open the FLOOR2 drawing from the IS DISK or reopen your FLOOR file.

 Open your FLOOR drawing.

Pull down **File** Select **Pen Info**	Set pen colors if you need to.
Pull down **File** Select **Plot Area**	
Drawing Units **48**	Set to 48.
Plotting Units **1**	Leave set to 1.
Select **Rotate 90 Degrees**	Turn it on.
Select **Create Plot Box**	Leave on.
Select **Create Clip Box**	Leave off.
Click **OK**	Select the OK box.
Pull down **Change** Select **Move**	Move plot box so it surrounds the space plan.
Pull down **File** Select **Save**	Save your work to an accurate scale.
Pull down **File** Select **Plot**	Plot the file.

After plotting the space plan to an accurate scale, you may also want to go back and fetch the MAP drawing and try plotting that. You will have to experiment with different size plot boxes, since this drawing was not drawn to scale. Use scaling and clipping to bring out different parts of the drawing.

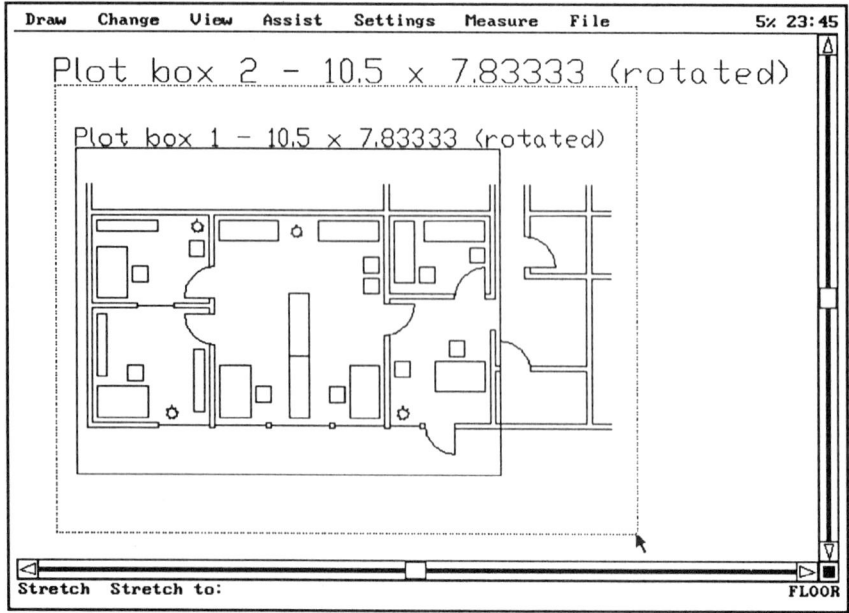

Adjusting the Plot Box

Summary

The normal procedure for getting printed or plotted output from AutoSketch consists of just two major steps: define a plot box, and select the Plot command. Using the plot and clip boxes, you can fully control the scale and cropping of the image on the page. On the other hand, if you're in a hurry you can simply select Plot without worrying about any of the optional settings, and still get a reasonably useful plot of your drawing.

If you are using a pen plotter, the Pen Info command lets you set up drawing speeds and associate plotter pens with the colors you used to create your drawing.

You should have a grasp of all the basic drawing techniques by now, as well as a good feel for how your drawing can be transferred to paper. In the next chapter, we'll look at some more technically oriented AutoSketch commands dealing with measurement and dimensioning.

PART THREE

Advanced Features

This final part aims to round out the information presented in the earlier two parts. If you've been following along in sequence, you should have a grasp of almost all the tools available in AutoSketch, and some idea of the best techniques for applying them. The remaining advanced features of the program are aimed mostly at more technical and specialized types of drawings.

The topics in this part include:

- **Technical Drawing Tools** looks at the last (and most powerful) of the drawing tools.
- **Technical Drawing Aids** contains discussion of AutoSketch's commands for verifying the precision of your drawings and adding professional-looking dimensions.
- **File Transfers** examines some of the file transfer options that allow you to transfer your work between AutoSketch and other programs.
- **Advanced Applications** approaches some common professional drawing projects with tips on putting AutoSketch to work at the office.

The exercises in the following chapters are based on a drawing of a machine part which demonstrates the advanced technical capabilities of AutoSketch. An appendix completes *Inside AutoSketch* with additional information and suggestions.

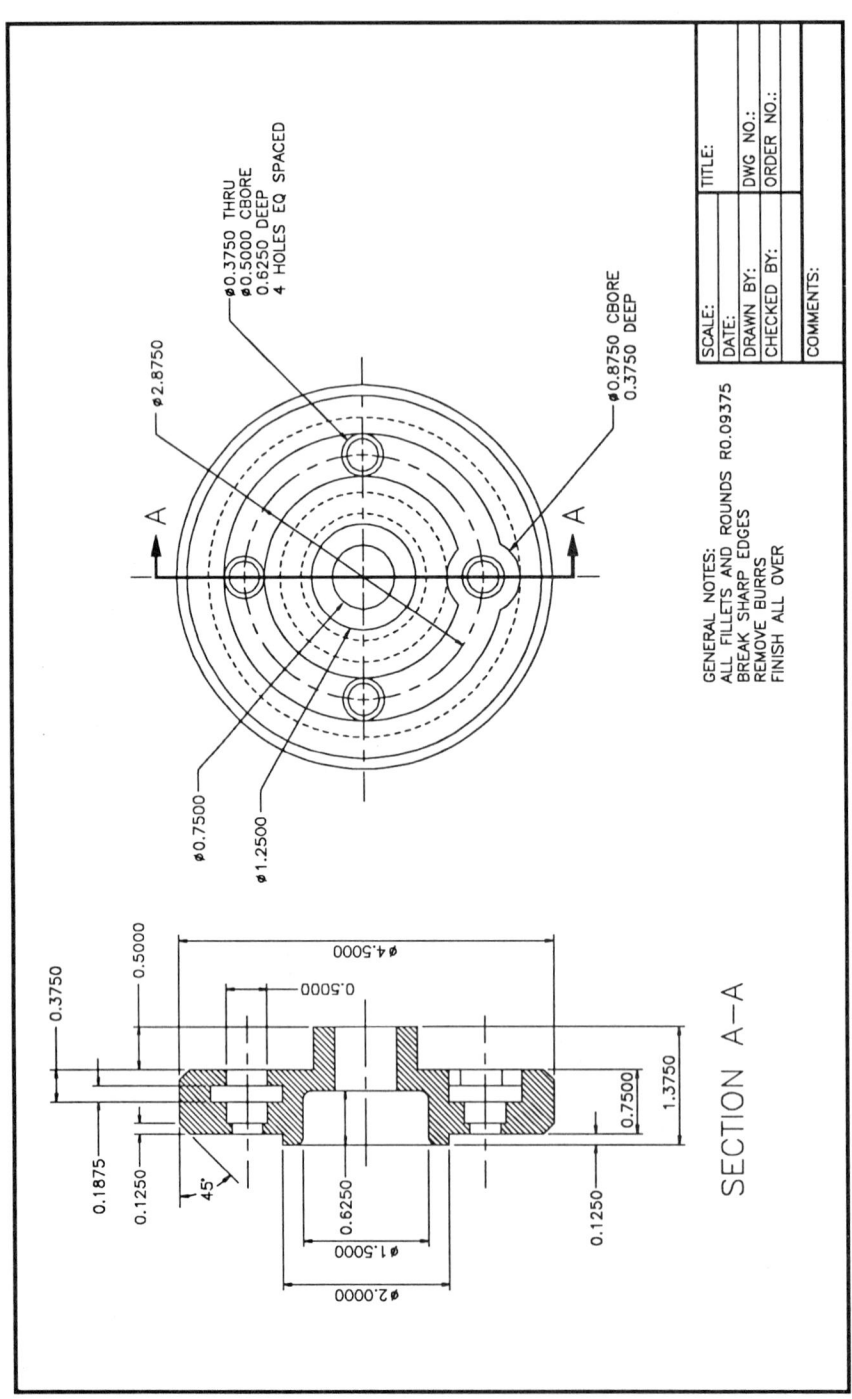

The Completed Machine Part

Chapter 9

Technical Drawing Tools

By now you should know the basic AutoSketch commands and be familiar with how they work. This chapter explores a variety of advanced drawing tools. For example, you will be shown how to use fillets and chamfers to clean up corners. In most manufactured parts, sharp edges are usually not desirable. Often they will be "knocked down" with either a fillet or a chamfer.

Also, techniques that let you create different line weights and various hatch patterns will be explored. Line weights and hatch patterns both add meaning when you have a complex drawing.

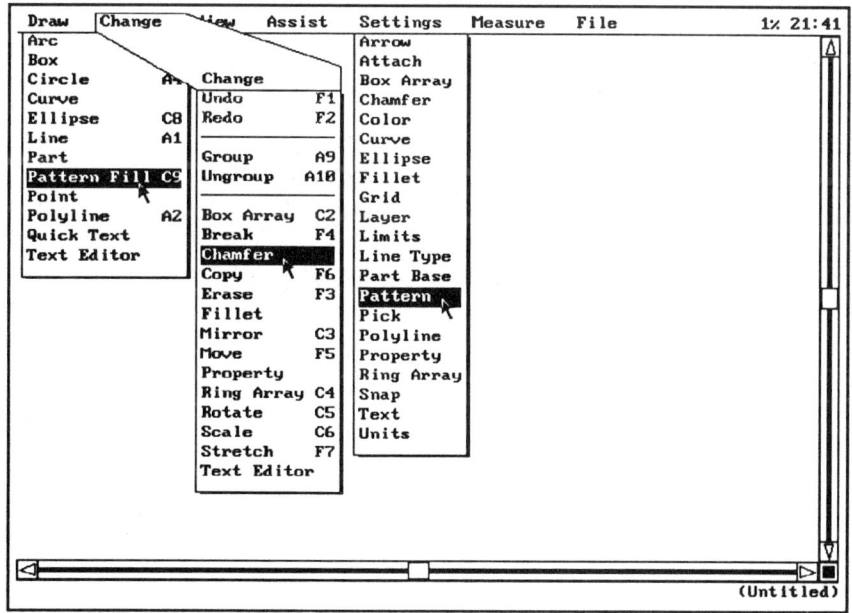

Advanced Draw and Change Commands

Instead of the simplified exercises we've demonstrated in past chapters, we're going to use the construction of a detailed, real-world mechanical drawing to illustrate the uses of some of these advanced drawing techniques.

Getting Started

We'll start by creating the rough outline of a machine part using the simple techniques covered in previous chapters. Use the dimensions shown in the illustration on the facing page of this chapter for reference. Don't worry about actually reproducing the dimension lines shown in the illustration; we'll pick those up in the next chapter. Any dimensions not shown are not critical and can be estimated.

With any drawing, your first thought should be to set some appropriate grid, snap, and limits values, and to plan how to use the ten available drawing layers. With this particular drawing, it's probably easiest to begin by drawing the outside circumference of the part. You could start anywhere, of course, depending on what you find most natural.

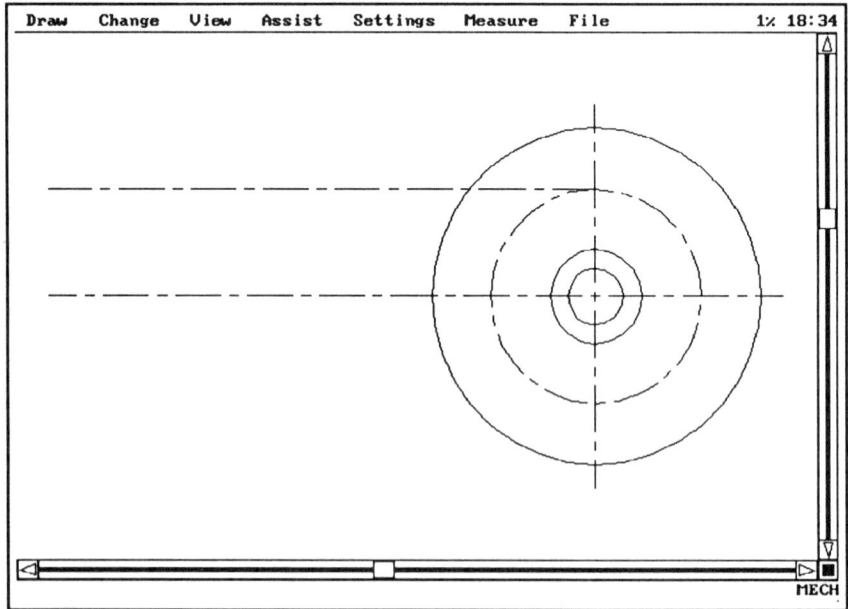

Circles and Center Lines

Beginning the Machine Part

Pull down **File** Select **New**	Start with a new file.
Pull down **File** Select **Save As**	Name the new file MECH.
Pull down **Settings** Select **Units**	Select 4 digits of precision.
Pull down **Settings** Select **Grid**	Set both X and Y to .25, and turn Grid on.
Pull down **Settings** Select **Snap**	Set both X and Y to .0625, and turn Snap on.
Pull down **View** Select **Zoom Box**	
First corner: **0,3**	
Second corner: **11,9**	
Pull down **Draw** Select **Circle**	
Center point: **8,6**	Absolute coordinates.
Point on circle: **R(0,2.25)**	Relative coordinates, using 1/2 of diameter.

Draw two more circles at center point 8,6 with radius .375 and .625.

Pull down **Settings** Select **Color**	Set color to blue.
Pull down **Settings** Select **Line Type**	Select Center type.
Pull down **Settings** Select **Layer**	Make layer 2 current.
Pull down **Assist** Select **Ortho**	Set Ortho mode on.
Pull down **Draw** Select **Line**	Draw horizontal and vertical center lines. If you can't find the center, use keyboard coordinates.
Pull down **Draw** Select **Circle**	Draw the circular center line at center point 8,6 and radius 1.4375.
Pull down **Settings** Select **Attach**	Turn on Intersection and Attach Mode. Turn off everything else.
Pull down **Draw** Select **Line**	Draw a line from the top intersection of the circle center line and the vertical center line to the far left.
Pull down **Settings** Select **Line Type**	Set line type back to solid.
Pull down **Settings** Select **Layer**	Make layer 1 active.
Pull down **Settings** Select **Color**	Set color to black.

Be sure to extend the horizontal center lines to the left. You can break any excess later. This will serve as a guide for the second, cross-sectional view of the part. Note that we've created these lines on a separate layer and in an alternate color, to set them apart from the actual drawing lines. Of course, if you're working in monochrome, you'll be able to tell the lines apart by their dashed style.

Arrays

To AutoSketch, an array is an evenly spaced group of identical objects, or groups of objects. This type of structure comes up often in technical drawing. Imagine a mechanical part with evenly spaced bolts, or the regular arrangement of components on a circuit board, or even the boxes in an organizational chart.

AutoSketch provides two different types of array commands. The Box Array command duplicates an object so that the copies are laid out horizontally and vertically in a grid — like soldiers on parade. The Ring Array command creates duplicates around the circumference of an imaginary circle — like the teeth on a gear, or petals on a flower. Both array commands provide numerous options that let you control the exact placement of the duplicate objects that form the array.

Once created, all arrays act like collections of individual objects. You can change any individual element of an array without affecting the rest. If you want the array elements to behave as a unit, you can group them together.

Box Arrays

Box Array is probably the easier of the two array commands to understand, because it has somewhat fewer options. Basically, it requires that you specify vertical spacing for array rows, horizontal spacing for columns, and the total number of rows and columns.

For our example, let's try adding an extra flange to the machine part in the drawing.

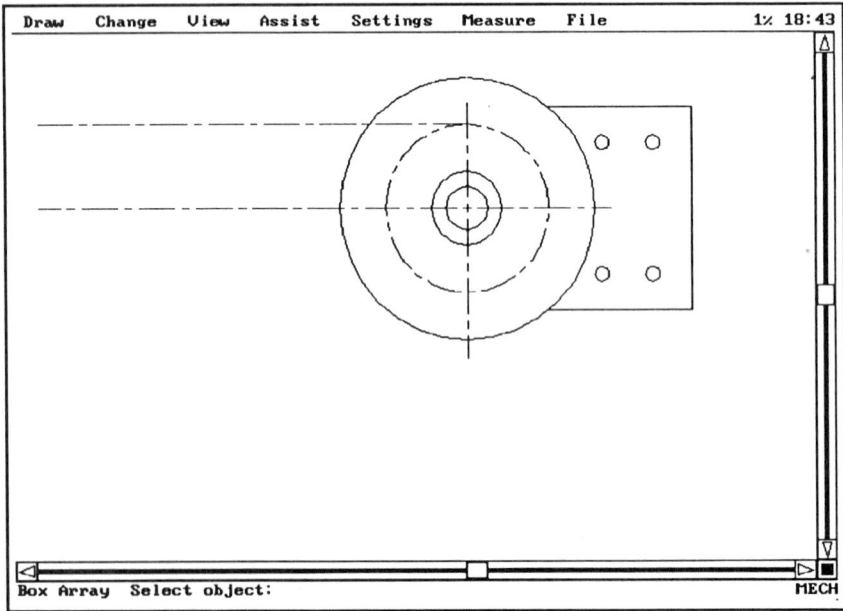

Drawing a Flange

Box Arrays

Pull down **View** Select **Zoom Limits**	Zoom out to get some working room.

Also, turn Snap on and Attach off. Use a solid, black line.

Pull down **Settings** Select **Layer**	Put the flange on layer 10.
Pull down **Draw** Select **Line**	Draw the flange.

If you draw as shown, the horizontal lines don't quite touch the outer circle.
To continue line drawing at each corner, double-click.

Pull down **Draw** Select **Circle**	Draw a hole.
Center point: **11.250,7.125**	Use absolute coordinates, or match the illustration.
Point on circle: **R(0,.125)**	Use .125 radius.
Pull down **Change** Select **Box Array**	
Select object:	Select the circle.
Column spacing First point:	Pick center of circle.
To point: **R(-.875,0)**	Absolute coordinate, or drag highlighted image left.
Row spacing First point:	Pick center of circle again.
To point: **R(0,-2.250)**	Or drag highlighted image downward.
Click **Accept**	Choose from Accept/Modify dialogue box.

Any variation on this simple Box Array procedure is handled by the Box Array Settings dialogue box. There are two ways to get into this dialogue box: use the Box Array command on the Settings menu or click on Modify in the Accept/Modify dialogue box from the Box Array command when you're drawing. Use the Settings route if you wish to preset some of the options; for example, when you know you'll be using the same options repetitively.

The most obvious control provided by the Box Array dialogue box is selection of the total number of rows and columns in your array. By default, you get a four-object array: two rows, two columns. You can enter larger values in the Rows (- - -) and Columns (| | |) numeric boxes, and thereby increase the size of your array.

AutoSketch offers several more options for specifying array spacing. By default, with the two Point boxes enabled, you specify row and column spacing by pointing on the screen. Disabling the Point boxes allows you to specify row and/or column spacing by entering exact measurements in the Row Distance and/or Column Distance boxes. You can combine the two techniques. AutoSketch shows the last distance you pointed out in the appropriate Distance box, so you can re-use the value by disabling Point the next time you create an array.

Furthermore, by default, the spacing value that you either point out on the screen, or enter as a numerical value, determines the spacing between individual rows or columns. Thus, if you enter a column spacing of, say, 2, AutoSketch will place columns two drawing units apart. However, if you check the Fit boxes, AutoSketch assumes that the spacing values should determine the *total* width and/or height of the array. If you enter a Row Distance of, say, 10, and a Rows value of 5, AutoSketch will fit the five array columns into a space ten drawing units across.

Finally, AutoSketch lets you specify the baseline angle of your array. If you change this value from its default of zero, AutoSketch creates the entire array at an angle. All of the row and column distances apply as before, but are measured at the specified angle from the horizontal. However, the individual objects in the array are not rotated; each one has exactly the same orientation as the original.

Ring Arrays

If you wish to arrange objects around a circle, the Ring Array command can be very convenient.

The Ring Array command has a corresponding Ring Array Settings dialogue box, accessed either by choosing the Ring Array command from the Settings menu or by choosing the Modify box while using the Ring Array command.

The Point box works much like the one in the Box Array Settings dialogue box. With Point enabled, you specify the array center point by pointing on the screen. With Point disabled, the center is positioned by values entered in the X Coordinate and Y Coordinate numeric boxes.

The number of items in the array is specified by a single numeric value. Positioning of the items is specified by the Included Angle option, which corresponds to the Fit option used with Box Array. The array objects are spaced evenly around the included angle. Thus, if the number of items is 3, and the included angle is 180 degrees, you'll end up with objects at three o'clock, twelve o'clock, and nine o'clock positions. (This includes your original, which will be at the three o'clock position.)

Specifying degrees between items is like disabling Fit with Box Array. AutoSketch copies the original object the specified number of times, moving each copy by the degrees between items angle.

Selecting the Draw Clockwise box lets you change the direction in which the array is drawn. If you've selected an included angle of less than 360 degrees, or if the number of objects doesn't divide evenly into 360 degrees, the objects may end up positioned quite differently, depending on the direction AutoSketch proceeds. The default is counterclockwise. Most often you'll use an included angle of 360 degrees, and a number of objects that spaces evenly — four, five, six, ten, and so on. In these cases, you can ignore the drawing direction.

The final two options allow you to control the orientation of items in the array. With Rotate Item as Copied enabled (the default), each copy will keep a constant orientation toward the center of the array — like the spokes of a wheel, which always point directly toward the center. If you disable this option, each copy keeps its orientation relative to the drawing page like the chairs on a ferris wheel, which always sit right side up as the wheel revolves.

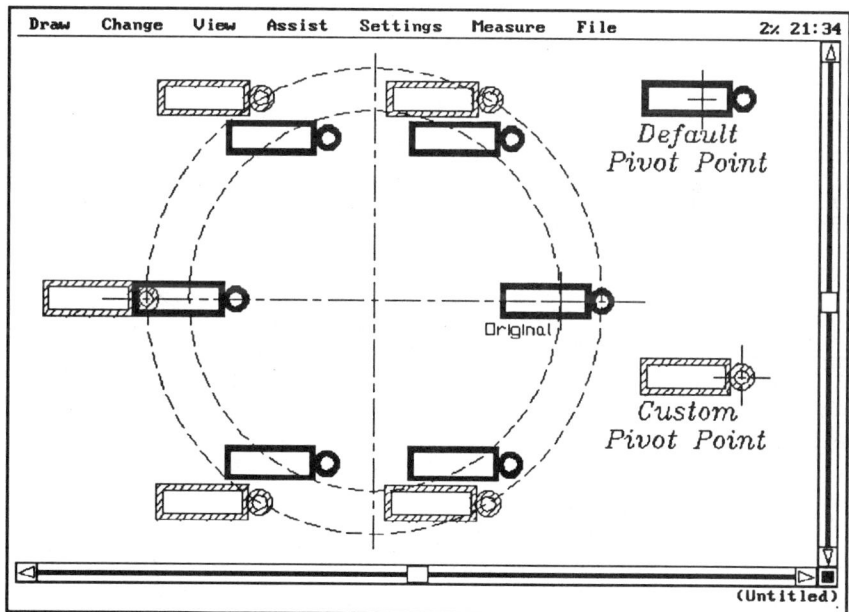

Effect of Pivot Point

The Pivot Point option works only with Rotate Items as Copied disabled. In fact, selecting the former option will automatically disable the latter. The pivot point works much like the from point or base point specified in many of the other Change commands. As AutoSketch creates a new element in the ring array, it first positions the pivot point, then draws a copy of the original object. If this seems confusing, refer to the illustration. You probably won't need this particular option very often, in any case.

Now, we'll draw a circle and then use the Ring Array command to duplicate and array the holes on the machine part.

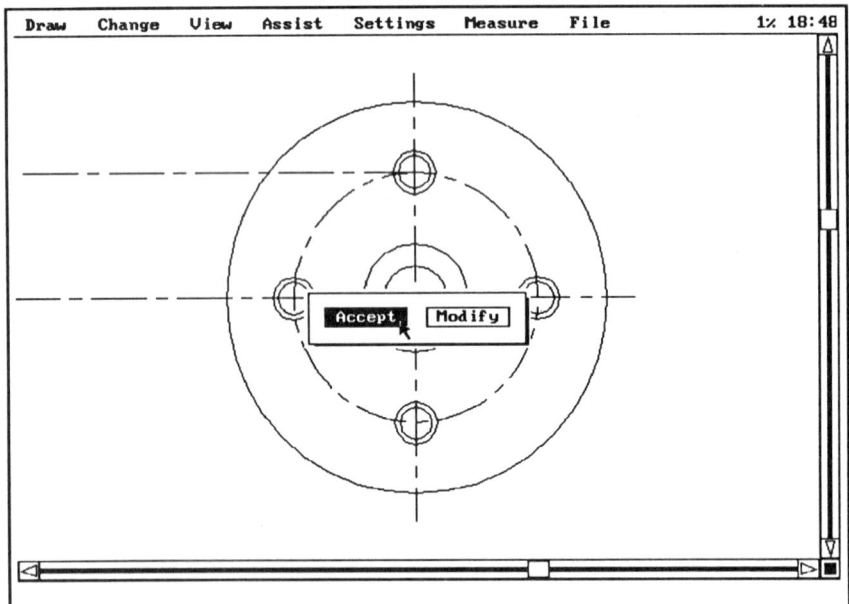

Adding Holes Using Ring Array

Ring Arrays

First change the layer back to 1 and make layer 10 invisible. We will come back to it later. Next, we need to create one of the small holes.

```
Pull down View Select Zoom Box          First corner 5,3. Second corner 11,9.

Pull down Assist Select Snap            Turn Snap off.
Pull down Settings Select Attach        Enable Intersect mode only, and turn Attach on.
Pull down Draw Select Circle
Center point:                           Intersection of circle center line and vertical
                                        center line.
Point on circle: R(0,.25)               Enter relative coordinate.
Center point:                           Select intersection point again.
Point on circle: R(0,.1875)             Relative coordinate.
```

Arrays 9-9

```
Pull down Change Select Ring Array
Select object:                    Use Window box to select both small circles.
Center point of array:            Select center of part.
Click Accept                      Select Accept from Accept/Modify dialogue box.
```

➥ *TIP: The AutoCAD ARRAY command controls both rectangular box arrays, and polar (ring) arrays. However, AutoCAD lacks the ability to fit objects into a specified rectangular array as AutoSketch can.*

Next, start the cross-sectional view. Just to be sure you're working on the same basis as our example, we'll place the first polyline point (the top left corner of the cross-section) at coordinates 1.500,8.250. Remember, use the drawing shown below for reference only, to help you draw the cross-section.

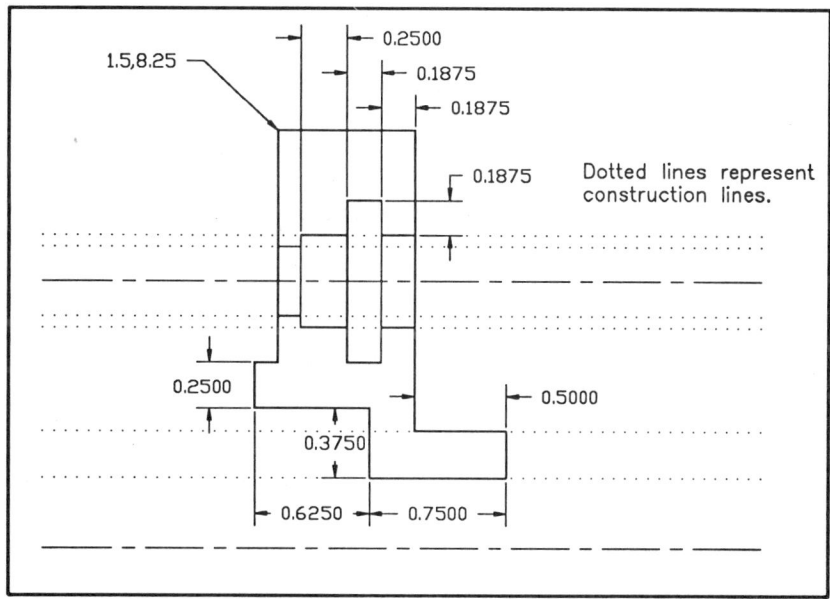

Dimensions for Drawing Top Half of Section

Drawing the Cross-Section View

```
Pull down View Select Zoom Box         First corner 0,3. Second corner 11,9.
Pull down Settings Select Attach       Quadrant and Attach Mode on. Everything else off.
Pull down Settings Select Color        Set color to cyan.
Pull down Draw Select Line             Draw construction lines from circles to the far left.
Pull down Settings Select Color        Set color back to black.
Pull down Assist Select Snap           Turn Snap on.
```

Turn Attach off.

```
Pull down Draw Select Line
First point: 1.5,8.25                    Absolute coordinates.
```

Complete the outline of one-half the cross-section. Look at the above illustration for dimensions.

```
Pull down Change Select Erase            Erase cyan construction lines.
Pull down Change Select Mirror
Select object:                           Select the top half of the section outline.
Base point:                              Place point on the center line.
Second point:                            Second point also on center line.
Pull down Draw Select Line               Draw three lines connecting the two section
                                         outlines.
```

Now that the section view is roughed in, it's time to do some editing and construction. First, draw the bore hole in the front view, then edit the section view to match. Next, add the visible channel lines to the front view and break out the portions for the bore hole. Finally, add the hidden lines to the front view and visible channel lines to the section view.

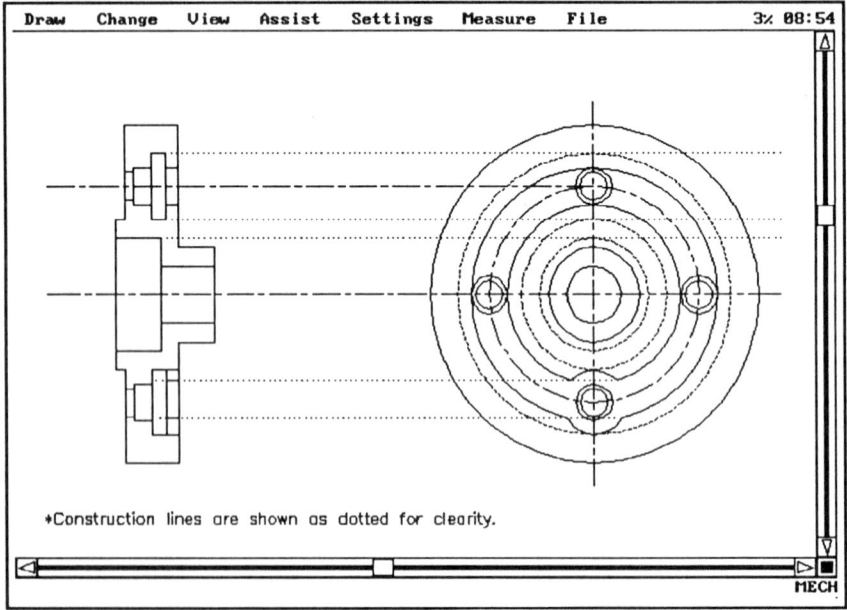

Machine Part After Editing

```
Pull down Draw Select Circle
Center Point:                              Pick the center of the two bottom small circles.
Point on circle: R(0,.4375)

Pull down Change Select Move               Move each channel line to the width of the bore hole.
Pull down Draw Select Circle
Center Point: 8,6
Point on circle: R(0,1.1875)
Pull down Draw Select Circle
Center Point: 8,6
Point on circle: R(0,1.6875)
```

Turn Snap off. Turn on Attach Mode intersection. All others off.

```
Pull down View Select Zoom Box             Zoom in.
Pull down Change Select Break              Break out channel lines from bore hole in front view.
Pull down Settings Select Color            Set color to cyan.
Pull down Draw Select Line                 Draw construction lines for hidden lines.
Pull down Settings Select Layer            Set layer to 3.
Pull down Settings Select Color            Set color to green.
Pull down Settings Select Line Type        Set line type to hidden.
Pull down Draw Select Circle               Draw the hidden lines in the front view.
Pull down Settings Select Layer            Set to 1.
Pull down Settings Select Line Type        Set to solid.
Pull down Settings Select Color            Set to cyan.
Pull down Draw Select Line                 Draw the construction lines for the channel lines
                                           in the section view.
Pull down Settings Select Color            Set to black.
Pull down Draw Select Line                 Draw the two visible channel lines in the section
                                           view.
Pull down Change Select Erase              Erase the cyan construction lines.
```

Break out the unnecessary portions of the center lines and copy the top center line to the bottom hole in the section view.

Pattern Fill

Various types of standard line patterns are used in technical drawing to represent specific types of physical entities. A stippled or dotted pattern might represent a swamp on a topographical map, and a diagonal hatch pattern represents a cross-sectional area in a mechanical drawing. Furthermore, various hatching patterns are used to denote specific types of materials.

The most natural method of applying a hatch pattern in AutoSketch is by means of the Pattern Fill command on the Draw menu. Pattern Fill doesn't actually fill in an area that you've already created. Instead, it creates a brand-new polyline and fills it with a hatch pattern, selected by the Pattern command on the Settings menu. Often, you'll find that it's convenient to create the outline of an object in one way, yet fill it in quite a different way.

There's a simple technique you can use to hatch areas on your drawing. We'll use this technique to hatch the cross-sectional view in our mechanical drawing.

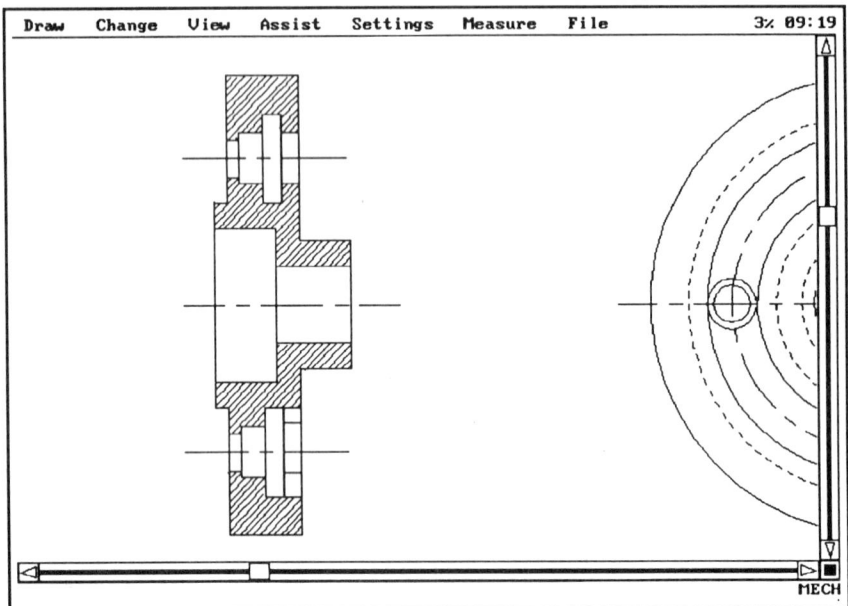

Hatching Section View With Pattern Fill

Hatching the Cross-Section View

```
Pull down View Select Zoom Limits          Get an overview of the drawing.
Pull down View Select Zoom Box             Zoom in on the entire cross-section.
Pull down Settings Select Color            Set color to magenta.
Pull down Settings Select Layer            Set layer to 4.
Pull down Settings Select Attach           Turn End Point, Intersect, and Node Point modes
                                           on. All others should be off.
```

Make sure that Attach is enabled.
Also, go to the Assist menu and turn Snap off; leave Ortho on.

```
Pull down Settings Select Pattern
Angle for Crosshatch 45                    Pattern is rotated at 45-degree angle.
Spacing between Lines 0.05
Click Double Hatch Area                    Turn off.
```

```
Click Boundary                          Turn Boundary off.
Click OK                                Close the dialogue box.
Pull down Draw Select Pattern Fill      Draw over the upper cross-section area.
Select Accept                           Select Accept from the Accept/Modify dialogue box.
```

Use Pattern Fill to trace each cross-section area.

```
Pull down File Select Save              Save your work.
```

Of course, it is much easier if you can simply use the Pattern Fill command instead of Polyline in the first place. But, as you've seen in this example, that's not always the simplest approach. It is often more convenient to draw a complex outline with other commands first, then hatch areas within the outline using Pattern Fill with Boundary turned off.

Each fill pattern is stored in a special file on disk with the extension PAT. Fill pattern selection follows the usual convention: the Pattern Settings dialogue box allows you to view the patterns as icons or by name alone. There are quite a few patterns included with AutoSketch. Also, since AutoSketch uses the same pattern files as AutoCAD, you'll find that many extra patterns are available commercially. You can even create your own pattern files, if you have the patience. (The procedure is a bit tedious, but it is amply explained in the appendix of your AutoSketch manual.)

The built-in patterns, including CRSSHTCH as well as the BLANK and SOLID patterns covered later, have slightly different options available than do the external, file-based patterns. CRSSHTCH expects you to specify the spacing between lines, while the external patterns ask for scale for pattern. The net result is roughly the same, but you should be aware that the numbers you enter will have slightly different effects, depending on which option is active. CRSSHTCH also provides a unique option of its own, Double Hatch Area. By default, CRSSHTCH consists of parallel lines; if you check Double Hatch Area, a second set of parallel lines is also drawn, perpendicular to the first set, creating a true cross-hatched grid pattern.

The Point option allows you to specify the origin point for the pattern. By default, all patterns are aligned to the (0,0) origin point. You will rarely need to change this. Once in a while, you may find that the placement of the pattern within an area is particularly inappropriate, and you can use Point to realign the pattern. However, bear in mind that *all* patterns on your drawing are aligned to the same point. Existing patterns will be redrawn if you select a new origin point.

Like other AutoSketch objects, patterns are drawn in the current color, on the current layer. All pattern options can be altered by the Property command on the Change menu. Just remember to set the appropriate options in the Property dialogue box on the Settings menu. Otherwise, pattern fill shapes behave just like polyline shapes, and can be edited in all the same ways.

Although you turned Boundary off in the exercise above, the hatch pattern you made still has a boundary (similar to a frame), only it is invisible.

An invisible boundary can be viewed by enabling the Frame option on the Assist menu. You can make hatch patterns themselves invisible by de-selecting the Fill option on the Assist menu. You can also place hatch patterns on separate layers, as we've done in the example. This is particularly helpful in keeping things straight when you're filling a separate outline with Boundary turned off.

> *TIP:* *AutoCAD's HATCH command, although similar to AutoSketch's Pattern Fill, has the ability to recognize composite objects and alternately hatch nested, closed regions. In order to do this though, the AutoCAD HATCH command does not use its own boundaries, but relies on existing objects to define the area to receive a pattern. As a result, AutoCAD does not enjoy the convenience of associative hatching as does AutoSketch. If the objects that contain a hatch pattern are modified, the resulting area must be rehatched.*

Chamfers, Fillets, and Rounds

Let's clean up some of the corners of the machine part by adding *chamfers* and *fillets*. In our example drawing, we'll chamfer the four outside corners and round off the 1.250" diameter hole cut into the part from the back side.

Chamfers

A chamfer is essentially a beveled edge. Showing a chamfer in an AutoSketch drawing is relatively easy, using the Chamfer command. Simply specify the lines to be chamfered, and AutoSketch does the rest.

Chamfers, Fillets, and Rounds 9–15

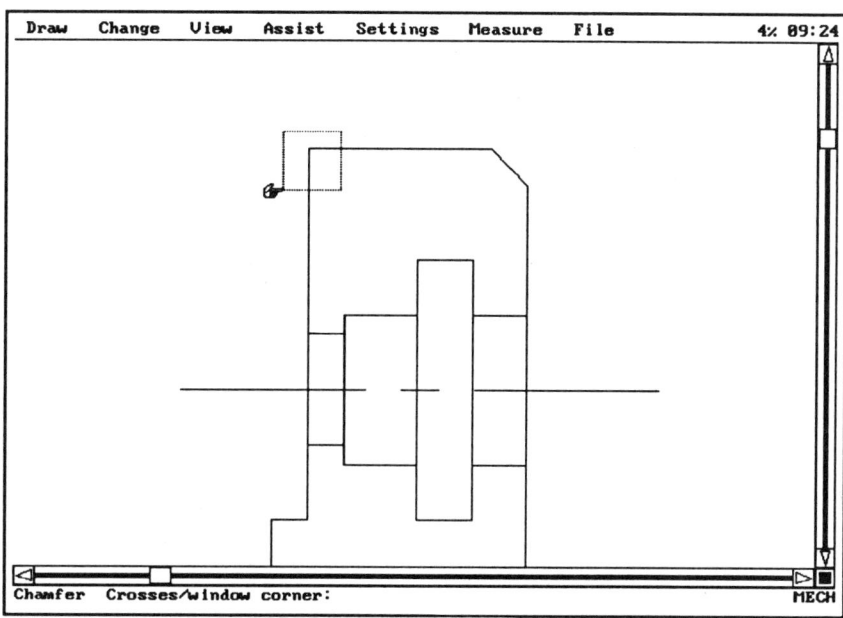

Zoom In and Chamfer the Corners

Adding Chamfers

Pull down **Settings** Select **Layer**	Make layer 1 active, layer 4 invisible.
Pull down **Settings** Select **Chamfer**	
First Chamfer Distance **0.125**	Type in chamfer distance.

The Second Chamfer Distance changes to match.

Click **OK**	
Pull down **View** Select **Zoom Box**	
First corner:	Zoom the top of the cross-section view.
Pull down **Change** Select **Chamfer**	
Select object(s):	Select upper right edge.
Select second segment:	Select top edge.

The chamfer is drawn in.

Select object(s):   Place a Crosses box around top left corner.

Zoom out and chamfer the bottom corners using the same process.

By default, AutoSketch provides 45-degree chamfers, automatically changing the second chamfer distance to match the value you enter for the first chamfer distance. You can enter a different value for the second distance, if you need a different angle. If you do select different first and second chamfer distances, you should select the two lines to be chamfered separately, rather than using the Crosses/window box. That's how you tell AutoSketch which line should be chamfered to the first distance, and which to the second.

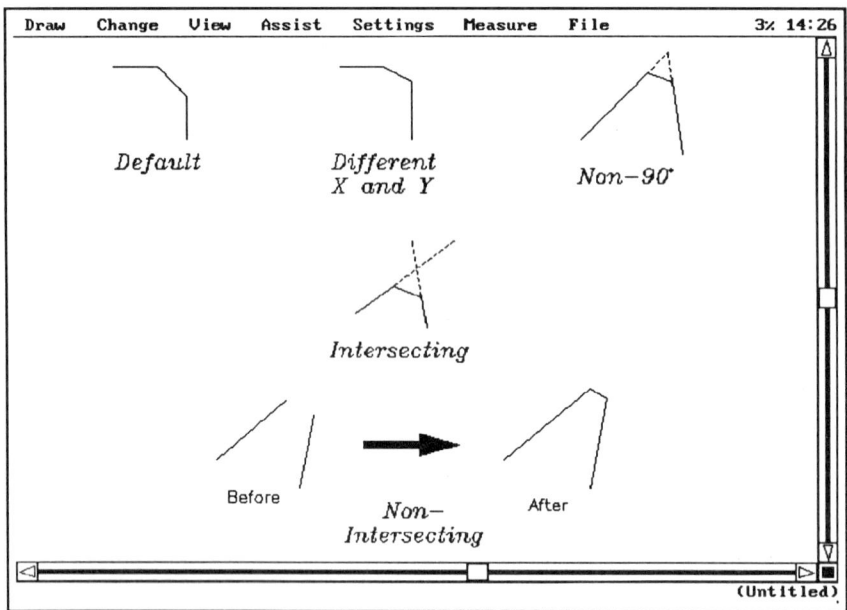

Chamfer Variations

Lines, or other objects, are not always broken back to the chamfer distance. If you try to chamfer lines that don't actually intersect, AutoSketch will extend them until they do, and then insert the appropriate chamfer at the intersection point.

➥ *TIP: Setting both first and second chamfer distances to zero creates a zero-length chamfer — essentially a sharp corner. The effect of such a chamfer will depend on the objects to which it is applied. If they already meet at a corner, there will be no apparent change. If the two objects don't actually meet, they will be extended until they intersect. If you seldom or never draw chamfers, leaving Chamfer set to zero distances can be a handy tool for quickly and accurately cleaning up intersections.*

Between most objects, the chamfer itself is simply a short line, and can be manipulated as such, using any of the usual Change commands. However, chamfering a polyline actually adds another segment to the polyline; it can't be removed, although the complete polyline can still be edited as usual.

There are a number of object combinations that cannot be chamfered. Most obviously, you cannot chamfer parallel lines. As you saw in the above example, you can chamfer corners within a polyline. If you chamfer corners of a box, AutoSketch automatically converts it to a polyline.

Fillets and Rounds

A rounded interior corner is called a *fillet*, while a rounded exterior corner is known as a *round*. AutoSketch provides a Fillet command, which is very similar in operation to Chamfer: you set the radius and then pick the two lines to which the fillet should be applied.

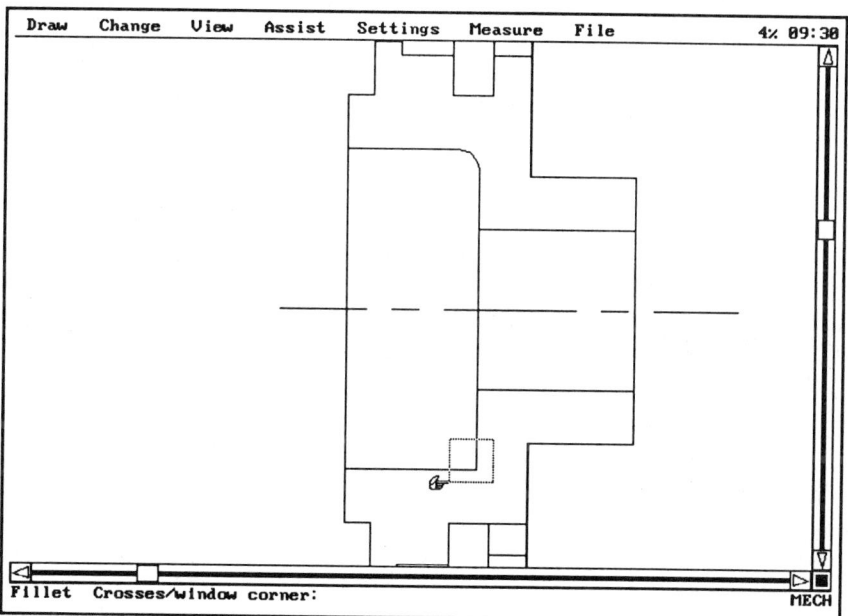

Filleting the Interior Corner

Creating Fillets and Rounds

```
Pull down View Select Zoom Limits
Pull down View Select Zoom Box
First corner:                          Zoom the middle of the section view.
Pull down Settings Select Fillet
Fillet Radius .09375                   Set radius to .09375.
Click OK
Pull down Change Select Fillet
Select object(s):                      Select one of the inside lines.
Select second object:                  Select the short outside line.
```

```
Select object(s):                    Use a Crosses/window box to select one of
                                     the inside corners.
```

Fillet the other outside edge and interior corner.
You'll have to stretch or redraw the outside line, which no longer connects to the filleted corners.
Now make the hatching layer visible, and layer 1 invisible. Apply matching fillets and chamfers to the pattern fill areas. Make layer 1 visible again when done.

```
Pull down File Select Save           Save the drawing.
```

Fillet entities are similar to chamfers. If you fillet two lines, the fillet itself is a short arc, and it can be edited separately. If you fillet two segments of a polyline, the fillet is inserted as an arc segment of the polyline.

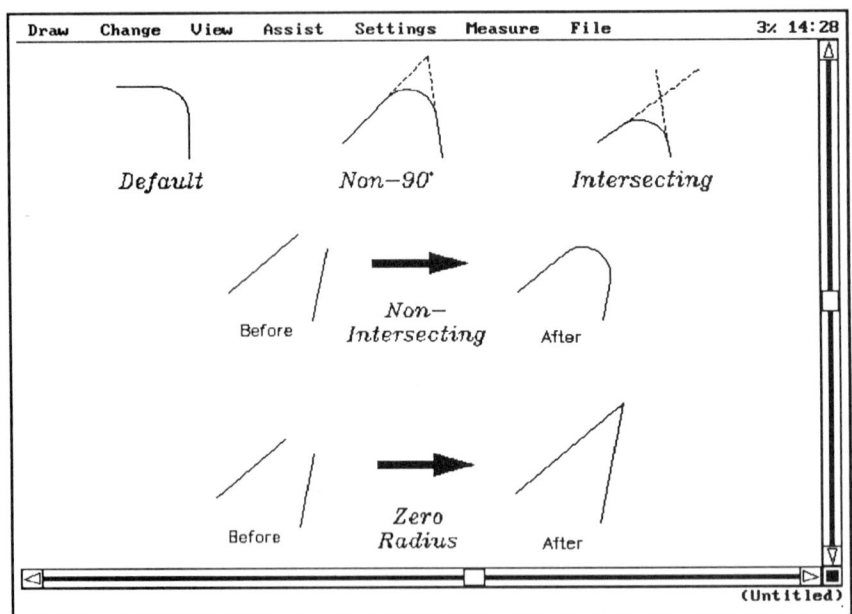

Fillets and Rounds

For both fillet and chamfer, you can either select the two lines — or polyline segments — separately, or you can use a Crosses/window box to select both at the same time. Avoid using the Crosses/window box if there's any chance of catching extraneous lines; these will confuse the Fillet or Chamfer command, resulting in either an incorrect result, or a dialogue box warning that you've selected an incorrect combination of objects.

As with Chamfer, you cannot fillet parallel lines. Also, there's a limit on the size of the fillet arc relative to the size and spacing of the selected objects. If there's no room to insert the fillet, you'll get a warning dialogue box. A zero-radius Fillet setting behaves similarly to a zero-length Chamfer, producing a sharp corner. This is an easy way to get exact intersections between objects.

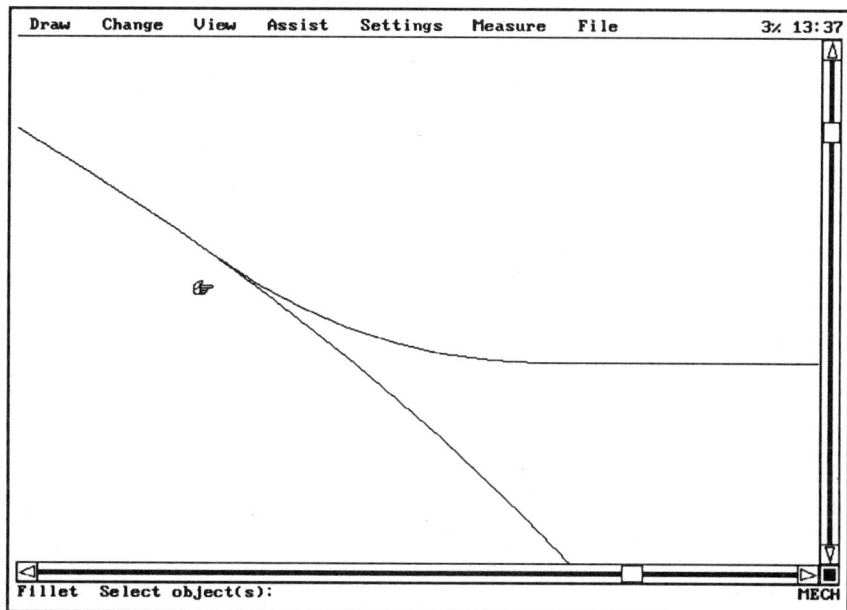

Filleting the Flange

Filleting the Flange

Pull down **Settings** Select **Layer**   Set layer to 10 and make it visible.
Pull down **View** Select **Zoom Limits**
Pull down **View** Select **Zoom Box**   Zoom into the gap between the flange and the
                                                 big circle.
Pull down **Settings** Select **Fillet**   Set radius to .5.
Pull down **Change** Select **Fillet**   Select horizontal flange line, then big circle.

Erase the flange or make Layer 10 invisible again.

Polyline Width and Fills

Until now, we've been working entirely with the default line width corresponding to one dot on your monitor screen, or one pen stroke on your plotter. This suffices for most technical work where a thin line is the most accurate. However, various line widths can be used to distinguish different types of drawing elements, in much the same way as Line Type.

One of the most powerful features added to AutoSketch version 3.0 is the ability to vary polyline width. The width is set from the Polyline command on the Settings menu. You can draw thick, heavy lines or even create wide hatched "lines" filled with the hatch pattern of your choice.

➥ *NOTE: If you are still using a version of AutoSketch prior to version 3.0, no control over polyline width is available. You must create wide lines by the more laborious expedient of drawing closely spaced parallel lines, offset by a distance equivalent to one pen width on your plotting device. An example of this procedure is included in the appendix.*

In our machine part drawing, we will add a section line to the front view. Such a line indicates the position of the particular "cut" that would produce the cross-sectional view of the part. The section line should be three times thicker than the rest of the lines.

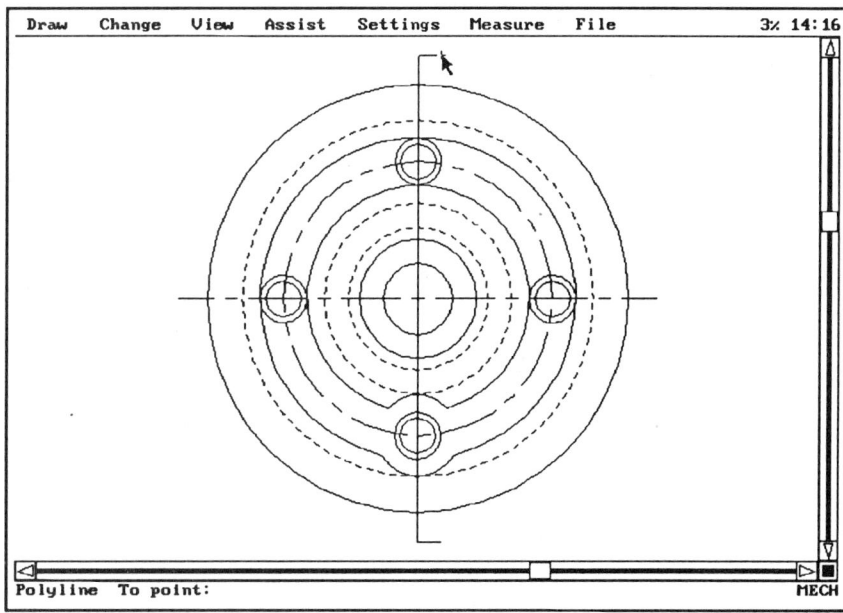

Adding a Wide Section Line

Line Weights

Ensure that Snap is turned on, layer 4 is current, and the color is magenta.

Pull down **View** Select **Zoom Limits**	Zoom back to get some elbow room.
Pull down **Settings** Select **Polyline**	
Polyline Width **.024**	Assumes a pen width of .008" (3 x .008 = .024).
Click **Solid Fill**	Select this option, then OK.
Pull down **Change** Select **Erase**	Erase the vertical center line.
Pull down **Draw** Select **Polyline**	Draw in the section line where the center line used to be.
Pull down **File** Select **Save**	Save your work.

There are three fill options in the Polyline dialogue box. The one we used above — Solid Fill — creates a solid line of the selected width, in the current drawing color. Blank Fill creates an outline of the selected width. These outlines could plot as solid filled, if you pick a polyline width finer than your plotting or printing device can handle. Pattern Fill creates an open outline, but it treats it like areas created with the Pattern Fill command on the Draw menu.

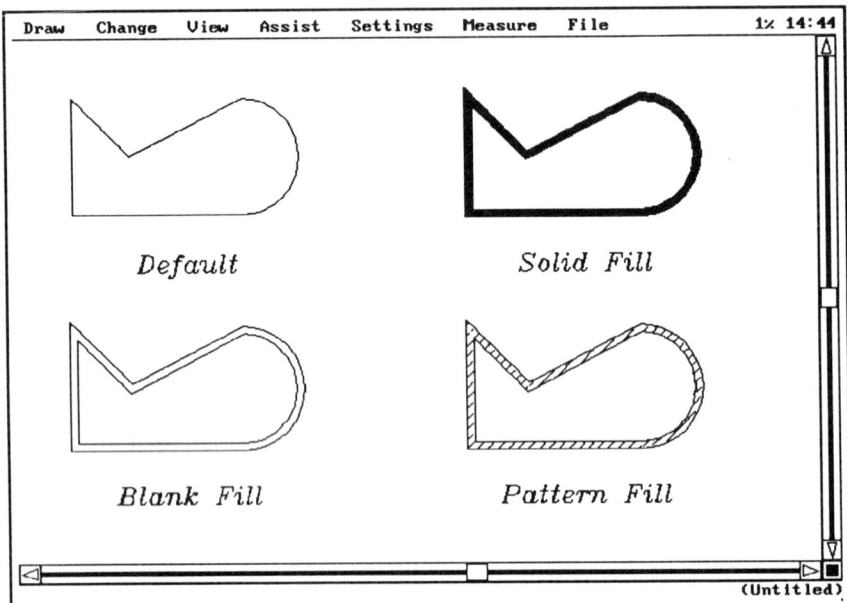

Polyline Fill Options

If you click on Change Pattern in the Polyline dialogue box, AutoSketch pops up the same Pattern Settings dialogue box you'd get by selecting the Pattern option on the Settings menu. You can fill wide polylines in exactly the same ways discussed earlier under *Hatching*. In fact, options set using the Pattern command on the Settings menu affect objects drawn using either Pattern Fill or Polyline.

The default line width for polylines is zero. To disable wide polyline drawing, use the Polyline command on the Settings menu to set the width back to this value. Note that a change in Polyline settings while you are actually in the process of drawing a polyline will have no immediate effect. You must re-select Polyline from the Draw menu for the new width settings to be recognized. This means that you cannot vary line width within a single polyline.

AutoSketch can vary line width only for polyline objects, which, of course, can contain both straight lines and circular arcs. Thus, you can create wide straight lines or even circles by using Polyline in Arc mode to draw a closed arc. But if you ever happen to need a wide curve, you'll have to use a procedure similar to that detailed in the appendix, offsetting multiple parallel copies of the curved line, so that they give the appearance of extra width.

Attach behaves somewhat unusually with wide polylines. When attaching to a wide polyline, you must click on the visible outline of the polyline. The actual attachment points will be located in the middle of the polyline as though there were a frame running through it.

A particularly important characteristic of wide polylines is that their width is in actual drawing units and will plot wider if you change the plotting scale. AutoSketch's default, zero-width lines, will always plot as a single pen stroke on a plotter, or a minimum thickness line on a printer. A wide polyline, on the other hand, will keep its dimensions like any other component of the drawing. You can verify this easily: try zooming in on the middle of the front view. The polyline you just drew will be magnified to much more than three times the width of the other lines, which remain as thin as ever.

This behavior is highly advantageous if you use wide polylines to represent actual objects within a drawing. For example, in a space plan, you could use wide polylines for the walls. If you plot a portion of the drawing at double its original scale, the walls will still be sized correctly. However, if you use a wide polyline to draw non-scaled drafting symbols, such as the section line in our mechanical example, the line will be abnormally thick if you plot at a larger scale than the line was intended for. Polyline widths should always be set according to the final plotted scale.

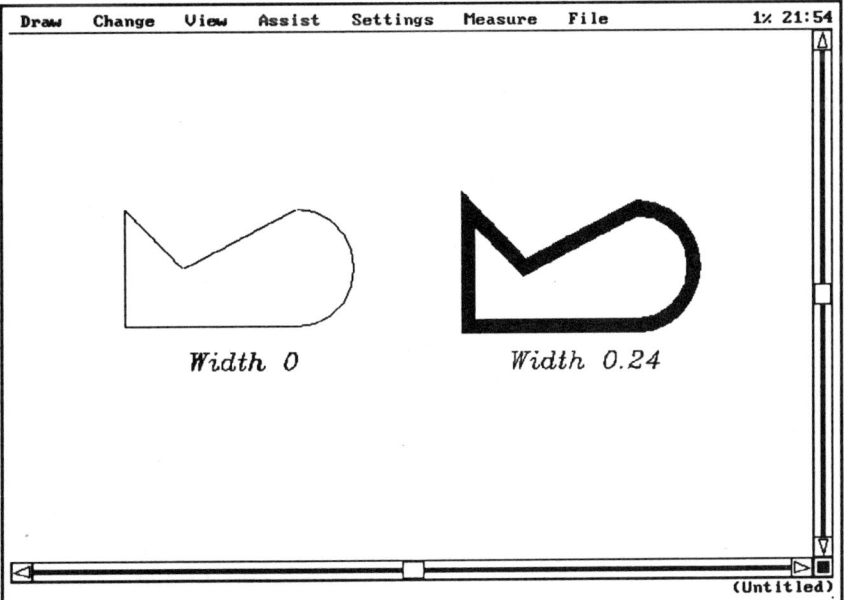

Triple-Width Polyline at Zoom Limits

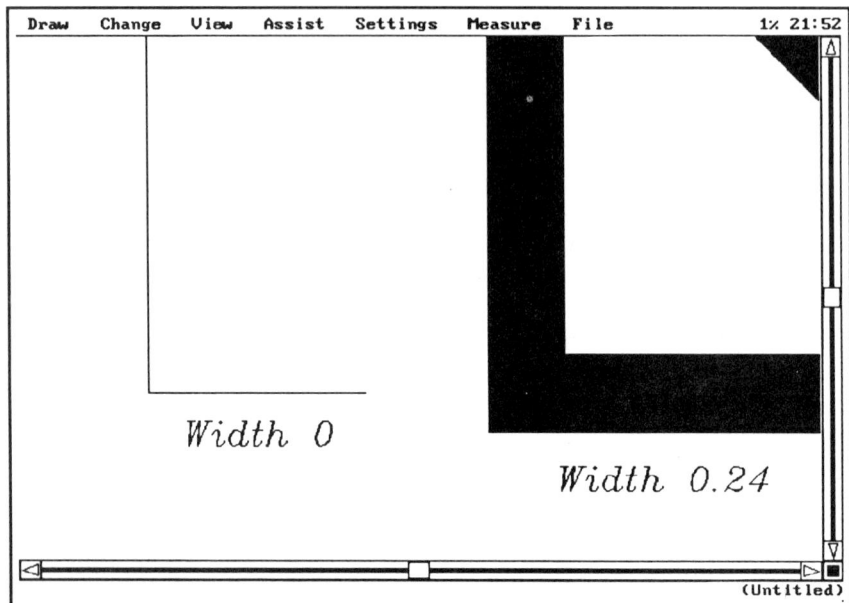

Triple-Width Polyline Close Up

You can easily change the width of existing polylines using the Property command on the Change menu. The Property command on the Settings menu lets you enable Polyline Width as one of the properties that will be affected by the Change command (in addition to properties such as color, line type, or layer). For information on line types, see Chapter 5, *Drawing Effects and Setup*.

If you want to change the width of drawing lines that were not created with the Polyline command, your best bet is to "trace" over them using a polyline. With practice you'll learn what Attach modes to turn off and on under different circumstances. When inserting a line segment it's best to have End Point on, and when tracing circles and arcs you should have Center on.

➥ *TIP: The AutoCAD PLINE command, in addition to making polylines like AutoSketch, has the ability to apply line types to polylines and taper them between vertices. AutoCAD polyline vertices may be edited individually, joined with other polylines, lines, and arcs into a single polyline, and have a curve or spline fitted to them. Also, they may be filleted and chamfered, whereas AutoSketch's cannot, and AutoCAD will calculate the area and perimeter of an existing polyline. However, an AutoCAD polyline cannot be filled with a pattern.*

If you feel like practicing now, try changing the line weight of some of the object lines in the front view of the machine part.

Command Practice

These advanced drawing commands have numerous options. The only way to get a proper feel for all the combinations is to experiment with them. Try them in a new SCRATCH drawing.

PATTERN FILL. Try creating various solid filled shapes: a square, a triangle, a circle, and so on. Try overlapping filled shapes of different colors and see what happens.

PATTERN FILL. Draw some shapes using various hatch patterns. Also, try giving some of your solid filled shapes from the previous exercise a hatch pattern, with the Change Properties command. Experiment with various pattern scale settings. You'll find that you can dramatically change the appearance of a pattern by varying its angle and scale.

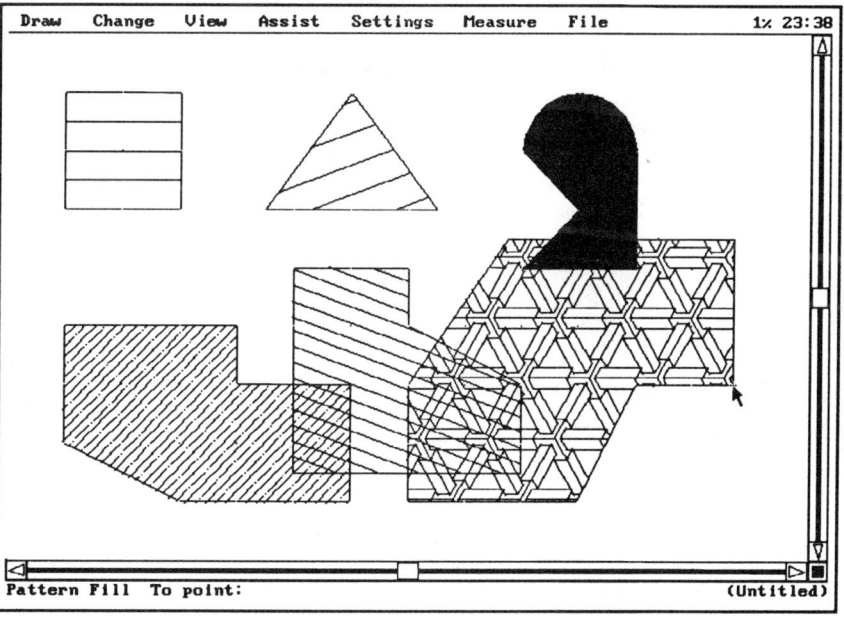

Various Pattern Fill Effects

PATTERN FILL. Use the Pattern Fill command to draw a filled circle. First, draw a circle with a radius of two units to use as a guide. Select Pattern Fill, and press <CTRL-F1> to enter Arc mode. Select a start point at the nine o'clock position on the circle. The next point on the arc goes at twelve o'clock. Finish the arc with a point at three o'clock. Then draw a second arc, placing points at six and nine o'clock.

PATTERN FILL. How would you create a filled shape with a hole in it like a flat washer? One easy way is to do it in two halves, as shown in the following illustration. Unless you are using solid fill, however, this will show unwanted horizontal lines where the halves join. A better technique would be to use a wide polyline. Draw the arcs just as described in the previous exercise, but remember to draw on a radius smaller than the desired final radius by one-half the polyline width.

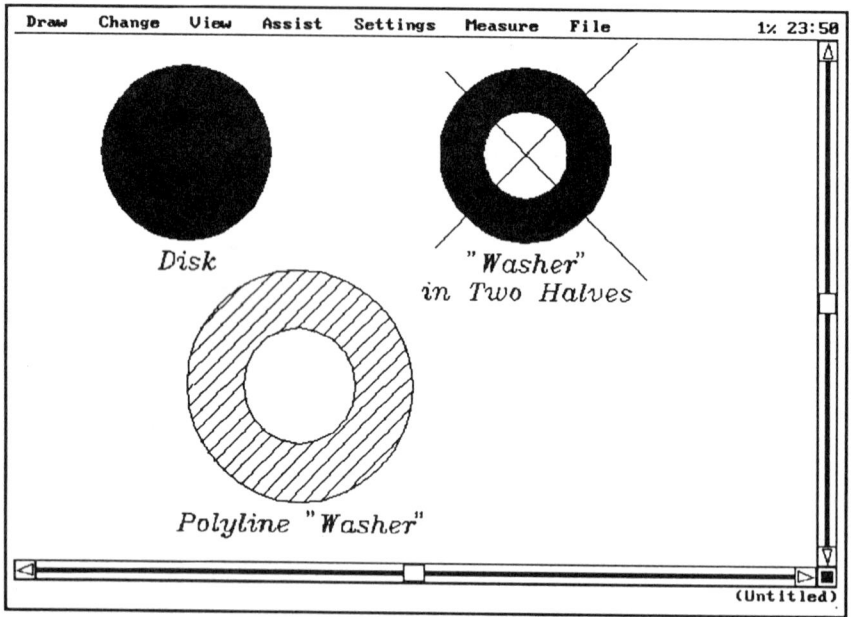

Filled Circles

ROUNDS AND CHAMFERS. Draw two lines at 45 degrees to each other, with the two nearer ends two drawing units apart. Chamfer the two lines. Notice that AutoSketch extends the lines as far as necessary, then adds the chamfer line to connect them. Try the same thing with a round.

BOX ARRAY. Draw a one-unit box. Create a box array with four items, and a spacing between items of one unit. Now try to do the same thing with a 45-degree baseline angle. Notice that although you are still asked to specify the spacing by positioning duplicate objects horizontally and vertically, the spacings are then applied at 45 degrees. You may find it easier to get accurate spacing if you disable the Point option and enter the spacing values numerically.

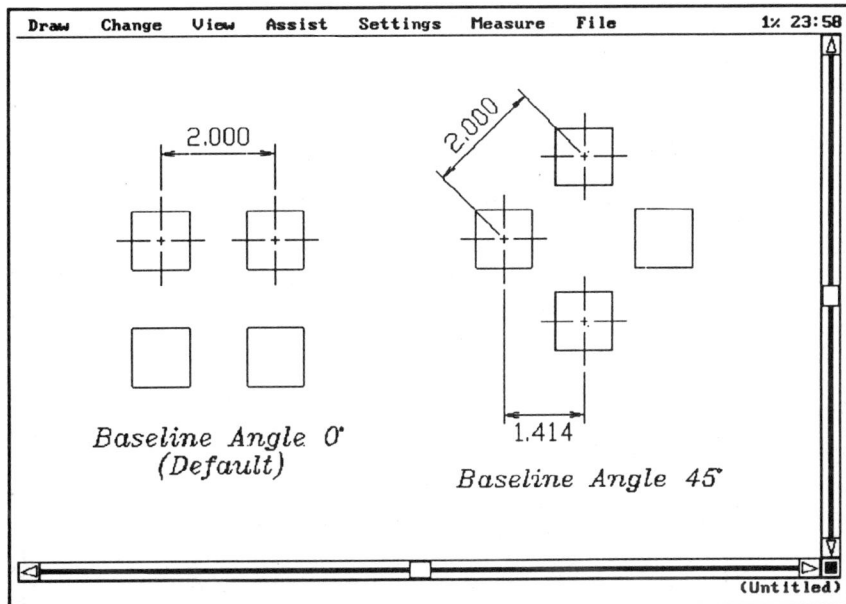

Effect of Baseline Angle on Item Spacing

RING ARRAY. How would you create a five-pointed star? The Ring Array command can help. Draw a base circle of two units radius. Draw a short, vertical line crossing the top of the circle at the twelve o'clock position. Use Ring Array to duplicate this short line, placing the center of the array at the center of the circle. When asked to accept or modify, select Modify. Change the number of items to five, then select OK. Your circle is now divided into five equal arcs. Connect the five intersection points with a polyline, using Attach in Intersect mode. You can then erase the base circle and the five short lines.

WIDE POLYLINE. Set polyline width to 0.5, with blank fill. Draw a slightly open box using the Polyline command, and then a fully closed one. Notice that when you complete the box, the edges of the wide polyline merge, producing a "picture frame" effect. If you leave the ends open, short perpendicular edges are added to close the polyline.

WIDE POLYLINE. Set polyline width to 0.2, with blank fill. Try creating a simple floor plan as shown in the illustration. You'll find this approach fast and easy. However, try cleaning up one of the wall intersections. You'll find that the edges of a wide polyline can't be broken individually. Both edges break together, and a new perpendicular edge is added to close the open ends of the polyline. Using the Change Property command, give the wall a solid fill. Note that with solid fill, the crossing edges in a T junction are no longer visible. However, such wide solid lines are not appropriate for all types of work.

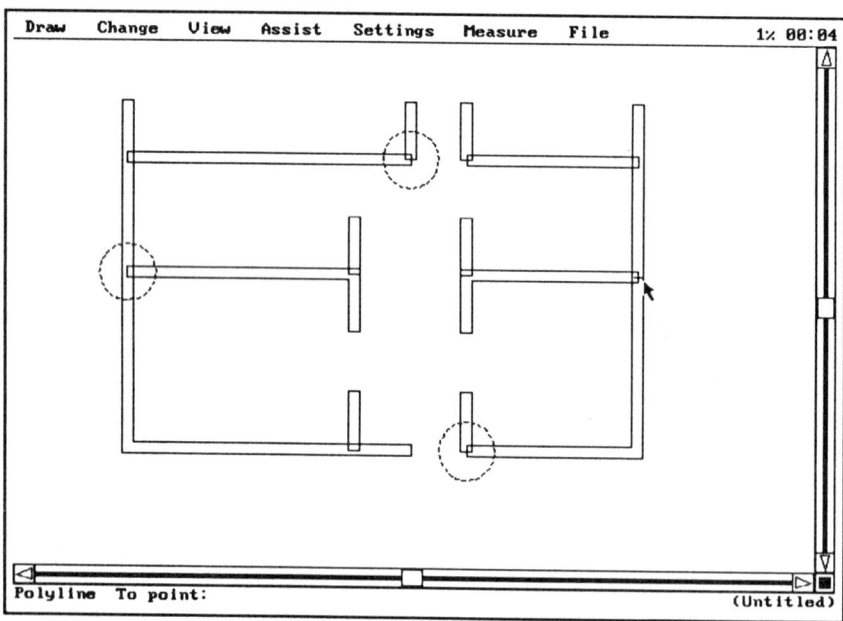

Simple Space Plan Using Wide Polylines

Summary

In this chapter, we've looked at some very high-level commands. These allow you to quickly create compound objects that would be tedious to draw manually. For example, cross-hatching a shape by drawing many individual lines could take hours. Similarly, you could duplicate objects by using Copy, but the two array commands make it easy to get many duplicates with accurate spacing. You could create fillets, rounds, and chamfers using the Polyline command and a lot of patience. Finally, you could create wide lines by placing many single lines side by side, but the polyline width options make this unnecessary — and provide extra power as well.

By now you have seen virtually all the drawing and editing commands that AutoSketch has to offer. The next chapter deals with measurement commands, which allow you to find exact positions and distances, and to add professional markings to the drawing.

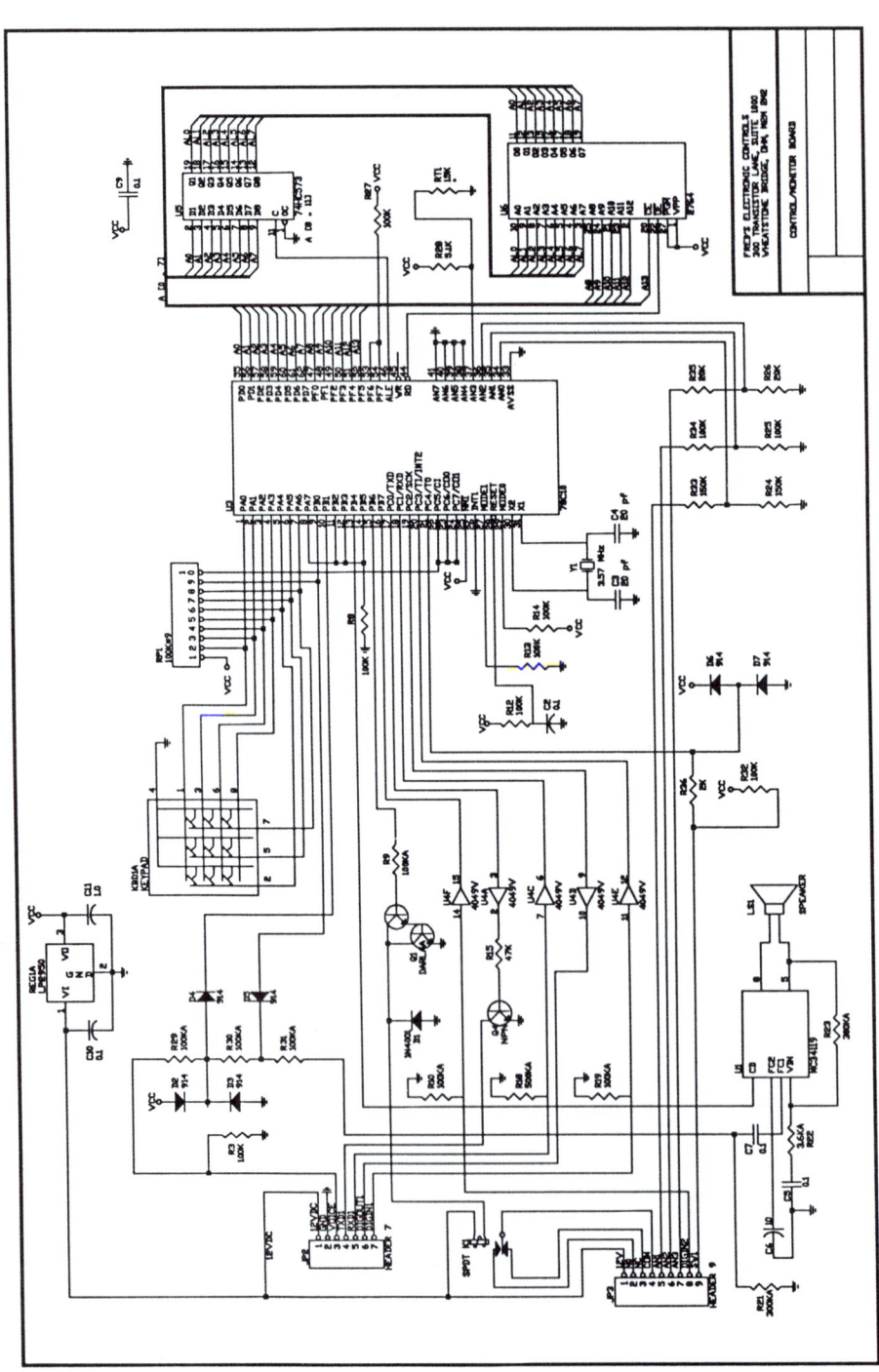

Control/Monitor Board, Courtesy Fred's Electronic Controls

Chapter 10

Technical Drawing Aids

This chapter deals with measurement. The AutoSketch Measure menu provides a number of useful tools to help you find out how large objects are, how far apart they are, their area, the angle between lines, and more. This same menu also provides dimensioning capabilities so you can place dimension markings right on your drawings.

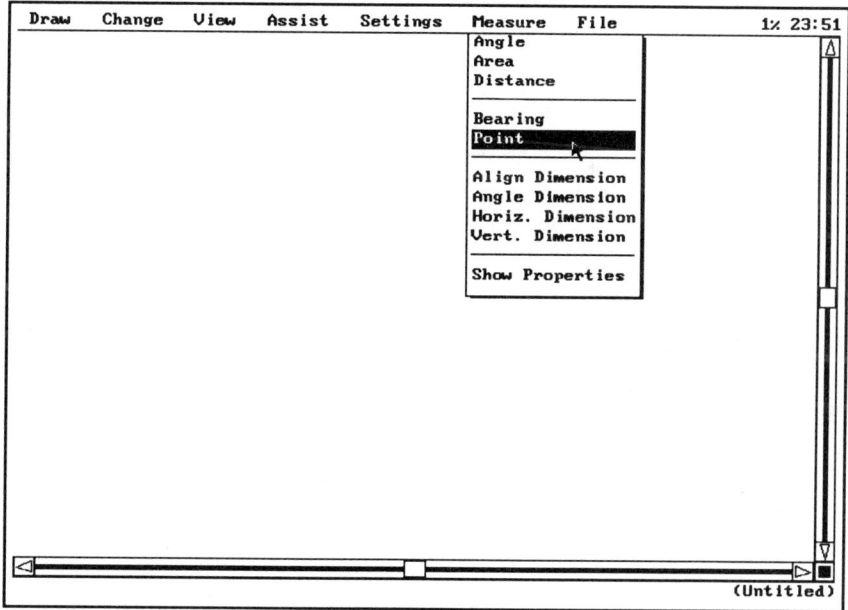

The Measure Menu

We've left these commands until last because you're not likely to need them in every drawing. For instance, AutoSketch lets you instantly find the area and perimeter of any polygon shape that you've drawn. This is a powerful capability, but it's not essential to most drawings.

Dimensioning, on the other hand, is crucial to many types of technical work. The dimension commands available in AutoSketch are particularly powerful and worth a close look.

Point

As you work with AutoSketch, you'll often want to know the exact coordinates of certain points. Using the Point command, you can get a report of your pointer's coordinates on the screen. AutoSketch will even keep pace with the pointer as you move it around, giving you a running readout of the X and Y values. When you click the pointer, AutoSketch pops up a dialogue box presenting the exact coordinates of the selected point.

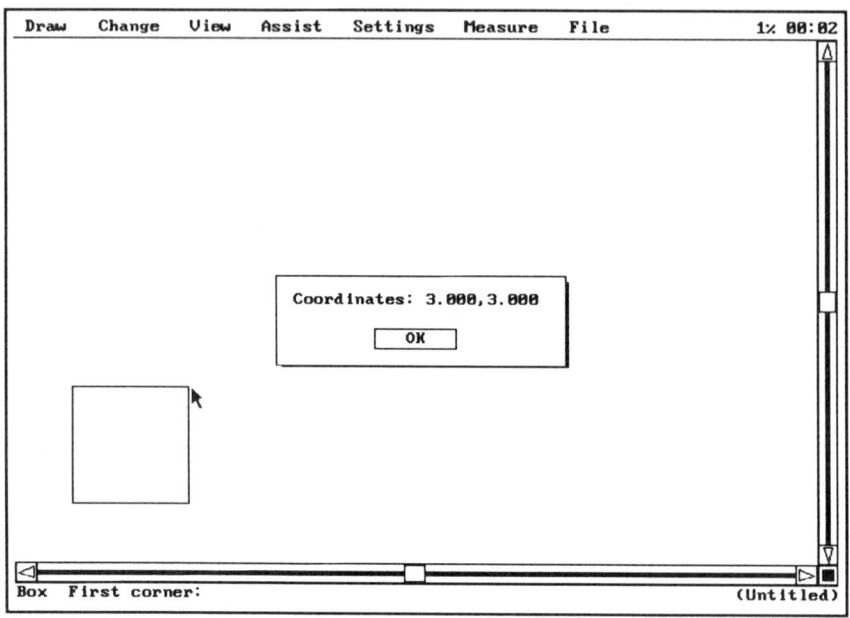

Getting the Coordinates of a Point

Point Coordinate Display

Pull down **File** Select **New**	Start with a new file.
Pull down **Assist** Select **Attach**	Turn Attach on.
Pull down **Settings** Select **Attach**	Turn all modes except End Point off.
Pull down **Draw** Select **Box**	Draw a 2-unit square box.
First corner: **1,1**	Absolute coordinates.
Second corner: **R(2,2)**	Relative coordinates.
Pull down **Measure** Select **Point**	Activates the command.

The command line displays your pointer coordinates.

Point coordinates:	Pick a corner point of the box.

The Coordinates dialogue box gives exact point coordinates.

`<ENTER>`	Same as selecting OK to close dialogue box.

Notice that if you pick a point close to a corner of the box you drew, the dialogue box will show the coordinates of the corner of the box. Since the End Point attach mode is in effect, the point you select is actually the endpoint of one of the lines that comprise the sides of the box. The ability to apply Attach mode to point selection sets the Point command apart from the Coords display, which we will look at next. For more on the available Attach modes, see Chapter 6, *Advanced Drawing Tools*.

Be sure not to confuse the Measure Point inquiry command with the Draw Point command, which actually draws a point.

The Point dialogue box is the easiest way to find the coordinates of a particular drawing point, especially if you use Attach with an appropriate Attach mode so that you can be sure your pointer has caught the point you're after.

By default, point coordinates are shown to three decimal places. You can have AutoSketch display up to six digits of precision, or none at all. Decimal display is controlled by the Units command on the Settings menu — discussed later in this chapter.

Once you've specified a point and the coordinate values have appeared in the Point dialogue box, you may want to note them down. Once you click on OK, the dialogue box will vanish and AutoSketch will drop you back into whatever command mode you were in before you selected Point.

➥ *TIP*: *AutoCAD's equivalent of the Measure Point command is the ID command.*

Coordinate Display

In addition to the Point command, AutoSketch also gives you a means of continuously displaying pointer coordinates, through the Coords command on the Assist menu. With Coords mode turned on, the pointer's X,Y coordinates will display on the prompt line at the bottom of the screen. The X and Y numbers will change constantly as you move the pointer across the screen.

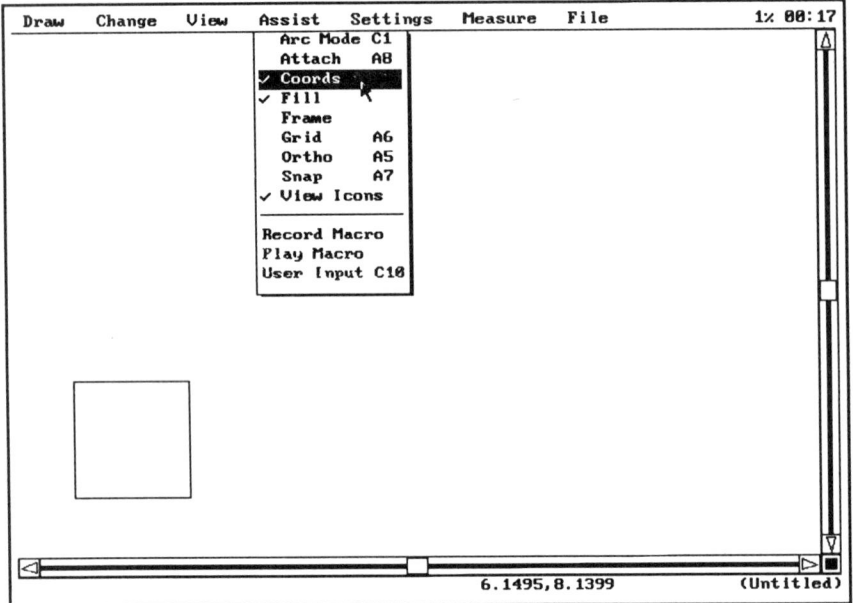

Coordinate Display

Coordinates Display

Pull down **Assist** Select **Coords**   Turn on coordinate display.

Move the pointer around the screen and observe the numbers changing on the prompt line.

Pull down **Assist** Select **Snap**   Coordinate values change in even snap increments.
Pull down **Measure** Select **Point**   Coords coordinate display is replaced by
Point command coordinates.

Select a point and end the Point command.
Coords display returns.

Since Coords display does not involve selection of any points on the screen, it can't utilize Attach settings. When combined with the Snap command, Coords can make it easy to quickly zero in on a particular point, even on a large, complex drawing. However, with proper settings, Attach and Snap are much easier and more reliable ways to ensure accuracy.

Bearing

The term *bearing* is usually associated with the use of a magnetic compass. Instead of the familiar north, south, east, and west, AutoSketch bearings are displayed according to the polar coordinate system with 0 degrees instead of east, 90 degrees pointing straight up or to the north, and so on.

After activating the Bearing command, you are prompted to pick the bearing base point. Once the base point has been chosen, Bearing displays the polar angle between the base point and your pointer. For instance, if you pick a point directly above the base point, you'll get a bearing value of 90. If desired, you can select a specific point and a dialogue box will appear giving the point's bearing. As with Point coordinates, bearings are shown to three decimal places by default.

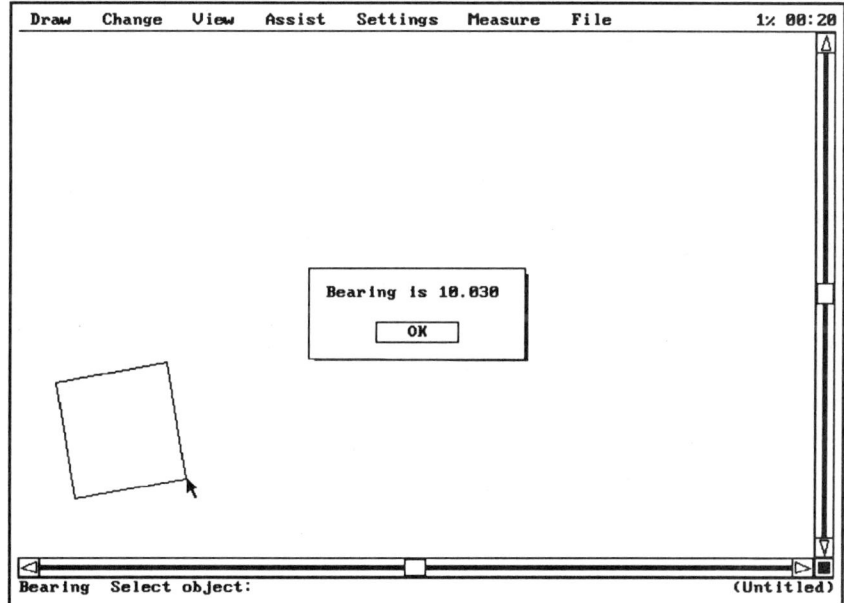

Measuring a Bearing

Bearing Display

```
Turn off Ortho and Snap
Pull down Change Select Rotate            Rotate the box you drew earlier.
Pull down Measure Select Bearing
Base point:                               Pick a corner of the box.
```

The prompt line gives a readout of pointer bearing relative to the base point.

`Enter point:`	Select an adjacent corner.

A dialogue box appears, giving exact bearing to the selected point.

`Click OK`	Click the OK box or press <ENTER>.

In practice, the Point command best supports conventional Cartesian keyboard coordinate entry. The Bearing command is most useful for polar coordinate entry.

Distance, Angle, and Area

These three AutoSketch measurement commands are quite straightforward. Their usefulness will depend on the type of work you do, and how well you set up your drawings. If you want to get accurate distance or area measurements from a drawing, you have to create an accurate drawing — one that is either actual size or to scale. Otherwise, measurements are only meaningful in the drawing, not in the real world.

Distance

If you work to scale, the Distance command can be handy. Distance reports the number of drawing units between any two points. Even if your drawing has extensive dimension markings (which we'll be covering next), you may still need specific, unmarked measurements.

After selecting the Distance command, pick the starting and ending points for the measurement. A dialogue box displays the distance, applying the current Ortho, Snap, and Attach settings.

Distance, Angle, and Area 10–7

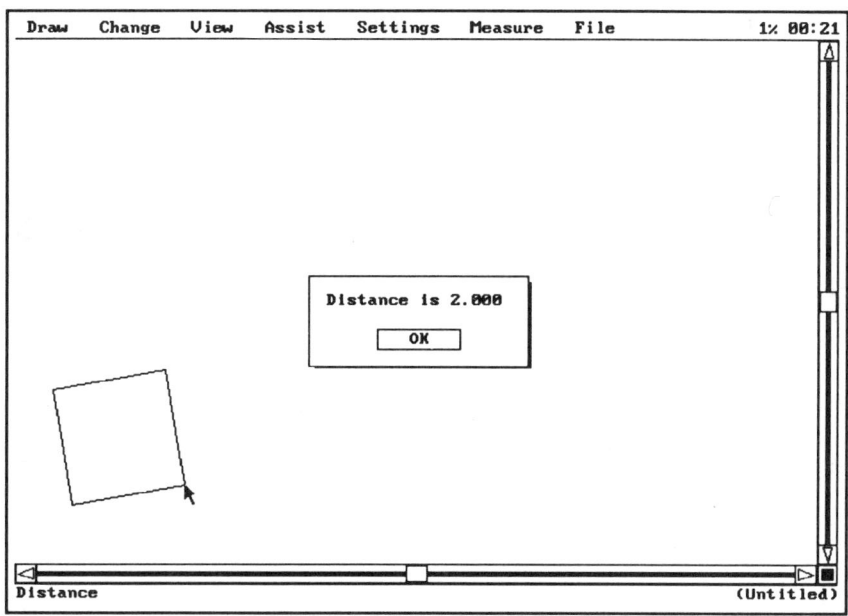

Measuring a Distance

Measuring a Distance

Pull down **Measure** Select **Distance**
From point: Pick a corner of the box.
To point: Pick another corner.

A dialogue box shows "Distance is 2.000."

Click **OK**   Click the OK box or press <ENTER>.

➡ *TIP: The AutoCAD DIST command reports the distance between two specified points and also displays 3D angle information about the points.*

Angle

The Angle command works like an electronic protractor to measure the size of any angle on your drawing.

After selecting the Angle command, you'll be prompted to select an angle base point. Select the vertex of the angle you wish to measure. A rubberband line follows the pointer, extending from the base point. Click the pointer on the base line of the angle to be measured. A rubberband line will continue to connect the pointer to the base point.

Click the pointer on the other line of the angle. A dialogue box will display the actual angle in degrees.

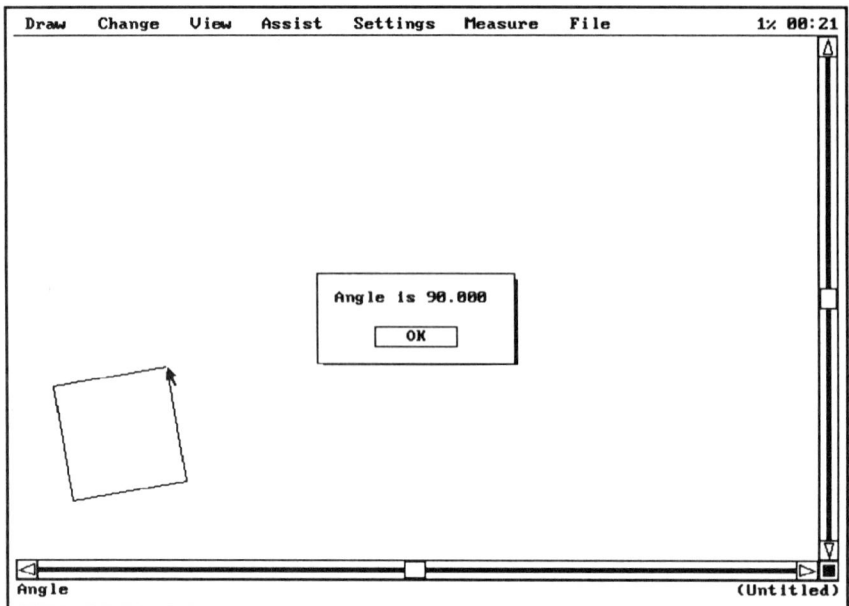

Measuring an Angle

Measuring an Angle

```
Pull down Measure Select Angle
Base Point:                         Pick lower right corner of the box.
First Direction:                    Pick lower left corner.
Second Direction:                   Pick upper right corner.
```

A dialogue box appears, stating that the angle is 90 degrees.

```
Click OK                            Or press <ENTER>.
```

Area and Perimeter

You are not likely to need area and perimeter readings very often. You might, for instance, draw a map of your irregularly shaped farm, then use Area to determine the actual number of acres you own. As with Distance, this command will work only if your drawing is drawn to scale.

Pull down the Measure menu, select Area, then select a point along the perimeter of the area to be measured. The first point is marked by a large X, in the same color used by rubberband or ghost lines. Continue to select points along the perimeter. Each additional point is marked by a smaller X. Close the perimeter by reselecting the first point. As soon as all the points are selected and you close the perimeter, a dialogue box appears displaying the area and perimeter of the enclosed shape.

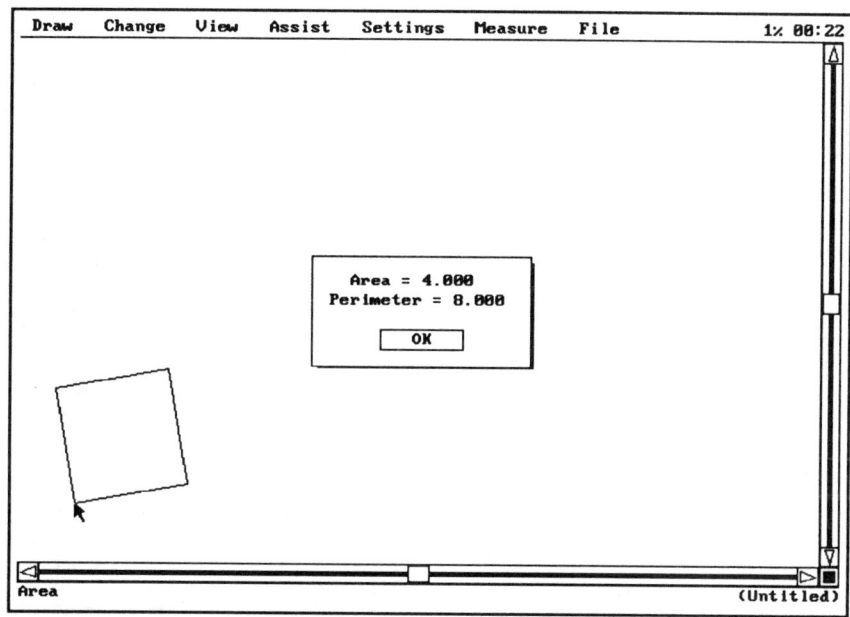

Measuring Area and Perimeter

Measuring Area or Perimeter

```
Pull down Measure Select Area
Area First perimeter point:            Lower left corner of the box.
```

A colored X-mark appears at each point as it is marked.

```
Next point:                            Lower right corner.
Next point:                            Upper right corner.
Next point:                            Upper left corner.
Next point:                            Lower left corner, closes the perimeter.
```

Dialogue box displays area as 4.000 and perimeter as 8.000.

```
Click OK
```

To get the area or perimeter of a curve, you will have to approximate it with a number of closely spaced points. The larger the number of points you use, the more accurate your measurement.

➥ *TIP*: *AutoCAD's AREA command allows you to pick multiple existing objects to calculate area and perimeter. It will also automatically calculate those properties for circles and closed polylines without tracing. Areas can be added to and subtracted from running totals maintained within AutoCAD.*

System Variables

Now that you are familiar with the measurement commands, you may find a number of AutoSketch built-in system variables useful. Each variable is a name by which you can ask AutoSketch to recall a value or measurement that was previously entered by you, or calculated by AutoSketch. A complete list of system variables is as follows:

\\	Table of System Variables
/angle	The last measured angle or bearing.
/area	The last measured area.
/dist	The last measured distance (or dimension).
/point	The last measured point.
/x	The X component of the last point entered.
/y	The Y component of the last point entered.

Unfortunately, /point is the only system variable that can be used on the AutoSketch command input line. The rest can be used only for input in dialogue boxes.

System Variables   10-11

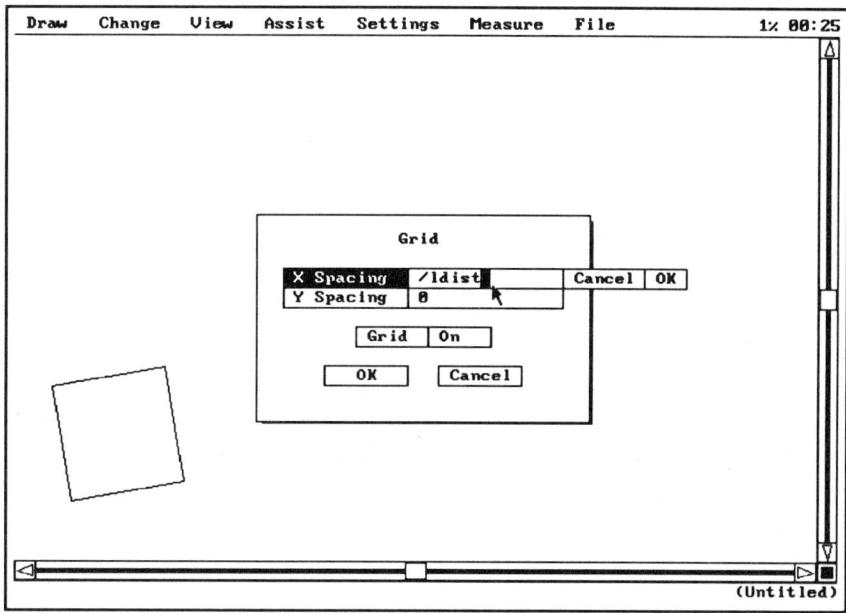

Using /ldist to Set Grid Spacing

Using a System Variable

Pull down **Settings** Select **Grid**	Click on the X spacing.
X Spacing **/ldist**	Type "/ldist," then click OK or press <ENTER>.
Click **OK**	The grid resets to 2, the last measured distance.

Once you get to know them, system variables can save keyboard strokes. They can also be immensely useful in the creation of command macros — allowing you to program generic macros that are independent of specific coordinates. For example, starting a macro using the /lpoint variable in place of an actual coordinate allows the macro to start at a position relative to your last drawing action. This macro would then be able to work correctly at any location within any drawing, rather than being tied to a specific coordinate position.

➥ *TIP: AutoCAD allows user access to dozens of system variables that describe the state of command, drawing setup, and configuration options. They are primarily used for programming in AutoLISP and menu macros.*

Dimensioning

Dimensioning is a very important element of any working drawing. For technical drafting applications, there are few AutoSketch functions more powerful than the four dimensioning commands grouped together on the Measure menu. Back in the dark days of paper and pencils, dimensioning a technical drawing could be an exhausting process. AutoSketch makes dimensioning an almost trivial matter (provided, that is, that the program's particular style of dimensioning suits your application).

To make drawings readable, dimension markings must be properly organized. There isn't space in this book to discuss all the intricacies of correct dimensioning, but fortunately AutoSketch takes care of the major details for you. If you want to place a dimension on your drawing, you specify two points on the object to be dimensioned and a position for the actual dimension line. AutoSketch automatically draws the dimension line, complete with arrowheads, and inserts numerals indicating the dimension value. It also draws in the extension lines (the short lines that extend from the dimensioned points perpendicular to the dimension line), properly offset from the dimensioned object.

All of these dimension components — extension lines, arrows and numeric text — are drawn as a single AutoSketch object, and can be manipulated with most of the normal editing commands.

You cannot, however, break a dimension line. AutoSketch dimensions are associative. Changes in their length will result in a recalculation of the dimension text.

Linear Dimensioning

To dimension a distance within your drawing, pull down the Measure menu and select Horiz. Dimension, Vert. Dimension, or Align Dimension. Then select one end point of the length to be dimensioned. A rubberband line follows the drawing pointer. Next pick the other end point of the length to be dimensioned.

After you have specified the length to be dimensioned, you'll be prompted to pick the dimension line location. Click the pointer at the desired location. Complete dimension lines and text will be drawn at the specified offset between the selected points.

Attaching a Dimension

```
Pull down Settings Select Attach        Enable Node Point mode, and turn Attach on.
```
Ensure that Snap is off.

```
Pull down Measure Select Align Dimension
Points to dimension:                    Lower left corner.
To point:                               Upper left corner.
Dimension line location:                To the left of the box.
```

Now rotate the box.

```
Pull down Change Select Rotate          Use a Crosses/window box to select both your box
                                        and dimensioning.
```

Notice how the horizontal and vertical dimensions change while the aligned dimension remains the same.

Now try dimensioning the top of the box, using Snap.

```
Pull down Assist   Select Attach        Turn Attach off.
Pull down Settings Select Snap          Set to .125 and turn on.
Pull down Measure  Select Horiz. Dimension
Points to dimension:                    Pick upper left corner.
To point:                               Upper right corner.
Dimension line location:                About .5 above top of box.
```

You may find it convenient to use Align Dimension most of the time. Align Dimension will automatically align to horizontal, vertical, or any angle without your having to constantly reselect another command. On the other hand, the Horiz. Dimension or Vert. Dimension commands can be handy when you wish to force exact horizontal or vertical dimensioning of a shape that has no true horizontal or vertical features. For instance, you could use a vertical dimension to show the height of the Great Pyramid.

If you use Horiz. Dimension or Vert. Dimension, then rotate the dimensions along with the object to which they refer, they will remain truly horizontal and vertical. Thus, if you dimension a horizontal line with a length of 3.000, then rotate it so that it is at 45 degrees, the dimension will read 1.500. If you make the line vertical, the dimension will be zero. If you want dimensions to follow the lines to which they refer, always use Align Dimension.

Angular Dimensioning

To dimension an angle, use the Angle Dimension command. It will prompt you to specify two lines that form the angle and provide a position for the dimension line. If the dimension text won't fit (for example, inside a very acute angle), you'll be prompted to provide an alternative position for the dimension text.

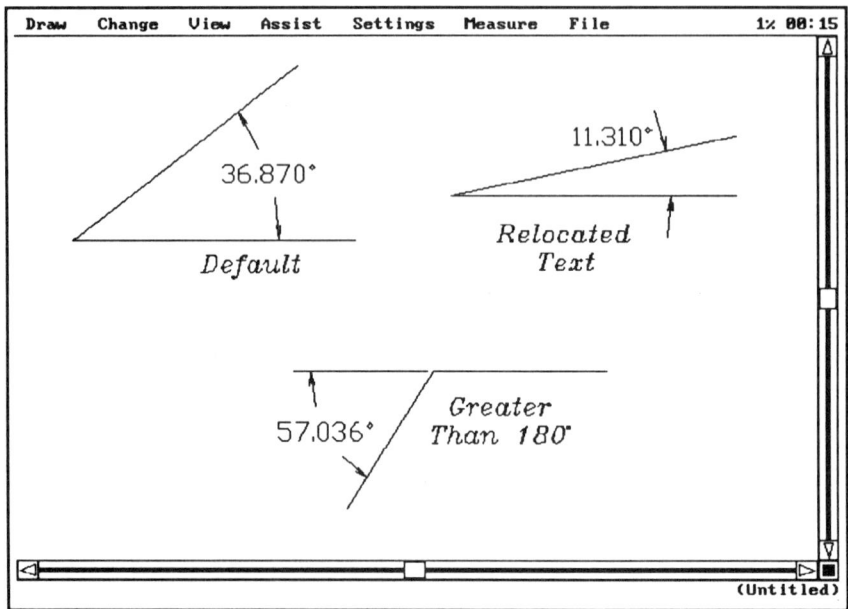

Dimensioning an Angle

Angle Dimensioning

Use Erase to clear some drawing area, or pan over to an empty area.

```
Pull down Draw Select Polyline              Draw a V-shaped polyline.
Pull down Measure Select Angle Dimension
Select first line:                          Pick one arm of the polyline.
Select second line:                         Pick the other arm.
Dimension line arc location:                Pick a location within the angle.
```

You'll find that you can't use Angle Dimension to dimension angles greater than 180 degrees. If you try, AutoSketch will automatically draw extension lines and dimension the smaller angle. This still specifies your angle completely, but it might not be what you really want. If you really must dimension the large angle itself, your only option is to draw the dimension by hand.

➥ *NOTE: Prior to version 3.0, AutoSketch had no facility for automatic angular dimensioning. If you are still using a previous version of AutoSketch and want to dimension angles in your drawing, you'll have to measure them using the Angle command, then draw in the dimension lines and text manually.*

Above all, remember that if you don't use Snap or Attach to pick dimension points, the dimension values produced by AutoSketch will not be very accurate.

Associative Dimensioning

If you scale or stretch objects to which dimensions refer, dimensions automatically change size and value to reflect the changes. Just be sure to use a Crosses/window box to select the objects for scaling or stretching, and include any dimension lines within the box. As you stretch the object, a highlighted image of both the object and the included dimension lines will appear. When you complete the operation, the dimensions will be redrawn with new dimension values.

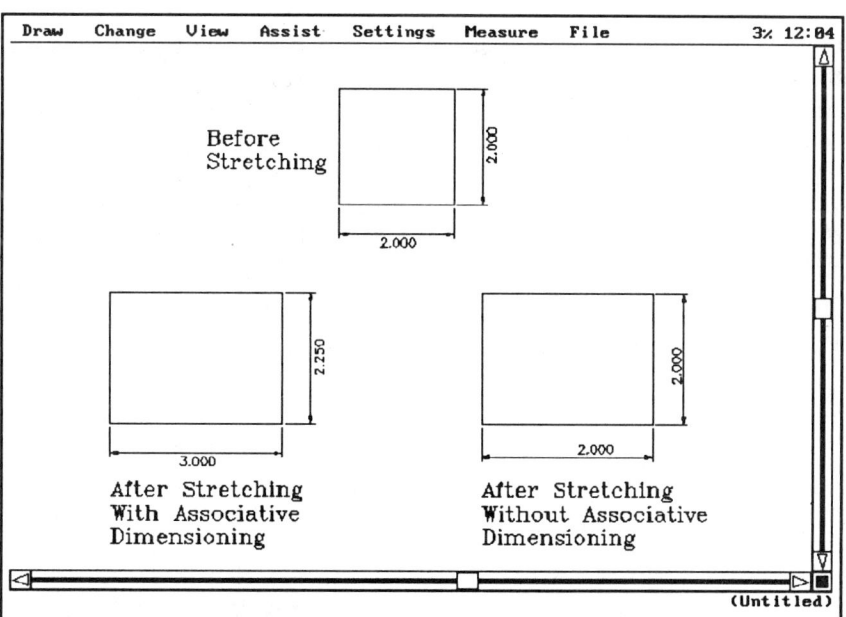

Associative Dimensions

Associative Dimensioning

Pull down **Change** Select **Erase**	Erase everything.
Pull down **Draw** Select **Box**	Draw a new 3-unit by 3-unit box in the middle of your screen.
Pull down **Measure** Select **Horiz. Dimension**	
Points to dimension:	Pick lower left corner.
To point:	Pick lower right corner.
Dimension line location: R(0,-0.5)	
Pull down **Measure** Select **Vert. Dimension**	
Points to dimension:	Pick lower right corner
To point:	Pick upper right corner.
Dimension line location: R(0.5,0)	
Pull down **Change** Select **Stretch**	Use a Crosses/window box to select the left side of the box.
Stretch base:	Pick a point.
Stretch to:	Pick a point to the left.

The dimension value changes to reflect new box size.

The relationship between the box and its dimension is called *associativity*; the dimension is associated with the box. Associative dimensions make it easy to maintain accurate dimensions if you include an object's dimension with it should you decide to change your design. If you simply drew a dimension manually, then stretched the dimension line, it would still contain the same numeric characters.

AutoSketch provides four different dimensioning commands for horizontal, vertical, and odd-angled objects, and for dimensioning angles between objects.

Dimension Text

Dimension text is created according to the Text options set from the Settings menu. You can control the size and style of dimension text by changing the Text settings before adding dimensions. Existing dimension text can also be changed with the Change Property command. Just be sure the Dimension Units option in the Property Settings dialogue box is enabled, as dimension text is not affected by the Text option.

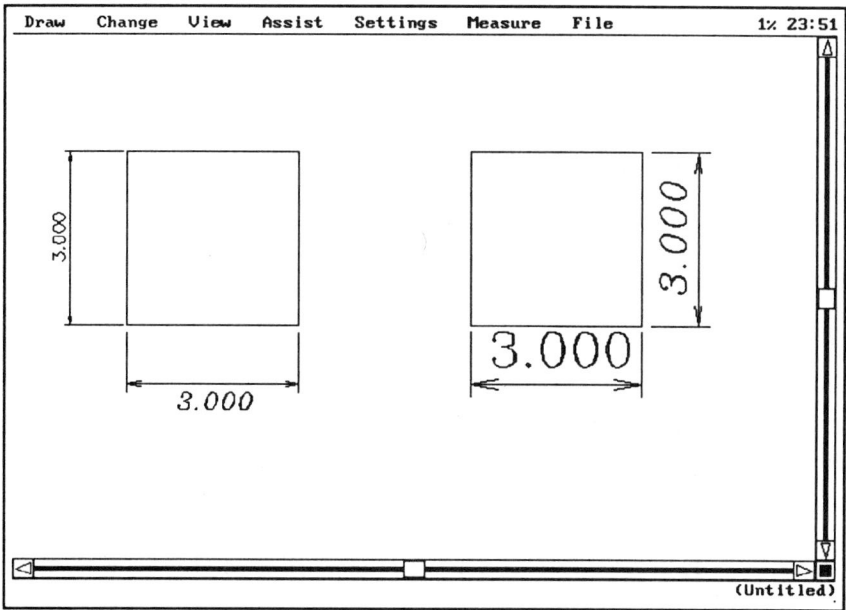

Varying Dimension Text Settings

Like any other AutoSketch entities, dimension lines and text can be drawn in an alternate color and on an alternate layer, depending on the Color and Layer settings. In fact, for clarity and organization, you *should* draw dimensions in a contrasting color and on a separate layer. Dimensions placed on a separate drawing layer can be made invisible when you want to get a clearer view of your drawing. If your pen plotter permits, you may also wish to plot dimension lines in an alternate line weight to further distinguish them from visible lines on the drawing.

The size and location of circular objects (including arcs) are generally specified by dimensioning to their center points. The centers of circles or the central axes of cylinders should be marked using the Center line type.

Arrow Styles

Beginning with version 3.0, AutoSketch provides a choice of five arrowhead styles. These include most of the types you are likely to need.

Arrow Styles

Pull down **Settings** Select **Arrow**	Select solid style.
Pull down **Settings** Select **Property**	Enable only Dimension Arrow mode.
Pull down **Change** Select **Property**	
Select object:	Pick one of your dimension markings.

The arrowheads change to the new style.

AutoSketch uses the current text height to determine the size of all arrowheads. AutoSketch arrowheads do not always remain the same size. By default, standard, solid, and tick arrowheads are drawn at 80 percent of the current text height. The dot arrowhead is drawn at 50 percent of text height. You can make arrowheads draw smaller or larger using the Text command on the Settings menu.

The standard and solid arrowheads are commonly used in all types of technical drawings. The tick style is used extensively in architectural drawings. The dot style generally indicates less accuracy, pointing out an area rather than the single point suggested by a triangular arrowhead.

➥ *TIP: AutoCAD provides an almost unlimited number of linear angular, diameter, and radius dimensioning options. They are controlled by dozens of AutoCAD system variables, many of them user-definable.*

Generally, use decimal units for all systems of measurement except feet and inches. If you want decimal feet — feet and tenths of a foot — set decimal units and use "ft" as a suffix.

Dimensioning 10–19

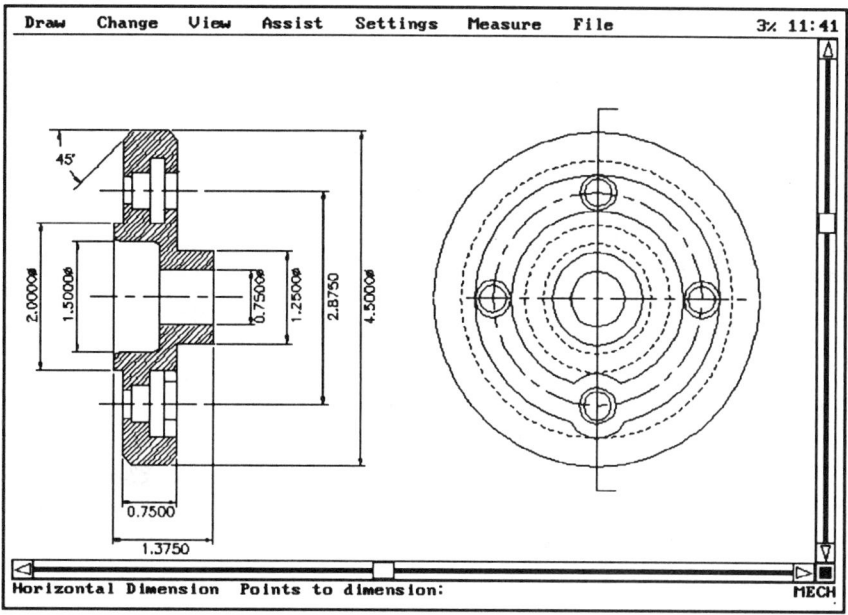

Fully Dimensioned Drawing

Dimensioning the Machine Part

 Load the MECH1 drawing from the IS DISK, or open the MECH drawing from Chapter 9.

 Load or continue with the MECH drawing from Chapter 9.

```
Pull down View Select Zoom Limits
Pull down Settings Select Text           Set Active Font to ROMANS and Height to .125.
Pull down Settings Select Color          Make red the current color.
Pull down Settings Select Arrow          Set to Solid.

Pull down Settings Select Layer          Make layer 5 active. Make layer 4 invisible.
Pull down View Select Zoom Box           Zoom in on the bottom end of the cross section view.
Pull down Measure Select Horiz. Dimension    Start dimensioning.
Points to dimension:                     Pick the outer corner of the lower left chamfer.
To point:                                Pick the outer corner of the lower right chamfer.
```

Continue to dimension the drawing until it resembles the above example illustration. The diameter symbol was added to the end of dimension values by use of the decimal suffix.

➤ *NOTE: If you are using AutoSketch version 2.0 or earlier, the angular dimension is one you'll have to make up by hand. First, draw in the extension lines at the two sides of the angle. Then draw an arc between the extension lines, breaking it in the middle to leave room for the text. Next put in the text. Finally insert your arrow head part twice, and rotate both copies to the proper angles.*

Custom Dimensioning

You may eventually find yourself faced by a situation that simply cannot be handled by the AutoSketch dimensioning system, flexible though it is. When the need arises, you can actually create your own dimensioning system.

Even if you don't need all of this extra dimensioning control, the following should serve as a good demonstration of how you can use advanced AutoSketch techniques to simplify a complex but repetitive task.

The drawback to forging off on your own is that you have to abandon the conveniences along with the limitations. For example, your custom-built dimensions will not be associative — that is, they will not change in value when you change the geometry of the dimensioned object.

Adding Center Marks

In the next exercise, you are going to continue dimensioning the mechanical part by adding center marks.

You can add the center marks to the holes in the front view using two different methods. You can either zoom in on every hole and draw two short crossing lines, or you can make a group that consists of two crossing lines and use Attach in Center mode to copy this group to the centers of the holes. You can even make this center mark into a Part. If you do, place the part base at the intersection point, and your center marks will snap easily into place.

Add center marks for all of the holes in the front view. This is done by breaking out the portions of the centerlines that cross at holes and drawing in the center marks. Adding the center marks has the added benefit of neatening the appearance of centerlines.

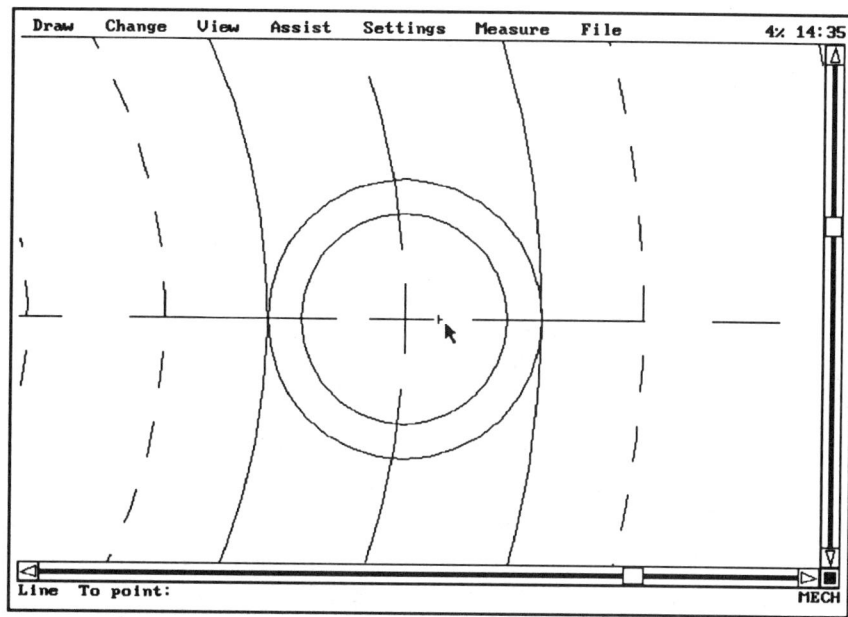

Add Center Marks

Center Marks

```
Pull down Settings Select Layer      Set layer to 2.
Pull down Settings Select Color      Set color to blue.
Pull down View Select Zoom Box       Zoom in on the center hole.
Pull down Change Select Break        Remove a portion of the center line to allow for
                                     the center mark.
Pull down Draw Select Line           Draw the center mark.
```

Now break out the center lines from the four outer holes. Remember to break the circle center line in the counterclockwise direction.

```
Pull down Draw Select Line           Draw the center mark on one of the outer holes.
Pull down Change Select Group        Group the two lines.
Pull down Change Select Copy         Copy center mark to remaining 3 holes.

Pull down Draw Select Line           Add short lines to either end of the section line
                                     to denote the center.
Pull down File Select Save           Save your work.
```

Dimension Orientation

To some extent, the order and orientation of the points you pick control the orientation of the dimension text. Horiz. Dimension text is always horizontal and right-reading, and Align Dimension text is always oriented with the dimension line and right-reading. Vert. Dimension text, however, can be inverted by placing the dimension points in the opposite order. The placement of the dimension line is somewhat a matter of judgment.

Dimension lines should be offset far enough for clarity, separating the dimension text from the object to which it refers. On the other hand, very long extension lines should be avoided, as they will clutter up the drawing unnecessarily.

Most people like their drawings to be readable either from the bottom or the right side, and dimension text always above or to the left of the dimension line. However, AutoSketch always places dimension text outside of the dimension line in the direction you use to show the dimension line location. If you drag a rubberband line to the right in a vertical dimension to show the dimension line location, the dimension text will be to the right of the dimension line. If you drag to the left to show a dimension line location, the text will be to the left, and so on. This makes it difficult, but not impossible, to create consistently bottom- and right-reading dimensions with the dimension text always above the dimension line. To achieve this format, always pick the bottom point first when using Vert. Dimension to place dimensions to the left of objects. For horizontal dimensions above objects, select the points in any order.

For dimensions along the bottom of an object, and for dimensions at the right side, things are not quite so straightforward with text to the left of the dimension line. You'll have to trick AutoSketch.

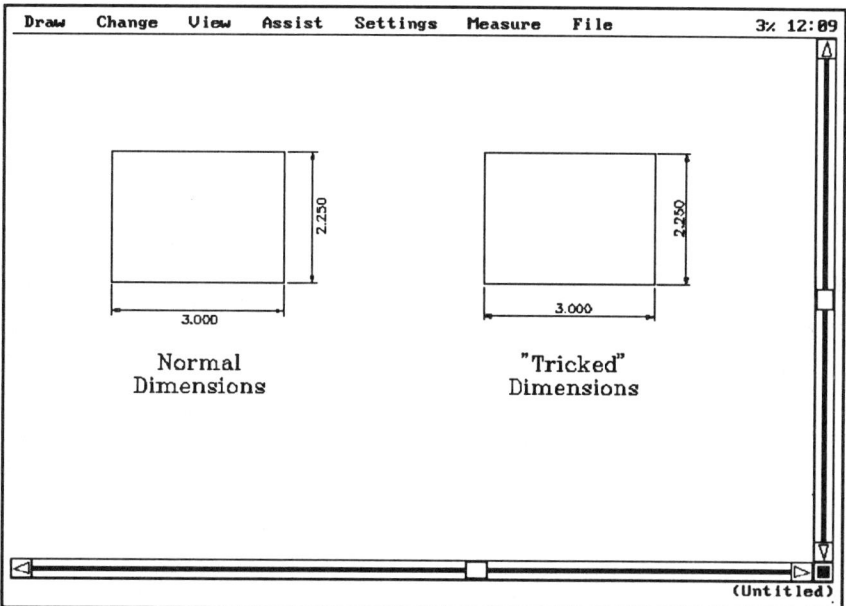

Normal and Tricked Dimensions

To dimension along the bottom, first draw in the extension lines manually, at their appropriate locations, using the Line command. When prompted for the points to dimension, pick points on these extension lines, where you want the dimension line to be located. These points must be chosen in the correct order. Pick the left side first and then the right side. Then, when asked to pick the dimension line location, simply click the last point again. In other words, pick the left side and then double-click on the right side.

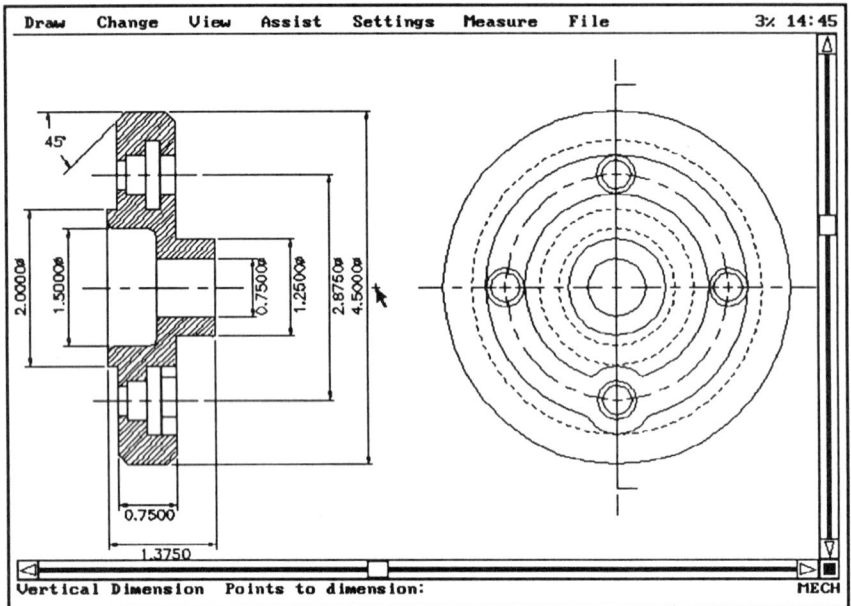

Tricked Dimension on Machine Part

Tricking AutoSketch For Dimensioning

```
Pull down Change Select Erase          Erase the outer 4.5-inch vertical dimension.
Pull down Settings Select Snap         Set Snap to .0625.
Pull down Draw Select Line             Draw in the extension linto replace the ones
                                       just erased.
Pull down Measure Select Vert. Dimension
Points to dimension:                   Pick the lower dimension.
To point:                              Pick the upper dimension.
Dimension line location:               Click the last point again.
```

Dimensioning along the bottom follows the same pattern. First draw the extension lines using the Line command, then pick the points. The only real difference is that now you are dimensioning horizontally.

When drawing extension lines manually, use an alternate color or line weight than you would normally use for dimensioning. Their appearance will help you to tell them apart from AutoSketch's associative extension lines. You can draw offset extension lines accurately using Attach, then break away a small segment so that the lines don't quite touch the dimensioned object. AutoSketch does this automatically with its own extension lines.

Constructing and Using Arrowheads

AutoSketch currently has no provision for drawing arrowheads with a leader attached to them in a single command — used for dimensioning a radius, or calling out a specification — so we will make two ourselves. The first thing we'll want to do is to create the arrowhead as a part. Then we can quickly insert copies of it, rotate them to the correct angle, and draw in leader lines. To review the AutoSketch concept of parts, refer to Chapter 7, *Advanced Editing Tools*.

Various arrowhead styles commonly used include hollow closed, solid closed, open, and others. For our example, we'll make a solid closed arrowhead. Creating solids is something you'll want to become familiar with as you continue to use AutoSketch. We'll use dimensions to match the arrowheads created by AutoSketch's dimensioning commands.

➥ *NOTE: If you are using AutoSketch version 2.0, use the Fill Region command where we mention Pattern Fill below. If you are using an even earlier version of AutoSketch, you'll have to fill in the arrowhead outline using single lines spaced one pen-width apart.*

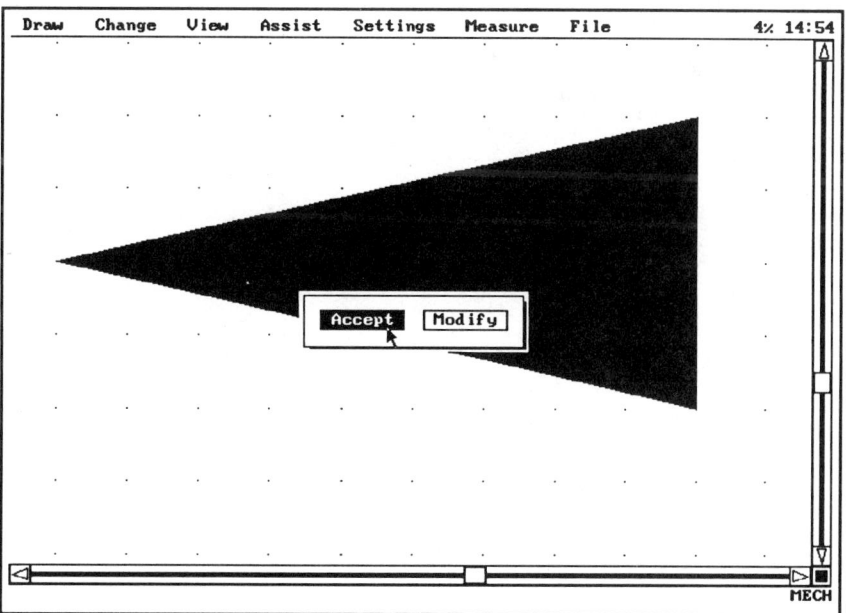

Reusable Arrowhead Part

Arrowhead Construction

Pull down **View** Select **Zoom Limits**	
Pull down **View** Select **Zoom X**	
Magnification Factor: **40**	Zoom in by a factor of 40. Pan to a clear area.
Click **OK**	
Pull down **Settings** Select **Snap**	Set to 0.015625 and turn on.
Pull down **Settings** Select **Grid**	Set to 0.015625 and turn on.
Pull down **Settings** Select **Pattern**	Select SOLID fill.
Click **SOLID**	
Click **OK**	
Pull down **Draw** Select **Pattern Fill**	Draw triangle.

Make it 8 snap points along the base, 16 snap points wide from point to base.

Click **Accept**

Now make it into a part.

Click **OK**	
Pull down **File** Select **Part Clip**	
Click Filename: **ARROW-LG**	Arrow, large.
Insertion base:	The point of the triangle.
Select object	Pick the triangle.
Pull down **Change** Select **Erase**	Erase the arrow.

Construct another arrowhead that measures 2 snap points by 6 snap points using the same method as above. Name it ARROW-SM. Set Snap back to .0625 and Grid to .25.

Now that you have the arrowhead as a part, you can finish off the section line you drew earlier.

Custom Dimensioning   10–27

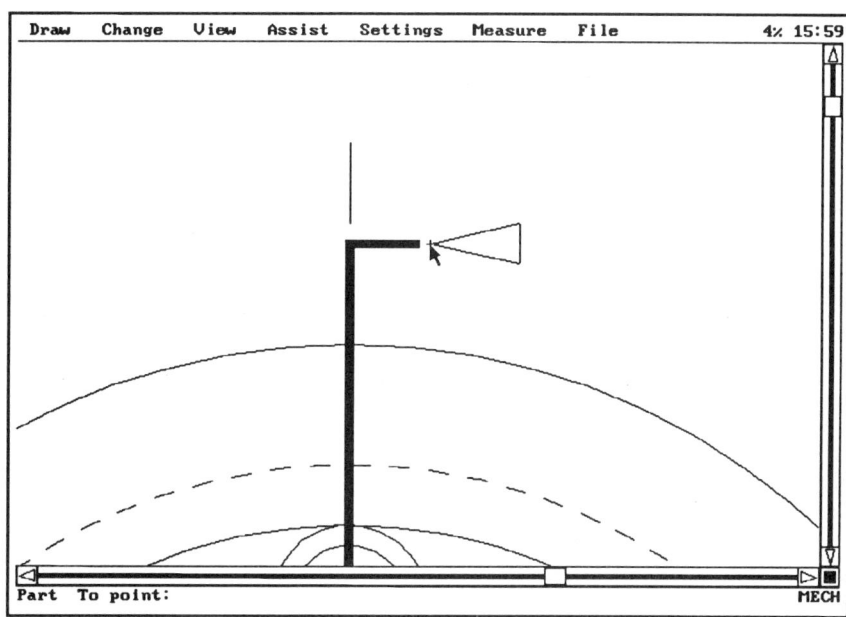

Inserting Section Line Arrowheads

Adding Arrowheads to the Section Line

Pull down **View** Select **Zoom Limits**
Pull down **View** Select **Zoom Box**   Zoom in on the top end of the section line.

Ensure that Snap is on, Ortho and Attach off.

Pull down **Draw** Select **Part**   Select ARROW-LG.
To point: Place at end of section line.

You'll probably need to rotate the arrowhead.

Pull down **Change** Select **Rotate**
Select object: **<ALT-F7>**   Turn Snap off, then select arrowhead.
Center of rotation: **<ALT-F7>**   Turn Snap back on, then select the middle of
                                                the arrow.
Second point: Rotate the arrowhead by 180 degrees.

Place another arrowhead on the other end of the section line.

Pull down **View** Select **Zoom Limits**
Pull down **File** Select **Save**   Save your work.

To finish up the mechanical drawing, label the two views, and label the section line.

Adding Leader Dimensions and Notes

Now that we have the arrowheads constructed, we can use them to build leader dimensions and add notes to a drawing. Leader dimensions are assembled from lines, parts, and text.

The process of constructing a leader dimension is simple. First, draw the leader line and its extension. Then insert the arrowhead and rotate it to the angle of the leader line. Selecting the arrowhead for rotation can be tricky. When rotating the arrowhead, turn off Attach and window select the arrowhead.

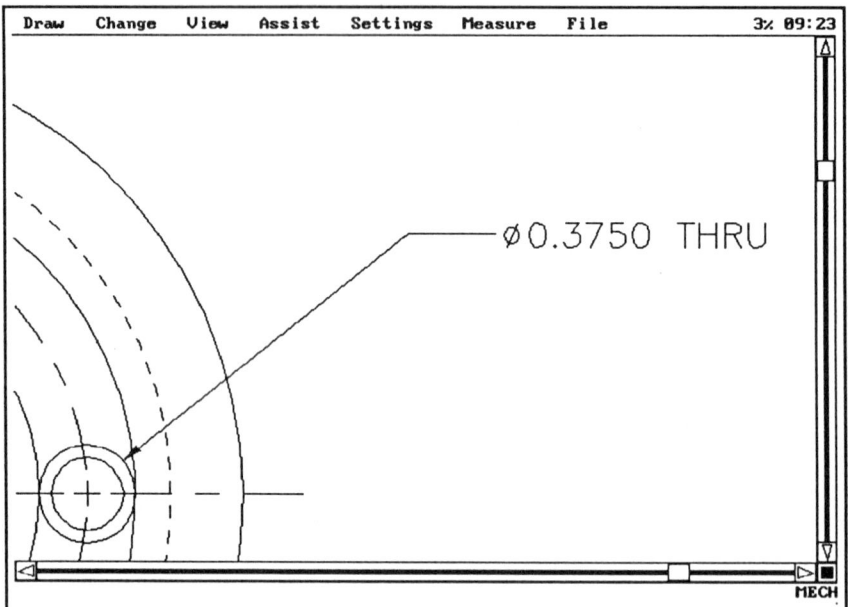

Finished Leader Dimension

Leader Dimension

Turn off Snap and Attach.

Pull down **View** Select **Zoom Box**	Zoom in on the right small hole.
Pull down **Draw** Select **Line**	Draw the leader line and extension.
Pull down **Settings** Select **Attach**	Turn on End Point and Attach Mode.
Pull down **Draw** Select **Part**	Insert ARROW-SM at the end of the leader line.
Pull down **Assist** Select **Attach**	Turn Attach off.

```
Pull down Change Select Rotate        Window the arrowhead.
Center of rotation:                   Pick the arrowhead point.
Second point:                         Rotate the arrowhead into position.
Pull down Draw Select Quick Text      Add the dimension text.
Enter text %%c0.3750 THRU
```

Now that you have the necessary skills, all that is left is to finish the dimensioning. Using custom dimensions as needed, add notes and labels, and add a title block. A completed drawing is on the facing page of this chapter.

Command Practice

Here are a few simple practice exercises to help you become more familiar with the commands covered in this section.

NEW. Pull down File and select New. Start with a clean slate.

DRAW. Set Snap to .25 and turn it on. Draw two circles, one with a radius of exactly two units and the other with a radius of exactly one unit. Use relative coordinate entry.

DISTANCE, ANGLE, AREA. Use the Area command to measure the perimeter and area of the two-unit radius circle. Compare these with the actual values (remember, area is πr^2 and circumference is $2\pi r$). Try again, using a greater number of points along the circle's circumference. (You'll need a dozen or more points to get close to the true values — about 12.57 for both area and circumference.)

DIMENSIONING. Turn Attach mode on. Dimension the circle diameters. Also dimension the horizontal distance between their centers.

> ➥ *TIP: One easy way to draw a circle and mark its center for dimensioning is to place center marks first, then draw the circle. Use Intersection Attach mode and pick the center mark for the circle's center point.*

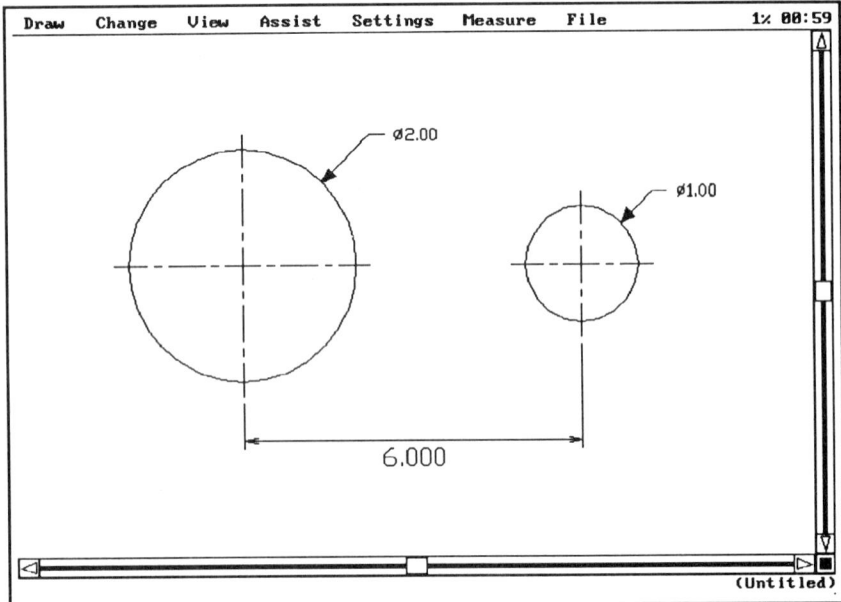

Dimensioning Circles

Map Drawing

Let's bring up the MAP drawing and label the back road with text at the same angle as the road.

Use the Bearing command to find the angle of the little back road you drew. Armed with this angle, you should be able to easily insert a text label parallel to the road by setting the text baseline angle. If the bearing is south of the zero mark, you'll need to do some arithmetic. Enter "35 miles" using Quick Text. To change the baseline angle in the Settings Text dialogue box, try simply entering the /langle system variable.

Map Drawing   10–31

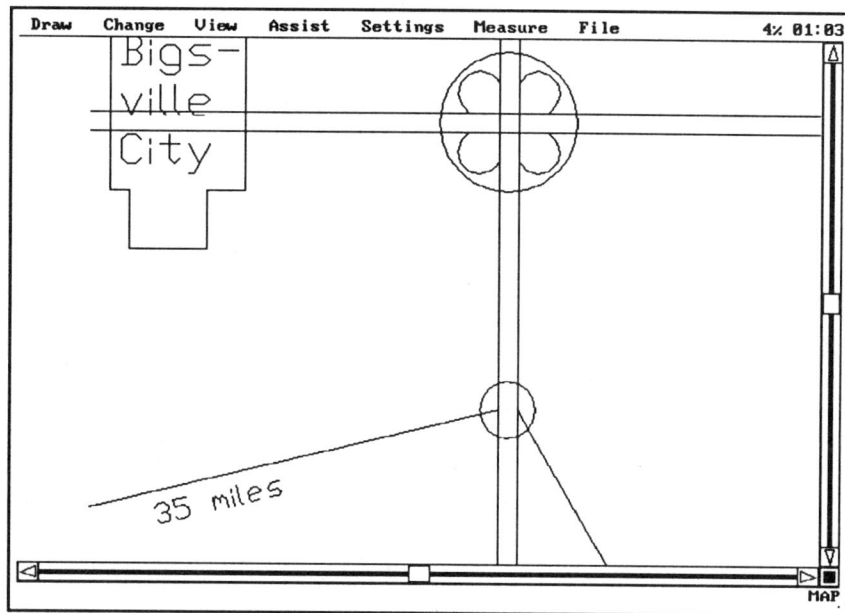

Text With a Baseline Angle

Map Drawing Exercise

   Complete this exercise with either your MAP file or the MAP3 files from the IS DISK.

   Open the MAP file.

```
Pull down Change Select Erase              Erase the plot box from Chapter 8.
Pull down View Select Zoom Full
Pull down Measure Select Bearing
Base point:                                On the road, in Bigsville.
Enter point:                               Somewhere on the highway.
```

Bearing should read 0, or due east.

```
Click OK                                   Close the dialogue box.

Pull down Settings Select Attach           Select End Point and Node Point modes;
                                           turn Attach on.

Pull down Measure Select Bearing
Base point:                                Left end of back road.
Enter point:                               First jog in the road.
```

```
Pull down Settings Select Text        The angle of the back road.
Angle /LANGLE
Pull down Draw Select Quick Text
Enter point:                          Pick point above road.

Enter text: 35 miles
Pull down File Select Save
```

Using the Bearing command, find out which direction you'd be going if you left Bigsville City. Remember that 0, in most cases, is equivalent to east. If you want, you can draw in a small compass rose such as you see on professional maps, showing that north is the top of the drawing. Check some of the other roads. You can add text notes to your map telling your guests which direction to go to find your country estate.

If you try using the Measure Point command on your map, the coordinates will be quite meaningless, since this drawing was not drawn with any particular scale in mind. You may find it an interesting exercise to use Scale and Stretch to mold this sketch into something like a real piece of cartography. We'll have a shot at this in the next chapter.

Space Plan

Now open the FLOOR drawing. How many square feet is the office? How much carpeting do you need for just one of the rooms? You can now use the Area command to find out.

Set the active layer to 5, and if you're using a color monitor or plotter, set the drawing color to green. Dimension the sides of the office plan. Snap should still be set to 6, so your dimension points will coincide with the walls easily. Use this spacing for your dimension lines.

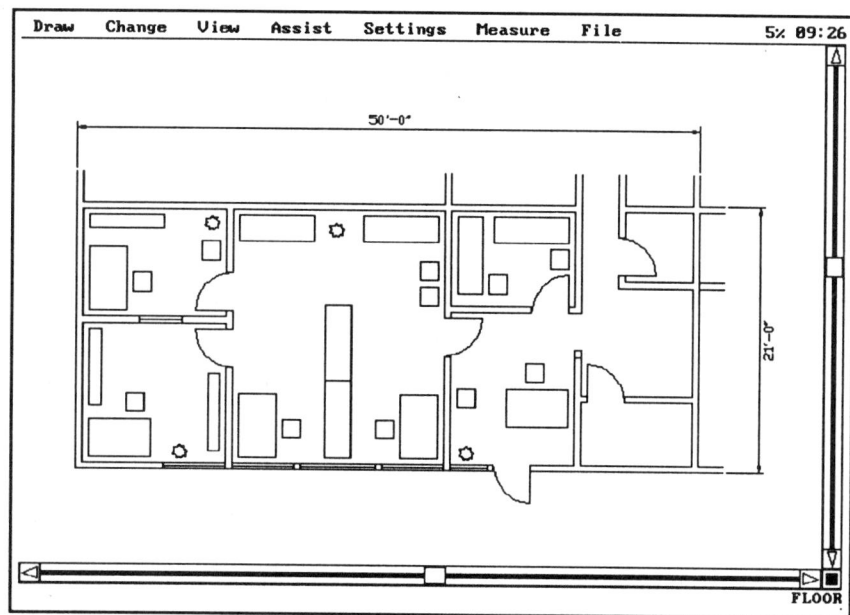
Dimensioning the Space Plan

Space Plan Drawing Exercise

 Open either the FLOOR3 file from the IS DISK, or your FLOOR drawing.

 Open the FLOOR file.

```
Pull down Change Select Erase           Erase any plot boxes from Chapter 8.

Pull down Measure Select Area           Select the four corners of the office space.
Pull down Measure Select Area           Select the four corners of one room.

Pull down Settings Select Layer         Set current layer to 5.
Pull down Settings Select Color         Set drawing color to green.

Pull down Measure Select Horiz. Dimension
Points to dimension:                    Left top corner of space.
To point:                               Right top corner of space.
Dimension line location:                Above top of space.

Pull down Measure Select Vert. Dimension
Points to dimension:                    Bottom right corner of space.
To point:                               Top right corner of space.
```

`Dimension line location:`	To right of space.
`Pull down` **`Change`** `Select` **`Erase`**	Erase the previous plot box.
`Pull down` **`File`** `Select` **`Plot Area`**	Adjust all settings to include your dimensions.
`Pull down` **`File`** `Select` **`Save`**	Save your work.
`Pull down` **`File`** `Select` **`Plot`**	Plot the drawing.

Summary

AutoSketch provides two types of measurement commands. The first set — including Point, Coords, Bearing, Distance, Angle, and Area — allows you to get information from your drawing wherever you need it. The second set of commands — Horz., Vert., Align, and Angle Dimension — allow you to add dimensioning information to a drawing, referencing the relationships between drawing objects.

Remember that none of your measurements will be accurate unless you take care to create your drawing precisely to scale. Proper AutoSketch grid, snap, and attach settings make it easy to draw with great accuracy. Once an accurate scale drawing is created, you can use the AutoSketch measurement commands to extract dimension information that you may not have known at all before creating the drawing.

The AutoSketch system variables are included as a final convenience. You can often use the /lpoint variable to save reentering a coordinate. The /lx and /ly variables can also be useful, allowing you to enter points matching a previous X or Y coordinate. The other variables are more important when creating macros.

With this chapter, you've completed your survey of AutoSketch drawing and editing commands. In the next chapter we'll look at several extended examples, focusing on higher-level techniques and shortcuts that can make your AutoSketch work more productive.

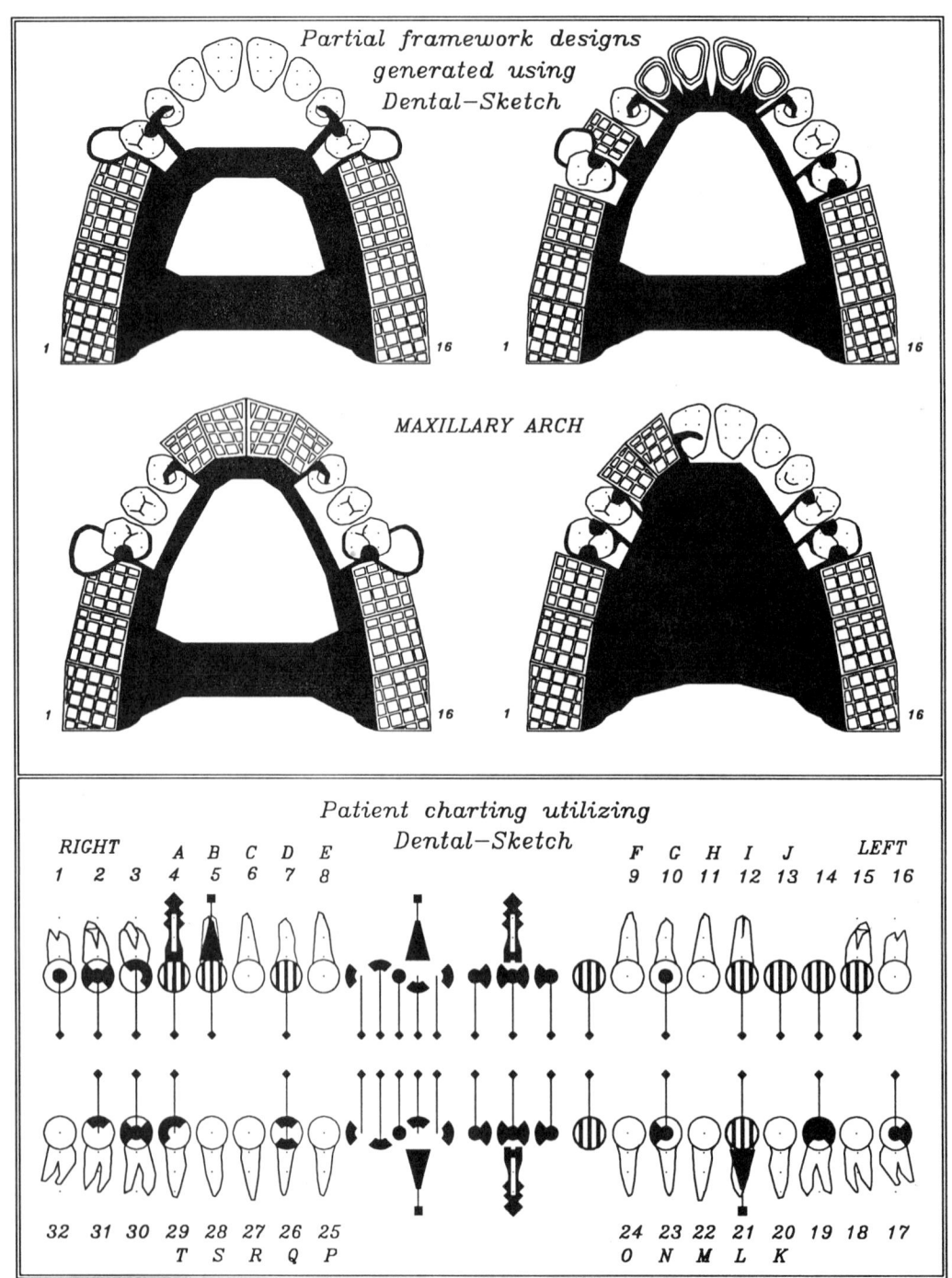

Example Dental-Sketch Drawing, Courtesy of Jeff Mildner

Chapter 11

File Transfers

This chapter covers the few remaining AutoSketch File commands. With them, you can convert your drawings into several different forms from the program's standard SKD files. Each file type has its own uses.

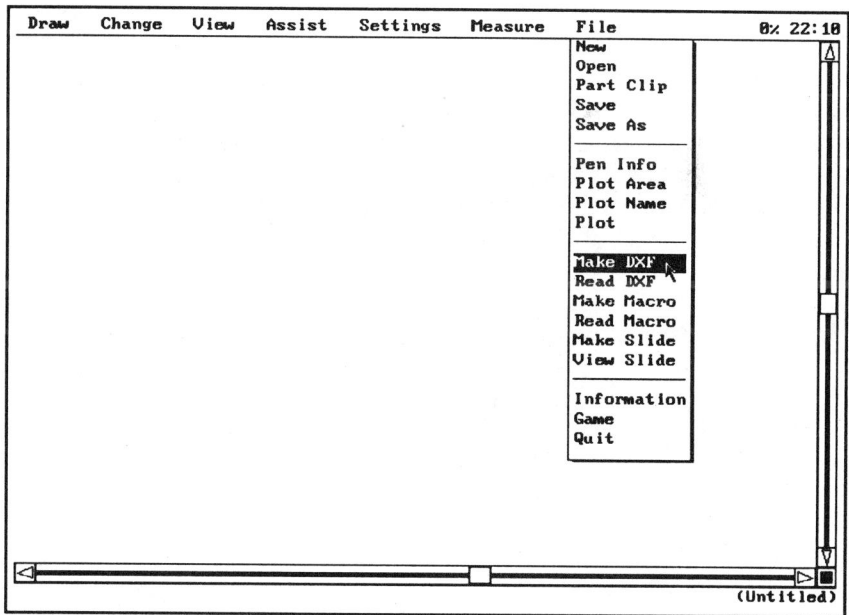

The File Menu

AutoSketch can create what it calls *slide* files — simplified vector representations of your drawings. Slides can be displayed more quickly than normal drawing files, but cannot be modified. AutoSketch slide files are interchangeable with those produced by AutoCAD and AutoShade. However, AutoSketch cannot currently display AutoCAD Slide Library SLB files.

AutoSketch also supports the well-established DXF file format. DXF files are extremely useful for transferring your work between various software programs, since they are supported by most major CAD, illustration, and desktop-publishing programs. Once saved in DXF form, an AutoSketch drawing can be read into programs such as AutoCAD or Ventura Publisher. Conversely, an AutoCAD drawing saved in DXF format can be read into AutoSketch. The results of DXF transfer are not always perfect, but they are usually good enough to save you from recreating the drawing.

Some programs, such as Ventura Publisher, can also import drawings plotted by AutoSketch to files in HP-GL or PostScript format. HP-GL is a particularly useful file format, because it provides excellent compatibility among a number of types of software.

Slides

If you want to store just the visual appearance of a drawing, you can take advantage of the AutoSketch Make Slide command. A slide is an image of your drawing as it appears on your screen at the time the slide is created. Slides are useful for taking a "snapshot" of the current drawing at a desired level of completion, or for reference while editing a different drawing. When displayed on your screen, the slide looks like the drawing, but its appearance is frozen. The slide can't be edited, plotted, or even magnified. However, it can be displayed very quickly by either AutoSketch or AutoCAD.

To make a slide, pull down the File menu and select Make Slide. When the Make Slide File dialogue box appears, enter a filename for your slide file. The dialogue box offers the same name as that of your drawing and automatically adds the SLD file extension (visible only from DOS). You can type in a different name if you wish.

Slides   11–3

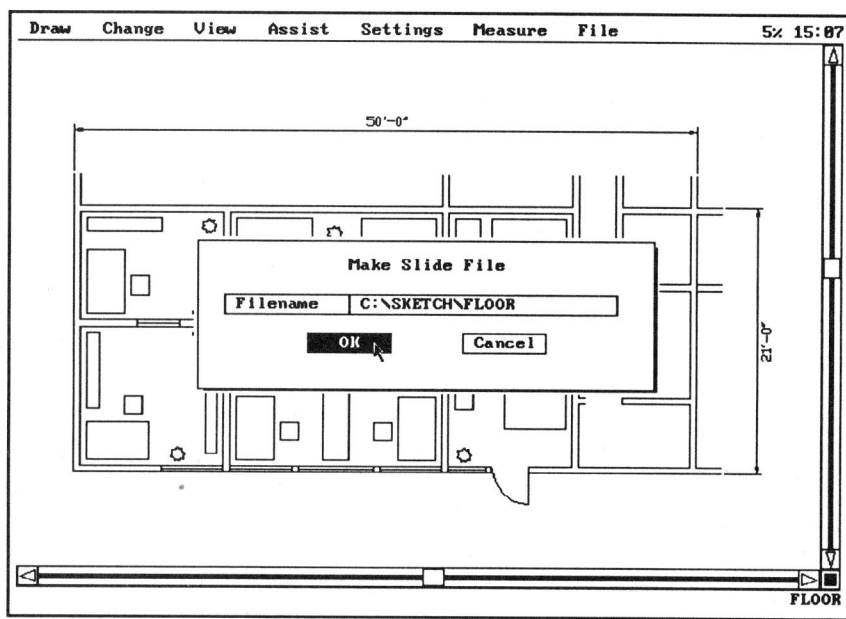

Making a Slide

Making a Slide

First, make a slide of your "space plan" drawing.

   Open the FLOOR4 file or continue in FLOOR4.

   Open or continue in the FLOOR file.

```
Pull down File Select Make Slide
Filename <ENTER>                     Accept the default.

Click OK                             Click the OK box.
```

To view a slide, all you have to do is pull down the File menu and select View Slide. A dialogue box appears labeled "Select Slide File." Select a filename from the menu, or enter a name directly. As usual, the file extension (SLD) is assumed and should not be typed in. Click on OK and the selected slide is displayed.

Viewing a Slide

Pan to the right until the space plan is out of sight and look at the slide you created.

```
Pull down File Select View Slide
File FLOOR                                    Check the box next to the current drawing name.
Click OK
```

The FLOOR slide appears on the screen. It should look just like your previous view.

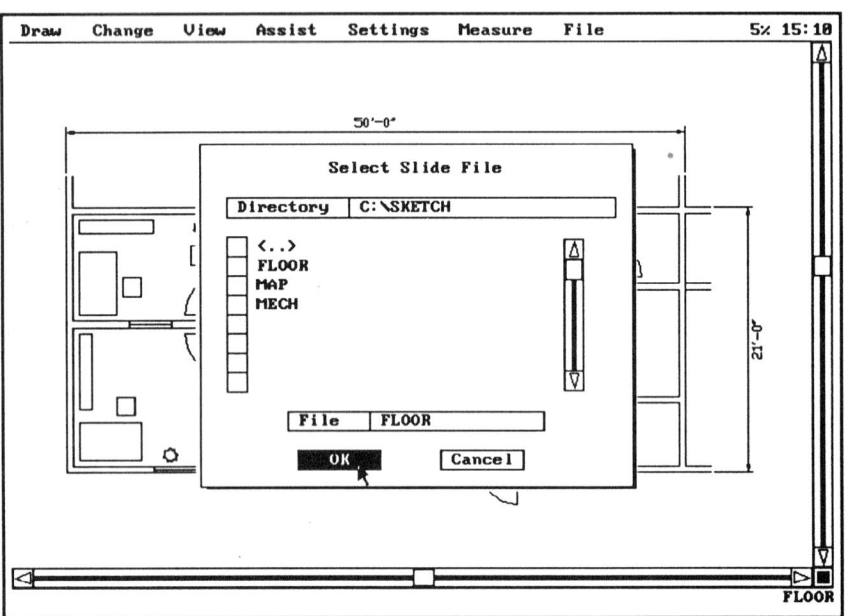

Displaying the FLOOR Slide

A slide will contain only the visible elements of your original picture. It preserves the specific view that was in effect when the slide was created. The slide will include any visible plot boxes or clip boxes. However, it will not include any objects on layers that are invisible when the slide is created, any parts of the drawing that are off the screen, grid dots, or any of AutoSketch's user interface.

When a slide is displayed, it merely overlays your current drawing, which remains in RAM. All editing, plotting, and viewing commands will have no effect on the slide, but will apply to the current drawing. To remove a slide display without disrupting your current drawing, use the Redraw command.

The major advantage of slide files is that they display more quickly than complete drawing files. Depending on the complexity of the original drawing file, the corresponding slide file can display up to five times more quickly. The fact that slides cannot be modified is also an advantage in some circumstances. For example, if you want to give someone a look at something you're working on without passing them the actual work itself, you could capture it as a slide. The person could view your work, but would be unable to modify or re-use any of it.

AutoSketch reads slide files without interfering with your current drawing work, and this is another advantage. You can quickly refer to a previously saved slide file and carry on drawing where you left off.

➥ *TIP: Since a slide is visible until you execute a viewing command, you can use slides as patterns or templates and trace over them onto the current drawing. When used this way, one drawing can be used as a sort of "disposable" layer in another.*

Slide files are also more portable than drawing files. For example, Ventura Publisher can read slide files (including color information), making them useful for illustrating technical documents. However, we recommend that you use the more robust HP-GL procedure described later in this chapter.

A final, but very important, use of slide files is for creation of slide *shows*. Although you cannot do this with AutoSketch alone, AutoCAD can display slide files in a pre-planned sequence, just like a series of film slides in a projector. This type of slide show has many applications, such as sales, demonstration, and training tools.

DXF Files

AutoSketch has the built-in ability to save and read drawings in the DXF (Drawing Interchange Format) file format. DXF files can be read directly by most micro-based CAD programs and many other types of software — notably the major illustration programs such as CorelDRAW! and Micrografx Designer.

To create a DXF file, select Make DXF. The Make DXF File dialogue box appears. Enter a filename, or accept the default of the drawing's original filename but with the DXF extension.

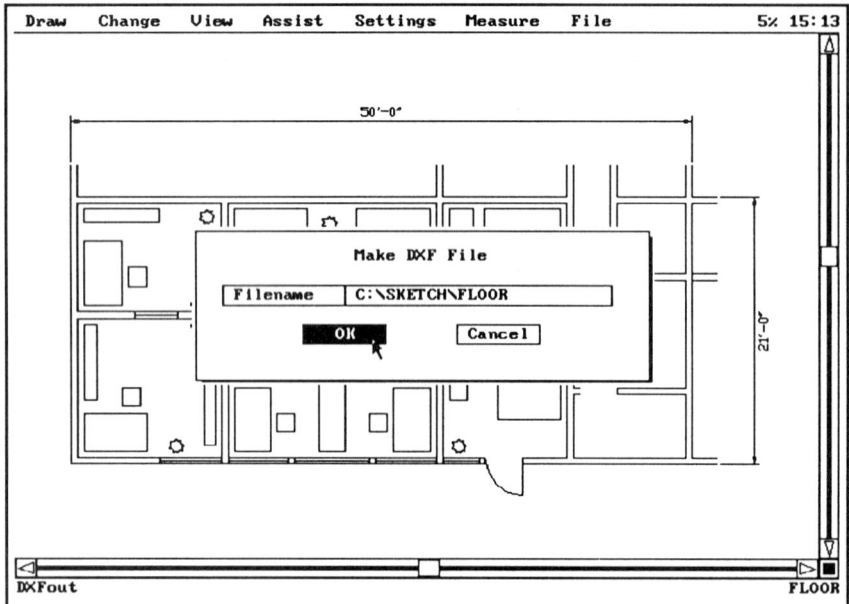

Making a DXF File

Making a DXF File

Pull down **File** Select **Make DXF**
Click **OK**   Use the default.

AutoSketch writes the DXF file.

DXF files are larger than either AutoSketch drawing or slide files. Be sure that you have sufficient free space on your disk drive to hold the DXF file before trying to create it. A DXF file contains almost the same information as a drawing file, but much more information than a slide file. If you view a DXF file, either with the DOS TYPE command or from a text editor, you'll find that it consists of a series of commands in ASCII text. These commands tell other programs how to re-create the entire drawing in a standard format. AutoSketch also has the ability to read DXF files produced by other programs.

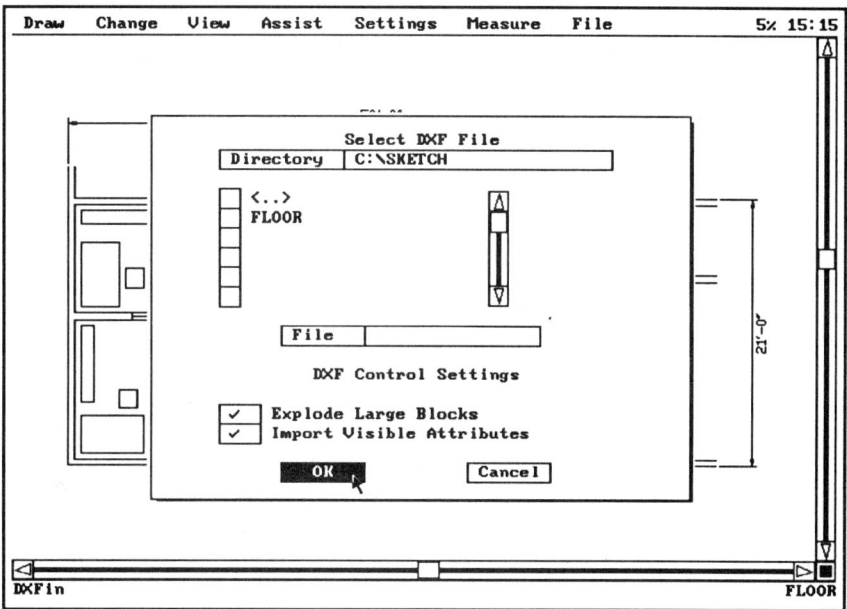

Reading a DXF File

Reading a DXF File

Pull down **File** Select **Read DXF**   Select the file you just made.
Click **OK**

The space plan appears on the screen, almost exactly as it looked originally.

The Read DXF dialogue box has no icon display because DXF files do not include the icon information that AutoSketch stores in drawing files. Also, you'll find that a few things are lost in the translation to DXF and back again. Dimensions, in particular, are disassembled into text and lines and are no longer associative.

➥ *TIP: You may be able to put this feature to good use, if you need to use an unusual dimension notation system that the AutoSketch Units suffix facility cannot handle. You can make a DXF file when your drawing is complete, then read it back into a new file and edit the dimension text to your own requirements.*

There are limitations on DXF drawing transfer. Some programs may be unable to recognize objects created by AutoSketch and saved in the DXF file. To get around these limitations, we recommend that you import drawings into CorelDRAW! using the HP-GL procedure described later in this chapter. AutoCAD will usually import DXF files from AutoSketch easily, since AutoSketch entities are a subset of those in AutoCAD. Even so, don't expect perfect results under all circumstances.

The same is true of DXF files read into AutoSketch. DXF files created in a more powerful drawing program such as AutoCAD will contain many elements that simply have no equivalent in AutoSketch, and therefore cannot be re-created. There are two options on the Select DXF File dialogue box that give you some control over how AutoSketch will interpret certain types of drawing elements.

The Explode Large Blocks option deals with blocks (the AutoCAD equivalent of AutoSketch groups) that have over 1000 elements, which is not permissible in AutoSketch. If you enable Explode Large Blocks (the default), these blocks will be broken up into their component objects. If you disable Explode Large Blocks, large blocks will simply be omitted from the drawing.

➥ *NOTE:* *AutoSketch 2.0 cannot translate AutoCAD blocks or AutoSketch 3.0 groups from a DXF file.*

The Import Visible Attributes option relates to text that AutoCAD can associate with drawing objects. If this option is enabled, this text will be read in; if the option is disabled, the labels are ignored.

DXF transfer can greatly extend the usefulness of AutoSketch. You can use DXF files to move drawings that have outgrown AutoSketch into more powerful programs such as AutoCAD, CorelDRAW! and Micrografx Designer. You can also use DXF files to exchange drawings with users of other CAD programs. Each of these advanced systems places at your disposal huge libraries of commercial and public-domain drawings, symbols, and clip-art images. Importing these via DXF can save you a great deal of time and allow you to add features to your drawings that would be difficult to create in AutoSketch alone.

Plot Files

When you install AutoSketch, you can tell it to send printer or plotter output to a file rather than to an actual output device. Drawing information captured in this way can be printed later or from another computer by sending it to the appropriate device. It can also be read in by many other programs.

Plot files are not particularly useful, other than for their original purpose, that is, plotting out at a later date or different location from your original AutoSketch installation. However, two types of plot files, HP-GL and Encapsulated PostScript, are extremely useful for transferring drawings from AutoSketch to other programs.

The HP-GL (Hewlett-Packard Graphics Language) file format is a plotter control language developed by Hewlett-Packard. You can create HP-GL files by configuring AutoSketch to send the output for any of the supported Hewlett-Packard plotters to a file — as shown in the following exercise.

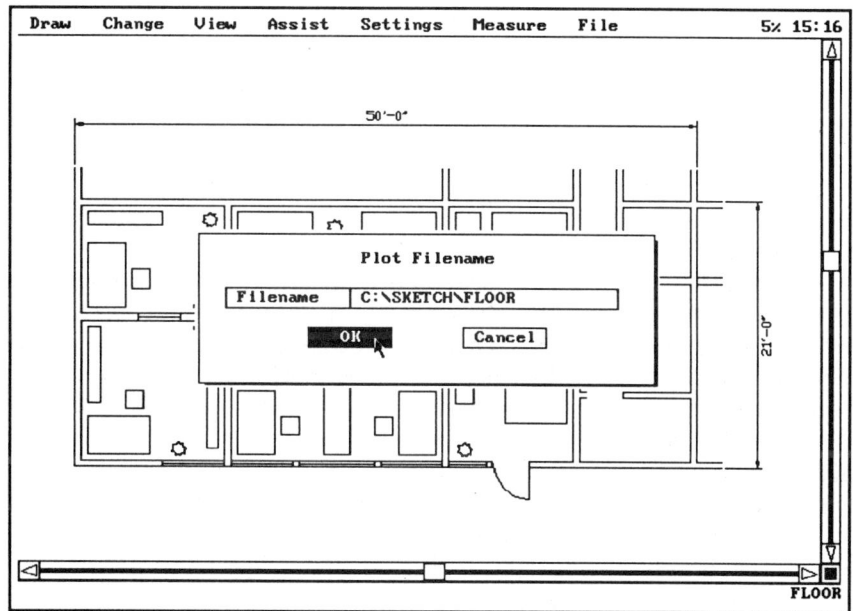

Creating a Plot File

Creating a Plot File

```
Pull down File Select Quit
Click Discard                    If you made any changes.
```

Assuming that you've installed AutoSketch normally, restart it from DOS using the following command:

```
C:\SKETCH3>SKETCH /R
```

You'll be presented with the same configuration questions you saw when first installing AutoSketch.

Answer the questions as you did originally, specifying your hardware configuration, until you reach Plotter selection.

```
Plotter or printer selection: 7     Select the number corresponding to Hewlett-Packard Plotter.
Model selection: 1 to 7 <1>: 3      Select 7475 plotter.
Connection Selection: 4             Select File as your plotter connection.
```

After this, AutoSketch starts normally.

  Reopen the FLOOR4 or FLOOR file from the IS DISK.

  Reopen the FLOOR file.

```
Pull down File Select Plot
Filename                            The Plot Filename dialogue box suggests the current
                                    drawing filename as the plot filename.
Click OK                            Click on OK to accept.
```

Your plot file is created. This can take some time.

An HP-GL file consists of instructions that will cause a compatible plotter to plot all the types of drawing objects found in a CAD drawing, whether created in AutoSketch or any other program. Because the HP-GL format has been in existence for so long, and because it has become a standard, it is particularly well-suited for transferring drawing information among various programs. Unfortunately, although virtually all drawing programs can create HP-GL files, not all can read them. However, major programs like Microsoft Word, WordPerfect, Pagemaker, CorelDRAW! and Ventura Publisher are capable of reading HP-GL files, and the results are generally superior to those obtainable with any other transfer method.

If you intend to use AutoSketch drawings in Ventura Publisher, we recommend that you transfer them in HP-GL format. Configure AutoSketch as described above, then plot the drawing as you wish it to appear in Ventura. In Ventura, create a new frame with the sizing and scaling options of your choice, and select the Load Text/Picture command from the Ventura File menu. Select the Line Art option and HP-GL file type. In the file-selection dialogue box, Ventura assumes that the HP-GL file will have an extension of HPG; change this to PLT, to match the extension supplied by AutoSketch. Click on the filename you created, and then the OK button. The file should load perfectly.

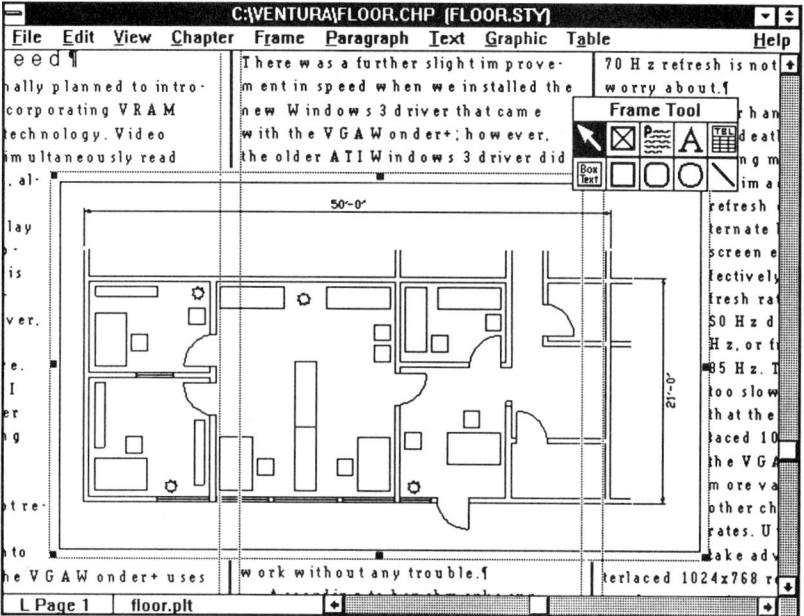

HP-GL Plot File Imported Into Ventura Publisher

You can control the amount of your drawing that you import with an AutoSketch clip box. However, bear in mind that you can also crop the drawing in Ventura. The method you use will depend on how much you need. If you want almost all of the drawing visible in Ventura, plot the entire extents of the drawing, and position and crop in Ventura as necessary. If you only need a small portion of a larger drawing, use a clip box to plot only what you need, then import. You'll save time and disk space.

Importing an HP-GL file into CorelDRAW! is a similar procedure, although CorelDRAW! doesn't use frames, so you can bring an HP-GL file directly into a CorelDRAW! drawing. Select the Import command from the File menu, and select HP-GL file type. The CorelDRAW! file selector is quite similar to that in AutoSketch; use it to specify the desired plot file. CorelDRAW! reads in the file and converts it to its native drawing format. Most AutoSketch objects transfer perfectly using the HP-GL method. The entire drawing will be grouped together and must be broken apart before it can be edited.

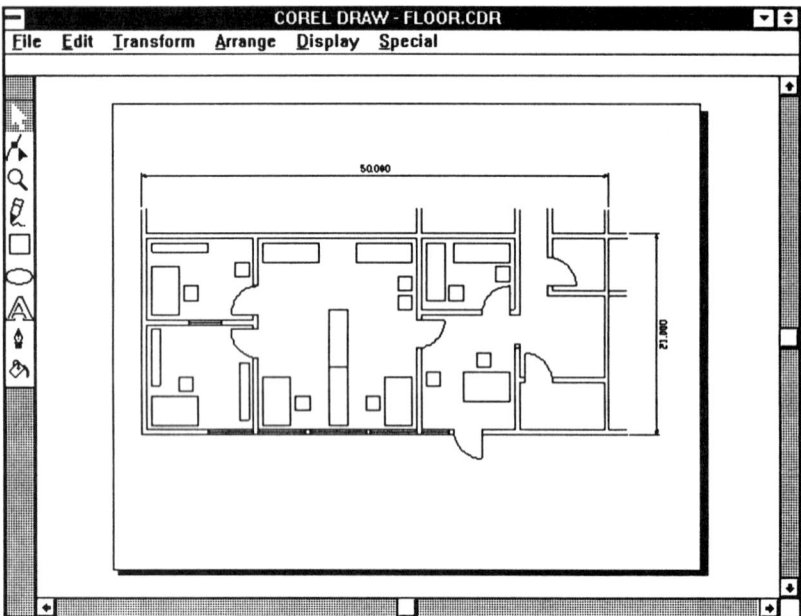
HP-GL File Imported Into CorelDRAW!

Unfortunately, Micrografx Designer currently has no HP-GL import facility. If you want to bring AutoSketch files into Designer, you'll have to work within the limitations of the DXF format.

Most illustration or publishing software has far better text capabilities than those available in AutoSketch. You may wish to replace some or all of your AutoSketch text with new text once the file is transferred.

For programs that don't support HP-GL files, you may be able to import AutoSketch drawings in Encapsulated PostScript (EPS) format. Simply configure AutoSketch for PostScript output and, again, direct output to files. Unfortunately, even though Encapsulated PostScript was designed to be the Esperanto of graphics formats, it has two limitations that make it less useful than HP-GL when used with AutoSketch. First, PostScript is primarily oriented toward publishing and is therefore better at reproducing text and illustrative graphics than the kinds of technical drawings produced by AutoSketch.

What's worse, most programs that profess to read the Encapsulated PostScript format (Adobe Illustrator and CorelDRAW! for example), really read only a limited subset of the PostScript commands normally included in an EPS file. Finally, PostScript files intended for import into desktop publishing programs usually incorporate a bit-mapped preview image; AutoSketch EPS files do not. Without this image, programs such as Ventura Publisher, Microsoft Word, and Wordperfect can read and print an Encapsulated PostScript file, but cannot display it on the screen.

➥ *TIP: If you're using AutoSketch version 2.0, you'll have to go through an additional step to encapsulate your AutoSketch PostScript plot files. The procedure for this is described in the appendix.*

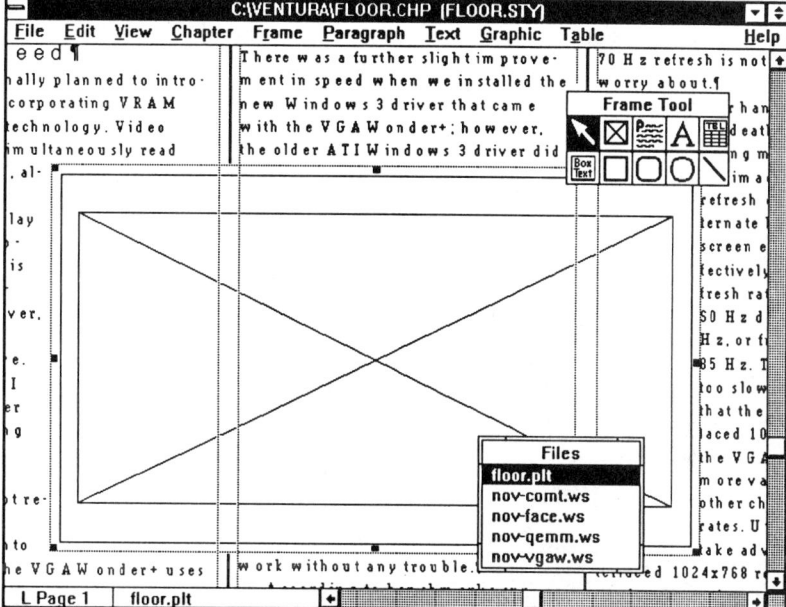

PostScript File Imported Into Ventura Publisher

For these reasons, we suggest that you use HP-GL plot files whenever possible. They convey AutoSketch drawing information just as well, and tend to transfer data more reliably. However, in some cases you will need to transfer drawings to programs that do not support HP-GL input, and Encapsulated PostScript is one solution that you might try.

Command Practice

Try a couple of other little things with slides and then finish up the FLOOR drawing.

NEW. Pull down File and select New to clear the screen.

VIEW SLIDE. Use View Slide to recall the space plan slide. Try to move or erase some of the shapes. (It won't work.) Try zooming or panning the image. It will disappear completely and you won't be able to get it back, short of reloading the file. Trace over a section of the slide with Draw commands, then issue a Redraw command.

MAKE DXF. Try loading some of your practice drawings, or the AutoSketch sample drawings, and exporting them as DXF files. If you are familiar with DOS, go to the DOS command prompt and compare the file sizes of the original drawing files with those of the DXF files. Also try using the TYPE command to examine the contents of a DXF file. Do you recognize anything?

READ DXF. Try reading back some of the DXF files you've created. Observe any changes — particularly what happens to dimensions.

Space Plan Viewing

Open your FLOOR drawing. Set layer 5 invisible to hide the dimension lines. Use Zoom Box to magnify just the two rooms on the left side of the plan. Use Make Slide to create a slide file. Use New to clear the screen. Now recall the slide file using View Slide. The slide looks exactly like your zoomed view. Remember that even if you have Grid on, it will not show in a slide. Now set layer 5 visible again. The dimensions won't reappear. They are not part of the slide.

If you've got access to a system running AutoCAD, try importing the DXF version of your FLOOR drawing.

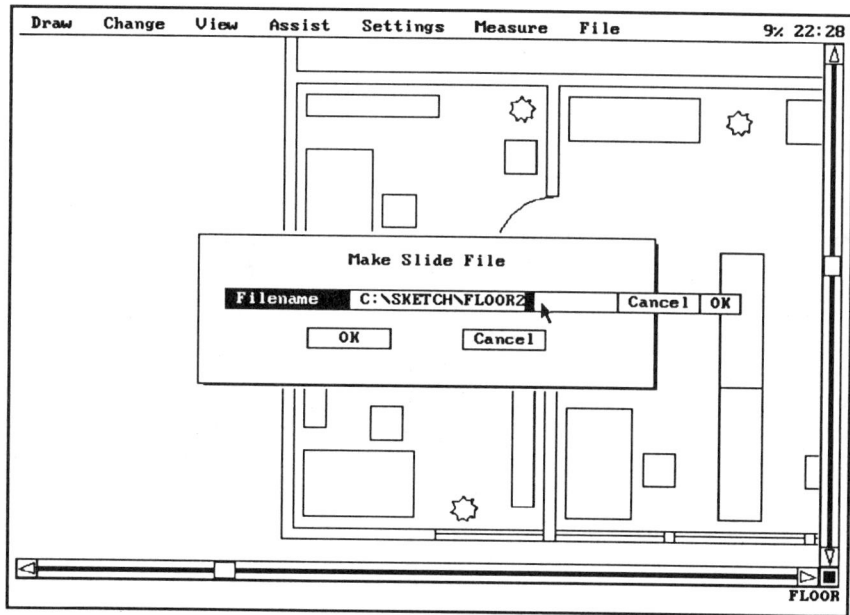

Making a FLOOR2 Slide

Space Plan Viewing Exercise

 Open or continue in FLOOR4 or FLOOR.

 Open or continue in the FLOOR drawing.

```
Pull down Settings Select Layer          Set layer 5 to invisible.
Pull down View Select Zoom Box           Zoom in on the left side.

Pull down File Select Make Slide
Filename FLOOR2                          Enter the name.
Click OK                                 Click the OK box.

Pull down File Select New                Clear the screen.
Pull down File Select View Slide         Recall the first space plan slide, then FLOOR2.
```

Summary

In this chapter you've seen the last of the AutoSketch commands pertaining to input and output of files other than the program's own file type.

Using Make Slide and View Slide, you can save and recall snapshots of the drawing screen, and pass specific views of your work to other users of AutoSketch or AutoCAD. The Make DXF and Read DXF commands let you pass editable drawings between AutoSketch and AutoCAD. You can also use DXF between AutoSketch and other programs, particularly illustration software such as CorelDRAW! and Micrografx Designer. Finally, you can use the AutoSketch capability of plotting to a file to create HP-GL and PostScript files for exporting to programs that don't support DXF, the former being particularly useful for transferring information into CorelDRAW! and Ventura Publisher.

Now that you've mastered all of the commands in AutoSketch, all that remains is to practice combining them creatively to solve real-world drawing problems. In the next chapter, we round off our exploration of AutoSketch with a few extended examples that may give you a better idea of how you can use the program in your daily work.

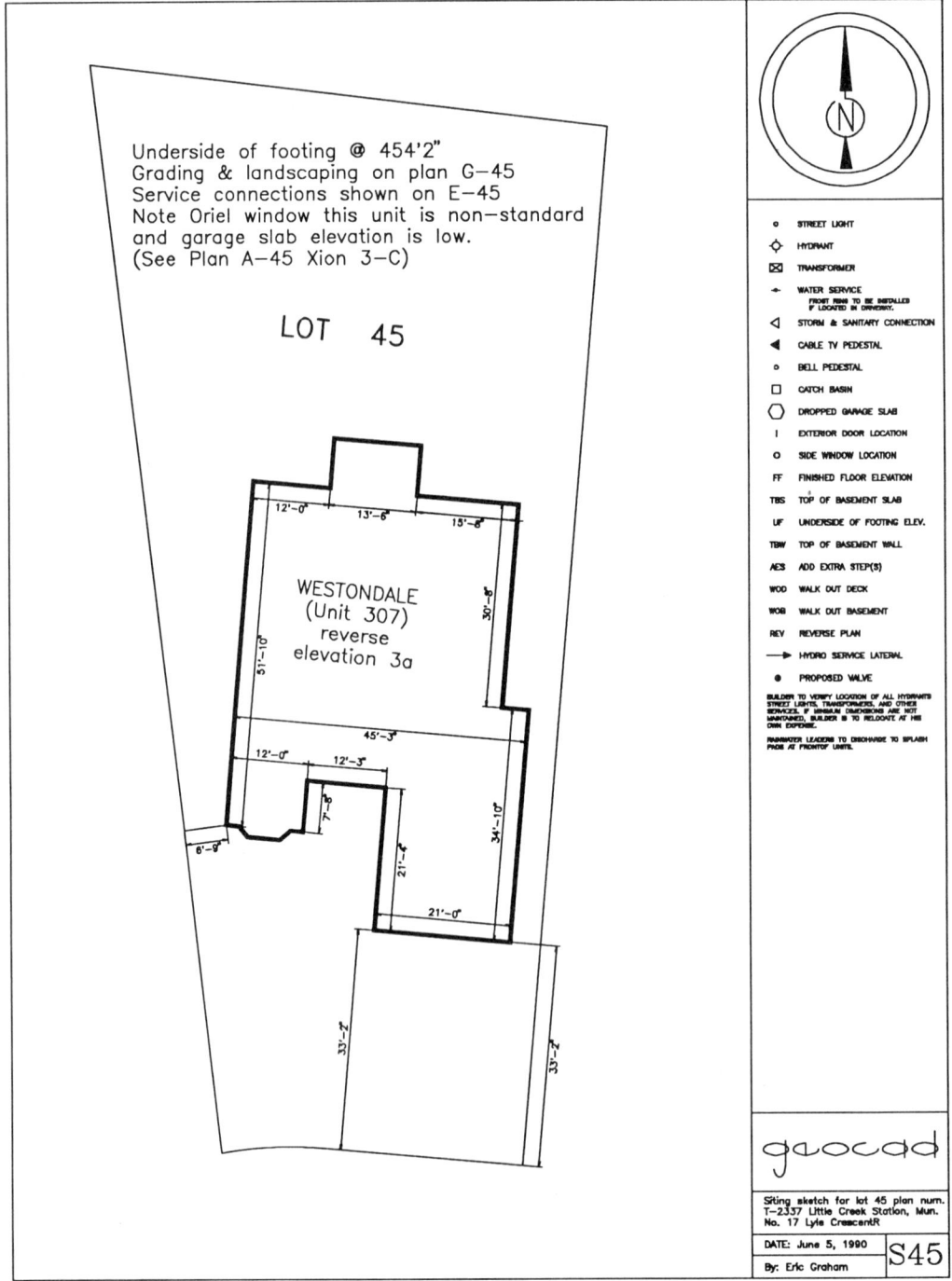

Site Plan Drawn in AutoSketch, Courtesy Eric Graham, GEOCAD

Chapter 12

Advanced Applications

It's one thing to learn all of the commands in a program such as AutoSketch. It's quite another to tackle a real-world project and apply those commands.

AutoSketch is such an easy program to use that most users can work their way through any task without problems. However, real efficiency is something that comes only with experience and planning. It pays to have a clear, logical procedure firmly in mind before you launch into any AutoSketch project. By all means, experiment on the screen; but before you get too far into a drawing, consider the overall process from start to finish. By taking a step back, you will often discover ways to save yourself a lot of time. This chapter provides a shortcut to efficient working in AutoSketch. We'll look at a number of different drawing jobs you might want to do in AutoSketch, focusing on proper approach and work habits. For each drawing type below, you'll find the approximate steps you need to complete that drawing together with suggestions and other tips.

Business Applications

AutoSketch may not seem to be a business-oriented product, but it can take on all sorts of common business-related graphic tasks. If you are already familiar with AutoSketch, you are way ahead of most business computer users. Rather than learn another piece of software to perform a specific task, you will probably find you can be just as productive using AutoSketch and a little ingenuity.

Organizational Charts

One typical business graphics application would be the creation of the infamous organizational or "org" chart. These are easy to create in

AutoSketch, if you pay special attention to the selection of text settings and proper use of attach modes.

The exact procedure is up to you; by now you should be evolving your own approach to AutoSketch. Even though an org chart doesn't have a real-world scale, you should use the expected sheet size of your final output as a guide to setting limits and a general scale for the drawing. As you make draft copies to check the final appearance, you can easily estimate the distances you need to move, stretch, and scale objects into place.

- Set limits, snap, and grid. For an 8 1/2" by 11" chart, set Limits to the effective landscape or portrait printing area of your output device. Try Grid at 1 and Snap at .125.
- Draw one box that you can copy and move into place where needed, according to the organizational structure you'll be diagramming. Decide how large you want the final text to be and how many lines of text you'll need to place in each box. Adding one line to the total will determine the height of each box. For example, a box three lines high will accommodate two lines of text.

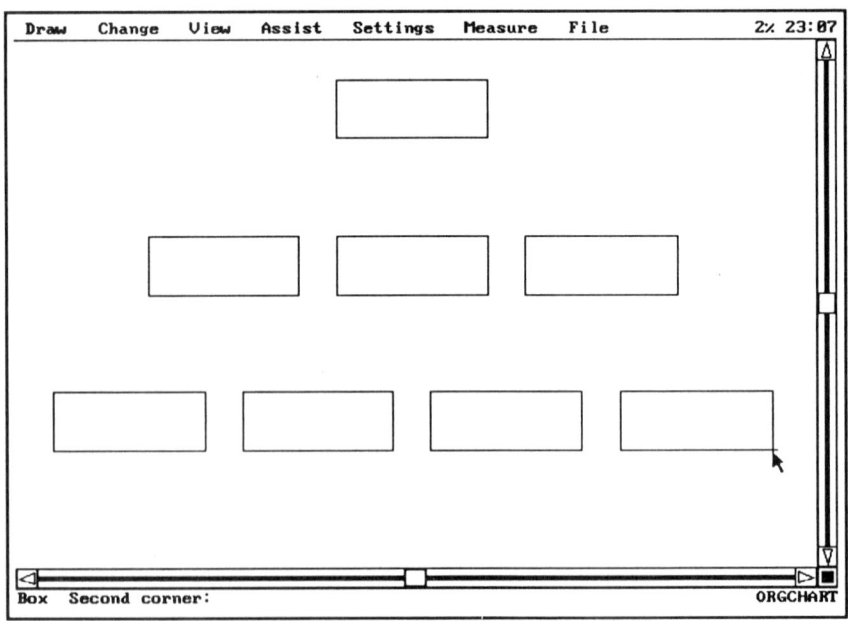

Rough Layout of the Org Chart

- Add text to the boxes. Use Text Settings to set text justification to Center and Middle. Try using one of the more formal-looking fonts, like ROMANC, rather than the very technical-looking default font. Use a text height of about .125".

- Set the Attach mode to Midpoint. Draw in connecting lines between the text boxes. You can use the Line command, but Polyline is more convenient for lines that have corners in them.
- Add arrows or other parts as embellishments. You can use the arrowhead we created earlier in this book or create your own decorative arrowheads.

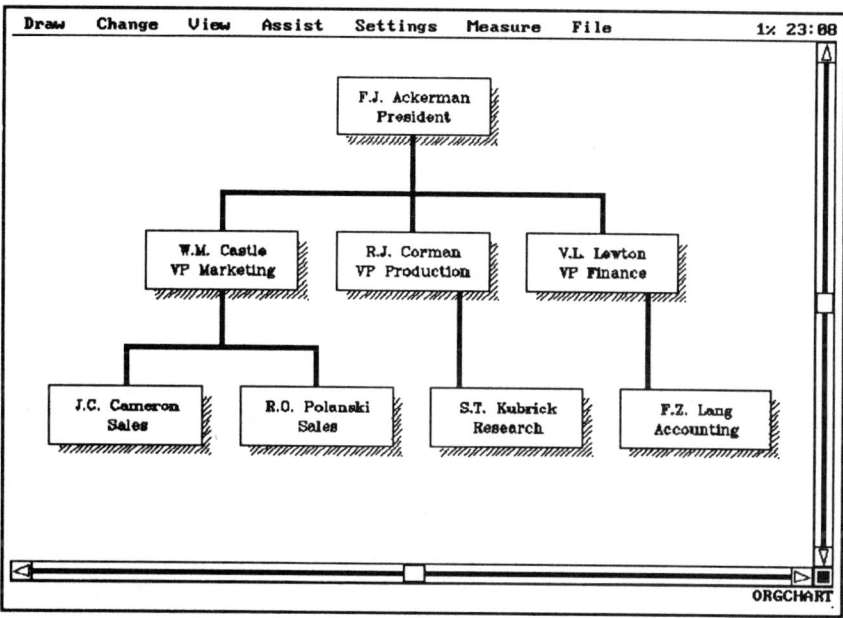

The Completed Org Chart

If you draw some or all of the boxes or connecting lines with the Polyline command, you can easily modify their width. This gives you a lot of flexibility in dressing up the appearance of the chart. Key positions in the chart can be highlighted with wide polylines or even pattern-filled boxes. Using a wide polyline with blank or pattern fill, you can easily create "open" connecting lines as shown in the illustration.

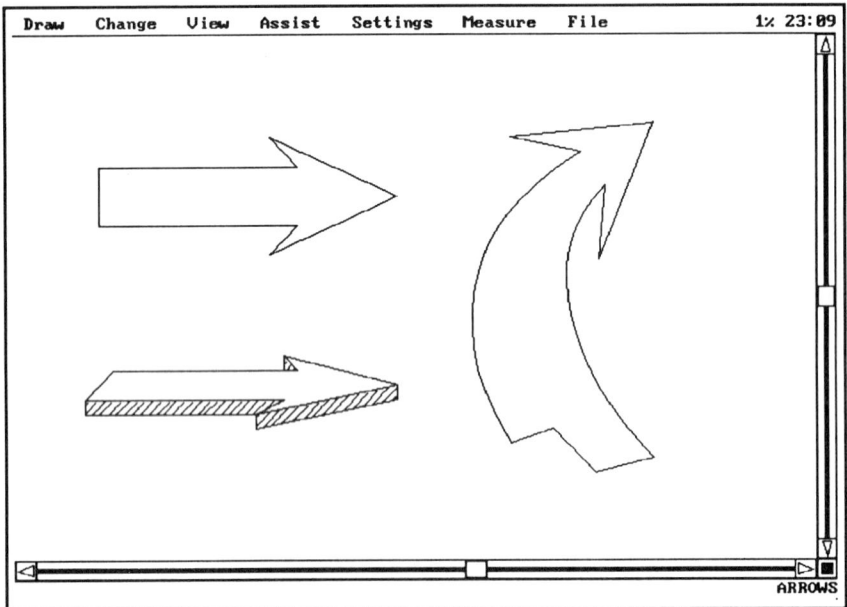

Decorative Arrow Styles

The advantage of doing this type of job in AutoSketch is that if things don't line up exactly as you expected, you can use the editing commands to quickly move text and boxes around and change the text size. Also, once you've created your org chart in AutoSketch, you can easily modify it each time there's an organizational change. You can even use plot and clip boxes to isolate portions of a large organizational tree for specific presentations, or use layers to add annotations that can be hidden or displayed as needed.

For this type of application, AutoSketch falls down only in the area of text. All AutoSketch's own text fonts are relatively simple vector shapes. Although the selection of text styles is reasonably good, text output quality isn't as good as software that takes full advantage of the built-in text capabilities of a laser printer. However, for all but the most appearance-sensitive applications, AutoSketch should be a more than adequate tool.

A similar, but more technical, application encountered in today's heavily computerized businesses is the software flow chart. There are relatively few good flow-charting software packages on the market. AutoSketch can handle these types of jobs very well. The procedure is a lot like creating org charts, but the flow chart is typically more complex. You will need to construct a library of standard symbols used in flow charts.

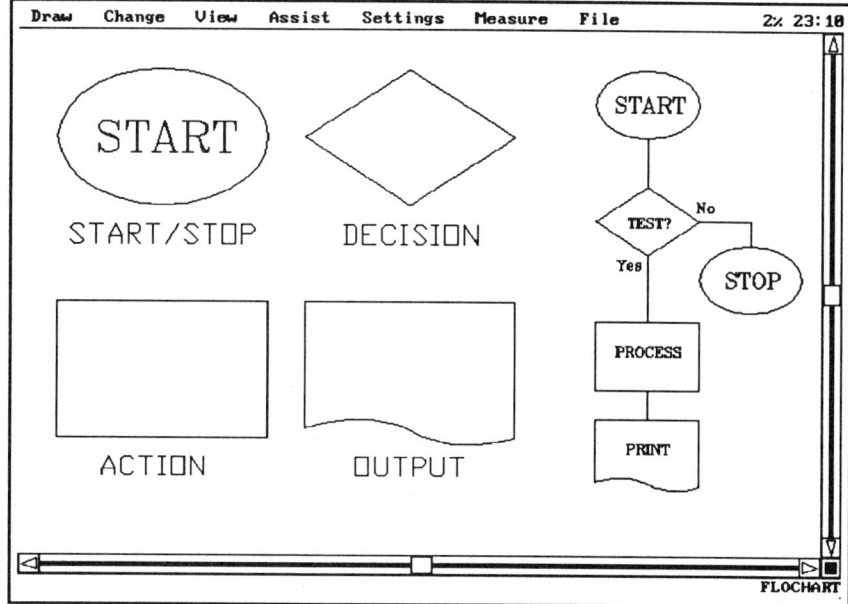

Flow-Chart Symbols

Pie Charts and Graphs

AutoSketch is not the ideal tool for creating charts and graphs. There are many software products on the market that have the ability to convert numerical information directly into graphical representations: bar charts, pie charts, line graphs, and so on. However, for occasional use AutoSketch is quite adequate and can save you the extra expense of one of these other programs.

Creating a pie chart is simply a matter of drawing a circle, dividing it into appropriately sized segments, and adding labels.

- First, draw the circle. The rest of your job will be easier if you enable Snap and place the center of the circle on a snap point. Give the circle a specific radius. Either place the circumference point on another snap point located orthogonally above, below, or to either side of the center, or use relative coordinates to specify the radius.

- Calculate the angles for each slice of your pie chart. If you have a series of percentages to graph, multiply each percentage by 360 degrees to get the included angle of that segment. Next, decide on the sequence of the segments, rotating counterclockwise around your pie. You don't have to start at zero degrees; just make sure you take the starting angle into account.

- Start the first segment. Place one end of a line at the center of the circle. Use polar coordinates to position the other end of the line, using the radius of the circle for the distance, and the starting angle of the first pie slice as the angle.
- Draw more lines. Each line should start at the center of the circle and use an angle value that is the starting angle plus the sums of the angles included in all the preceding segments.
- Label the pie chart with Quick Text.

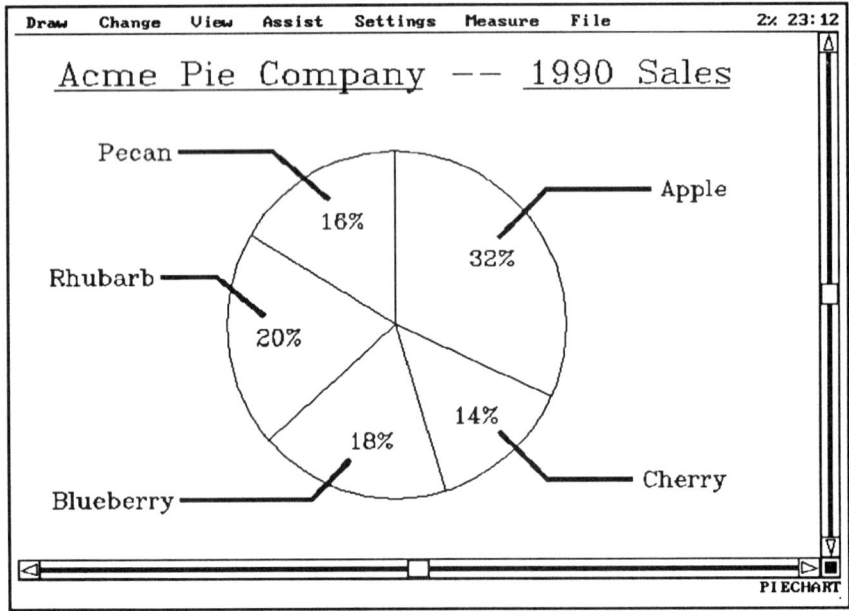

Creating a Pie Chart

Obviously, you need to do some calculation to draw graphs in AutoSketch. However, the mathematics involved are certainly not difficult.

Theoretically, you could use Snap (to place one end of the radial lines), then toggle Snap off and use Perpendicular Attach mode to place the endpoints precisely on the circle. Unfortunately, AutoSketch has trouble calculating exactly which point perpendicular to the circle to use. For this reason, we suggest that you use a specific radius distance to ensure that the radial lines meet the circumference accurately.

If you want a pie chart with an "exploded" segment, first copy the pie. Use Break to remove the appropriate section of the original circle. Then use Break to remove all but that section of the duplicate pie, and Erase to remove the extraneous radial lines. You should end up with a perfect pie slice that you can offset from the gap in your original pie. Copying the entire pie and erasing the unwanted parts is much easier and more accurate than trying to build a new pie slice using lines and an arc.

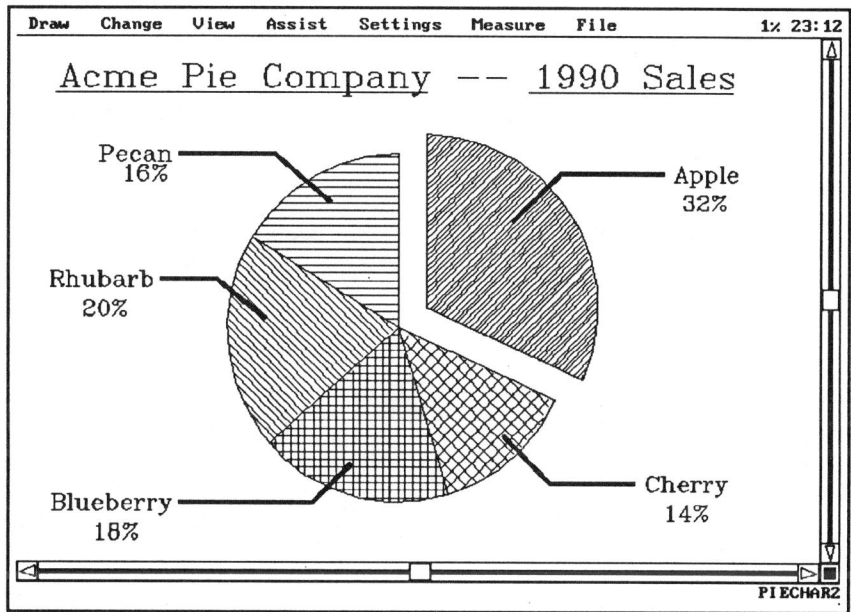

Pie Chart With an Exploded Segment

Drawing a line graph presents a different challenge. In this case, you can use Snap and Grid to help you graph the data. The scale for these drawings can be one of those cases we mentioned in Chapter 1 where you are using both unusual standard units and enormous scale. Since numeric data has no real-world scale, you can use a direct relationship between drawing units and the data.

For example, suppose you are working for the Acme Widget Company, and you want to graph your sales for 1990. Assume that in your best month you sold 30,000 widgets. Since you'll be graphing thousands of widgets sold, you can let the maximum Y distance be 30. The X distance should be 12, one drawing unit for every month, but that would give you a very tall graph. To give it better proportions, use three units horizontally per month. Leave a few units of space at the sides to make room for captions. Notice how we ended up with a unit scale for this drawing of 1000 widgets for Y and one-third of a month for X. Unusual drawing jobs like this often end up with seemingly arbitrary scales because the objects you are drawing really have no scale. Simply use whatever scale makes your job easier. If you are consistent and accurate, plotting to the extents of your drawing will ensure it fits on the paper.

- Set your drawing limits to -2 and -2 for left and bottom, 31 and 37 for top and right. These settings will let you use the visible grid as a guide for entering sales amounts accurately. Zoom limits. Set Snap to 0.5 and Grid to 1.0.
- Draw the axes, using Line. Extend the axes by one-half unit at the lower left so that they cross slightly. Add tick marks extending half a unit to either side of each axis to indicate the major divisions — months on the X axis, 5000 units on the Y axis.

➥ *TIP: After creating several tick marks on each axis, you can use a Window box to grab just the marks and copy them. This saves a lot of time.*

As opposed to using tick marks on the axes, there are a lot of other options. For instance, you may want to draw a grid of lines across the graph area itself. You can use an alternate line type for these: dashed or dotted. For the sake of clarity, you might want to use a wide, solid polyline to draw the axes. Bear in mind that if you're drawing an area chart, you'll need to break away the hidden grid lines or they'll show through a patterned area fill.

- That's the hard part. Now all you have to do is draw in objects to represent the sales for each month. You can use several methods depending on the type of graph you want.

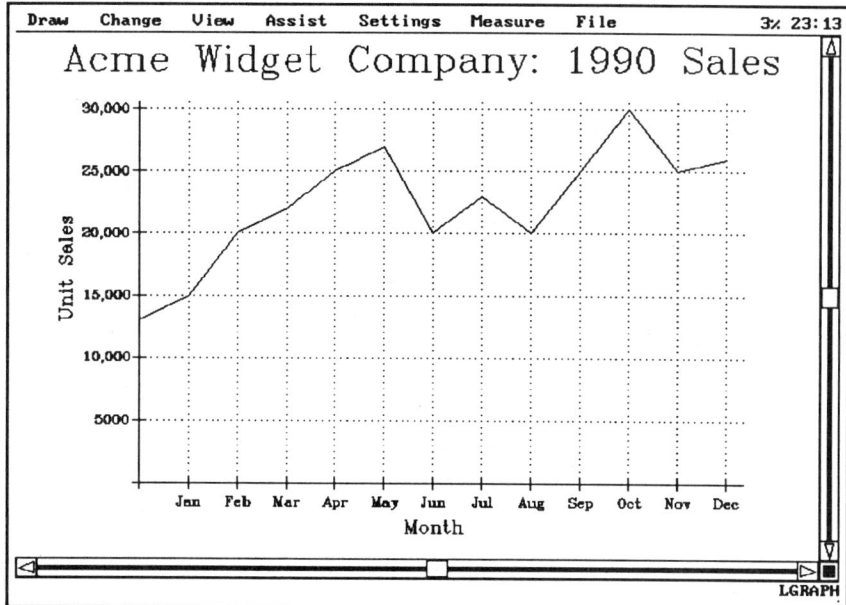

A Simple Line Graph

Scatter plots are a straightforward variation on this technique. Use small markers — squares, circles, triangles — to show values on the graph. You can use symbols from the SYMAP text font as data-point marks; the upper-case A, B, C, I, J, K, L, M and N are particularly appropriate. If you place these characters directly on the graph, be sure to set text justification to Center and Middle. Otherwise, the characters will be offset from the point you pick for Quick Text.

For an area graph, use Pattern Fill instead of Polyline to draw the graph line.

A column graph is very little extra trouble. Instead of drawing a graph line, you can draw columns at each X location. Draw one column and copy it, or save it as a part. Once the copies are in position, use Stretch to extend each one to the correct Y height.

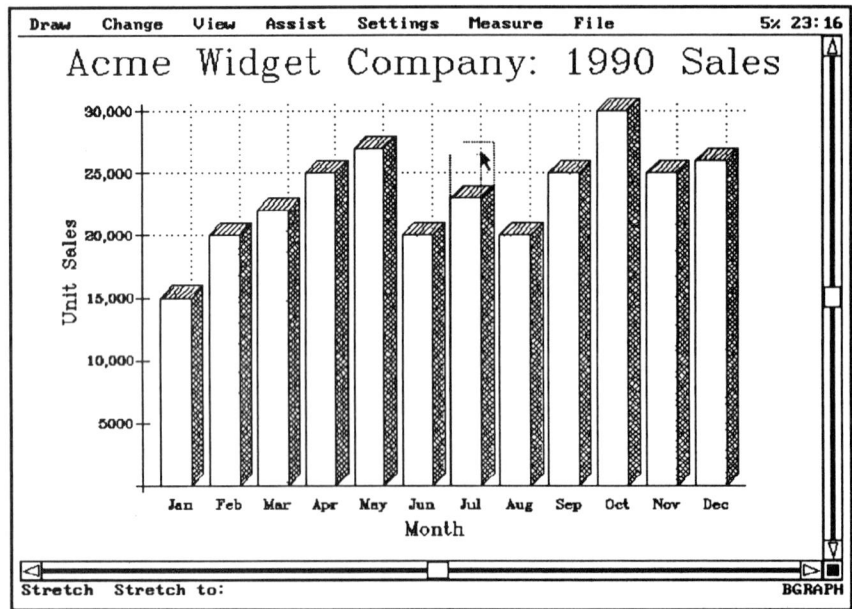

Using Stretch on Column Graphs

Isometric Drawings

There are numerous ways to represent a three-dimensional object on a flat surface. Each involves some sort of compromise. One of the most popular ways is isometric projection. Although AutoSketch has no specific aids for isometric drawing, it is still much easier to use than a pencil, T-square, protractor, and other traditional drafting tools. In previous chapters, we alluded to some of the techniques you'll need for drawing isometric views. We'll expand on them further here.

In the three-dimensional world, the three axes X, Y, and Z are at 90 degrees to each other. In an isometric drawing, the axes are flattened out onto the page and drawn 120 degrees apart.

Isometric drawings provide a realistic representation of relatively small objects and are therefore frequently used in mechanical design. A simple example should help. The following is a procedure for drawing the 35mm camera shown in the illustration. It demonstrates most of the principles you need to draw just about anything.

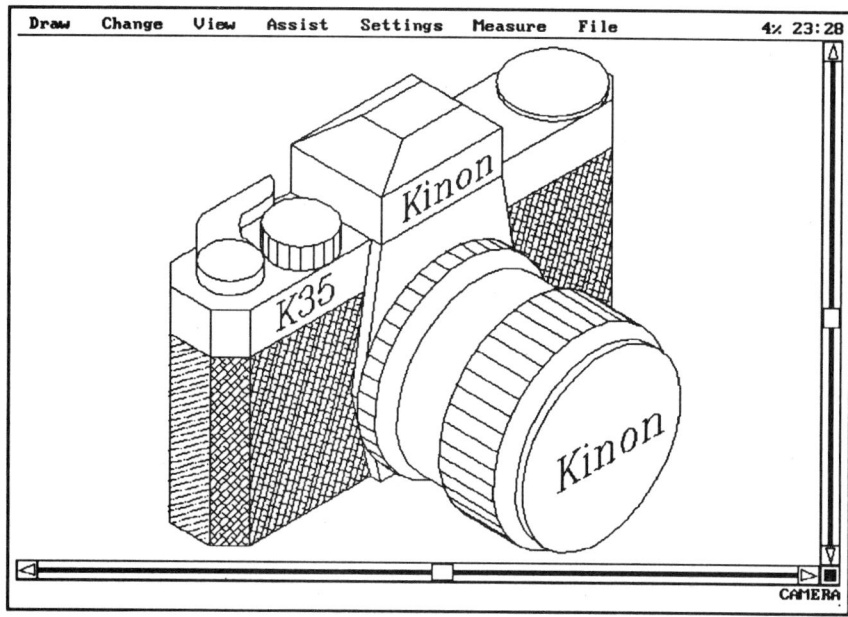

The 35mm Camera

- Set Snap and Grid to isometric proportions as described in Chapter 6: Grid X to 1.732051, and Grid Y to 1; Snap X to 0.1732051, and Snap Y to 0.1. Set Limits on the right to 24, top 16.
- Draw the top surface of the camera body, using the Polyline command. Place the front left corner, then enter the polar coordinates: P(10,30), P(2,150), P(10,210) and P(2,330).
- Chamfer the corners of the polyline using a chamfer size of 0.5.
- Copy the chamfered polyline, placing the copy 5.0 units above the original.
- Turn Snap off. Turn on Attach in End Point mode. Connect the corners of the two polylines using the Line command.
- You'll need to locate the center of the front face of the camera to position the lens. One easy way is to use Line to draw in two diagonal construction lines. Change to Intersect Attach mode, and draw a vertical construction line through the intersection of the two diagonals. Start it at the base of the camera, and make it 4.0 units high.

- Copy this line in place, and rotate the copy to parallel the top edge of the camera body. Set Midpoint Attach mode, and start to move the rotated line with its midpoint as the from point. Change to End Point Attach mode, and place the midpoint of the rotated line at the top of the original vertical line. Measure the distance between the upper right end of the rotated line and the midpoint of the vertical line, once more switching Attach modes from End Point back to Midpoint. You should get 3.464.

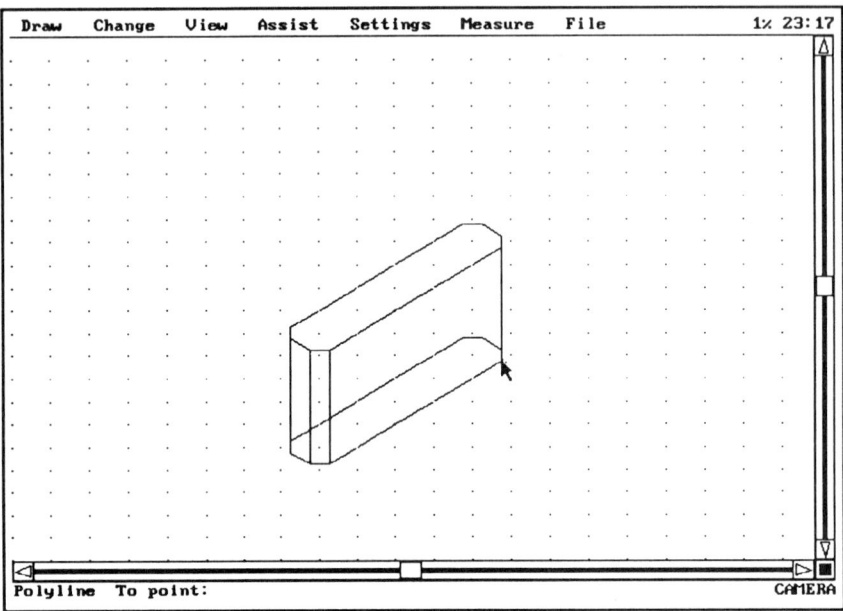

Drawing the Camera Body

- Set Midpoint Attach mode. Set Ellipse mode to Axis and Planar Rotation. Select the Ellipse command from the Draw menu. Place the center of the ellipse at the midpoint of the vertical line. The equation to calculate the major axis distance is Sin(45) x 3.466. Therefore, enter the polar coordinate P(2.450832,60) to specify the major axis endpoint. For planar rotation, enter the coordinate P(1,45) to specify a 45-degree angle.

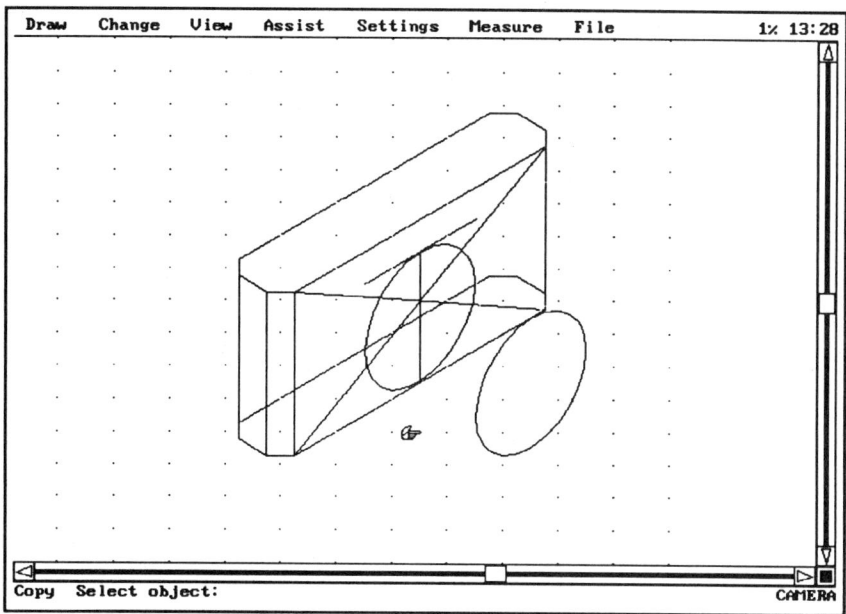

Positioning the Ellipse

- To position the other end of the lens, copy the ellipse from its center point to P(4,-30).
- Next, use Tangent Attach mode and Line to construct the lens barrel.
- Using Zoom as needed, break away the lines hidden behind the lens and camera body. Erase the various construction lines: the two diagonal construction lines, the horizontal and vertical ellipse construction lines, and the lens center line.

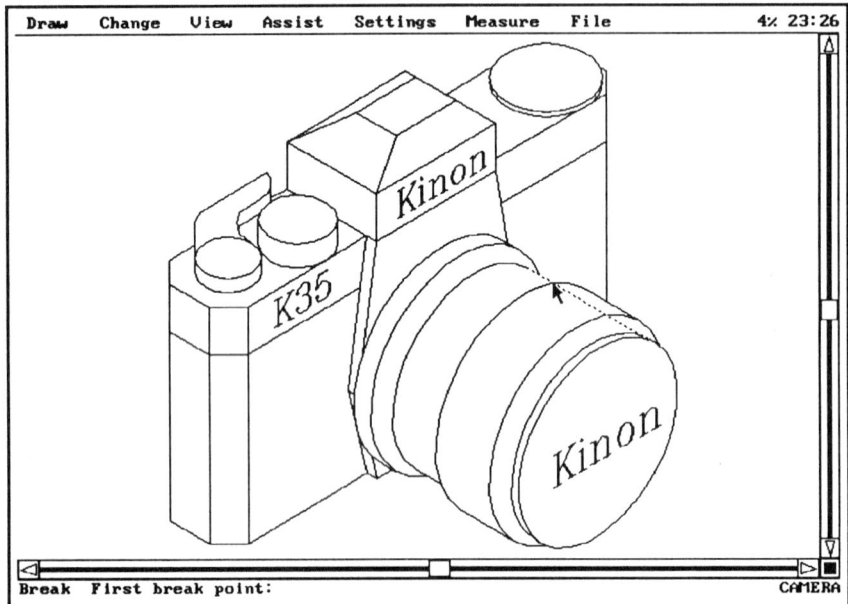

Breaking Away Hidden Lines

This covers all the basic techniques you need. Using these few construction line and Attach mode tricks, you can draw just about any isometric shape. Try continuing the exercise: add the eyepiece housing, shutter-speed dial, and film advance lever to the top of the camera body, and focus and aperture rings to the lens. As you can see, even though AutoSketch doesn't have built-in 3D features or automatic hidden line removal like the more advanced CAD programs, it can still be used to create effective isometric projections.

Maps Made Easy

Try cleaning up the map exercise you did in the early chapters of this book, using some of the more advanced techniques you've learned since then to make this into a more professional drawing. Here are a few suggestions:

- First, draw a border around your map.
- Draw in a more realistic shoreline using the Curve command.
- Replace the dot pattern in Lake Clearwater with a pattern fill. Zoom in on the upper right corner of the map. Set Intersection Attach mode. Using the Pattern Fill command, trace along the shoreline from where it intersects the box. Follow just on the water side of the shoreline; you don't need to get too close. When you reach the right side of the border, draw upwards a short distance, then cross over the

middle of the water area. Make a 90-degree corner and rejoin the box along the upper edge, then close the pattern area. When the Accept/Modify dialogue box appears, select Modify. Change the pattern to DASH, and turn Boundary off. Draw a second pattern to fill the upper right portion of the lake, but leave a blank rectangle in the middle to accommodate a label.

- Enlarge the original text "Lake Clearwater" if necessary and change the font to ROMANS. Place the text in the blank area you've prepared for it.

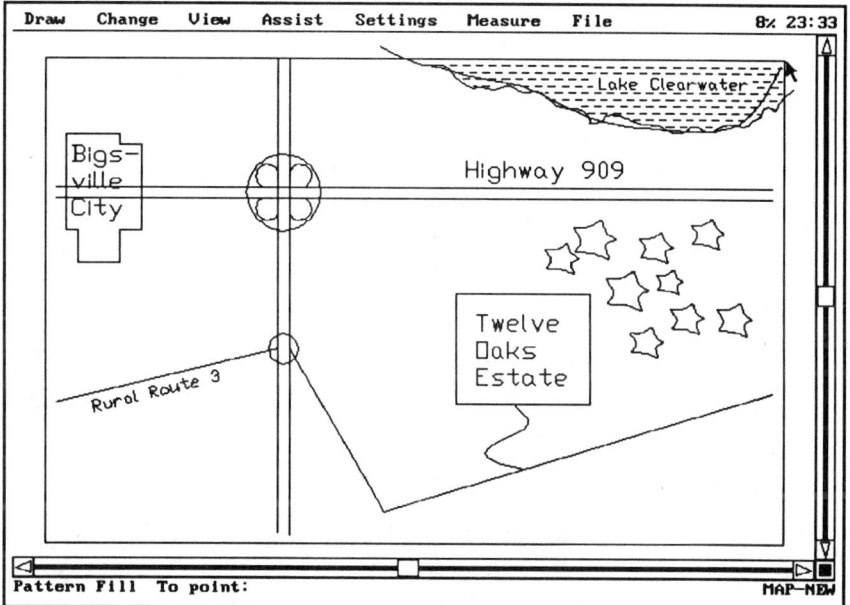

Adding a Pattern to the Water

- Use a similar technique to rebuild Bigsville City. Hatch it with the CRSSHTCH pattern, an angle of 45 degrees, and a spacing of 0.1.
- There's no ideal pattern in AutoSketch to represent forest, but CROSS at a 30-degree angle and 0.6 scale will do the job reasonably well. Use it to replace the trees you drew in originally. An alternate technique would be to use the tree symbol corresponding to lower-case b in the SYMAP text font. Draw one using Quick Text, then copy it repeatedly. We've used both techniques in our illustration; one to represent heavy forest, the other, brush country.

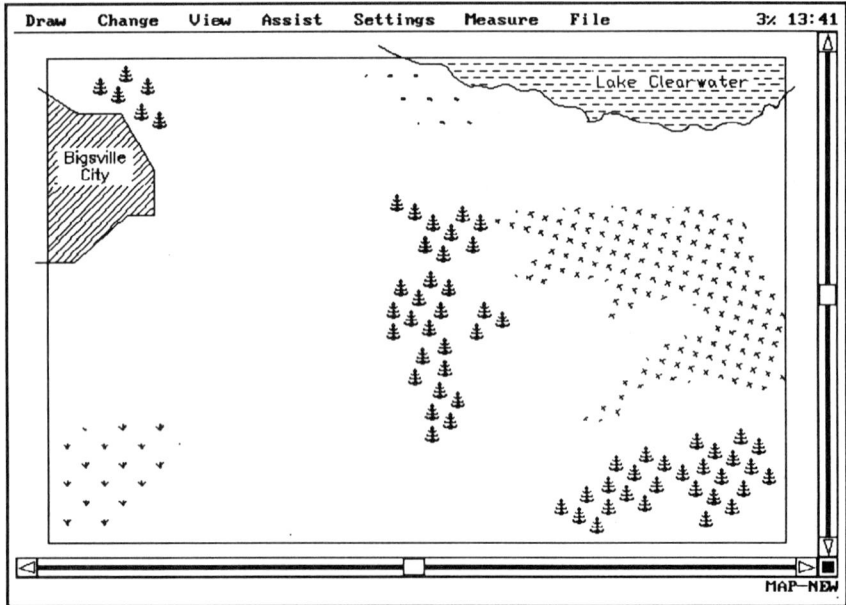

Two Techniques for Representing Forest

- AutoSketch does provide a SWAMP pattern. Add some swamp using this. There's also a GRASS pattern you can use. The amount of these patterns you place on the map will depend on the type of map you are trying to create. A road map, for instance, will have relatively little detail of the terrain.
- Unless you can work with colored plotter pens, the best way to represent the major highways is with double lines. However, you'll want to draw more realistic curved highways, rather than the simple straight ones used originally. The Polyline command is the only tool for the job. Set the polyline width to 0.1 with Blank Fill. Use Arc mode to insert curved segments. Unfortunately, when you complete the polyline at the map border, you'll find that there's no easy way to make the square polyline ends mate cleanly with the border line.
- The local road should remain a single line, but can also be replaced with a more complex polyline.
- To label the highways, use the SYMAP text font with a height of 0.3. The lower-case o and p on your keyboard will produce the typical highway number "shield" symbols. Add text using the ROMANC font at 0.2 height.
- The simple box originally used to represent your country estate should be redrawn to a more accurate shape using the Polyline command as shown in the illustrations.

- A north arrow should be inserted, pointing to true north. And a scale rule should be added. A proper map would also include a complete legend, showing all the symbols you've used.

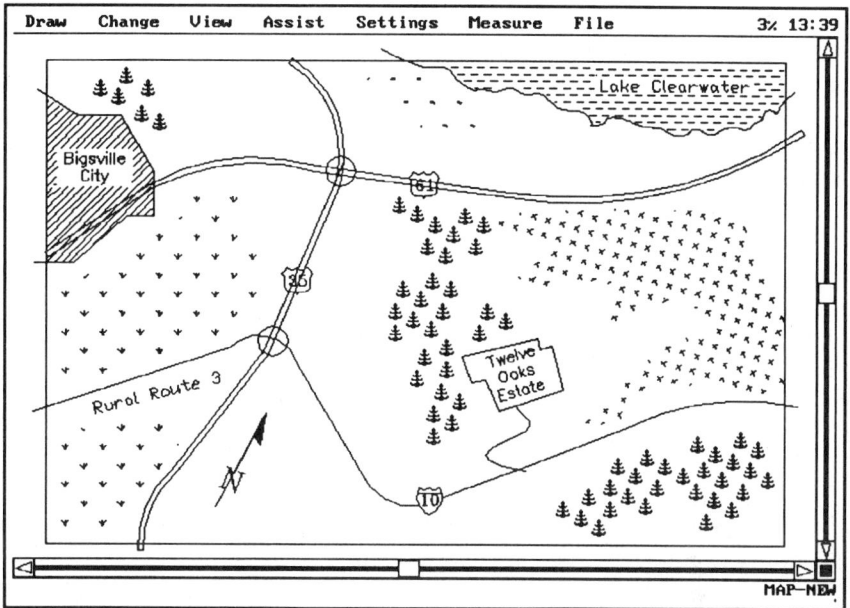

The Rebuilt MAP Drawing

Obviously, if you had accurate survey information, scaling would be critical in drawing your map. Each detail would need to be represented according to its true position. To do this, you would first set up Snap and Grid. You would probably want one drawing unit to represent something like one mile on the map. In the case of our map, that would require the entire drawing to be enlarged using the Scale command. Alternatively, you could define one unit to equal, say, ten miles. In this case, grid spacing should be 1.0 and snap spacing 0.1.

This certainly doesn't exhaust the cartographic possibilities of AutoSketch. For example, you can create detailed topographical maps using the Curve command to draw contour lines. Weather maps are drawn in much the same way, with the addition of special symbols to represent air flows.

Site Plans

Just as mechanical drawings communicate the design of a machine part, site plans are used to communicate various design parameters relevant to the construction of a house: the position of the house on its lot, the routing of services such as water and electricity, and even landscaping details such as the location of bushes and flower beds.

There are really no new techniques involved in drawing a site plan in AutoSketch. Drawing an accurate site plan is mostly a matter of transferring survey data to drawing coordinate locations. Dimensioning is very important, since the placement of houses involves complex legalities.

The example drawing on the facing page of this chapter is a working site plan, one of many that made up the plans for a new urban subdivision. It shows positioning of the house on its lot — something that is rigorously controlled by an array of local building codes. These codes specify factors such as the percentage of the lot that may be covered by the house, the minimum setback of the house from the front, and the clearances at the sides and back. All of these values vary, depending on proximity to major roadways, whether the lot is on a corner, and so on.

In creating a site plan such as the one in the illustration, the draftsman would be presented with survey information for the lot in the form of distances and bearings for each of the boundaries. The house plan would be supplied by the architect or developer. Here are the major steps:

- First, draw the lot boundary. Each corner is a specified survey point, and each side can be easily drawn as a polyline segment, translating the given location and bearing information into a polar coordinate.
- Assuming that the house plan was created on a computer, it might be inserted as a DXF file. If it is not, then an outline would be created as a polyline, using the hand-drafted dimensions. In our example, a wide polyline with solid fill has been used.
- Dimensioning should be carefully applied, primarily using the Align Dimension command. Some dimensions may have to be constructed manually, using the techniques described in Chapter 10.
- Other annotations and a title block are added. Note that the example drawing includes a complete legend of symbols, most of which are not used in this case. The title block is actually a standard part, added automatically to all the site plans generated by this company.

Tips for Schematic Diagrams

One common example of a schematic drawing is the electronic schematic diagram, which shows the design of a working circuit. Again, there are programs on the market that are optimized for creating two types of drawings. However, AutoSketch costs only a fraction of the price of these highly automated programs, and can produce equally workable results with a bit of care.

Schematic diagrams are particularly easy to create in AutoSketch. The process is similar to that for drawing an organizational chart, but more complex.

- Set up Snap and Grid. Use the default spacing of one unit for the grid. Set Snap to a smaller value, either .05 or 0.1 units, to draw small parts.
- Draw one of each electronic symbol used in the circuit, making sure each electrical connection point ends on a snap interval. Group each one and save as a part file for use in other schematics.
- Label the ratings and part numbers of the components. Set text justification to Center and Left for text along the left side of a symbol, Center and Right for text along the right side.
- Draw the electrical connections. The most useful tool is Polyline, since it can go around corners as needed, and works for single segments as well. Copy and rotate symbols as needed for each component and move them into place.

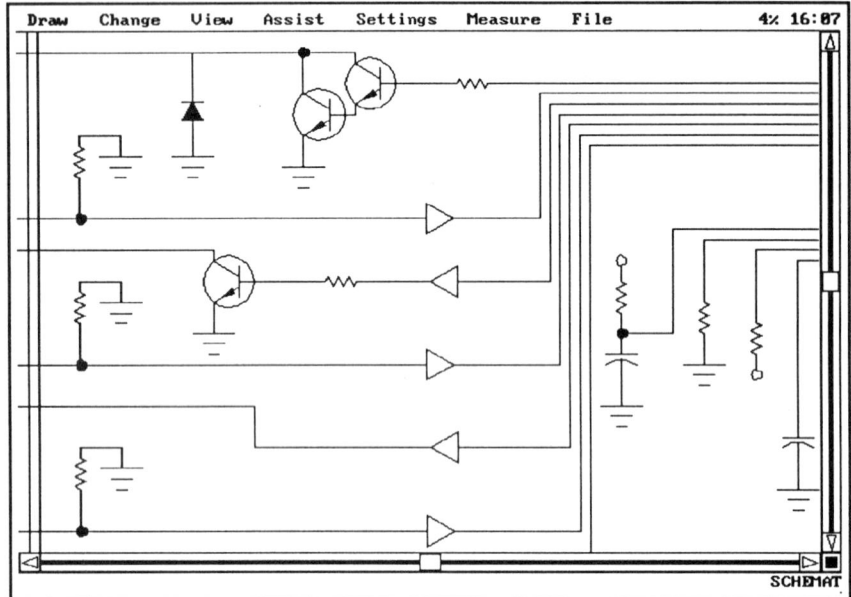

Section of a Schematic Drawing

When creating parts, zoom in on them before using the Part Clip command to store them for re-use. This will ensure that the corresponding icon on the Part menu is large enough to be useful. You should either store parts in a separate directory on your disk, or give them distinctive names — perhaps all beginning with a P. Parts that are used in two orientations (such as resistors and capacitors) can be saved twice, one 90 degrees from the other to save a rotation step later. By covering all the possible combinations of orientation and insertion points, you can save quite a bit of time and effort.

If you are using AutoSketch as a design tool — that is, if you design the circuit as you draw it — the layout will almost certainly bog down at various points. You may often find, for example, that two components have been placed too close together to allow for others to be placed between them. AutoSketch makes it easy to rearrange sections of the drawing. Just use the Stretch command, rather than Move. Components entirely enclosed within the Crosses/window box will be moved; any lines crossing the box will stretch to maintain all your connections. If you make the stretches parallel to connecting lines, they will remain neatly orthogonal.

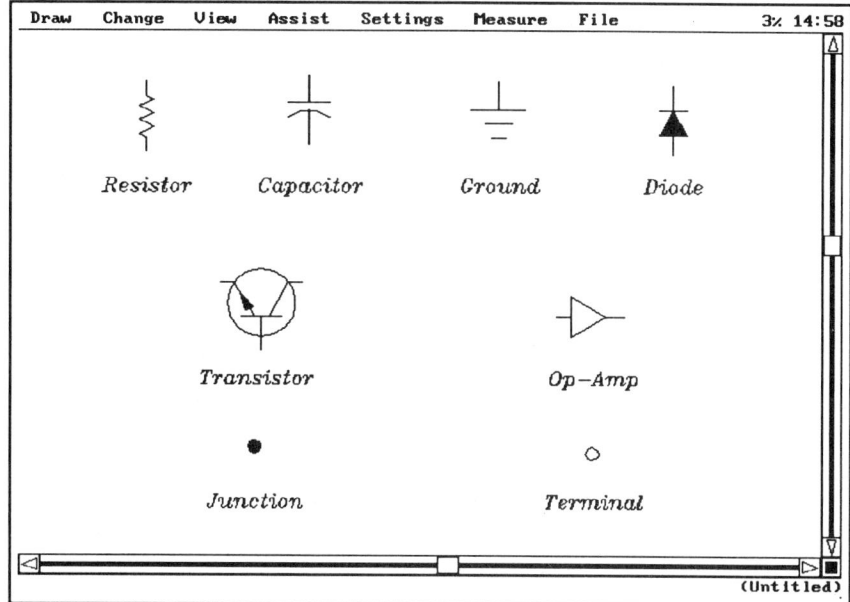

Various Parts Used in the Schematic

All of the techniques given here can be applied equally well to other types of schematic diagrams. For example, hydraulic systems diagrams use similar symbology, where the resistors, transistors, and integrated-circuit chips of electronic diagrams are replaced by symbols representing valves, pumps, and related mechanical components. Once you've built up (or purchased) an appropriate symbol library, you can use drawing techniques exactly like those described above.

Summary

All these procedures may sound intimidating, but they shouldn't. We're not suggesting that you should make work for yourself. Over time you may find that some of the procedures we've described really are not ideal for you, and you'll probably end up modifying them to suit yourself. That's great — this book is, after all, only a starting point. Still, in the long run you'll probably find that the careful, disciplined way of working is also the easy way.

Happy AutoSketching!

Appendix

The main part of this book contains all the information you need to use AutoSketch itself. However, there are a lot of other things to know about the correct use of your computer system, and these will also affect the usefulness of AutoSketch. This appendix covers the following areas:

- Work-arounds for AutoSketch 2.0 users
- Tips on configuring AutoSketch for multiple devices
- Hardware tips
- File management tips
- Using AutoSketch command line options
- Use of prototype drawings
- Support and CompuServe

This appendix cannot be a substitute for a good, basic manual on MS-DOS computing, but what we *can* do is to discuss how AutoSketch fits into the rest of the computing world.

Work-Arounds for AutoSketch 2.0

AutoSketch version 3.0 is a very powerful piece of software. We strongly recommend that users still working with version 2.0 (or earlier) get in touch with Autodesk to obtain an upgrade to the current version. Most of the exercises in this book depend on the advanced features available only in AutoSketch version 3.0. However, based on our past experience with AutoSketch, we can provide a few tips for users of earlier versions. Even users of AutoSketch version 3.0 can learn something from these tips.

Creating Hatch Patterns

Hatch patterns come in handy under many circumstances. For example, they are used to distinguish between different materials or to show that a particular view is a cross section. By creating various hatch patterns that represent materials such as brickwork, grass, or wood, you can spice up the simplest of drawings.

Creation of hatch patterns in AutoSketch version 3.0 is simply a matter of using the Pattern Fill command. AutoSketch version 2.0 offered only solid fill, via the Fill Region command. But with patience, it is possible to create reusable hatch patterns that can be used in any version of AutoSketch. We'll do this using AutoSketch's Part facility to save an array of predrawn objects that can be used later.

The following exercise demonstrates the creation of a simple hatch pattern that consists of horizontal lines. We'll use a 0.0625 (1/16-inch) spacing, which will plot at 1:1 as fine ruled lines. For other plot scales, you'll need to scale the pattern after you insert it. If you use some of the larger pens, you may also want to scale the pattern or make the spacing wider.

The quickest way to draw a large group of evenly spaced lines is to use the Box Array command with a single column and many rows. Note that if you have a low-resolution display, you'll almost certainly need to zoom in to see the results, or use a wider line spacing.

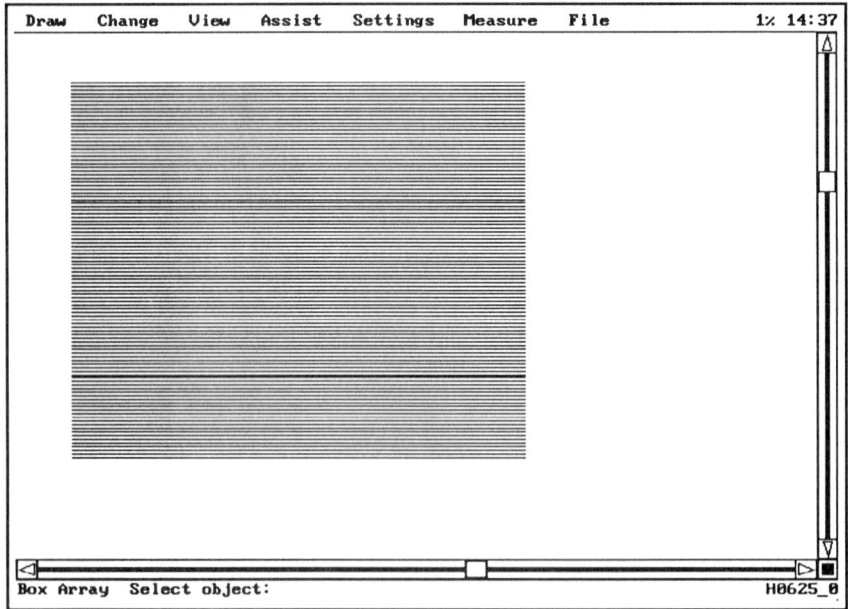

Creating a Hatch Pattern

Creating a Hatch Pattern

```
Pull down File Select New
Pull down File Select Save As          Save as H0625_0.
```

This filename makes the drawing recognizable as a hatch pattern (H) with .0625 spacing (0625) at a zero degree angle (_0). You can use this naming convention to describe many other line spacing and angle combinations.

```
Pull down Assist Select Ortho              Turn on Ortho mode.
Pull down Assist Select Snap               Use Snap.
Pull down Draw Select Line                 Draw an 8" horizontal line.
Pull down Settings Select Box Array
Row Distance .0625                         Enter the row spacing.
Column Distance 0                          A zero column distance yields one column.
Rows 104                                   104 rows will yield a square pattern.
Columns 1
Click Fit                                  Put a check mark in the Fit box of the Columns
                                           option.
Click OK

Pull down Change Select Box Array
Pick                                       Anywhere on the line you drew.

AutoSketch builds the array.

Click Accept                               If your drawing looks like the illustration above.

Pull down Settings Select Part Base
Set by pointing:                           Click the box.
Insertion base:                            Click the lower left corner.
Pull down Change Select Group              Select all of the lines.
Pull down File Select Save                 Save the new pattern.
```

Horizontal lines can be used in a variety of ways. Since you made a part out of a group of horizontal lines, it can be inserted into any drawing. Once inserted, you can rotate it to a specific angle, copy it to other areas of your drawing, or make minor placement adjustments by selecting just one object. You can copy it onto itself and rotate the copied pattern 90 degrees to create a cross-hatch pattern that can, in turn, be rotated. Before you finalize your pattern, be sure to scale it for the desired line spacing at your intended plotting scale.

Once you've positioned your hatch pattern correctly, ungroup the part and break away any unwanted portions or stretch the pattern to fit . The procedure is easier if you place the hatch pattern on an otherwise unused layer.

Remember, the Break command lets you use the Crosses/window box to select as many objects as you like. It will then prompt you for break points on each selected object, until everything that was selected has been broken. This characteristic is ideal for working with hatch patterns. Select Break, then select all the lines in the pattern. Use

Attach with Intersect mode, and break outward from the boundary of the area to be hatched.

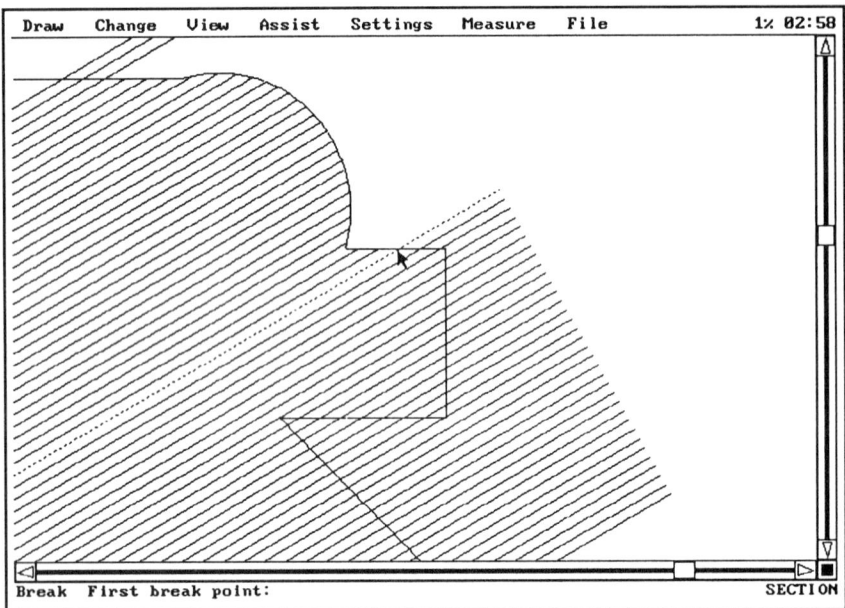

Breaking Away the Excess Pattern

Since zoom commands are transparent, you can zoom in and out and pan back and forth without interrupting the Break command.

More complex patterns take longer to draw initially, but can be used in exactly the same way. For example, notice the knurl pattern on the lens of the CAMERA drawing in Chapter 12. This was created separately, then laid over the isometric outline of the camera and the unwanted portions broken away — exactly as described above.

Constructing Wide Lines

Until version 3.0, AutoSketch had no provision for drawing lines of different widths. However, it is possible to create thick lines by combining multiple thin lines.

Say you have a single vertical line, and you want to triple its width. You would copy the line twice, once to the right and once to the left. But at what spacing? The spacing between the copied lines must vary depending upon plot scale and the width of the pen or printer dots used in the finished product. You'll want the spacing between each copied line to be a little bit under one pen width at a 1:1 plot scale.

The best thing to do is to figure out what spacing would be correct at full scale, then scale it up from there so that when you plot the drawing it will come out right again. For example, if a spacing of .02″ works at 1:1 and you plot at 1/2″=1′ (1:24), then .02 x 24 gives a spacing of .48″.

You can have different line widths for anything that you can draw (arcs, circles, curves, boxes, polygons, and lines). Some are easier to draw than others. If you'd like to make a bold arc, it would probably be easier to make a bold circle and then break it. Curves are a little tricky but possible with some time and practice.

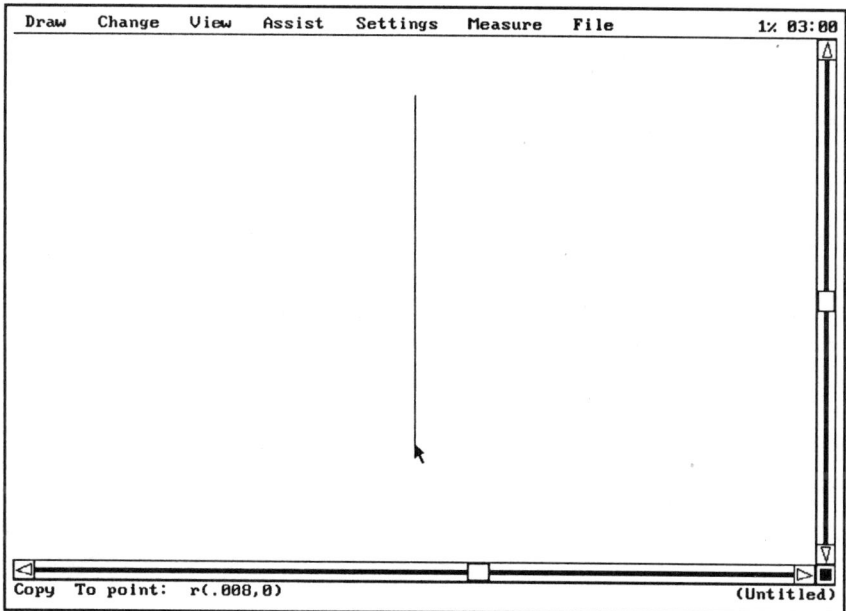

Creating a Thick Line

Line Widths

```
Pull down File Select New
Pull down Draw Select Line                  Draw a 1″ vertical line.
Pull down Change Select Copy
Select object                               Select the line.
From point                                  Using Snap or Attach, select a point on the line.
To point: R(.48,0)                          Using relative coordinate, copy .48 to the right.
```

Repeat the process, using the coordinate R(-.48,0) to move the copy to the left.

You probably don't want to have to copy a line three or four times every time you need a different line weight. Here's a shortcut using the Part command again.

You can make different parts that are just short segments of a set of lines. Locate the part base at the end point of the middle line of the set. You'll find that if you try to attach to the endpoint of a line set, you may get any one of the lines. The solution is to always make the middle line first (since AutoSketch usually selects the oldest object) or to zoom in close to each end of the line and place a point at the ends of the middle line. Then you can snap right to the middle of the line set, using the Node Point Attach mode.

To make your parts, figure out the correct spacing for the different pens that you use and make a set of thick lines that correspond to each different pen size. If you work with scaled drawings, take each individual full-scale line set/part, scale it up to the appropriate size, then save it using a different name. You should end up with a library of descriptively named line set/part files.

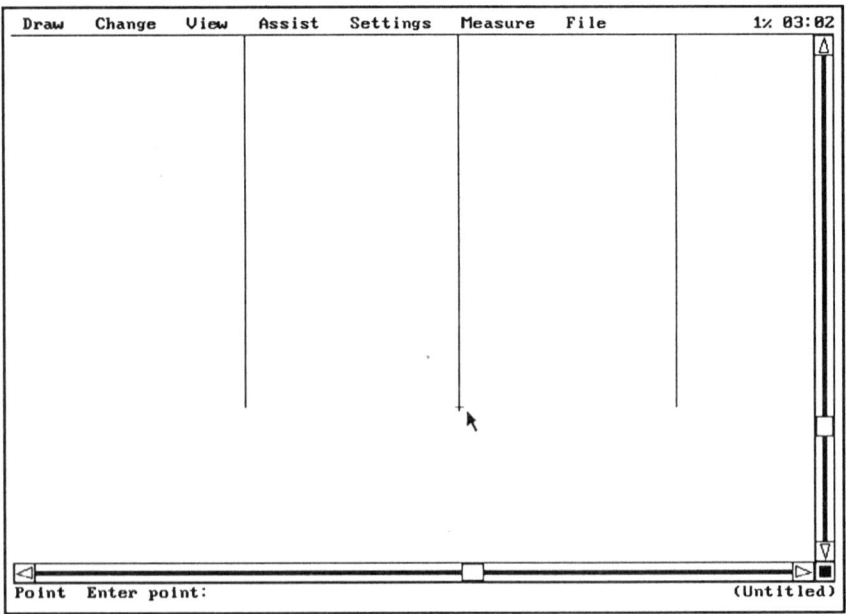

Make the Line a Part

Making the Part

```
Pull down View Select Zoom Box            Zoom in on the lines.
Pull down Draw Select Point               Draw in the point.
Pull down Settings Select Part Base       Select by pointing.
Insertion base:                           The endpoint of the middle line.
Pull down File Select Save                Save as LINE_48.
```

Once the parts have been created, all you have to do is insert the desired line set/part and move it to its correct starting location. Then use the Stretch command to give the line set its desired length. Note that we didn't group the lines, because you cannot stretch a group.

This method of storing varying line widths really only works well for bold lines and boxes. Drawing other bold entities is only a little more difficult, but since you can't stretch them to a different size without altering the spacing between the lines, making parts out of them doesn't save time.

Encapsulated Postscript Conversion

Many of the best laser printers use a powerful built-in programming language called PostScript, designed by Adobe Systems. PostScript is a page description language, which simply means that a series of PostScript statements can completely describe what is to appear on a printed page — formatted typeset text, complex graphics, or both.

AutoSketch can be configured to output to a PostScript printer and send the plot to a PostScript file on your disk. This file will contain all the PostScript instructions required to recreate your image. Many other programs will accept PostScript files and allow you to do further processing that is impossible in AutoSketch itself.

However, AutoSketch 2.0 PostScript output is not in the encapsulated format expected by most other PostScript-compatible programs. To create Encapsulated PostScript files, first configure AutoSketch to plot PostScript to a file, then use the following conversion procedure.

First, copy or rename the PostScript plot file, changing the original PLT extension to EPS. Then edit the file as ASCII text. To actually place the renamed file in proper encapsulated form, there are just a few small changes to make. You must change the version information on the first line, move the %%Bounding Box line from next to the end of the file up to the second line, then add an %%EndComments line just after the last line that starts with the %% comment marker. The rest of the file remains unchanged.

The following example files — before and after — show this more clearly. Changes are marked in bold.

SAMPLE.PLT File Before Modification

```
%!PS-Adobe-1.0
%%Creator: AutoSketch by Autodesk, Inc.
%%Pages: 1
/m {moveto} def
/l {lineto} def
/s {stroke} def
/n {newpath} def
20 20 translate
0.240000 0.240000 scale
0 setlinewidth
n
1500 1134 m
1500 2088 l
2349 2088 l
2349 1134 m
1500 1134 l
706 925 m
706 1760 l
1292 1760 l
1292 925 l
706 925 l
s
%%BoundingBox: 189 242 584 522
showpage
```

SAMPLE.EPS File After Modifications

```
%!PS-Adobe-2.0 EPSF-1.2
%%BoundingBox: 189 242 584 522
%%Creator: AutoSketch by Autodesk, Inc.
%%Pages: 1
%%EndComments
/m {moveto} def
/l {lineto} def
/s {stroke} def
/n {newpath} def
```

```
20 20 translate
0.240000 0.240000 scale
0 setlinewidth
n
1500 1134 m
1500 2088 l
2349 2088 l
2349 1134 m
1500 1134 l
706 925 m
706 1760 l
1292 1760 l
1292 925 l
706 925 l
s
showpage
```

Once you've made these few changes, you should be able to import the new file into most PostScript-compatible programs with their normal PostScript file import facilities. Some programs, such as Ventura Publisher, may not display an Encapsulated PostScript file on the screen. However, the image should print out correctly.

Saving Multiple Configurations

The initial installation and configuration of AutoSketch is explained in your *AutoSketch Installation Guide*. However, there is an easy way that you can use MS-DOS batch files to run several different configurations of AutoSketch. This could be particularly useful if you want to use more than one output device.

To begin with, install AutoSketch normally for one of your desired configurations if you haven't already. All of the configuration information is stored by AutoSketch in a small file named SKETCH.CFG. Using the DOS rename command, you can store this file under an alternate name, thus:

`C:\SKETCH3>REN SKETCH.CFG EPSON.CFG`

You can use any valid DOS filename for the duplicate file; choose one that will help you remember what is special about this particular configuration. For instance, EPSON.CFG could be your name for a version that will drive your Epson-compatible dot-matrix printer.

Next, re-install AutoSketch for your alternate configuration — for instance, a Hewlett-Packard plotter. AutoSketch will automatically put you into the configuration routine the next time it is run, because it won't be able to find the file SKETCH.CFG any more. After quitting AutoSketch, rename this second configuration as well:

`C:\SKETCH3>`**`REN SKETCH.CFG HP.CFG`**

Now that you have two configuration files, you can create a pair of batch files to start AutoSketch up with one or the other. See your DOS manual if you need a complete explanation of batch files. For instance, for the Epson configuration, create a batch file named SKEPSON.BAT with the following commands:

```
C:\SKETCH3>COPY CON SKEPSON.BAT
CD \SKETCH3
COPY EPSON.CFG SKETCH.CFG
SKETCH %1 %2
<CTRL-Z><ENTER>
```

When you press <ENTER> after the final line, DOS will create a file named SKEPSON.BAT containing the commands entered on the second through fourth lines above. You can also use an ASCII text editor to create batch files like this. Now if you type SKEPSON at the DOS prompt, AutoSketch will be run with the Epson configuration.

Create similar batch files to match each configuration file. For example, you could set up your Hewlett-Packard plotter by repeating the above commands, substituting the names SKHP.BAT where we said SKEPSON.BAT and HP.CFG where we said EPSON.CFG. When you type SKHP, DOS will execute that batch file, change to the AutoSketch directory, copy the Hewlett-Packard configuration file to the default configuration file SKETCH.CFG, and start AutoSketch.

You can repeat this process as many times as you like, for as many different configurations as you need. You'll still be able to enter a drawing filename and macro name on the command line, if you like, and AutoSketch will recognize them automatically because of the %1 and %2 replaceable parameters. When the batch file is run, they are replaced by any options you put after the batch filename. Just type the drawing filename and/or the macro switch and filename after the name of the batch file. DOS takes care of the rest.

If you are uncertain about the procedure, check your DOS manual or, better yet, get a more experienced friend to run through it for you. It shouldn't take more than five minutes, but can make life a *lot* easier if you're trying to manage a complicated hardware setup.

Hardware Help

Although AutoSketch will run on virtually any IBM-compatible microcomputer system, there are a number of factors you should consider if you want to get the best performance. AutoSketch is designed to perform adequately on minimum hardware. However, if you will be doing extensive work with the program, you should consider investing in the most appropriate configuration.

Math Coprocessors

Whatever class of MS-DOS computer you use, the most cost-effective way of achieving adequate performance is to ensure that your computer is equipped with a *math coprocessor chip*. This chip relieves your computer's main processor (CPU) of most arithmetic calculations, and vastly improves the performance of programs like AutoSketch, which are designed to take advantage of this capability.

The impact of the math coprocessor chip is so great that AutoSketch is supplied in two versions. One version is specifically tailored to run *only* on computers equipped with the extra chip, and it runs several times faster than the standard version. The AutoSketch installation procedure automatically installs the correct version of the program. However, if you add a math coprocessor chip to your computer after AutoSketch has already been installed, you'll have to re-install AutoSketch in order to get the appropriate program version. Either version of AutoSketch will work with the math chip installed, but only the specially designed version will give you the extra speed.

Video Options

AutoSketch supports all of the current video display standards, and then some. Because of its object-orientation and zoom capabilities, AutoSketch is quite usable on even low-resolution displays. A Hercules-compatible monochrome graphics adapter plus a TTL monitor is still the cheapest way to go. However, a VGA display adapter together with a matching monochrome or color monitor will work much better. If you are planning to do a lot of detailed work in AutoSketch, a higher resolution SuperVGA adapter and multiscanning monitor will make those jobs even easier.

If you do decide to use a higher resolution display adapter, try to get a good AutoSketch software driver for it from the hardware manufacturer. These are usually included on a floppy disk with the display adapter card itself.

Few adapters include a proper AutoSketch driver for their high-resolution display modes (although they will still work in standard VGA mode). Higher resolution modes are usually supported by means of an ADI (Autodesk Device Interface) driver. Often, the ADI driver that is included with the card will be designed primarily for AutoCAD, rather than AutoSketch. Such a driver may not be completely compatible with AutoSketch, especially with the scroll bars of version 3.0. You might also find that text appears improperly positioned on menus or colors are unreadable. Many ADI drivers work well enough, but update the screen very slowly, so that you find menus taking several seconds to drop down. Your only recourse is to complain to the manufacturer about updating the driver.

Fortunately, most users should find standard VGA display more than adequate — and virtually any VGA or Super VGA display adapter on the market will work perfectly in this mode.

Disk Drives

AutoSketch will run adequately on most any type of disk. A hard disk is recommended but not required. A hard disk will improve file loading times and provide far more convenient storage if you deal with large numbers of drawing files. Hard disks are no longer expensive, and if you still don't have one, we highly recommend installing one. Many portable computers don't include a hard disk; most of these include reasonably high-capacity floppy disk drives, or large internal electronic storage that can act like a hard disk. Any of these computers should run AutoSketch very well. In fact, AutoCAD users may find that AutoSketch is an ideal travelling companion.

Input Devices

Although AutoSketch supports keyboard entry, we recommend you use a digitizer or mouse. Most of the popular brand name mice will work well. Digitizer tablets provide a similar feel to the mouse, but have greater accuracy — and a higher price. For most people, the mouse is adequate. As with video displays, many digitizers are supported through the ADI interface, so your selection is virtually limitless. (However, they don't tend to have the compatibility problems that video displays do.)

Output Devices

AutoSketch can output to most of the common dot matrix printers. These are inexpensive and provide adequate results for many applications. AutoSketch also works with the two most common types of laser printers — the Hewlett-Packard LaserJet series (and compatibles), as well as PostScript printers such as the Apple LaserWriter. Laser printers produce excellent results and are becoming very affordable. If you only need black-and-white output, the laser printer is your best choice. It will also be the most all-around useful addition to your computer system.

However, for professional, high-volume or precision work, a pen plotter is the recommended device. Plotters can be expensive, but they give clean, sharp lines, accurate curves, and can work in color or with multiple pens on large sizes of vellum, film, or paper.

File Management

Managing AutoSketch files is pretty easy in version 3.0. Its icon menus make it easy to see what your files contain, and the file dialogue boxes make it easy to find any drawing on your disks. Nevertheless, there are still some precautions you can take that will make you drawings even easier to work with and more secure.

Basic file management isn't difficult, and you don't need expensive utility software. You can get by just fine with DOS. All of the techniques given below use DOS. Each of the examples assumes your DOS programs are in a directory on your DOS search path. Try them for yourself and see if they don't help you work more safely and efficiently. If you have problems, consult your DOS reference or an experienced friend.

Backing Up Files

Even once saved to disk, a drawing file is at risk. The most common way to lose a drawing is to save another drawing — or another version of the same drawing — under the same name. It is also possible to erroneously delete files from DOS. Worst of all, it is possible for any disk — hard or floppy — to fail and simply become unreadable. Fortunately, these disasters are rare. Wwhen they do strike, however, they can be devastating if you are not prepared. The only sure protection against lost work is to follow a regular backup regimen, making duplicate copies of all your important drawing files.

The procedure is not difficult. The following command will copy all the drawings in the current directory to a floppy disk in drive A:

```
C:\SKETCH3>COPY *.SKD A: /V
```

If your disk drives are not drives A: and C:, substitute your drive names. The optional /V parameter provides an extra measure of protection, causing DOS to verify that information is being placed on a readable area of the target disk.

If your drawings are on a floppy disk in drive A:, this command will back them up to a second floppy disk in drive B:. (If you have only one floppy drive, use the same command and follow the disk-swapping instructions that appear on your screen.)

`A:\>COPY *.SKD B: /V`

The COPY command will work fine as long as all of the drawing files in the directory will fit on a single floppy disk. If not, you can use more precise filename and wildcard combinations in place of the * shown, to back up only specific files. A better alternative, if you have DOS 3.2 or later, is to use the XCOPY command. The XCOPY command can be made to fit a directory full of files onto several diskettes if their total size is larger than one diskette. Use the command as follows:

`C:\SKETCH3>XCOPY *.SKD A: /M/V`

In this form, the XCOPY command will only copy drawings that have been modified since they were last backed up. The next time you modify one, it will be eligible for backing up again. If all the files won't fit on one diskette, you will receive an "insufficient disk space" error message. Simply repeat the above command with a fresh disk, and it will continue to fill as many disks as needed to back up all the specified files. If you want to use XCOPY to back up all the specified files whether they have changed or not, enter the following command before the first XCOPY command.

`C:\SKETCH3>ATTRIB +A *.SKD`

The ATTRIB command above will make all your AutoSketch drawing files look to DOS as if they have been changed (your drawing won't change, though). See your DOS manual for other XCOPY options, and an explanation of ATTRIB.

If you wish to duplicate a complete floppy disk, the DISKCOPY command is your best bet. The following command will duplicate the floppy disk in drive A: onto the disk in drive B:. The two drives will have to be the same capacity though. You cannot copy from a high-density drive to a low-density one (or vice versa) or from a 5.25" drive to a 3.5" drive (or vice versa).

`C:\SKETCH3>DISKCOPY A: B:`

There are many products on the market to make backup procedures more painless. Fastback, from Fifth Generation Systems, Inc., can rapidly back up specified directories, with many time-saving options. PKZIP, from PKWare, Inc., can combine large numbers of files into a single compressed file, greatly reducing the amount of disk space needed for storage. AutoSketch drawing files compress very well.

It's not a bad idea to keep two separate floppy backups of all important drawing files. When you back up your files at the end of each day or each week, simply use two sets of floppy disks in alternation. That way, even if disaster strikes while you are backing up and obliterates both the original and backup (this *does* happen, although rarely), you will still have a copy left. Keep one copy away from the computer — preferably in another building!

All this may seem like paranoia, but if you total up the many hours that are invested in your drawings, you'll begin to appreciate their value, both emotionally and in monetary terms. Computer storage media are delicate and all too easily destroyed.

Handling AutoSketch Drawing Files

Getting rid of unwanted files is a less delicate problem, but still worth doing. Keeping your disks cleaned up gives you back the storage space you've purchased for more important uses. Naturally, you'll want to be absolutely certain that you're done with a file before you wipe it away from your disk. The appropriate DOS command is:

`C:\SKETCH3>DEL FILENAME.SKD`

Obviously, you should substitute the name of the file you wish to delete for the word FILENAME in the example.

AutoSketch automatically makes secondary backup copies of your files whenever you save them a second or subsequent time. Active drawing files all have the extension SKD; the backup files end in BAK. If your data disk is filling up and you need more room, you could use the following command to eliminate all the backup files:

`C:\SKETCH3>DEL *.BAK`

These backup files can be useful. For example, if you mess up your drawing and then accidentally save it, you can still recover the previous version. Quit, return to DOS, and change to your drawing directory or floppy disk. Then type the following command:

`C:\SKETCH3>COPY FILENAME.BAK FILENAME.SKD`

Once more, substitute the name of your drawing file for FILENAME. This same procedure can also help in the unlikely event that your file becomes damaged. If the original drawing is unreadable for some reason, the backup file may be intact.

Working With Directories

The basic unit of data storage in MS-DOS is the file. To help you deal with very large numbers of files on a hard disk, DOS lets you organize files into separate directories. Directory names are usually distinguished by a leading backslash character, as in \SKETCH3.

As described in the *AutoSketch Installation Guide,* you'll certainly want to place the AutoSketch program in a special directory — named something like SKETCH3. By default, your drawing files will automatically end up in this same directory. However, you might want to sort things out a bit further, particularly if you're dealing with large numbers of drawings relating to different projects. If so, it would be a good idea to create several subdirectories to store your drawings.

Directories are structured like the roots of a tree. Except for the highest directory, each new directory is located under some previous directory. In fact, the first (highest) directory on your disk is called the root directory. The first new directories you create will be under the root directory. However, if you create a directory named ONE, change to that directory, then create another directory TWO, you'll find that TWO is below ONE. That is, from the root directory you can see only ONE; if you enter ONE you can see the listing for TWO and the root directory. Directories are specified according to their path within this branching structure. In this case, the complete name of TWO would be \ONE\TWO. The root directory has no literal name and is, therefore, not specified.

Although you can change drawing directories easily when using the AutoSketch Open or Save As commands, you cannot create new directories. To do this, exit to DOS, make sure you are in the SKETCH directory. Then use the DOS command for making directories (MD) to create a new directory for each of the types of drawings you work with. For example:

`C:\>CD SKETCH3`	Change to the AutoSketch directory.
`C:\SKETCH3>MD ELECTRIC`	Make a new directory for electronic schematics.
`C:\SKETCH3>MD MECHANIC`	Make a new directory for mechanical drawings.
`C:\SKETCH3>MD CHARTS`	Make a new directory for charts and graphs.

Within AutoSketch, you use the Open dialogue box to select the desired directory. Directory names are shown surrounded by angle brackets.

Directory icons are blank except for the word DIR. Once you select a directory, the Open dialogue box will show only the drawing files (and any subdirectories) available from that directory. If you follow a logical procedure when saving your drawings, you'll see only the drawings dealing with one project or topic, making it much easier to find the drawing you want. Logical directory storage also makes backup procedures simpler.

If you use many directories to store your drawings or if they are widely separated in your directory structure, even the AutoSketch File dialogue box may be inconvenient. You can use the power of a DOS batch file to make staying in one directory easier. To do this, make a batch file that will start AutoSketch without your having to change to the directory where AutoSketch is installed. Make one line of the file specify the full drive and path location of the AutoSketch executable file. The batch file will also need a line that tells AutoSketch where to find its configuration file SKETCH.CFG. You can do this by making use of two DOS environment variables. Environment variables are simply labels that you tell DOS to equate with a certain directory. AutoSketch automatically checks with DOS when it executes to see where these labels are assigned (as do many other programs). The environment variable to show AutoSketch the location of SKETCH.CFG is ASKETCHCFG. Create a batch file for these two lines like this:

```
C:\>COPY CON SK.BAT
SET ASKETCHCFG=C:\SKETCH3        Labels directory so AutoSketch finds it.
C:\SKETCH3\SKETCH %1 %2          Executes AutoSketch from home directory.
SET ASKETCHCFG=                  Erases label when you quit AutoSketch.
<CTRL-Z><ENTER>                  Saves the SK.BAT file.
```

Now you can change to a directory anywhere on any drive, execute this batch file, and AutoSketch will start up right where you are.

You can use other AutoSketch environment variables to:

- Segregate AutoSketch's pattern, font, and icon library files.
- Segregate your own part files away from drawing files.
- Direct AutoSketch's temporary files to a virtual disk for better performance.
- Control AutoSketch's use of expanded memory.

The ASKETCH environment variable tells AutoSketch where you've stored the pattern, font, and icon library files. The AutoSketch installation program puts them in a directory named SUPPORT, below SKETCH3 by default. This is the directory (and files) displayed by the Pattern Settings, and Text and Font Modes dialogue boxes. If you move them later, or want AutoSketch to only use your own files in a different directory, you can tell AutoSketch where they are without disrupting your default installation.

You can use ASPART and store all your part files in one directory for use in drawings saved anywhere. The directory you specify with ASPART is displayed by the Select Part File dialogue box.

For very large drawings, you should install additional memory for AutoSketch to use. The additional memory will allow you to create much larger drawings than you could without it.

If you have *extended* memory installed (such as comes with 286 and 386 PCs), AutoSketch cannot use it directly. You will either have to use an expanded memory manager to convert it into expanded memory, or use it to create a virtual disk. If you set up a virtual disk, you can specify a location for AutoSketch's page file (which would otherwise use expanded memory or a physical disk) with ASMEMPATH. The VDISK.SYS driver that comes with later versions of MS-DOS can do this for you. See your DOS manual for instructions on how to set one up. Once you have a working virtual disk, you can tell AutoSketch to use it with ASMEMPATH.

You can also use this virtual disk to store two other files that AutoSketch would normally put on your hard or floppy disk drive. Telling AutoSketch to place them on the virtual disk will improve performance, especially when plotting to a printer.

The first file is AutoSketch's undo file. This is the file we mentioned in Chapter 2, that keeps a record of all your commands in case you want to back up. Every time you issue a command, it is recorded in this file. Putting the file on a virtual disk will make this happen very quickly. You direct the undo file with the ASUNDO environment variable.

The other file is the AutoSketch vector file. We've taught you that AutoSketch deals with objects, not pixels. However, printers deal only with pixels. Therefore, AutoSketch must translate every object into pixels when it plots to a printer that only understands pixels. To do this, AutoSketch has to create a temporary file to store all the object information in while it performs the translation. This file can be as large or larger than your drawing. Placing it on a virtual disk can greatly decrease your printing time. The vector file destination is specified with the ASVECT environment variable.

If you have *expanded* memory installed in your computer (or are using an expanded memory manager to convert extended memory), AutoSketch will use up to 2 megabytes worth. If you need to use some, or all, of it with another program, you can control how AutoSketch uses it with the ASLIMEM variable by turning it off or on.

The easiest way to use each of these environment variables is in a batch file. Below is an example batch file using all of the environment variables we have discussed. Use the following commands to create SK.BAT with all the variables:

```
C:\>COPY CON SK.BAT
SET ASKETCH=C:\SKETCH3\SUPPORT
SET ASKETCHCFG=C:\SKETCH3
SET ASPART=C:\SKETCH3\MYPARTS
SET ASMEMPATH=D:\
SET ASUNDO=D:\
SET ASVECT=D:\
SET ASLIMEM=OFF
C:\SKETCH3\SKETCH %1 %2
SET ASKETCH=
SET ASKETCHCFG=
SET ASPART=
SET ASMEMPATH=
SET ASUNDO=
SET ASVECT=
SET ASLIMEM=
<CTRL-Z><ENTER>
```

Each drive and directory specified with an environment variable must exist before you execute the batch file, and you must substitute your directory names for the ones shown above. Also, if your virtual disk is other than drive D:, substitute its letter in your batch file. Notice how we cleared all the environment variables when AutoSketch is done. This makes the memory that they occupy available to your other application programs, which may use their own environment variables.

If you see the error message: Out of environment space when your SK.BAT file runs, you will need to allocate more memory for environment settings. If you are using DOS 3.2 or later, place a statement in your CONFIG.SYS file:

```
SHELL=C:\COMMAND.COM /E:256 /P
```

This statement expands your environment space to 256 bytes, which should accomodate the batch file above, depending on the length of your DOS search path and other settings. For more information on the SHELL statement and environment space, see your DOS manual.

Command Line Options

AutoSketch has several options you can execute from the DOS command line when you start it that affect the way the program executes. Each one is entered on the DOS command line after the program name. The first option lets you specify a drawing file to be opened automatically. Type the program name SKETCH as you would normally at the DOS prompt, but follow it with the name of the drawing. It is not necessary to type the extension.

C:\SKETCH3>**SKETCH FILENAME**

If you've stored the drawing in a directory other than the AutoSketch program directory, you'll have to include the directory specification. For instance:

C:\SKETCH3>**SKETCH ELECTRIC\DRAWING1**

Another AutoSketch command line option allows you to see your current hardware configuration without reconfiguring. You can use this option to verify that the correct devices are configured if you are using the multiple configuration technique described earlier. Simply add the configuration option on the command line:

C:\SKETCH3>**SKETCH -C**

AutoSketch will display a message on the screen containing your current configuration choices and return you to the DOS prompt. If you need to reconfigure AutoSketch, you can by using the reconfigure option.

C:\SKETCH3>**SKETCH -R**

AutoSketch will take you through the same installation process it did when you first installed it.

The final AutoSketch command line option allows you to start AutoSketch and automatically load and play a macro. You can use this option with macros that set all your favorite command options for different types of drawings, insert a part file for a title block, or zoom to a specific view. In a DOS batch file, a macro could plot a group of drawings without human assistance. Simply follow the AutoSketch command with the macro option and the name of the macro file:

C:\SKETCH3>**SKETCH -MFILENAME**

Again, substitute your macro name for FILENAME, and make sure the option and filename are not separated by a space. Note that the macro capability is not available in AutoSketch 2.0 or earlier. For information on making macros, see Chapter 7, *Advanced Editing Tools*.

Prototype Drawings

Another way to automate some of the tedious steps you go through in setting up each new drawing is with prototype drawings. Chances are that you have favorite values for settings such as Snap, Grid, and Limits. You may also have a set layout format, with borders and title blocks, that you'd like to appear on all your drawings.

A prototype drawing is simply an "empty" drawing with all your normal settings already in place. This drawing could be entirely blank, or it could contain standard elements such as titleblocks and borders. You could even have the title block on an invisible layer. It's all up to you.

Once you establish a prototype drawing, you can create a batch file to call it up automatically each time you begin a new project. The following is a variation of SK.BAT. You can create it from the DOS command prompt with the following commands:

```
C:\>COPY CON SK.BAT
CD \SKETCH3                  Changes to the AutoSketch directory.
COPY PROTO.SKD %1.SKD        Copies the prototype drawing to a new file.
SKETCH %1                    Starts AutoSketch and loads new drawing.
<CTRL-Z><ENTER>
```

To execute the batch file so that AutoSketch loads your prototype drawing when you start up AutoSketch, type:

```
C:\>SK FILENAME
```

Substitute the title of your new drawing for FILENAME.

In the above batch file, we've used PROTO.SKD as the name of the prototype drawing. However, you can have as many prototype drawings as you want. All you have to do is make some more batch files, substituting your various prototype file names where we've shown PROTO.SKD. For instance, a batch file called SKELEC.BAT might copy the prototype file PROTELEC.SKD, containing the setup you like for electronic schematics. SKMECH.BAT might do the same with PROTMECH.SKD for mechanical drawings.

If you want to run AutoSketch without loading a prototype drawing, type SKETCH just as you normally would.

You can accomplish the same thing without a batch file by opening the prototype drawing in AutoSketch and immediately saving it as your new drawing name with the Save As command.

Support and CompuServe

In general, it can be difficult to obtain support and help for low-cost programs. However, AutoSketch is particularly blessed in this regard, having the solid Autodesk organization behind it. Calls to the AutoSketch support line — listed in your manual — *should* get you through most conceivable problems. The number is (415) 331-4030. Be sure to ask specifically for *AutoSketch* support.

In addition to its regular phone support line, Autodesk maintains an information, file, and message exchange forum on the CompuServe Information System. Access to this service requires a modem, any communication software package, and a CompuServe Starter Kit available at most bookstores and computer dealers. Follow the Starter Kit instructions to log on, type GO ADESK, and you will be plugged into the world's largest CAD user group. If you're at all serious about getting the most out of your software, the investment in equipment and connect fees is very much worthwhile.

Index

A

Accuracy, 6-2
   Snap, 6-13
Align Dimension command, 10-12
Alternate key, 1-5
Angle command, 10-7
   Base point, 10-7
   Dialogue box, 10-7
Angles
   Dimensioning, 10-14
Arc command, 2-15
   Rubberband, 2-15
   Using coordinates, 2-30
   Using pointer device, 2-30
Area command, 10-8
   Dialogue box, 10-8
   Measuring perimeter, 10-8
   Perimeter points, 10-8
Arrays
   Box, 9-4
   Definition, 9-3
   Ring, 9-6
Arrow command, 10-18
Arrowheads
   Drawing, 10-25
Assist menu, 2-20, 6-1
Attach command, 6-2, 6-14
   Dialogue box, 6-14 – 6-15
   Intersect mode, 6-17
   Attachment modes, 6-15
   Center mode, 6-16
   End point mode, 6-17
   For Part base, 7-11
   Midpoint mode, 6-17
   Node point mode, 6-17
   Perpendicular mode, 6-17
   Pick spacing, 6-20
   Quadrant mode, 6-16, 6-18
   Tangent mode, 6-18
   Using only one mode, 6-19

AutoCAD
   DXF files, 11-6
AutoSketch
   Version 2.0, A-1
AutoSketch display, 1-3, 1-5, 1-7

B

B-spline curve, 2-19
Backup protection, 1-19
Bearing command
   Base point, 10-5
   Dialogue box, 10-5
   Polar coordinates, 10-5
Box Array command, 9-4 – 9-5
Box command, 2-6 – 2-7, 2-27
Break command, 7-2
   Alternative drawing methods, 7-2
   Compared to Stretch, 7-4
   Direction of break, 7-4
   Multiple breaks, A-3
   Using Frame, 7-4
Business applications, 12-1
   Org chart, 12-1
   Flow chart, 12-4
   Pie charts, 12-5
   Graphs, 12-5

C

Canceling a command, 1-23
Chamfer, 9-1
   Command, 9-15
   Definition, 9-14
Change menu, 2-4, 5-1, 7-1
Charts
   See Graphs, 12-5
Circle command, 2-9
   Aligning, 2-11
   Fractional coordinates, 2-28
   Polar coordinates, 2-10

Radius, 2-10
Relative coordinates, 2-10
Color command, 5-2 – 5-3
   Color code, 5-2
   Color coding, 5-3 – 5-4
   Color vs monochrome display, 5-4
   Dialogue box, 5-2
   Display, 5-2
Commands
   Align Dimension, 10-12 – 10-13
   Angle, 10-7 – 10-8
   Angle Dimension, 10-14
   Arc, 2-15
   Area, 10-9
   Attach, 6-2, 6-14, 6-16, 6-20
   Bearing, 10-5
   Box, 2-6 – 2-7
   Box Array, 9-4 – 9-5
   Break, 7-2 – 7-3
   Chamfer, 9-15
   Circle, 2-9 – 2-10
   Color, 5-2 – 5-4
   Coords, 10-4
   Curve (Draw), 2-18 – 2-19
   Curve (Settings), 6-3
   Distance, 10-6 – 10-7
   Ellipse, 2-11 – 2-13
   Ellipse alternate methods, 2-14
   Erase, 2-4 – 2-5, 2-26
   Fillet, 9-17
   Frame, 6-4 – 6-5
   Grid, 5-19, 6-2, 6-7 – 6-10, 6-13
   Group, 7-5
   Horizontal dimension, 10-12 – 10-13
   Last View, 4-14 – 4-15
   Layer, 5-13 – 5-15
   Limits, 5-2, 5-19, 5-21
   Line, 2-3
   Line Type, 5-2, 5-5
   Macro Record, 7-14
   Make DXF, 11-5 – 11-6
   Make Macro, 7-18
   Make Slide, 11-2 – 11-3
   Move, 8-10
   New, 1-16
   Open, 1-16, 1-19, 1-21
   Ortho, 6-6
   Pan, 4-2, 4-11 – 4-13
   Part, 7-7, 7-12
   Part Base, 7-10, 7-12
   Part Clip, 7-9
   Pattern Fill, 9-11 – 9-12
   Pen Info, 8-10 – 8-11
   Pick, 6-20
   Play Macro, 7-16 – 7-17
   Plot, 8-2
   Plot Area, 8-5 – 8-6
   Plot Name, 8-12
   Point (Measure), 10-2
   Polyline, 2-8, 2-16 – 2-17, 9-20
   Print, 8-2
   Print Area, 8-5
   Property, 5-2, 5-14, 5-17, 5-18
   Quit, 1-22
   Read DXF, 11-7
   Read Macro, 7-18
   Record Macro, 7-15
   Redo, 2-4, 2-26
   Redraw, 4-16
   Ring Array, 9-6, 9-8
   Save, 1-16, 1-18
   Save As, 1-16, 1-18
   Scale, 8-10
   Show Properties, 5-14 – 5-16
   Snap, 6-2, 6-7, 6-10 – 6-13
   Stretch, 8-10
   Text, 2-21, 2-23
   Text (Settings), 5-2, 5-7 – 5-12
   Undo, 2-4, 2-26
   Ungroup, 7-7
   Vertical Dimension, 10-12 – 10-13
   View Slide, 11-4
   Zoom, 4-2
   Zoom Box, 4-3 – 4-5
   Zoom Full, 4-8
   Zoom Limits, 4-9 – 4-10, 5-19
   Zoom X, 4-6 – 4-7

Index I-3

Configuring AutoSketch
   Multiple configurations, A-9
Construction lines, 7-27 – 7-28
Coordinates, 1-9, 1-11, 1-13
   Bearing command, 10-5
   Default, 1-10
   Display, 1-11, 10-3
   Entry, 1-11
   Keyboard input, 1-10
   Plotting, 5-21
   Point (Measure) command, 10-2
   Polar, 1-10
   Relative, 1-10
   Snap mode, 6-11
Coords command, 10-3
Crosses/window box, 1-8, 1-9
   Selecting curves, 6-4
Curve (Draw) command, 2-18 – 2-19
   B-spline, 2-19
   Control points, 2-30
   Display speed, 6-4
   Frame, 2-30
   Points, 2-20
Curve (Settings) command
   Dialogue box, 6-2, 6-4

D

Data files, 1-15
   Extension (.SKD), 1-15
Dialogue boxes
   Angle, 10-7
   Area, 10-8
   Attach, 6-14 – 6-15
   Bearing, 10-5
   Color, 5-2
   Curve (Settings), 6-2
   Distance, 10-6
   Grid, 6-8, 6-9
   Layer, 5-13
   Line Type, 5-5 – 5-6
   Make DXF, 11-6
   Make slide, 11-2
   Part, 7-11
   Pen Info, 8-11

Pick, 6-20
Plot Area, 8-5, 8-9
Point (Measure), 10-3
Property, 5-17, 5-24
Show Properties, 5-16
Snap, 6-11
Text (Settings), 5-8
View slide, 11-3
Digitizer, 1-3
Dimensioning
   Accuracy, 10-15
   Angles, 10-14
   Angular dimensioning, 10-14, 10-27
   Arrow styles, 10-18
   Associative dimensions, 10-15
   Color & layer, 10-17
   Commands, 10-12
   Custom, 10-20
   Drawing extension lines, 10-24
   Lines, 10-12
   Manual, 10-25
   Point sequence, 10-22
   Rotated objects, 10-13
   Text alignment, 10-22
Discard option, 1-23
Disk drives, 1-15
Display
   ADI compatibility, A-11
   Color, 5-4
   Low resolution, 6-10
   Monochrome, 5-4, 5-17
   Recommended, A-11
   Screen, 1-3, 1-5, 1-7
   Speeding up, 5-15, 6-4
Distance command
   Dialogue box, 10-6
   Scaling, 10-6
Dragging the rubberband, 1-9
Draw menu, 2-1, 2-3
Drawing objects
   Arcs, 2-1
   Boxes, 2-1
   Circles, 2-1
   Curves, 2-1

Lines, 2-1, 2-3
Points, 2-1
Polygons, 2-1
Text, 2-1
Drawing pointer
   Selecting objects, 1-8

E

Editing a macro, 7-19
Electronics
   Schematic diagram, 12-19
Ellipse command, 2-11, 2-13
Erase command, 2-5, 2-26
   Erasing text, 2-31
   Selecting, 2-5

F

File commands
   New, 1-16, 2-25
   Open, 1-16
   Save As, 1-16
   Save, 1-16
File menu, 8-1, 11-1
Filename indicator, 1-6
Filenames, 1-23
File transfer
   CorelDRAW!, 11-11
   Ventura Publisher, 11-10
Files
   Backing up, A-13
   Configuration, A-9
   Data, 1-15
   Description, 1-14
   Directories, A-16
   Directory organization, A-16
   Disk full during plot, 8-4
   Drawing exchange format, 11-5
   Drawing (.SKD), 11-1
   Encapsulated PostScript (.EPS), A-7
   Erasing, A-15
   File extension, 1-15
   File management, A-13
   Filenames, 1-15

HP-GL, 11-2
IS DISK, 10-19
Loading, 1-19
Making space on floppy disks, A-15
Part files, 7-11
Plot files, 8-12
PostScript, 11-2
Printing plot files, 8-14
Prototype drawings, A-19
Saving a new file, 1-17
Saving an existing file, 1-18
Slide library (.SLB), 11-1
Slide (.SLD), 11-2
Storage, A-13
Types, 11-1
Using DOS to copy, 8-12
Ventura Publisher, 11-5, A-7
Fillet, 9-1
   Definition, 9-17
Fillet command, 9-17
Fonts, 5-9
Frame command, 6-4 – 6-5
   Curve, 2-19
   Dialogue box, 6-4
   Selecting curves, 6-4
Function keys, 1-5

G

Graphs
   Area graphs, 12-9
   Column graph, 12-9
   Introduction to, 12-5
   Line graph, 12-7
   Pie chart, 12-5
   Scatter plots, 12-9
Grid command, 6-2, 6-7, 6-10
   Dialogue box, 6-8
   Drawing limits, 5-19
   Grid spacing, 6-8
   Inches & feet, 6-14
   Prototype drawings, A-19
   Spacing too small, 6-9
   Using with Snap, 6-13

Group command, 7-5
    Grouping groups, 7-6
    Maximum number of objects, 7-6
    Modifying a group, 7-6
    Selecting objects, 7-5
    Selecting within a group, 7-6
    Terminating, 7-6

H

Hardware, A-11
    Disk drives, A-12
    Dot-matrix printers, A-12
    Laser printers, A-12
    Math processor, A-11
    Mouse, A-12
    Plotters, A-12
    Pointing devices, A-12
Hatching, 9-11
Horizontal Dimension command, 10-12

I

Installation
    Plot to file, 11-8
IS DISK, I-5
Isometrics
    Advanced exercise, 12-10
    Settings, 6-13

K

Keyboard
    Break key, 7-3
    Coordinates, 1-9 – 1-13, 2-9, 6-11
    Zoom box key, 4-3
Keyboard input
    <CTRL-ENTER>, 2-22
    <CTRL-J>, 2-22
    <ENTER>, 2-23
    <INS key>, 1-4

L

Landscape mode, 8-7
Last View command, 4-14 – 4-15
Layer command, 5-13, 5-15
    Active layer, 5-13, 5-15
    Allocating layers, 5-14
    Changing an object's layer, 5-13 – 5-14
    Checking layer, 5-14
    Dialogue box, 5-13
    Grid, 6-8
    Invisible layers, 5-13 – 5-14, 5-23 – 5-24
    Prototype drawings, A-19
Leaders
    Drawing, 10-25
Limits command, 5-2, 5-19, 5-21
    Coordinates, 5-21
    vs Zoom limits, 5-22
Line command, 2-3
    Construction lines, 7-27 – 7-28
    Double-clicking, 2-26
    Line width, A-4
    Orthogonal lines, 6-6
Line Type command, 5-2
    Coding, 5-6
    Creating heavy lines, A-4
    Dialogue box, 5-5 – 5-6
    Plotting, 5-5
    Scale factor, 5-5 – 5-6
    Text, 5-7
Loading a file, 1-19

M

Macros
    Definition, 7-14
    Editing a macro, 7-19 – 7-20
    Playing a macro, 7-16 – 7-17
    Reading a macro, 7-18
    Recording a macro, 7-14 – 7-15
    Restoring a macro, 7-18
Make DXF command, 11-5
    Dialogue box, 11-6
Make Macro command, 7-18
Make slide command, 11-2

Dialogue box, 11-2
Invisible objects, 11-4
Maps
    Advanced exercise, 12-14
Measure menu, 5-1, 10-1
Memory
    Meter, 1-6
    RAM, 1-15
Menus
    Assist, 6-1
    Change, 5-1, 7-1
    Draw, 2-1
    File, 8-1, 11-1
    Measure, 5-1, 10-1
    Settings, 5-1, 6-1, 7-1
    View, 4-1
Messages
    Dialogue boxes, 1-7
    File name indicator, 1-6
    Memory meter, 1-6
    Prompt, 1-3
Mouse, 1-3
MS-DOS
    Batch files, A-10, A-20
    Change directory command, A-16
    Copy command, A-13
    Del command, A-15
    Diskcopy command, A-14
    Directories, A-16
    Rename command, A-7
    Xcopy command, A-14

N

New command, 1-16

O

Objects
    Filled shapes, 5-4
    Viewing, 4-2
Oblique angle, 5-9
Open command, 1-19, 1-21, 1-23
Ortho command, 6-6

Orthogonal lines, 6-6
Output, 8-1

P

Pan command, 4-2, 4-11, 4-13
    Scroll bars, 4-13
Part base command, 7-10
    Default base, 7-10
Part Clip command, 7-9
Part command, 7-7
    Dialogue box, 7-11
    Grouping a part, 7-8
    Inserting a part, 7-11
    Part properties, 7-13
    Preparing parts, 7-7
    Setting Part base, 7-10
Pattern Fill command, 9-11 – 9-12
Pen Info command, 8-10 – 8-11
    Dialogue box, 8-11
    Pen speed, 8-11
Pick command, 6-20
    Dialogue box, 6-20
    Setting spacing, 6-20
    Units, 6-21
Play Macro command, 7-16
Plot Area command, 8-5
    Create crop box, 8-5
    Create plot box, 8-5
    Dialogue box, 8-5, 8-9
    Editing plot and clip boxes, 8-10
    Manipulating plot & crop boxes, 8-10
    Multiple plot & clip boxes, 8-8
    Paper size, 8-9
    Plot margins, 8-8
    Plot orientation, 8-7
    Scaling, 8-7
Plot command, 8-2
    Color, 5-4
    Device on-line, 8-3
    Disk full, 8-4
    Layers, 8-3
    Line weight, 5-4
Plot extents, 8-3

Plot files
    Creating, 11-8
    Encapsulated PostScript, 11-12
    HP-GL, 11-9
    PostScript, 11-12
Plot Name command, 8-12
    Installing AutoSketch, 8-13
    Printing plot files, 8-14
Plotting
    Black and white, 5-5
    Color, 5-4
    Coordinates, 5-21
    Device on-line, 8-3
    Disk full, 8-4
    DOS MODE command, 8-14
    Dot matrix printer, 8-4
    Editing plot and clip boxes, 8-10
    Layers, 8-3
    Line type & scale, 5-7
    Margins, 8-8
    Paper size setting, 8-9
    Pen selection, 8-10
    Pen speed, 8-11
    Plot orientation, 8-7
    Plot to a file, 8-12
    Practice exercises, 8-15
    Printing plot files, 8-14
    Scale, 5-20, 8-7, 8-9
    Selecting pen number, 8-11
    Setting plot area, 8-5 – 8-6
    Setting print area, 8-5
    Starting plot, 8-2
    Using DOS to copy plot files, 8-12
Point (Draw) command, 2-32
Point (Measure) command, 10-2
    Dialogue box, 10-3
    Using Attach, 10-3
Pointing devices
    Digitizer, 1-3
    Mouse, 1-3
    Pointer, 1-3
    Snap mode, 6-11
Points, 2-1
    Keyboard entry, 2-25

Pointing device, 2-25
Polar coordinates, 1-10
Polygon command
    Using relative coordinates, 2-27
    Line weight, A-5
    Points, 2-20
    Using polar coordinates, 2-27
Polyline command, 2-8
    Arc mode, 2-28
    Using relative coordinates, 2-27
    Arcs, 2-16 – 2-17
    Terminating construction, 2-9
    Using polar coordinates, 2-27
Polylines
    Wide, 9-20
Portrait mode, 8-7
Print Area command, 8-5
Print command, 8-2
Printers
    ADI compatibility, A-12
    Dot matrix, A-12
    Laser, A-12
Prompt message, 1-3, 1-5
Property command, 5-2, 5-14, 5-17
    Changing properties, 5-17
    Dialogue box, 5-17, 5-24
    Text, 5-18
Pull-down menus, 1-4
    Assist, 2-20
    Change, 2-4
    Draw, 2-3
    File, 2-2
    Measure, 5-1, 10-1
    Settings, 5-1, 6-1, 7-1
    View, 4-1

Q

Quit command, 1-22

R

Read DXF command, 11-7
Read Macro command, 7-18
Record Macro command, 7-14

Recover from errors, 2-4
Redo command, 2-4, 2-26
Redraw command, 4-16
Relative coordinates, 1-10
Ring Array command, 9-6, 9-8
Rubberbands, 2-3, 2-34
    Angle measurement, 10-7
    Dimensioning, 10-12
    Dotted lines, 7-3, 7-5
    Ortho mode, 6-7

S

Save As command, 1-17 – 1-18, 1-23
Save command, 1-17 – 1-18
Saving a new file, 1-17
Saving an existing file, 1-18
Scaling
    Calculations, 5-20
Scroll bars, 4-13
Selecting drawing commands, 1-3
Selecting objects
    Crosses/window box, 1-8
    Drawing pointer, 1-8
Settings menu, 5-1, 6-1, 7-1
Show properties command, 5-14 – 5-16
    Dialogue box, 5-16
    Monochrome display, 5-17
Site plans
    Advanced exercise, 12-18
Snap command, 6-2, 6-7, 6-10
    Dialogue box, 6-11
    For Part base, 7-11
    Inches & feet, 6-14
    Isometric settings, 6-13
    Pointing device, 6-11
    Prototype drawings, A-19
    Snap spacing, 6-11
    Using with Grid, 6-13
Special text characters, 2-23
Spline, 2-19
Starting AutoSketch, A-16
Support
    Autodesk phone line, A-20
    CompuServe modem conference, A-21

System variables
    Listing, 10-10
Sytem setup, I-5

T

Text command, 2-21, 2-23
    Effects, 2-23
Text font, 5-9
Text formatting, 5-11
Text (Settings) command, 5-2, 5-7, 5-9, 5-11
    Font, 5-9
    Dialogue box, 5-8
    Height, 5-9
    Italics, 5-9
    Oblique angle, 5-9
    Size, 5-9
    Width factor, 5-9

U

Undo command, 2-4, 2-26
Ungroup command, 7-7
    Nested groups, 7-7

V

Vertical Dimension command, 10-12
View menu, 4-1
View Slide command
    Dialogue box, 11-3

W

Width factor, 5-9
Window selection, 1-8

Z

Zoom Box command, 4-3, 4-5
    Proportions, 4-6
    Zoom in, zoom out, 4-3
Zoom Full command, 4-8

vs Zoom Limits, 4-9
Zoom Limits command, 4-9
   Setting drawing limits, 5-19
   vs Zoom full, 4-9
Zoom X command, 4-6 – 4-7
   Maximum, minimum, 4-7
   Reference exercise, 4-7
   Zoom factor, 4-7

New Riders Library

New Riders Publishing consistently delivers the best tutorials and references for understanding your personal computer and its programs.

INSIDE CompuServe®
The Easy Start Guide to Online Information and Communication

By Julie Anne Arca and Richard T. Lindstrom
320 pages, includes communication programs disks
ISBN 0-934035-83-0, **$29.95** (Book/Disk Set)

INSIDE CompuServe will escort you through today's largest and most diverse information source. This book and disk set contains all the guidance you need to connect your telephone, modem, and PC to CompuServe's on-line telecommunications service. Whether you're just getting started or exploring new realms, *INSIDE CompuServe* is a valuable resource to help you get the best out of the most popular computer information service, CompuServe.

Comes with two 5 1/4" disks. See coupon to order 3 1/2" disk.

For fast service, call New Riders at 1-800-541-6789

STEPPING INTO AutoCAD®   Fourth Edition—Release 10
A Guide to Technical Drafting Using AutoCAD

By Mark Merickel
544 pages, over 140 illustrations
ISBN 0-934035-51-2, **$29.95**

This popular technical drafting tutorial has been completely rewritten with new exercises for Release 10. The book is organized to lead you step by step from the basics to production of industry standard dimensioned drawings. Handy references provide quick setup of the AutoCAD environment. Improve your drawing accuracy through AutoCAD's dimensioning commands. It also includes extensive support for ANSI Y14.5 level drafting.

Optional ANSI Y14.5 tablet menu disk available.

AutoCAD® for Architects and Engineers
A Practical Guide to Design, Presentation and Production

By John Albright and Elizabeth Schaeffer
544 pages, over 150 illustrations
ISBN 0-934035-53-9 **$29.95**

Master your AutoCAD project using high-powered design development with AutoCAD Release 10. Learn to construct working drawings using techniques from real-life projects. Export crucial data for credible report generation. Generate stunning computer presentations with AutoLISP, AutoShade, and AutoFlix. The ONLY AutoCAD book specifically written for the architectural, engineering, and construction community.

Optional companion disk available.

INSIDE AutoDesk Animator®
The Complete Guide to Animation on a PC

By Leah Freiwald and Lee Marrs
480 pages, over 500 illustrations
ISBN 0-934035-76-8 **$29.95**

Exploit the power of the Autodesk Animator program, guided by an Emmy-winning graphics animator and a computer training expert. With a series of hands-on tutorials, they take you from basic to advanced animations, so that you will be capable of producing professional animated graphics for everything from presentations to your own cartoons. The book also includes coverage of the Autodesk ATK to easily create animated presentations from your 3D AutoCAD drawings. With the help of *INSIDE AUTODESK ANIMATOR,* you can tame this exciting program and make it work for you in real world presentations!

Optional companion disk available.

CUSTOMIZING AutoCAD®   Second Edition — Release 10
A Complete Guide to AutoCAD Menus, Macros and More!

By J. Smith and R. Gesner
480 Pages, 100 illustrations
ISBN 0-934035-45-8, **$27.95**

Uncover the hidden secrets of AutoCAD's Release 10 in this all new edition. Discover the anatomy of an AutoCAD menu and build a custom menu from start to finish. Manipulate distance, angles, points, and hatches — ALL in 3D! Customize hatches, text fonts, and dimensioning for increased productivity. Buy *CUSTOMIZING AutoCAD* today and start customizing AutoCAD tomorrow!

Optional companion disk available.

For fast service, call New Riders at 1-800-541-6789

INSIDE AutoLISP®   Release 10
The Complete Guide to Using AutoLISP for AutoCAD Applications

By J. Smith and R. Gesner
736 pages, over 150 illustrations
ISBN: 0-934035-47-4, **$29.95**

Introducing the most comprehensive book on AutoLISP for AutoCAD Releases 9 and 10. Learn AutoLISP commands and functions and write your own custom AutoLISP programs. Numerous tips and tricks for using AutoLISP for routine drawing tasks. Import and export critical drawing information to/from Lotus 1-2-3 and dBASE. Automate the creation of scripts for unattended drawing processing. *INSIDE AutoLISP* is the book that will give you the inside track to using AutoLISP.

Optional companion disk available.

AutoCAD® Reference Guide
Everything You Want to Know About AutoCAD — FAST!

By Dorothy Kent
256 pages, over 50 illustrations
ISBN: 0-934035-57-1, **$11.95**

All AutoCAD commands are arranged alphabetically and described in just a few paragraphs. Includes tips and warnings from experienced users for each command. This is the instant-answer guide to AutoCAD.

Optional companion disk available.

Inside CorelDRAW! ™
The Practical Guide to Computer-Aided Graphic Design

By Daniel Gray
424 pages, over 175 illustrations including eight pages in full color
ISBN: 0-934035-33-4, **$24.95**

Make impressive graphic design easy with *Inside CorelDRAW!* This handy, by-your-side tutorial shows you how to get the most from Corel's fabulous graphic arts and typography software for the PC. Learn how to produce your own projects by following the hands-on practice examples and by studying the full-color samples from the CorelDRAW! masters. Whether you're an artist, a designer, or a PC enthusiast, you'll quickly be creating eye-catching artwork of your own.

For fast service, call New Riders at 1-800-541-6789

INSIDE AutoSketch®   Second Edition — Version 3.0
A Guide to Productive Drawing Using AutoSketch

By Frank Lenk
384 pages, over 120 illustrations
ISBN: 0-934035-96-2, **$24.95**

INSIDE AutoSketch gives you real-life mechanical parts, drawing schematics, and architectural drawings. Start by learning to draw simple shapes such as points, lines and curves, then edit shapes by moving, copying, rotating, and distorting them. Explore higher-level features to complete technical drawing jobs using reference grids, snap, drawing layers and creating parts. *INSIDE AutoSketch* will help you draw your way to succes.

Add to your New Riders library today with the best books for the best software!

Yes, please send me the productivity-boosting material I have checked below. Make check payable to New Riders Publishing.

❏ **Check enclosed**

Charge to my credit card:

❏ **Visa #** ❏ **Mastercard #**

Card # _____

Expiration date: _____

Signature: _____

Name: _____

Company: _____

Address: _____

City: _____

State: _____ Zip: _____

Phone: _____

The easiest way to order is to pick up the phone and call 1-800-541-6789 between 9:00 AM and 5:00 PM EST. Please have your credit card available and your order can be placed in a snap!

Quantity	Description of Item	Unit Cost	Total Cost
	Inside CorelDRAW!	$24.95	
	Inside AutoCAD, 5th Edition*	$29.95	
	Inside AutoCAD, 5th Edition (Metric)*	$29.95	
	Customizing AutoCAD, 2nd Edition*	$27.95	
	AutoCAD for Architects and Engineers*	$29.95	
	Inside Autodesk Animator*	$29.95	
	Inside AutoLISP*	$29.95	
	Stepping Into AutoCAD, 4th Edition*	$29.95	
	Inside AutoSketch, 2nd Edition*	$24.95	
	AutoCAD Reference Guide*	$11.95	
	Inside CompuServe (Book-and-Disk set)	$29.95	
	*Companion Disks available for these books	$14.95 ea.	
	Shipping and Handling: See information below		
	Sales Tax: Indiana residents please add 5% sales tax		
	Total:		

Shipping and Handling: $4.00 for the first book and $1.75 for each additional book. Floppy disk: add $1.75 for shipping and handling. If you need to have it NOW, we can ship product to you in 24 to 48 hours for an additional charge and you will receive your item overnight or in two days. Add $20.00 per book and $8.00 for shipping up to three disks overseas. Prices subject to change. Call for availability and pricing information on latest editions.

New Riders Publishing • 11711 N. College Avenue • P.O. Box 90 • Carmel, Indiana 46032
1-800-541-6789   **1-800-448-3804**
Orders/Customer Service   Fax

Add to Your New Riders Library Today with the Best Books for the Best Software

Yes, please send me the productivity-boosting material I have checked below. Make check payable to New Riders Publishing.

❑ **Check enclosed.**

Charge to my credit card:

❑ **VISA**　　　　❑ **MasterCard**

Card # _____

Expiration date: _____

Signature: _____

Name: _____

Company: _____

Address: _____

City: _____

State: _____ ZIP: ____

Phone: _____

The easiest way to order is to pick up the phone and call 1-800-541-6789 between 9:00 a.m. and 5:00 p.m., EST. Please have your credit card available, and your order can be placed in a snap!

Quantity	Description of Item	Unit Cost	Total Cost
	Inside CorelDRAW!	$24.95	
	Inside AutoCAD, 5th Edition (for Release 10)*	$29.95	
	Inside AutoCAD, 5th Edition (Metric)*	$29.95	
	Inside AutoCAD, 6th Edition (for Release 10 and 11)*	$34.95	
	Customizing AutoCAD, 2nd Edition*	$27.95	
	AutoCAD for Architects and Engineers*	$29.95	
	Inside Autodesk Animator*	$29.95	
	Inside AutoLISP*	$29.95	
	Stepping Into AutoCAD, 4th Edition*	$29.95	
	Inside AutoSketch, 2nd Edition*	$24.95	
	AutoCAD Reference Guide, 2nd Edition	$14.95	
	AutoCAD Reference Guide on Disk, 2nd Edition	$14.95	
	Inside Compuserve (Book-and-Disk set)	$29.95	
	*Companion Disk available for these books	$14.95 ea.	
	Shipping and Handling: See information below.		
	TOTAL		

❑ 3½" disk

❑ 5¼" disk

Shipping and Handling: $4.00 for the first book and $1.75 for each additional book. Floppy disk: add $1.75 for shipping and handling. If you need to have it NOW, we can ship product to you in 24 to 48 hours for an additional charge, and you will receive your item overnight or in two days. Add $20.00 per book and $8.00 for up to three disks overseas. Prices subject to change. Call for availability and pricing information on latest editions.

New Riders Publishing • 11711 N. College Avenue • P.O. Box 90 • Carmel, Indiana 46032

1-800-541-6789　　　　　　　　　　**1-800-448-3804**

Orders/Customer Service　　　　　　　　**FAX**

To order: Fill in the reverse side, fold, and mail

BUSINESS REPLY MAIL
FIRST CLASS PERMIT NO. 6008 INDIANAPOLIS, IN

POSTAGE WILL BE PAID BY ADDRESSEE

NO POSTAGE
NECESSARY IF
MAILED IN THE
UNITED STATES

NEW RIDERS PUBLISHING
P.O. Box 90
Carmel, Indiana 46032